www.wadsworth.com

www.wadsworth.com is the World Wide Web site for
Thomson Wadsworth and is your direct source to dozens
of online resources.

At *www.wadsworth.com* you can find out about supplements, demonstration software, and student resources.
You can also send email to many of our authors and preview new publications and exciting new technologies.

www.wadsworth.com
Changing the way the world learns®

FROM THE WADSWORTH SERIES IN COMMUNICATION STUDIES

Communicating with Credibility and Confidence

Communicating with Credibility and Confidence

Third Edition

Gay Lumsden
California Polytechnic State University, San Luis Obispo

Donald Lumsden
California Polytechnic State University, San Luis Obispo

WADSWORTH
CENGAGE Learning

Australia • Brazil • Japan • Korea • Mexico • Singapore • Spain • United Kingdom • United States

Communicating with Credibility and Confidence, Third Edition
Gay Lumsden and Donald Lumsden

Communication Editor: Annie Mitchell

Publisher: Holly J. Allen

Assistant Editor: Aarti Jayaraman

Editorial Assistant: Trina Enriquez

Senior Technology Project Manager: Jeanette Wiseman

Senior Marketing Manager: Kim Russell

Marketing Assistant: Andrew Keay

Marketing Communications Manager: Shemika Britta

Project Manager, Editorial Production: Jennifer Klos

Executive Art Director: Maria Epes

Print Buyer: Becky Cross

Permissions Editor: Sarah Harkrader

Production Service: Ruth Cottrell

Photo Researcher: Roberta Broyer

Copy Editor: Pam Suwinsky

Illustrator: G & S Typesetters

Cover Designer: Roy R. Neuhaus

Cover Image: Getty Images/Taxi: Ken Chernus; Index Stock Imagery/Benelux Press; PhotoEdit, Inc./Tom Carter

Compositor: International Typesetting and Composition

For product information and technology assistance, contact us at
Cengage Learning Academic Resource Center, 1-800-354-9706

For permission to use material from this text or product, submit all requests online at **cengage.com/permissions**
Further permissions questions can be e-mailed to **permissionrequest@cengage.com**

Library of Congress Control Number: 2005922131

ISBN-13: 978-0-495-00385-4

ISBN-10: 0-495-00385-9

Wadsworth Cengage Learning
25 Thomson Place
Boston, MA 02210
USA

Cengage Learning products are represented in Canada by Nelson Education, Ltd.

For your course and learning solutions, visit **academic.cengage.com**

Purchase any of our products at your local college store or at our-preferred online store **www.ichapters.com**

Printed in Canada
4 5 6 7 8 9 11 10 09 08

Brief Contents

Detailed Contents

Part I   Understanding Communication Processes

Part II   Creating Dialogue

Part III   Building Interpersonal Relationships

Part IV Communicating in Groups and Teams

Part V Speaking to Public Audiences

Preface

We believe that communicating should be challenging, effective, and fun. Yes, fun. Your everyday communication—conversing, working with a team, even giving a speech—should be stimulating and interesting and gratifying.

We hope this book and course will help you develop communication skills that will make your communication, both personal and career, satisfying and effective. There's more. We hope to help you develop keen skills in speaking and listening that reflect a high standard of ethics and critical thinking. With these abilities, when leadership opportunities come along—and they will—you will be ready. Being an excellent communicator who makes good choices and can lead others to do so is one way you can make your world better.

For right now, though, we guess you sometimes feel comfortable and successful in your communication and sometimes feel awkward or ill at ease. That's natural, because effective communication is so important to you. Communication is the vehicle for making your life what you want it to be, both in personal relationships and career goals.

We've written this book to help you make that vehicle work for you. Everything we hope you will learn—theories, facts, feelings, approaches, and abilities—all add up to two critical attributes that we want you to *own* by the end of this course:

1   *Credibility*. Other people will want to listen to you because they trust you and believe in you. Your credibility is critical in all forms of communication, whether you're talking to one person or a thousand. This book develops credibility as an overriding theme so you can, first, recognize the credibility you now have and, then, start working to develop your credibility further.

2   *Confidence*. You will learn how to manage nervousness, turn it to your advantage, and be able to speak confidently to others—one on one, in groups, or to large audiences. Confidence is based on knowing you've been successful in the past and anticipating success in new experiences. Whatever your confidence level is now, you can build it by practicing the strategies presented in this book, including relaxation and visualization techniques, to reduce your stress and improve your performance.

Fortunately, confidence and credibility are attributes that develop as you increase your competence in a range of communication situations. This book is designed to help you do that. It is based on several assumptions—first, about students and patterns of learning and, second, about the common threads that weave through all types of communication.

About the Third Edition

The philosophy and the substance of the previous editions remain, but we have tightened the prose and, as much as possible, made it more conversational. For the most part, we have continued to make the language friendly for the many English-as-a-second-language students who use the book, using few colloquialisms and slang, although we have left in common language devices that clearly have roots in identifiable metaphors. Our own experience has been that students can track metaphors and find this useful in developing their English usage.

Of course, we have updated resources and research and have provided more information on using technology effectively for both research and presentation. Some of this content is included in the text, and some appears in new boxes, instructions, exercises, and on the Internet through the Cyberpoints.

About Students and Learning

Students, even well-prepared ones, have some hurdles in common, for example:

- *Overcoming nervousness.* Almost everyone gets anxious about communicating at one time or another, and almost everyone believes she or he is the only one who feels this way. That means there are a lot of people in the same situation. So this book starts with where you may be right now—shaking in your boots. Our intent is for you to learn that you do, in fact, have things worth saying and the talent to say them well—no matter how unsure you might feel right now. Students often say they know nothing worth listening to (that is, they are not credible) and think they can't make people want to listen to them (that is, they are not confident). These are lonely feelings, and we know how you can change those perceptions.

- *Acquiring knowledge and skills.* Students become good communicators when they acquire knowledge, develop positive feelings, and practice specific skills. Knowledge helps you explain, with theory and facts, how people communicate. Positive feelings about yourself and communication situations enable you to approach communication confidently and wisely. Finally, both your knowledge and your feelings provide the foundation for practicing and implementing specific communication skills. To help you develop all three strands of learning, each chapter begins with a list of objectives categorized according to "knowledge," "feelings and approaches," and "abilities."

Tracking Common Threads through Communication Experiences

If you can talk to a friend, you can talk to an audience. It's true. Or you can learn to make it true. Certain basic skills are common to every type of oral communication: with yourself, with another person, with a group, with an audience. In fact, all types of communication are more alike than they are different. This is true across cultures and across experiences. Often students believe their foreign accent, American dialect, or vocal or physical characteristics will block their communication. Students even worry about their gestures because they reflect a particular culture. Not one of these individual characteristics means the student has a communication problem. It's only a matter of learning to turn what *seems* to be a disadvantage into an advantage, and you already have the foundation for doing that.

This book develops common skills first, step by step, so you can adapt them later to each type of interaction. Presentational speaking is discussed at the very end of the book, but when you get there you will have already developed communication strength in other contexts—and that strength will be the base for speaking to an audience. As your confidence grows in using these approaches with one person or a few, you will find it easier to communicate with more people. Some important common threads among all communication situations include ethics, adaptation, and creative and critical thinking.

Ethics. Any time you communicate, you make ethical choices about what to say, how to say it, and how to act. Those choices reflect how you regard yourself, your listeners, and your subject; they have consequences that affect you and the people with whom you communicate. In this book, we explain why we believe dialogical ethics provides the best approach to communication by helping you to build relationships, to work cooperatively in groups and teams, to involve audiences deeply in your public presentations, and to establish a sound base for your credibility and confidence.

Adaptation. Communication in today's world requires understanding and adapting to diverse individuals. Both personally and professionally, you will communicate with people who vary widely in background, ethnicity, culture, abilities, gender, and sexual orientation. Diversity can enrich communication with multiple perspectives; when you understand how to communicate with people different from yourself, you can transcend potential barriers to communication. That's why the book integrates issues and information about diversity—especially in culture and gender.

Critical thinking. Communicating effectively, both as a giver and receiver of ideas, demands good critical thinking in analyzing, understanding, creating, organizing, phrasing, and supporting ideas. Whether you are talking to yourself about a problem you must solve, working out an idea with a friend, brainstorming an idea with a team, presenting a persuasive speech, or simply listening intently, you should be using critical thinking. This book will help you develop these skills in every context of communication.

Features

We've tried to make this book user-friendly for you. *Communicating with Credibility and Confidence* has some special features to help integrate and apply the concepts. These include:

- *Terms* boldfaced and defined in the text and included in a glossary at the end of the book.

- *Objectives* listed at the beginning of each chapter so you can see what you're trying to accomplish.

- *Boxes* to stimulate discussion by presenting brief excerpts from contemporary publications on technology, culture, communication in business, interpersonal relationships, and so on.

- *Short quotations* as marginal inserts to stimulate thought and discussion.

- *Exercises and activities* that systematically develop competency through individual, dyadic, and group work and presentations. The exercises are designed to achieve two goals: to introduce a wider range of communication genres and to build skills incrementally.

- *Integrated technology activities*, called *Cyberpoints*, that direct you to interesting and relevant World Wide Web sites relating to concepts discussed in the text, to the student resources at the *Communicating with Credibility and Confidence* website, and to InfoTrac College Edition® to research communication issues and find speeches to read and critique.

- *Website* that provides self-assessment and observation forms, resources, and examples for students to use as supplementary information.

- *Workbook* containing self-paced exercises and experiences for students.

- *Instructor's manual* that develops the course so your instructor can choose a traditional approach to the class or a collaborative learning approach, together with syllabi, schedules, assignments, new activities and experiential exercises, examinations, and resources.

- *Art* that includes photo case studies, cartoons, models, diagrams, and illustrations of concepts.

Overview of the Book

The book will lead you to achieve three major goals: develop your credibility to yourself and to others; develop your confidence in your own communication; and develop skills that enable you to achieve your goals through communication.

That starts with the experience and abilities you already have, so Part I focuses on what communication is, how it functions, and how it influences your present and future life. We use this foundation for examining the nature of credibility and confidence. From there, we explore the essential roles of perception, critical thinking, and creative thinking in your communication.

Part II discusses creating dialogue with others. Here you will strengthen your listening and questioning abilities as well as your nonverbal and verbal communication skills—a background that applies to all communication situations.

Part III examines your communication in interpersonal relationships, including situations that help communication with another individual grow and develop, personal relationships with friends and family, and relationships in college and in your professional life.

Part IV develops your abilities to work in groups and teams. Group communication involves all the knowledge and skills covered in the previous chapters and applies them to achieving common goals through teamwork. Your communication helps you build effective teams, provide leadership, analyze problems, and develop solutions in group settings.

Part V prepares you to make speeches. Public presentations involve speaking to inform an audience about a topic and persuading an audience to change its attitudes, beliefs, or behaviors. Everything you have learned to this point serves as the foundation for the extensive preparation and effective practice that develop your skills as a credible, confident public speaker.

Acknowledgments

Many kind, patient, and insightful people have helped us develop this book. Our students—past and present—have provided the "proving ground" for much of the material, and they have contributed excellent ideas and enormous inspiration and encouragement. We especially thank the students who gave their time and thoughtfulness to reading and evaluating early drafts. The text reflects their suggestions for material and revisions to make it better and more student-friendly.

We also appreciate our department colleagues at Kean University and at California Polytechnic State University, San Luis Obispo. We feel we have worked with the finest faculty—personally and professionally—anywhere. Not only have they always been open and willing to share their great ideas, but they have been extremely patient as we have grappled with this project. Specifically, our colleagues at Kean University—Bailey Baker, Cathy Londino, Chris Lynch, Kristine Mirrer, Freda Remmers, and Ernest Wiggins—gave us helpful feedback based on their extensive experiences using this text in their classes.

Faculty members across the country made excellent contributions to this text through their thoughtful reviews of multiple drafts. Our thanks go to Blanton Croft, Northern Virginia Community College–Woodbridge Campus; Rita M. Miller, Keene State College; Victoria Orrego, University of Miami; Ingrid L. Peternel, College of DuPage; and Carole Shaffer-Koros, Kean University.

The work by these reviewers built on that provided by those who worked with the text's first edition. We also thank them for their contributions: Martha Ann Atkins, Iowa State University; Ruth Aurelius, Des Moines Area Community College; Melissa L. Beall, University of Northern Iowa; Marco Benassi, College of DuPage; Mary Bozik, University of Northern Iowa; Barbara Breaden, Lane Community College; Diane Casagrande, West Chester University; E. Neal Claussen, Bradley University; Michael Eaves, Valdosta State University; Robert Edmunds, Marshall University; Michael Elkins, Southern Illinois University; William E. Lewis, High Desert Christian College; Stephen A. March, Pima Community College; Robert W. Martin, Ithaca College; Tracy McAfee, Blue Ridge Community College; Lee McGaan, Monmouth College; Sheila Merritt, Mesa Community College; Diane L. Rehling, St. Cloud State University; and Deborah Shelley, University of Houston–Downtown.

Thomson Wadsworth has supported us with an outstanding cast. We appreciate the enthusiasm and direction from Annie Mitchell, our acquisitions editor. We are also well supported by her editorial assistant, Trina Enriquez, and we always enjoy working with Holly Allen, publisher, who was with us at the beginning of our association with Thomson Wadsworth.

We would like to thank Mark Lewis, Riverside Community College, for his significant contribution to this project. We appreciate the time and efforts he has dedicated to making this edition a success.

We were pleased to work again with Pam Suwinsky and Ruth Cottrell. Pam combines exceptional editing skills with a delightful sense of humor, and Ruth magically brings all the pieces together to create the product you are now reading. This is our third book with this team, and the process seems to work better each time.

Finally, we want to thank our family and close friends for their love, support, and tolerance. Although we are always with them in spirit, we'd rather be together in person—and we hope we can compensate for some of the time we have sacrificed in the process of developing this edition. It's to our kids and grandkids—Tom, Diana, Carolyn, Bill, Maria, Zoe, Savannah, Rita, Rita D., Anna Maria, and especially in memory of Eddie—that we dedicate this work.

Communicating with Credibility and Confidence

Chapter 1

Communication Dynamics: Exploring Concepts and Principles

Objectives for This Chapter

Knowledge

- Know how communication affects success in relationships and careers
- Understand the concepts of communication processes
- Explain the components of a model of human communication
- Know the qualities of effective communication

Feelings and Approaches

- Appreciate the challenge and potential satisfaction of communicating effectively
- Want to create transactional communication with others
- Approach communication as an ethical process

Communication Abilities

- Begin monitoring and adapting your communication to people and situations
- Consider the receiver when planning to send messages

Key Terms

intrapersonal communication
interpersonal communication
dyadic communication
group and team communication
presentational communication
mediated communication
communication
process

verbal cues
nonverbal cues
transactional process
sender
encode
transmit
channel
noise

receiver
decode
feedback
communication dilemma
effective communication
ethics
dialogical ethic

How do you spend most of your awake time? The answer is communicating—perhaps for fun, maybe for school or work, even to manage a conflict or sell a point. You may really enjoy the process and feel pretty confident about your skill, or you may find communication a little scary. Or, like most people, your feelings and skills in communication may vary from situation to situation. The purpose of this book is to make your communication (whether just to yourself, or to someone else, or to a whole audience of others) not only easier but more effective and more fun. We intend to help you:

- Know you are credible both to yourself and to others
- Feel confident of your ability to communicate in different situations
- Be skillful in achieving your goals through communication

You will reach these goals through a gradual, step-by-step process. You'll add knowledge about communication at every step; you'll learn how to harness your feelings and approaches to communication situations; and you'll practice communicating in different contexts to develop both skill and confidence. We begin each chapter with a list of objectives for each type of learning: knowledge, feelings and approaches, and abilities.

This chapter begins with how communication influences your life. Then we take a detailed look at what the communication process is, how communication works (and why it frequently doesn't), and what qualities make communication more effective.

Why Communication Affects You

We weren't kidding when we said most of your awake time is spent in communicating. Look, for example, at one of Tanisha's days:

At 8:30 AM, Tanisha opens one reluctant eye and looks at the clock. "Oh, no!" she yelps. "My paper was due at eight o'clock!"

As she tears out the door, juggling her backpack and laptop, her roommate smiles and hands her a cup of coffee to go. "Thanks—you're awesome!" Tanisha responds gratefully as she heads for her car. Listening to the traffic report on her car radio, she avoids a traffic tangle by taking an alternate route. She calls Dr. Saunders's office on her cell phone and leaves a message that she'll be late. At 8:50, she wheels into the parking lot and, at the first empty space, another car noses in just ahead of her. She yells at the driver, who yells back. Tanisha decides not to waste time arguing and, after cruising around, finally finds a parking place. She reaches Dr. Saunders's office at 9:10, apologizes, and persuades her to accept the late paper. Then Tanisha goes to her communication class and gives her PowerPoint report. She hates the idea of being videotaped, but discovers it's really not so bad. (Later, she'll see the videotape of her performance and discover that she did much better than she thought.) She gets a high grade, so she feels pretty good. In her history class, she listens carefully, takes notes, and asks questions to clear up the foggy points. Then, in sociology, she works with a group of students to plan a term project, entering their next meeting time on her electronic Day-Timer. Between classes, she checks her e-mail and then has a quick conference with members of her service club.

When classes are over, Tanisha goes to her job as a server. At 6:00 PM, she takes a break, pulls her cell phone out of her pocket, and calls home to tell her roommate when to expect her and to thank her again for being so quick with the rescue coffee. At work, her charm and skill earn her a healthy set of tips and a customer's report to her manager that she's an excellent employee. At 10:00 PM, she arrives home, exhausted but pleased by the day's successes. She spends a few minutes on the Internet to examine some reports for a paper assignment that's due next week. Finally, she turns on the television to get a quick update on the news and to relax by watching her favorite comedian before turning in.

Communicating in Contexts

Notice the variety of contexts in which Tanisha communicated: with herself, one to one with another person both in person and on the telephone, in a group setting, with an audience, and through media. Each context has distinct characteristics, but in all of them, communication uses closely related knowledge, feelings and approaches, and abilities.

Intrapersonal communication Communication to yourself in response to your environment, other people, or yourself

Intrapersonal communication is within yourself, as you respond to stimuli from the environment, from others, and from yourself. Tanisha talked herself into getting up and going to school; she stopped herself from arguing with another driver; she deliberated about how to approach Dr. Saunders. During the day, she had many conversations with herself—about everything from "It's time to eat" to "Now, be calm; you'll do fine on this report." You communicate with yourself constantly, even while you are also communicating with others.

Interpersonal communication Dynamic process among two or more people

Interpersonal communication is a dynamic process between or among people that touches people emotionally and psychologically.[1] Tanisha's interpersonal communication included expressing appreciation to her roommate, persuading Dr. Saunders, and talking with friends and customers. Interpersonal communication is sometimes called **dyadic communication** because often two people, or a dyad, are involved, although interpersonal communication may occur among more participants. More important, whereas dyadic communication may be as superficial as,

Dyadic communication Interactions between two people

"Hey, lady, where's the nearest phone?" interpersonal communication generally involves personal sharing of issues ranging from discussing your career aspirations with a friend to agonizing with your mate about where your relationship is going.[2]

Group and team communication Socializing or working with a small number of other people

Group and team communication involves socializing and/or working with a small number of other people. In her class project team, Tanisha communicated with several people to achieve a specific goal; she also had a quick meeting with her service club between classes. In group and team communication, you do all the same things as in intrapersonal and interpersonal communication. However, the communication is more complex because you can't interact as intimately with several people at once as you can with one.

Presentational communication Speaking before an audience

Presentational communication occurs when a person addresses an audience: a small group, a class of 20 students, or an auditorium full of people. In her communication class, Tanisha used a computerized slide presentation program, PowerPoint, to give her classmates information; she talked and explained while showing the slides. *Her skills in communicating interpersonally and in groups carried through into her skills in presenting to an audience.* As a speaker, Tanisha adapted interpersonal skills to make her message clear to a larger group of people. That required her to organize, plan, and rehearse her communication differently and to design PowerPoint slides that would clarify and enhance her message. In Tanisha's history class, her role in presentational communication was as an audience member who listened, questioned, and took notes on the speaker's information. Both as speaker and listener, she applied her abilities in intrapersonal and interpersonal communication in the context of her classroom group setting. Like Tanisha, you will learn to adapt your interpersonal skills to public situations as this course proceeds.

Mediated communication Communication channeled through written or electronic medium

Mediated communication is channeled through a written or electronic medium such as newspapers, magazines, telephone, computer, radio, or television. Tanisha listened to the radio so she could adjust her route to school; she checked her e-mail; she was videotaped giving her report; she used her computer for her PowerPoint presentation; she used the Internet, her cell phone, her electronic Day-Timer; and she watched television for news and entertainment when she got home. She probably saw an infinite number of billboards, glanced at or read newspapers and magazines, listened to commercials, entertainment, and news on the car radio, and perhaps read flyers left on her car windshield.

As you listen to and watch media, you are a single member of an enormous public audience. The messages you receive filter through to your talk with yourself (intrapersonally), with others (interpersonally), or in groups. You refer to mediated information in your research for presentations. As an audience, you listen to a speaker's information, much of which was gathered from media sources. Media messages strongly influence what you think about, what you talk about, and how you think and talk about it. Finally, you use media to reach others with your information or ideas.

Speech is civilization itself. The word, even the most contradictory word, preserves contact—it is silence which isolates.

Thomas Mann

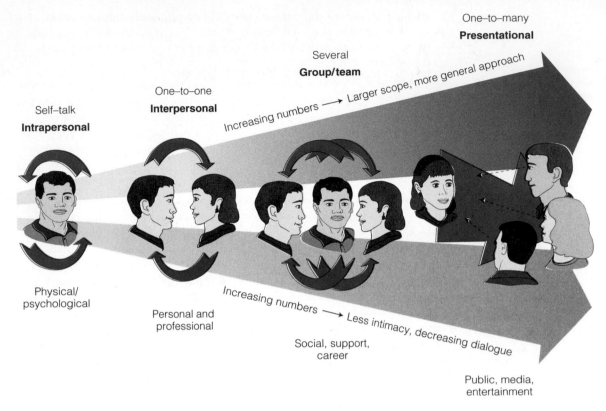

Figure 1.1 *Continuum of communication types*

These various communication contexts are distinguished mainly by numbers of participants, individual roles, the medium, and the settings or environments in which they occur. Figure 1.1 shows these types of communication as a continuum of communication experiences. At each stage, the communication enlarges and changes according to the situation.

The preceding discussion suggests some basic principles of communication contexts:

- Intrapersonal communication is ongoing and interacts with all other types and contexts of communication at all times.

- Communication abilities are closely related in each type of communication event, yet each context requires its own special skills and adaptations.

- In any communication context, the characteristics, needs, and goals of the other person(s) should influence a communicator's choices and adaptation of messages.

Try examining these principles in your daily communication. As this course proceeds, you will see how the knowledge, feelings, and skills you develop early in this book carry through into each type of communication you develop later.

Communicating and Your Success

If you were asked what you want most in life, what would you say? A happy relationship? Family? Spiritual development? Education? Successful career? Financial security? How do you achieve any of these? John Stewart says, "There's a direct link between the quality of your communication and the quality of your life."[3] Good communication can help develop and nurture both personal and professional relationships; poor communication can sabotage them. In addition, your communication experiences actually can affect your emotional *and* physical well-being. Positive intra- and interpersonal communication can strengthen your health, self-esteem, and self-confidence; *negative communication is directly correlated to stress-related diseases.*[4]

In your work, skilled communication can make you successful. Employers say that employees must be able to speak, listen, know how to learn, think creatively, solve problems and make decisions, negotiate with others, work in teams, provide leadership, and choose ethical and honest courses of action.[5] Each of these is an ability to communicate with oneself as well as with others in interpersonal and organizational settings.

Both in personal and professional relationships, effective communication is becoming more important every day. Why? Because society changes.

Changing relationships and families. Expectations and roles for men and women are changing rapidly, and so are family structures and ways of living. Children may have one parent or several; they may have no siblings or a variety of full, step-, and half-brothers or sisters. Both parents may work away from home, one may work while the other stays home, or one or both may work from home and stay connected with the office electronically. Families may be spread across the continent or the world.

Organizational demands. Whether you work in a corporate, nonprofit, or academic environment, your organization will expect you to take on more responsibility and involvement, to communicate at all levels and in many ways. More and more organizations are using teams to make and implement decisions. People who used to compete against each other now must cooperate, and that requires a whole new set of leadership and teamwork communication skills.[6]

Diversity at work and in the community. You will live and work with people of every color, religion, and sexual orientation, which requires that you bridge many differences. The Bureau of Census projects astonishing demographic changes in the United States in the next 50 years. The white majority will have dropped from 74% in 1995 to 53% in 2050, and some other groups will have more than doubled their proportion of the population during that time period. People of

Hispanic origin will increase from 10% of the total population to 25%, Asian and Pacific Islanders from 3% to 8%, and blacks from 12% to 14%.[7] Communicating successfully takes more work than it once did. Understanding people whose backgrounds differ from yours requires thinking more deeply about how they see things, how they express their ideas, how they listen and respond.

How Communication Works

Communicating effectively in your relationships and your career demands more than skill. You need to understand just what communication is and how it functions, in terms of its processes; of its transactional nature; and of its characteristics. Let's discuss that here.

Communicating Is a Process

Communication Using verbal and nonverbal cues to transact meanings

Communication is the process of using verbal and nonverbal cues to transact mutually understood meanings between two or more people within a particular context and environment. That is:

Process An ongoing, constantly developing and changing operation

Process. As a **process,** communication constantly develops and changes. For example, someone's remark makes you laugh, but the speaker is hurt; she didn't mean to be funny. You apologize and explain your response, but she has to be persuaded you weren't laughing at her. You try again to achieve an understanding. Eventually, you manage to work it out. That's a complex process that moves, doubles back, and moves again in a widening spiral, as more and more ideas, feelings, and information go into the transaction between or among people.[8]

Verbal and nonverbal clues.   **Verbal cues** are messages using words and structure in speaking, listening, and questioning, to convey and interpret ideas. You might say to your professor, "Could you explain what this means?" The specific words and the way they are ordered convey your request.

Verbal cues Words used to convey and interpret ideas

   Nonverbal cues are vocal characteristics, speech patterns, body postures, facial expressions, space, time, touch, and other personal behaviors or objects that convey some meaning. As you ask for clarification, you might lean toward the professor and point to confusing material in the book; you may underscore your puzzlement by wrinkling your brow, tilting your head, and raising your voice at the end of the question. The professor would interpret your verbal and nonverbal cues according to many factors, including his or her needs, interests, culture, and experience.

Nonverbal cues Body postures, facial expressions, and other personal behaviors or objects that communicate

Transaction.   A **transactional process** exchanges bits of meaning to arrive at a mutual understanding. Think about a shopping transaction. When you leave a store, you have less money and an item you didn't possess before. The store is down one item in its inventory and up some in income. The exchange involves intangibles, too. If you are satisfied, you will recommend the store to someone else. If you and the clerk both feel good about the transaction, that may affect how you interact with someone else in the next few moments.

Transactional process Interaction in which each person gives and takes to achieve understanding

   A transaction is more than simply giving and receiving information; it builds something between or among the communicators, whatever the context. Whether you're working out an understanding with a friend, trying to incorporate ideas from several team members into one plan, giving a public speech, trying to buy or sell a product, in any context, you notice others' nonverbal cues (A puzzled look? A nod? A smile? A glance at the watch?) and you send dozens of your own. You adapt your messages, both verbal and nonverbal, to help the other to understand and accept you and your ideas, and he does the same. Communication transactions actually alter each person, maybe only in mood or only for a moment, but sometimes in something as deep or long-lasting as a belief or value.

Mutually understood meanings.   Mutually understood meanings are in the heads of the communicators. Words don't have meanings—people do. Your words and nonverbal cues represent what you mean, but your listeners' backgrounds and experiences with the language shape their understanding of your meaning. As your communication transaction proceeds, you each take bits of meaning from one another to create a new mutual understanding.

   People too often assume that everyone in a transaction agrees on exactly what something means, but they're wrong. There are different understandings for each individual. Often differences are extreme. Haney calls this "bypassing."[9] For example, your friend asks, "How was the wedding?" and you respond, "Beautiful!" What neither of you realizes is that your friend was referring to the wedding you attended three weeks ago, which was a disaster, but you're thinking of the one you attended last night, which was wonderful. You've bypassed, but you each leave confident that you have a clear understanding.

Context.   *Context* refers to whether an interaction is intrapersonal, interpersonal, group, public, or mediated communication. The purpose or goals, the occasion, and the communicators all influence expectations for message content and communication behavior within that context. A job interview and a marriage proposal, for example, are both interpersonal and have many communication factors in common, but participants' specific goals and role expectations affect how transactions proceed.

Environment.   Environment includes physical conditions surrounding communication. The room, furniture, lighting, decor, acoustics, colors, scents—all create a social and emotional environment that affects people's interactions. Think how different interaction is, for example, in a classroom with chairs arranged in strict rows than in one with chairs in a circle.

Here's an example of how your message might be affected by environment, context, and your friend's understanding when the two of you engage in a process of transacting a meaning. You enter a restaurant to have lunch with your friend. You greet her with, "How's it going?" as a casual way of saying "Hello." She, however, interprets your question in terms of what's on her mind—a problem with her new boyfriend. "Terrible," she answers. "What's the problem?" you ask, and she tells you she's upset. Of course, you ask, "Why?" At the beginning, there was a wide gap between your idea of the context and your friend's understanding, but now the gap begins to narrow. As she explains her problem, you listen, question, and finally comprehend what's bothering her. You have negotiated an understanding of her message.

The process and your messages would have been different in another context or environment. If you'd been meeting with a work group to plan a project, for instance, your friend might not have responded, "Terrible," preferring to discuss her problem later. Or you might have simply clucked sympathetically without asking what the problem was, because it was neither the time nor place to pursue the issue.

A Step-by-Step Model   Let's take one small interaction segment of the process and break it down into still smaller components to focus on some factors that affect a transaction's success. Such a brief segment may take no more than a nanosecond, and the interaction we show is only one of many that could occur simultaneously as the two people transact their meanings.

We jump into the transaction at the point where one person responds to stimuli and gets an idea. The classic cartoonist's use of a light bulb is not a bad

Sender's idea

Sender Person who transmits a message

Encode

Encode Represent an idea with a symbol

Transmit

Transmit Speak or act so that symbols are available to the other person

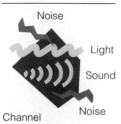

Channel

Channel Means by which cues are carried from sender to receiver **Noise** Stimuli that compete with a message in a channel

way to represent an idea—after all, thoughts *are* a system of chemical-electrical impulses within our brains. The brain creates a specific impulse pattern when some cells fire and others do not. To communicate an idea, one person must stimulate a pattern of chemical-electrical impulses in the other's brain so the listener generates a similar thought. You could liken the thinking process to that of computers, of course, but linked computers can communicate with perfect clarity. Human brains are more complex than computers and cannot be linked directly, so people must rely on a complex, roundabout route to make a connection.

With that in mind, let's take a "frame-by-frame" look at how one person tries to get an idea into another person's mind.

Sender's idea.   The message **sender** has an idea to express. If the idea is not clear in the sender's mind, it is difficult for the sender to communicate it. People frequently speak or act before being fully aware of their own thoughts, putting their mouths in action before their minds are in gear. Participants can work together to clarify ideas, but it's easier when the sender knows what his or her thoughts are before starting to talk.

Encoding.   To share the idea, the sender must **encode** it—that is, represent the idea with a symbol for another to interpret. Both words and nonverbal behaviors represent codes that humans use to convey what they mean. The sender searches mentally for symbols that best represent his or her thoughts. It's not easy, however, to select just the right words or behaviors to represent an abstract brain activity. Language is imprecise. Many words have multiple meanings, and a variety of words might represent any one idea. Nonverbal cues are often even less precise. A large working vocabulary and awareness of nonverbal cues improve one's chances of selecting the most appropriate symbols.

Transmitting.   Selecting a symbol to represent an idea, however, doesn't get the message outside the sender's head. The code is **transmitted** through speaking and/or acting so those symbols can be available to the other person. Oral transmission depends on the sender's abilities to speak with sufficient volume, vocal clarity, and emphasis. Nonverbal cues require expression and movement skills to illustrate and represent ideas and feelings.

Channel.   Speaking or acting puts symbols into the communication **channel,** the means by which cues are carried. In face-to-face communication, message symbols travel from sender to receiver as sounds through air waves and as visual cues carried by light waves. In mediated communication, cues travel via electronic codes or broadcast frequencies.

Once in the channel, symbols encounter **noise,** which means more than loud sound. Noise includes all other stimuli present in the channel—visual, aural, olfactory—that can disrupt, distort, or totally block a message. The sender's message must have enough attention-getting properties to compete with all these distractions and reach and win the ears and eyes of the receiver.

Vision

Hearing

Receive

Receiver Person who picks up cues using the senses

***

Want to go out Saturday?

Decode

Decode Translate symbols and cues into meaning

***

Receiver's idea

Feedback Responses from message receiver that give the sender information about how symbols were received and interpreted

***

Receiving. If cues are transmitted with enough intensity to overcome competing noise, they reach a **receiver,** who picks up verbal and nonverbal stimuli through sensory organs. The receiver may or may not attend, depending on her or his abilities, habits, and motivations. A person's psychological state may create another kind of noise that distorts the sender's cues, or a person may be hearing- or sight-impaired or simply be distracted by other stimuli or noise in the channel. The cues, as perceived by the receiver, travel to the brain as nerve impulses.

Decoding. Now the receiver translates the nerve impulses back to symbols and **decodes** these cues in terms of his or her background and experiences. In decoding, the receiver gives symbols meanings, which can differ considerably from the sender's intended meanings. Speaking the same language does not ensure that any word means the same thing to different people. Sometimes, too, people see and hear what they anticipate, which could differ from actual symbols the sender transmitted. People often misunderstand others' messages to the extent that George Bernard Shaw once described the United States and England as "two countries separated by a common language."

Receiver's ideas. The ways a receiver decodes symbols create brain patterns that stimulate specific ideas. Communication is successful if ideas the receiver creates are substantially similar to the sender's original thoughts. Even the clearest idea, transmitted skillfully with appropriate symbols, relies on the receiver's mind for successful communication. Receivers' backgrounds and experiences shape interpretations, value judgments, and feelings with which they react to messages. If communication stops here, there is no avenue to clarifying or correcting their impressions.

Feedback. The only way to ensure a receiver's understanding matches the sender's is for the receiver to provide **feedback**—possibly questions, a look of puzzlement or a nod of understanding, or a restatement of the idea—to let the sender know how symbols were received and interpreted. Then the original sender becomes the receiver, and the whole process continues as each strives to understand the other and to be understood. Good feedback requires careful listening, thinking, encoding, decoding, and *checking* for accuracy. Feedback may fail because people don't want it (it takes time and effort) or because they assume the understanding is clear and bypass one another's meaning.

In the "filmstrip" presented in the margin, each individual has a different symbolic system associated with "go out Saturday." Fortunately, human communication doesn't usually demand exact recreations of ideas. Some people believe it is nothing more than a "happy accident" when any two communicators create messages that are exactly the same. With thoughtful encoding and sending, feedback, and cooperative transactions, however, mutual meanings are not accidental. They are achieved because people work at them.

Figure 1.2 *A transactional model of communication*

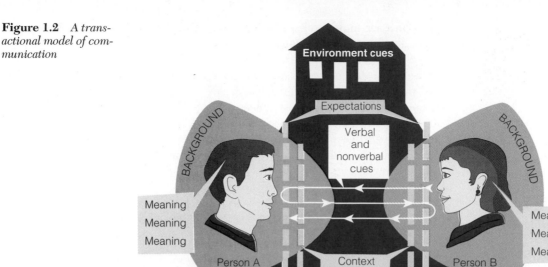

Environment cues

BACKGROUND

BACKGROUND

Expectations

Verbal and nonverbal cues

Meaning
Meaning
Meaning

Meaning
Meaning
Meaning

Person A

Context

Person B

Transactions

A Transactional Model   Sometimes, a model or diagram helps to picture how a process works. Figure 1.2 uses a model to show the processes whereby Raj and Melody transact meaning. Either person could start the communication process, or they might start talking at the same time. Here we show Raj, on the left, starting the conversation. Raj and Melody each have expectations and understanding of the context of the event, and each has a personal screen built by his or her own life experiences and conditions such as gender, culture, beliefs, education, values. Their backgrounds may be similar, though never exactly the same, or very different. Each communicator's personal screen influences how she or he puts together a message. In this case, Melody receives Raj's cues through her personal filter and constructs what she thinks he means, responding with verbal and nonverbal cues based, again, on her interpretation and her personal filter. With each exchange, Raj and Melody each adapt and refine their understanding of the other's meaning. If the process is working well, the two understandings come closer together until the participants believe they understand each other adequately to meet their personal goals for the exchange.

Communicating Is Not Transferring Ideas

The oft-repeated phrase "But I *told* you . . ." reflects some mistaken assumptions people make about communicating. To avoid falling into this trap, remember that:

Sending does not guarantee receiving.   People often conclude erroneously that if they've said it or written it, they've communicated. Sending a message only means it was transmitted; it ensures nothing about what happens after that.

Your message must reach a receiver, who in turn must perceive and interpret it correctly, for communication to have occurred.

Ideas cannot be "given" to another person. Even when the receiver receives and processes your cues, you can't say you transferred something from yourself to another as if handing over a piece of cake. When you serve the cake, you no longer have it, and the other person does. When you express an idea, you still have it—with, perhaps, some revisions and new insights provided by the receiver's feedback—and the receiver has it, too, as she or he understands it. The sender provides stimuli for receivers to create thoughts but does not actually deposit his or her own ideas in their heads. Communication is like education: We teachers provide stimuli, but learning happens only in the student's mind. Teachers don't make learning happen—we just provide opportunities. But every time we teach, we learn, too, from you, and from the process. That, too, is a transaction.

Communication cues are not always intentional. Sometimes, you send *unconscious* cues via facial expressions, posture, clothing, or even the tune you're whistling. When others observe those behaviors, they may assign meanings to them—and those meanings may be wrong. Such situations are *not* interpersonal communication, because there's no sharing and feedback. Those interpreting your cues are communicating *intra*personally, however, reacting internally to messages as they interpret them, and possibly assuming the cues were sent intentionally.

Communicating Can Be a Dilemma

To communicate or not to communicate, that is the question. If you do choose to communicate about something, how should you do it? What might you win? What might you lose? Everyone faces a dilemma sometimes—the choice between satisfying needs and meeting goals versus taking risks with their communication.

People communicate because they *need* to; consciously or unconsciously, you communicate to fill some need or reach some goal. Your goal may be simple—perhaps to get directions to someone's house. Or it could be more complex—to satisfy a psychological need, give or get crucial information, give or receive help, influence others, or even entertain others.

You might have multiple goals in one transaction, although some could be more important than others. For example, when Ron, a student of ours, worked on a team project, his primary goal was to get an A. In his teamwork, Ron communicated to give and get information, give and receive help with his teammates, and influence the team's choice of project presentation. Ron was just beginning a career as a comic in local comedy clubs, so he had the additional goal of entertaining his classmates.

Ron was both funny and effective; he took a risk in incorporating comedy into a serious group report, but it was worth it. He got the satisfaction of making

You already live in a computerized, electronic communication world, and changes that lie ahead will radically affect how you communicate in the future. Consider these ideas suggested by Ray Kurzweil who, on March 14, 2000, was honored at the White House as recipient of the National Medal of Technology, the nation's highest technology award. Mr. Kurzweil makes some interesting projections about how we may experience human communication, perhaps as soon as 2019:

- Computers are largely invisible and are embedded everywhere—in walls, tables, chairs, desks, clothing, jewelry, and bodies.
- Three-dimensional virtual reality displays, embedded in glasses and contact lenses, as well as auditory "lenses," are used routinely as primary interfaces for communication with other persons, computers, the Web, and virtual reality. . . .
- People are beginning to have relationships with automated personalities and use them as companions, teachers, caretakers, and lovers.

Projections for 2029:

- Permanent or removable implants (similar to contact lenses) for the eyes as well as cochlear implants are now used to provide input and output between the human user and the worldwide computing network.
- Direct neural pathways have been perfected for high-bandwidth connection to the human brain. A range of neural implants is becoming available to enhance visual and auditory perception and interpretation, memory, and reasoning. . . .
- A majority of communication does not involve a human. The majority of communication involving a human is between a human and a machine.

From Ray Kurzweil, *The Age of Spiritual Machines: When Computers Exceed Human Intelligence*. New York: Penguin, 2000.

---

people laugh, successfully getting his information across, and he earned an A on his presentation.

Taking a risk can be worth it, but you do sometimes have to weigh options. Risk taking is part of growing, developing, reaching goals, and meeting your needs, but you want to be sure your choice is right for a given situation or time. Sometimes the need and the risk are both so strong that individuals face a **communication dilemma,** a conflict between the need to communicate and the desire to avoid the risk involved. What risks do people fear to take? Some of the following may sound familiar to you:

Rejection.   Most people are motivated to gain the approval and acceptance of others. "Hey, I got an A on my paper!" you announce at home, expecting congratulations. But what if they shrug and turn away or say, "It's about time"? That's a risk.

Communication dilemma Conflict between need to communicate and desire to avoid risk

Telling Your Story

*E*verybody listens to and tells stories—anecdotes, jokes, fantasies—both from their personal lives and from other source, and a wonderful place to start as a communication student is by examining the process people use to tell stories. This process exemplifies good communication techniques as well as the ways people connect with others in other formats. Storytelling, like other forms of communication, uses detail and images; organization and emphasis; it is rich in ideas and simple in its direct contact of person to person. "Storytelling is connecting—teller to tale, then teller to audience, and finally audience to story."

In fact, in today's corporate world, the phrase "Tell your story" is used to guide employees who must write reports or make oral presentations. Storytelling has become a technique to involve employees in problem solving and to teach new techniques of management and teamwork. It's an approach for finding the best ways to create, understand, and share ideas. That's the heart of the communication process.

Telling a story is a good place to start thinking about how to describe your images and feelings and experiences so another person can start to imagine them. Stories provide the human experience of person-to-person understanding. The following story illustrates the importance of the personal connections when "telling your story."

I was working in central Africa as a Peace Corps volunteer when the trucks rolled into our village. On the side of the trucks were the words "RURAL ELECTRIFICATION." Many of the elders spoke

Obligation.   Communication may demand something extra from you. When you urge your friend to join a walk for charity, you'll be expected to walk, too. When you listen and learn how to perform a task, you may be expected to do it well. Frequently, people are more motivated *not* to comprehend a message than to get it correctly. For example, people used to think little about drinking and driving until media campaigns made them aware of the potentially lethal consequences and, therefore, that "friends don't let friends drive drunk." Now, people who have paid attention to the message know they should take keys away from a friend under the influence. But a drunken friend may be tough to handle. That's a risk, yet having understood the message, their responsibility is to make sure their friend gets home safely.

Change.   Either hearing or giving a message may lead to change, and that, too, is risky. People tend to feel more comfortable keeping their attitudes and beliefs than modifying them. Suppose, for example, you're thinking of changing your major. You could talk with a career counselor to help you figure it out, and the conversation could lead to a change. Or, the prospect might make you apprehensive; you might fear different course work, your family's response, or your ability in the new subject. Sometimes, it's easier to avoid communication that might influence you to change.

out against the changes this new electricity would bring, but Nkundi, the wise old storyteller of the village, pointed out that change need not always be feared. Soon there was light even in the middle of the night. Electricity had not been in the village long before a television set arrived. It was quickly installed in a gathering place for all to see. When I went to the storytelling circle, I saw the television on top of Nkundi's stool, surrounded by listeners agape with curiosity. Nkundi stood alone away from the circle.

I wasn't able to return to the circle for a couple of weeks, but when I did, things had changed again. The television set had been moved to the side; it was covered with a cloth. Nkundi had resumed his place on the storytelling stool and again was surrounded by listeners. No longer were their faces filled with curiosity; now they were alive with wonder. Nkundi paused as the children laughed, and I asked a small boy, "Is the television set broken?" "No," he said and went back to listening. Again I tapped him. "What," he said, clearly annoyed at the prospect of missing any of the story, which I knew he had heard before. I asked, "The television set . . . doesn't the television set know more stories than Nkundi?" The boy thought for a moment. "Yes, the television knows more stories. But my storyteller," he smiled a gap-toothed grin, "my storyteller knows me." And again the child left me for the world of the story.

From P. M. Cooper and R. Collins, *Look What Happened to Frog: Storytelling in Education.* Scottsdale, AZ: Gorsuch Scarisbrick, 1992, pp. 26–27.

Irreversibility. It's scary to realize that you can't take back what you said. A judge may instruct the jury to disregard a witness's statement, but that doesn't erase the experience. A friend may demand, "You take that back!" but the words have been spoken. You can say, "I'm sorry" or "Forgive me." You can add more layers of communication—talking about the talk—in hopes of giving the words a different slant or of burying them deep enough to reduce their impact. Still, scar tissue may remain. That's risky, too.

Failure. You may be motivated to communicate about something, but fear of failure, which may involve all of the preceding and more, may stop you. If your communication fails you might then be rejected, or obligated to try again, or simply frustrated. Sometimes, people even fear success—because it can lead to change, obligation, or others' higher expectations, which, in turn, raise the stakes even higher. Fears of failure or success can be enormous stumbling blocks for people in all aspects of life, especially in their willingness to communicate.

Being aware that communication involves a dilemma between need and risk is helpful in two ways. First, it helps you identify choices you must make yourself. Second, it helps you understand when others may be reticent, unclear, or defensive in their communication; they, too, must weigh their needs and their risks. Effective communication often demands that you take this risk but that you minimize it with careful preparation. The cliché "Nothing ventured, nothing gained" is good advice to keep in mind when you face most risks.

What Makes Communication Effective

Effective communication Communication that achieves its objectives, enriches people involved, and provides foundation for future communication

We now have a theoretical picture of how communication works. But what makes communication *effective*? We use **effective communication** to mean communication that achieves its objective, enriches the people involved, and provides a foundation for future communication. Three qualities in particular influence your communication effectiveness: responsibility, ethicality, and credibility. Because credibility rests in part upon your responsibility and your ethics, and because developing credibility and confidence are the theme of this book, we develop them at greater length in Chapter 2.

Here, we explore the vital elements of responsibility and ethicality.

Responsibility

Communication, like marriage, is more than a 50–50 proposition. Effective communication is a 100–100 proposition: Each person has to give 100%. Each participant must be deeply invested in the success of a transaction and take responsibility for achieving understanding. Each must ensure both the process and the results of communication. If you're talking to someone who isn't listening, you need to find a way to get that person's attention. If you're listening and don't understand someone, you need to work at the interaction until you do.

Process Responsibility   If each communicator takes responsibility for the quality of a transaction with strong and competent involvement, that's when good communication can result. Your involvement requires these qualities:

1   *Attentiveness*: Focusing on important cues from others in the environment

2   *Perceptiveness*: Being aware of and assessing accurately meanings of others' cues and responses

3   *Responsiveness*: Evaluating a social situation and adapting to it appropriately "by knowing what to say and when to say it."[10]

Your involvement shows that you're highly absorbed, you care, and you're a partner in the transaction. Developing ability to involve yourself, furthermore, enables you to communicate both confidently and credibly in different situations and contexts. Try practicing these three special skills in your daily communication:

1   *Understanding others*. Focus on perceiving others' needs, wants, and beliefs—their emotional and intellectual states—correctly. Your accuracy in understanding

demands that you listen carefully, watch how others respond, seek feedback, and check your perceptions.[11]

2 *Self-monitoring.* Pay attention to how your own behavior affects others.[12] When you see someone's response to you, ask yourself, "What am I doing that gets this reaction? Is it what I want? Should I change my approach to help her or him receive my ideas more positively or understand them better?"

3 *Adaptability.* Be flexible in responding to another person. As a self-monitor, you can develop a wide repertoire of possible behaviors to adapt as necessary to make communication work.[13]

Here is an example of positive involvement. At work, your coworker seems cranky, while you're tired and worried about tomorrow's exam. You snap at her over a minor problem. She becomes even more annoying, and you want to snap at her again, but you monitor your response. You think, "If I go off the handle, I'm not going to find out what's going on here. I'm going to drive a wedge between us. Is that what I want?" So you take a deep breath, put your own weariness on hold, and say, "Hey, I'm sorry I was so abrupt. Can we talk about it?"

In so doing, you are intensely involved in the interaction; you understand accurately (your coworker's unhappy about something); you self-monitor (check your own behavior); and you adapt (modify your response). In sum, you help to develop your relationship.

It's true that if you adapt your communication simply to manipulate or deceive others, you're being hypocritical and unethical. In contrast, however, when you self-monitor and adapt to make it easier for others to share ideas and feelings and to enlarge understanding, you act according to an ethical code that respects the interests and rights of others. In this context, your ability to understand others, to self-monitor, and to adapt behavior can contribute to your communication confidence and effectiveness.

Outcome Responsibility   Does the following exchange sound familiar?

"If *you* would just listen, you'd understand me."

"If *you* would say it clearly, I would understand."

Who is at fault? Who knows? Sometimes, people won't take responsibility for the outcome of communication and seek to blame someone else when it fails. They tend to feel vindicated if they can account for having sent the message, even though, as we pointed out earlier in this chapter, sending a message does not ensure anyone's receiving it. You've heard people shrug off their responsibility by saying things such as, "It was in the memo I sent last week," "It's in the college catalog," "We covered that at our last meeting," "It was on the bulletin board," "Didn't you read the instructions?" That is, "Not *my* fault! I *told* you!"

The "I told you" syndrome reflects a refusal to take responsibility for the results—to work through communication until a message has been understood. You can't guarantee another's agreement or compliance or even full understanding, but *outcome responsibility* means a communicator works hard to ensure the idea is comprehended.

A few years ago, there was a tragic example of poor communication and blame assignment—of a lack of outcome responsibility. Several children in the state of Washington died of food poisoning from undercooked hamburgers served by a quick-service restaurant chain. Investigators concluded that the meat wasn't cooked as required by new government standards. The chain's management initially responded that it had not received new guidelines. Then it stated that it had indeed received them but had misplaced them, and consequently had not communicated them to the restaurants' cooks. The government had "sent" the guidelines, but in this case, "telling" failed to ensure communication. Communication had failed between government and restaurant management and between management and workers.

Ethicality

If you say, "Wait a minute—that's not fair," you're talking about ethics. If you say, "Hey, give Johanna a chance to speak," you're talking about ethics. If you say, "We can't use that source in our report—it isn't credible," you're talking about ethics. Communication constantly involves conscious or unconscious reactions to ethical issues. Your **ethics** are codes or beliefs that your upbringing, religion, culture, and experience have given you for judging "what is right or wrong, fair or unfair, caring or uncaring, good or bad, responsible or irresponsible, and the like."[14] In communication, you apply these codes both to process (how you treat people in transactions) and to decisions about the content of your messages.

Ethics of Process   An *ethic of process* refers simply to how participants treat one another as they communicate. Are they open and sharing and honest? Or are they manipulative and deceptive and closed? We, your authors, believe that a **dialogical ethic** is your best approach to communication. A dialogical approach creates a climate in which people are able to be authentic about who they are. Communicators include and confirm the worth of others; they are "present" (accessible and attentive); and they share a spirit of mutual equality.[15] In a dialogical ethic, each person's right to be heard—and to be different—is respected and protected. If you must "hold your own ground" in a discussion, you still can respect and listen to the other.[16]

Communication ethicists say that you can know what *you* believe is right and wrong, good or bad—and still be tolerant, still see shades of gray in issues, and still have respect for others' beliefs and ways; in other words, you can create dialogue and learn from one another without compromising what you believe.[17]

Think of dialogue in contrast to monologue. *Monologue* is one-way, self-centered communication; it is not concerned with the listener. Monologue is akin to giving a speech to a mirror or into a tape recorder. *Dialogue* involves mutual commitment, give and take, listening, negotiating new meanings, and shaping ideas together. Dialogical communication is more evident in interpersonal and small group communication, but its spirit also infuses public speaking when you talk *with* rather than *at* your audience, when you are sensitive to their feedback, and when you adapt to their needs.

Ethics Codes or beliefs used for making moral judgments and determining acceptable behavior

Conscience: A small, still voice that makes minority reports.

Franklin P. Adams

Dialogical ethic Process based on the value of sharing ideas and feelings with another

Ethics of Message Content   *Ethics of content* determine what you will say, how much you reveal, how honest you are. Democratic societies rely on an ethic of content that gives people the best and most complete information possible in order to make reasonable personal and civic decisions. All too often we see these expectations violated. A recent survey of opinion leaders found that "only 20% in the US, 24% in the UK, 20% in France, and 18% in Germany" would find information credible from high ranking corporate executives.[18] Ethical communicators should provide messages that respect listeners' need for:

- *Truth*. Before speaking, weigh alternative statements for their accuracy, so you can make the most honest statement possible. Be authentic; keep from "projecting a false image, or 'seeming' to be something [you're] not."[19]

- *Individual freedom*. Phrase ideas so your listeners can see what choices are available. Avoid manipulating others in ways that subvert their rights to decide for themselves.

- *Fairness*. Present messages so they show more than one perspective and acknowledge the value of ideas other than your own.

- *Respect*. Consider how messages might reflect on your character and on that of others. If words might make anyone feel diminished or inferior, replace or modify your message to respect others' feelings.

Summary

Whether you're communicating intrapersonally (with yourself), interpersonally (with another), in a group or team, or giving a presentation, your effective verbal and nonverbal communication are important to your success in your life and your career. Understanding communication provides the foundation for developing attitudes and abilities that will increase your personal effectiveness.

Communication is the process of using verbal and nonverbal cues to transact mutually acceptable meanings between two or more people within a particular context and environment. The communication process involves senders who encode ideas with words and actions and transmit them through a channel that includes distorting and competing noise. Receivers pick up and decode cues in context of their backgrounds, expectations, and experiences. They create meanings from them and send feedback to develop successful transactions.

Communication helps people meet needs and goals, yet communication involves taking risks. People need to interact, but their desire to avoid discomfort can create communication dilemmas.

The challenge that this course and this book present is to learn and implement qualities that make your communication effective. These include taking responsibility for the process and the results of your transactions, applying ethical principles to guide the processes and content of your communication, and developing your personal credibility and believability of your messages.

Exercises

 1 Meet with two other people and get to know one another. Find out about your majors, interests, goals, likes, and dislikes. In addition, find out the answers to these questions:

- How would you describe communication in your family (open, limited, loud, quiet, funny, serious)?
- Where do you think your family communication habits come from (your culture or other background traits, experiences, and so on)?
- How do you think your family communication has influenced your own communication habits and feelings?

After you've gotten to know one another, introduce each other to the class. Make your introduction fairly short but interesting. Make sure the class learns the *name* of the person and something by which to *remember* him or her.

 2 In a group, share some of your funniest or most ridiculous communication experiences. These can be anything from misunderstandings to conflicts to embarrassing situations. Then do the following:

a Choose one or more of these situations to share with the class.

b Create a short skit that portrays the situation. Be sure every member of the group is in the skit.

c Perform the skit for the class.

 3 In a small group, examine the frame-by-frame communication model in this chapter on pages 11–12. In what ways would the model change if people were sending and receiving in languages other than their native language? Assume, for this exercise, that these people still think only in their first (or native) languages. Draw the new model.

The icons for the exercises throughout this book identify the types of communication activities each involves:

Intrapersonal—individual work; planning and analysis activities

Interpersonal—dyadic; one-to-one experiences

Small group—working with a few classmates

Presentational—sharing information with your class or other group

4 Choose an experience you have had or one you would like to have. Review the "Telling Your Story" box in this chapter. Remember the personal connections used by the storyteller as you prepare to tell your story to the class as a brief presentation. Think about the images in your mind, and choose the most appropriate verbal and nonverbal messages to help listeners to create clear images and meanings in their minds. Will you need to set the scene? What sequence will help you keep the ideas clear? What details will help them "get the picture"? Practice telling your story out loud until you are comfortable with the material. Then, share the experience with the class.

5 Observe a televised public speech or reference one of the links for *Historic Speeches on the Web* found at *Communication Links* under *Book Resources* at the *Communicating with Credibility and Confidence* website at http://academic.cengage.com/communication/lumsdenccc3. For a period of 10 minutes, analyze the following:

- To what extent does the speaker exemplify dialogical ethics or content ethics as these are developed in this chapter?

- In what ways does the medium of television affect the speaker's application of these ethical concepts?

Be sure you identify the specific aspects of the speech that lead you to your conclusions. Write a brief report of your findings, and prepare to discuss them in class.

Cyberpoints

The following Cyberpoints can be easily accessed from the Student Companion website for this text at http://academic.cengage.com/communication/lumsdenccc3. Click on *Student Book Companion Site* and select this chapter from the pull-down menu at the top of the page that says "Select a chapter." Click on *Cyperpoints* under *Chapter Resources* and you will find links for the exercises following.

1 Communication can be a frustrating experience. Go to the *Communicating with Credibility and Confidence* website following the directions in the previous paragraph. Then click on *knots,* by R. D. Laing. Why do you believe the author pretends to know everything? Why do you think he wants you to tell him everything? When was a time that you felt something similar to the *knot* the author describes?

2 Go to the *Communicating with Credibility and Confidence* website following the directions given. Then click on "If a tree falls in the forest." It is hard to believe that trees respond to the presence of humans. Do you communicate differently in the presence of others? Why or why not?

3 Use InfoTrac College Edition to locate and examine one of the following articles on ethics.

Communication Quarterly, Wntr 2003 v51 i1 p57(16) "Difficult Conversations as Moral Imperative: Negotiating Ethnic Identities During War," by Spoma Jovanovic.

Bulletin Northwest Public Power Association, Sept 2003 v57 i9 p19(1), "Communication Ethics Coming to the Forefront," by Nelson P. Holmberg.

Public Health Reports, May-June 2003 v118 i3 p193(4), "Health Communication Ethics and CDC Quality-control Guidelines for information," by Jeffrey W. McKenna, Terry F. Pechacek, and Donna F. Stroup.

How are communication and ethics important in the article you read? What principles from the article can you use in your own communication?

Chapter 2

Your Communication: Developing Credibility and Confidence

Objectives for This Chapter

Knowledge

- Understand factors of communication credibility
- Know ways to enhance your credibility
- Understand what influences communication confidence
- Know ways you can increase your confidence

Feelings and Approaches

- Want others to perceive you as a credible communicator
- Feel greater confidence as a credible communicator

Communication Abilities

- Set and work toward personal communication goals
- Visualize and develop personal attributes of credibility
- Visualize and develop confidence in communication

Key Terms

credibility	trustworthiness	relaxation techniques
ethos	coorientation	visualization
competence	dynamism	self-talk
objectivity	communication apprehension	affirmation

On the last day of the semester, our student Miriam walked to the front of the room, looked around, smiled, and confidently proceeded to give an outstanding speech. She was in command of the room, of herself, and of her topic. Her classmates listened eagerly, believing in her and what she had to say.

Miriam, who was an immigrant from Colombia, had started the term nervous about making speeches in English. She mumbled, she couldn't look at her audience, she forgot what she planned to say. Her classmates were kind and supportive—but unimpressed. What happened? Miriam developed confidence in herself and became aware that she was a credible person with something valuable to communicate.

How would you feel in Miriam's shoes? To what extent do you think others believe in you and what you say? How deeply do you believe in yourself and your message? The purpose of this chapter is to give you a framework for increasing both your credibility and your confidence in communicating. It introduces you to elements of credibility and ways to develop it, then helps you examine your present level of confidence, how it has developed, and how you can improve it in communication situations.

Communicating with Credibility

Suppose you're listening to a lecturer. Do you view everything she says as suspect? Or are you paying careful attention because you trust her goodwill and expertise? Whichever it is depends on your assessment of the speaker's credibility. Of course, someone else in the audience may see that lecturer differently.

Credibility is a matter of how one person perceives another and his or her message. In all communication situations, your credibility is in the listener's judgment of your character and affects how he or she responds to your message. A summary of credibility research confirms that "a high-credibility source is more persuasive than is a low-credibility source in both changing attitudes and gaining behavioral compliance."[1]

Obviously, credibility is closely tied to a communicator's ethics, but the two are not the same. Ethics are in a *communicator's* thoughts and behavior, credibility in the *receiver's* perception of the communicator. Unfortunately, ethical messages are not always believable, and credible messages are not always ethical. Because credibility for both speakers and messages lies in the minds of listeners, different receivers may perceive the same speakers and messages very differently,

Credibility How your message and character are perceived

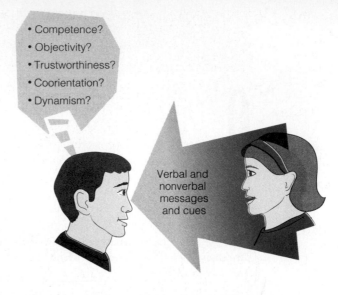

Figure 2.1 *How a receiver perceives another person's credibility*

- Competence?
- Objectivity?
- Trustworthiness?
- Coorientation?
- Dynamism?

Verbal and nonverbal messages and cues

but factors that influence their perceptions are much alike. That gives you a set of criteria to develop as a communicator.

Credibility Factors

More than 2,000 years ago, Aristotle explored what made speakers credible to their audiences. He identified credibility, or **ethos,** as the way an audience brings both prior knowledge of a speaker and what they see and hear in his communication to judge his good character, good sense, and goodwill.[2] The ancient Greeks viewed credibility a lot like people in the United States do today.

Contemporary researchers have investigated what makes a speaker credible to listeners, finding factors a little more specific than Aristotle's. Using those factors for our definition, we would say that credibility is how people judge a person's competence, objectivity, trustworthiness, coorientation, and dynamism.[3] Figure 2.1 illustrates how one person might see another and evaluate both the individual and the message using these criteria.

Ethos A speaker's believability: "good character, good sense, and goodwill"

Competence   **Competence** is the degree of expertise and qualifications, authoritativeness, and skill a person demonstrates. Your competence is reflected in your preparation, information, ability to adapt to and work with others, and ability to think creatively and critically.

How to develop and demonstrate competence? Like this:

Competence Perception of a person's expertise, authoritativeness, and skill

- Recognize what you know and do well. This involves specific content information, but also your ability to work with people. You already have *content competence* in some areas. You may be excellent in math but mediocre in literature, or weak in music but strong in sports history. Your competencies reflect your interest in and knowledge of these topics.

What do you think when you see a picture of a woman pastor? How do you think people might assess her credibility? Would she have to work harder than a male pastor to establish her credibility? To what extent would all members of a given place of worship agree on her credibility? To what extent do you think members of various religious groups might agree?

Don Lumsden

- Identify your *process competence*, which may vary according to the context. For example, you might already be excellent in face-to-face communication but terrified and bumbling in a presentation, or good at explaining but less effective at persuading.

- Develop both content and process competence by finding areas in which you're effective and practicing those behaviors—keep improving on your strengths.

- Build new strengths. Work on content through preparation and study; work on process through considering, analyzing, and practicing the communication abilities that help you work with others.

Objectivity Perception of a person's ability to look at different points of view and suspend personal biases

Objectivity   Objectivity, like Aristotle's concept of "good sense," is looking at various points of an issue; suspending personal biases; being reasonable and dispassionate; showing respect for others' opinions; and examining evidence, reasoning, and values before taking sides. In democratic societies, where discussion and debate are the means by which issues are decided, the ability to be an objective judge of ideas is particularly crucial.

You can develop objectivity by disciplining your thinking and phrasing your thoughts in everyday life. As you read, study, research, and write for classes or for pleasure; as you listen to lecturers, radio, and television; and as you interact with others, practice the following habits:

- Try to look at every issue from more than one side. You might feel strongly about an idea, but analyze how someone might justify other positions.

- Look for reasons and evidence to support various points of view on any issue.

- Read and listen to viewpoints other than your own, and evaluate them honestly and fairly. Look for points on which you can agree with underlying values, evidence, or reasoning on the other side. This may not change your own opinion, but it will help you maintain your objectivity about others.

- When you interact, be receptive to what others have to say, and phrase your own responses to acknowledge their points of view before you argue for your own. Withhold judgment until you've heard all sides of an issue.

Trustworthiness Perception of a person's consistent and honest behavior

Trustworthiness   **Trustworthiness** is the result of consistent and honest behavior, or "good character." Your ethical beliefs and choices shape your trustworthiness. People will trust you if they see you are sincere and ethical. Would a friend tell you a personal secret, knowing you will never, ever tell anyone else? That's trustworthiness.

Trust is a fragile attribute, and communication cannot get very far without it. In personal relationships, violation of trust often is the beginning of the end. In public life, loss of trust can destroy careers. As a communicator, therefore, you must guard your character and reputation closely. Ask yourself:

- Do I live up to what I say? Can I be trusted to fulfill a promise or commitment? To protect another person's confidentiality? If I hear a rumor, do I pass it on or stop it?

- Do I speak up for the ethical choice? Do I choose the truth when a lie would be easier?

Coorientation Perception of a person's similarities to and concern for listeners

Coorientation   **Coorientation** is your similar orientation with listeners and your concern for their well-being. Coorientation is similar to Aristotle's concept of "goodwill." It's easier for people to identify with you when they see you share some interests, beliefs, values, objectives, and needs with them. Here are some ways to develop coorientation:

- Consciously look for ways in which you and others *are* similar—backgrounds, attitudes, values, beliefs, or, perhaps, goals.

- Find ways to express that coorientation with others. Don't assume others are "just like you"; that can be a terrible mistake. Rather, seek to understand differences among people of other orientations, backgrounds, and cultures. Value insights of people with different experiences, building your opinions and ideas on that enlarged foundation.

- Listen carefully to others and express your support, if not your agreement.

- Show, verbally and nonverbally, openness, friendliness, and supportiveness that says, "We're working this communication out together."

Dynamism Energy with which a person compels the interest of others

Dynamism   **Dynamism** is energy, vigor, or intensity that compels the interest of others. It's probably a big part of charisma. Dynamism influences others, but

You're Such a Charmer

You may be baffled when someone who has no real credibility to you (in terms of the factors we discuss in Chapter 2) simply bowls people over with some kind of personal force. What is that, anyway? Maybe it's what this author is describing as charisma. Here are two thoughts to ponder: Can you really develop charisma? Is it always a good thing?

You know who they are. They're the people in the office who seem to have legions of fans from every department. For instance, it may be the person who can stop by the office of his boss—

or any other senior manager for that matter—for an informal chat on a whim, while everyone else on staff seems to have to set up a meeting at least a week in advance. "What is it he has that I don't?" you may wonder. What he has, in a word, is charisma.

A recent University of Pennsylvania study shows that charismatic leaders get better performance from their employees and have more influence within an organization. But you don't have to be born with charisma. You can develop it. . . .

From Phaedra Brotherton's article in *Black Enterprise* 30: 9 (April 2000): 152.

it is a tricky element of credibility. Individuals' reactions vary widely with personal experiences, cultures, and contexts. If someone is too loud or intense, those from quieter cultures may find such dynamism offensive, or if a leader conveys negative messages too intensely, group members may achieve less consensus and satisfaction.[4] Dynamism may have a strong voice, grand gestures, and colorful language, but quiet passion and strong convictions can be dynamic, too.

Do you remember Mother Teresa? Her communication reached around the world, yet she was as soft-spoken as a breeze. Her incredible intensity, her commitment, made her dynamic. She had that magical quality called "charisma"—drawing others to her and making them want to follow her lead.

You can develop and adapt dynamism by using these guidelines:

- Believe in what you communicate, and talk about it with an enthusiasm, reflecting your beliefs and feelings.

- Relax and energize before speaking (we discuss techniques further on in this chapter).

- Connect with others by using eye contact, facial expressiveness, gestures, and body position.

- Be sensitive to feedback. If listeners seem overwhelmed or offended, something's wrong. If they light up and seem to key in to you, you're probably doing fine. If you're speaking in a loud, intense voice, for example, a

North American might find it authoritative and dynamic, but a Thai might draw back, thinking that you're aggressive, perhaps even angry.[5]

■ Adapt to the situation. If you're listening sympathetically to a distressed friend, keep your energy under control. If, however, a business meeting is sagging, vitalize it with humor, gestures, and an expressive voice.

If you think you're generally a little too low-key, work on using your eyes, face, body, and voice to communicate energy and enthusiasm. If you're naturally dynamic, that's great—but be careful. Watch for responses; don't bowl people over, don't dominate, don't keep the emotional pitch at a constant high. The idea is to let dynamism energize your messages, not to let it overwhelm other people.

All of these credibility factors can come together at once. Suppose you are trying to persuade someone to vote for your candidate. In your explanation, you truthfully acknowledge the opposing candidate's strong points, demonstrating your trustworthiness and objectivity. You explain why your candidate's attributes serve values and beliefs that you and your listener share, showing both your competence and coorientation. As you present a logical, reasoned argument, you demonstrate your competence and objectivity. If you speak with passion, sincerity, and energy, honestly attending to your listener's feedback, your dynamism helps you to establish your credibility on all five factors.

Credibility Influences

It's important to realize that individuals also weigh credibility according to the situation and their individual constructs. For example, a comedian who keeps you in hysterics may be morally corrupt, but maybe you don't really care too much—you're just interested in being entertained. Possibly your friend Jeff is flaky and incompetent, but he's a good guy and your coorientation with him is more important to you than his reliability. Or Professor Sullivan might be objective, competent, and trustworthy, but boring because she lacks coorientation and dynamism. You might not go to the comedian for advice, nor ask Jeff for help on an exam, nor care to socialize with the professor. Perhaps you overlook some deficiencies because other characteristics are more important to what you want in each situation.

You might also have an individual standard of credibility that excludes some criteria and includes others. A gang member may find a tough, chain-swinging, domineering leader credible, but perhaps you would find that same person *in*credible.

An individual's response to someone's credibility is influenced by many other things, too, including cultural values and norms. A young western Apache, for example, listens to the "wise words" of elders who are credible because of their "reputation for balanced thinking, critical acumen, and extensive cultural knowledge."[6] Many Anglo North Americans, however, grant little credibility to older people because they believe aging is associated with the loss of intelligence and memory.[7]

Communicating with Confidence

If you are completely, absolutely confident in your communication, you probably don't understand all that is involved. Communicating, as we have said, is risky, and it's perfectly normal to be apprehensive about communicating. It's managing the anxiety that matters. That's why this book emphasizes confidence so heavily. Even in the United States—where people are great talkers and value communication highly—virtually 100% of the population is anxious about communication in *some* context.[8] Many businesses are so concerned about managers' confidence that they hire trainers to help them develop self-assurance in their abilities as managers.[9] You need that confidence in any career. Besides, communicating is easier and more fun when you are confident.

Where does your level of confidence come from? Maybe some of the following factors have influenced your feelings about communicating.

Influences on Confidence

Who you are now is, at least in part, a product of your lifelong experiences and the influence of such factors as your culture, gender or social status, family norms, role models, special people, and your own perceptions.

Culture In every culture and identity group, group norms affect how people communicate, norms that reflect their worldview, religious and political structure, and fundamental values. Overall, for instance, people in Hong Kong and Micronesia are very reticent, although they are more willing to communicate in groups than face to face—as opposed to the United States or Australia, where people are most comfortable in dyads.[10] Even how *much* people talk may be culturally influenced. In the United States, for example, talkativeness is considered a virtue. In Sweden, people are expected to be more judicious in their conversation.[11] In the United States, therefore, a Swede might be thought to be shy, whereas in Sweden, a North American might be thought to be a bit too outgoing.

Gender or Social Status Your gender and class ranking in society may largely affect your communication opportunities and confidence. In each society, a "power elite . . . those who *dominate* culture, those who historically or traditionally have had the most persistent and far-reaching impact"[12] maintains position over others who hold less political, economic, and social influence—frequently, women and various ethnic groups. One way the dominant culture maintains power and prestige is through downplaying the communication of subordinated groups. When subordinate members realize dominant members won't listen to them, they may see themselves as inferior. That perception undercuts their confidence, which weakens their communication, creating a vicious circle. That may explain why women public speakers experience more apprehension than do men.[13]

Family Norms   Every family, too, has its own ways—noisy or quiet, open or closed, supportive or defensive—and anything in between. Family norms teach children expectations of themselves they carry into adulthood.[14] Compare two kids, Erin and Tyler. Erin's family expects each member, including children, to share in decision making. At family meetings, all are encouraged to speak out and are listened to respectfully. In Tyler's family, one adult makes all the decisions, and no one—especially not children—can discuss or question them. Later in life, these family experiences may influence Erin's joy and confidence in leadership and Tyler's apprehension and followership.

Models   Parents, family, friends, public figures, media—all give children models to copy, and adolescents also imitate peers and television characters. In fact, media heavily influence self-image and interpersonal communication. If models are credible, confident, and competent communicators who interact ethically and humanely, that's great, but media are known for perpetuating racial and gender stereotypes, both in fiction and nonfiction programming.[15] People may model their communication after stereotypes they see, thereby reinforcing others' stereotypes of who they are. That, then, can diminish their credibility and weaken their confidence in interacting with diverse people. Although television and film show you many more professional, intelligent women and people of color than they used to, they still provide plenty of models of inept, stupid, or sociopathic stereotypes to imitate. And these stereotypes do say to people, "Look—this is what *you* are, and that is what *they* are." And, yes, this affects behavior and self-confidence, not to mention credibility.

Special People   Your sense of self might be influenced strongly by your brother or sister, your mother or father, your teacher, your pastor, or perhaps a family friend. One authority calls these important people "wizards."[16] Wizards are people in your life whom you believe much more than you believe others or yourself. With such power, your wizards' words and responses to you can shape your perceptions of yourself and your communication.

You may have been reinforced in your idea of who you are and how you communicate, too, by special people in your life. Reinforcement through rewards or punishments—whether physical or emotional and psychological—shapes your behavior and your perceptions of yourself. As a child, your family and primary groups reinforced your behavior. In adolescence, your most important reinforcement may have come from your peers.[17] As an adult, your behavior is reinforced by many people and events, but especially by your personal wizards and your own self-talk.

Sometimes reinforcement has the reverse effect; instead of repeating the actions that were rewarded and avoiding the ones that were punished, you could conclude that you "just are that way." Such thinking can lead to *self-fulfilling prophecies*, whereby individuals predicted to behave in a certain way then fulfill those expectations. That behavior, in turn, further reinforces their expectations and actions to the point that it becomes a vicious circle.

Here's an example of these influences: Rosa gave a poor report in class because she had insufficient information. She was embarrassed and told herself she just wasn't a good speaker. Her father, a very special wizard in her life, wants to help, so he keeps reminding her, "Don't make a fool of yourself again," reinforcing her bad feelings about herself.

Rosa takes that to heart. For the next speech, she does excellent research and prepares thoroughly. It works; when she gives her speech, her teacher and classmates praise her research, her reasoning, and her overall presentation. But does Rosa believe them? She wants to—*but she doesn't*. Why? Because *she* knows her presentation wasn't perfect. She was nervous and forgot some things. Her listeners don't know that, but she does. So she believes the speech was not really good; she just fooled them. Her wizard's voice in her mind says she is an imposter who made a fool of herself again. Rosa tells herself the teacher and class are wrong, that they're just trying to cheer her up.

They are *not* wrong. Rosa doesn't realize that forgetting something does not necessarily ruin the research or the speech. More important, she can't see what she did well because her well-meaning wizard's warnings are drowning out her successes. All she can see is the negative.

If you've ever had such an experience, however, be of good cheer. First, some wizards are great influences. Like the Wizard of Oz, they can show you that you have a heart, or brains, or courage and then send you out to use them. Second, you can stop listening to the negative influences and become your own wizard, find your strengths, and build on them.

Influences from You   What words do you use to describe yourself? "I am a good communicator"? "I'm a lousy speaker"? "I'm a good listener"? Your own experiences combine with influences from others to create your self-concept— the mental picture you have of who you are.

Your *self-concept*, consisting of the attitudes and beliefs you've developed about yourself over your lifetime, affects your credibility and your confidence as well as your actions and your perceptions of others. Research has found, for example, that success in school is greater for young African American and Mexican people whose self-concept includes a wide variety of possibilities than for those who see themselves in stereotypical terms.[18]

One theory suggests each person has three "selves":[19]

1   Your *looking-glass self* reflects views of you in the eyes of others, especially your wizards. Seeing that reflection, you may think, "Oh, that's how I am," creating a self-fulfilling prophecy, for better or for worse.

2   Your *self by social comparison* is how you compare yourself to others. "I'm just stupid," one child thinks, seeing that classmates solve math problems more quickly, or, "I'm a good artist!" as she sees that her pictures are better than others'.

3   Your *self in social roles* is your perception of how you respond to what you believe society expects of you. As society evolves and expectations change, it's increasingly difficult to know how to fulfill them. It can be frustrating, for

example, to juggle roles requiring "quality time" with kids, attentiveness to a spouse, and career demands.

Martin Luther King Jr. created an image of a child forming self-perceptions when he wrote, "You seek to explain to your six-year-old daughter . . . that Funtown is closed to colored children, and see the ominous clouds of inferiority beginning to form in her little mental sky."[20] King sensed how his daughter must have seen herself, not as she truly was, but drawn by the stereotypes and negative comparisons and expectations of a prejudiced world. Society was showing her a clouded looking-glass self, and her parents' task was to let her see her real worth, to provide her with a looking glass of clarity and beauty.

The way you perceive yourself and your communications also may draw on other factors, such as:

Self-attributions.   Did you ever see yourself do something, ask yourself "Why?" and then attribute characteristics to yourself as the cause of your behavior? People do that.[21] "I speak well, so I must have a self-confident personality," you might reason, or, "I can't communicate with my family without fighting because I am basically a high-strung person." An attribution may be false, but all too real in a person's self-image.

Language.   Are you fluent in your native language? The more fluent you are, the easier it is to get a point across and the more confident you become. In another language, you might be much less confident. Constantly trying to translate thoughts can be exhausting and frustrating, and often listeners are impatient. Sometimes foreign speakers just give up. Even in their own language, however, people sometimes feel they have an inadequate vocabulary and, therefore, lack confidence in their ability to express themselves. Lacking confidence, they are silent. What a pity; frequently, their vocabularies are better than they think. Besides, vocabulary can be developed.

Skills.   Have you ever looked back at a communication experience and seen only your faults—or only your virtues? A more realistic assessment can better help you improve your skills and confidence. Many of our students, for example, worry that they "talk with their hands too much," a belief that undercuts their confidence when they make a speech. Yet, rarely is excessive gesturing a problem for one of these students. In fact, their tendency to move and gesture is a great basis for developing dynamic communication. Recognizing that fact can help them to build skills *and* confidence.

Communication Apprehension

Do you relish a chance to communicate? Sometimes you do, sometimes you don't? Do you shake at the prospect? Sometimes yes, sometimes no? People vary in their *willingness to communicate*, but researchers have found that people who like to communicate are perceived by others as more credible, sociable, composed,

Communication Anxiety

Roger Fluet, a volunteer at Covenant House in New York City, wrote the following poem about his apprehension as he completed his training and was about to take his first call on the "Nineline" (1-800-999-9999), a hotline that runaway kids and teens are encouraged to call from the United States, Canada, and Mexico.

This is horrible.
I'm thinking like a child again.
This is all new to me.
This training is too overwhelming.
Am I supposed to remember all of this?
I'm not sure if I understand.
Is anybody else getting all of this?
Is *everybody* getting all of this?
These feelings are really scary.

How can I be expected to be able to help a
kid in crisis?
What if the caller is smarter than me?
What if they realize that I'm unsure of what
I'm doing?
Maybe I will know what I'm doing.
Am I ready?
I am definitely not ready. Well, maybe.
Am I supposed to know?
God, I wish I knew.

I'll never be able to answer those phones.
What am I supposed to say?
What do they expect of me?
What if I say the wrong thing?
I don't want to screw up.
What if I get a drug call?
Or a pregnancy call?
Oh, my God, a suicide call.
I can't handle this.
"RING . . . RING . . . "
"Covenant House Nineline . . . "
Stick to the model.
The supervisor is only a touch-of-a-button
away.
Hey, this isn't so bad.
I think I'm really helping this kid.
Wow, thank goodness for the model.
Maybe I am ready.
This is all new to me.
I'm thinking like a child again.
This is great.

How do you think Roger's credibility and confidence were developing as he took his training? What do you think happened as he took that first call?

Reprinted by permission of Roger Fluet

---

competent, extroverted, and attractive.[22] Others have found that people who are *reticent* experience anxiety about communicating that leads to holding back, feeling like (and possibly perceived by others as) an incompetent communicator.[23] That all makes it worth the effort to acquire a taste for interaction.

Sometimes, people are really anxious about communicating; they say, "I'm so shy," or "I'm just too nervous," or "I have such butterflies, such stage fright."

These responses all reflect **communication apprehension,** "an individual's level of fear or anxiety associated with either real or anticipated communication with another person or persons."[24] Most people are apprehensive about communication in some contexts, but extreme apprehension can contribute to poor communication and to loneliness,[25] or to students' lower grades and even to the probability they will drop out of school.[26] Most communication apprehension is a temporary problem; sometimes it's deeper. There are four basic types of communication apprehension.[27]

1   *Context communication apprehension.* You may be comfortable talking with a friend, okay with a group, terrified to make a speech. Or you might love making a speech, but horrified at the thought of asking someone to buy a raffle ticket. That's context. As you might expect, the context that scares most people most is public speaking.[28]

2   *Audience communication apprehension.* Possibly you, like almost 95% of the U.S. population, could be intimidated by a specific audience (of one person or many) at some point in your life.[29]

3   *Situational communication apprehension.* You might be breezily confident in just about any situation but suddenly choke up on, say, your wedding vows. Situational apprehension is a transitory response to one particular situation.

4   *Traitlike communication apprehension.* This is like a personality trait— a gnawing, constant anxiety about communicating in almost any context. Fortunately, traitlike apprehension can be alleviated with professional help.

As you can see, communication apprehension ranges among individuals from an occasional emotional spasm to a seriously problematic condition. Sometimes people are apprehensive because they feel they lack the necessary communication skills.[30] Some become more apprehensive in intercultural communication situations.[31] Yet some students enroll in a required speech class— and then drop it because of apprehension—every semester up to their senior year. That kind of apprehension is demoralizing, but there are ways to get it under control. Many colleges have learning centers and/or counseling centers that can help with this problem. In most instances, no matter how awful communication apprehension feels at the moment, it can be alleviated. As this book progresses, you'll learn ways to manage your stress and develop confidence in your communication abilities.

Realistic Confidence

As we have seen, it's possible to be too timid, too quiet, and/or too anxious. It's also possible to be too confident, too brazen, too sure. People need to assess their skills and to develop confidence to pursue their opportunities. In the United States, for example, women may be at a disadvantage, because, while they tend to be better at identifying their own limitations than men are, they more often underestimate what they *can* do.[32] As a consequence, they often lack the confidence to pursue challenging careers for which they would have been well suited.

A *little* anxiety is a good thing. Some apprehension probably reveals that you understand the situation and your responsibilities. Before giving a speech, you may think, "If I quote this statistic incorrectly, I'll give all 25 people in my audience the wrong idea." Or, before giving your best friend some difficult advice, you may say to yourself, "If I say this in the wrong way, our relationship may be damaged." Your logical concern over possible consequences may make you nervous; at the same time, you may prepare your message more carefully, think through your ideas more thoroughly, and consider your listeners' needs with greater sensitivity.

Sometimes, students' confidence actually slips a bit as they begin to learn more about communication. The more they know, the more they realize communication isn't a simple matter of "just talking." As they develop skill, however, they learn how to prepare better and their confidence becomes better founded, stronger, and more convincing to others.

To get a quick picture of your own feelings about communicating, fill out Form 2.1 at the end of this chapter. The results can indicate your starting point for confidence, pleasure, and effectiveness in communicating.

Developing Communication Confidence

We're going to offer you a proven method that we have seen work over and over again. Relax—Visualize—Practice: Do these and you'll be more confident and more effective.

Relax Away Your Stress

In dread of what you must do, you might postpone a difficult call or procrastinate interminably your research for a speech. You might see yourself with a fluttery stomach, shaky knees, sweaty palms, and dry mouth when you face an interview, perhaps, or a speech. These are normal reactions to communication stress, but you can turn them around, be confident, and make that energy serve you.

Communication stress is a circular set of relationships between psychological factors and physical symptoms that lead back to psychological responses. Figure 2.2 shows what happens.

Hao is about to go to an interview. He feels unprepared and anxious. His body receives this message about his feelings from his mind and interprets it as a threat. When people are threatened, their instinct is either to flee or to fight. Hao's sympathetic nervous system, which doesn't know the difference between the emotional threat of communicating and the physical threat from a gun, prepares for "fight or flight." His adrenaline surges and his heart beats faster; the

Figure 2.2 *How psychological stress and physiological symptoms are interpreted negatively to increase apprehension or stage fright*

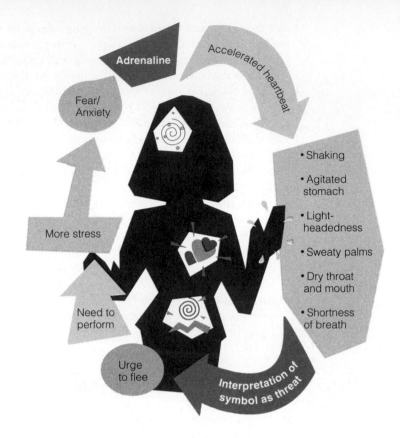

- Shaking
- Agitated stomach
- Light-headedness
- Sweaty palms
- Dry throat and mouth
- Shortness of breath

Adrenaline

Accelerated heartbeat

Fear/Anxiety

More stress

Need to perform

Urge to flee

Interpretation of symbol as threat

increased adrenaline makes him a little nauseous and shaky in the knees and stomach; his head feels fuzzy and his mouth goes dry.[33] Hao becomes aware of these symptoms and thinks, "I'm scared—I can't do this—I'm going to be sick." As his mind wrestles with anxiety, it sends another SOS to his body, which reacts by pumping yet more adrenaline.

The problem is, Hao's mind and body are interpreting every response negatively, and his anxiety is increasing rapidly. "I'm just too nervous," he tells himself. He doesn't realize confident communicators *also* feel anxiety, and they also get a good shot of adrenaline from their systems, but they interpret it positively. The adrenaline gives them the vitality and dynamism to do a good job; it makes the situation exciting and challenging. So stress isn't the problem; you can learn to accept normal stress and use it to your advantage.

The first step is to relax. "Impossible!" you say? Not so; it's possible and essential. Research has shown that **relaxation techniques,** when used *before* you actually get into specific situations, help you develop confidence and effectiveness in your communication.[34] Relaxing slows breathing, lowers pulse rate and blood pressure, eases muscle tension, and focuses your attention. By consciously relaxing, you can help clear your mind for studying, reduce stress before an

Relaxation techniques
Methods used consciously to help you reduce anxiety

exam, counteract exhaustion during the course of a long day, and prepare for a difficult talk with another person or a presentation to a group.

There are a number of approaches to relaxation. Here is one called "deep-muscle relaxation":

1   Get comfortable, close your eyes, and concentrate on relaxing your muscles.

2   Breathe slowly and deeply. Imagine the oxygen flowing through your blood-stream, reaching all parts of your body.

3   Now begin relaxing your body, starting with your toes. Envision them relaxing. Think of the blood as circulating freely around your toes, making them relaxed, warm, and comfortable.

4   Continue this process up into your feet, ankles, and legs. Work slowly, thinking of each muscle relaxing, all the way through your body.

5   Concentrate on areas where you have the greatest tension—perhaps your back, shoulders, or neck. Tell yourself you feel them relaxing, feel the blood circulating, feel the tension flowing out of them.

6   When your entire body and mind feel relaxed, allow yourself a few moments of floating in that easy, comfortable state.

7   Now, tell yourself that the muscle relaxation will continue and that you will feel comfortable, at ease, and energized for your communication. Picture energy flowing back into your body.

8   Open your eyes, and you're ready to communicate with confidence.

As you work through your relaxation exercise, actual physiological changes take place. Your adrenal glands are calmed, so they pump out less stimulation to your nervous system. As you feel the reduced physiological stress, your comfort level increases. *With practice, you can relax yourself in a matter of seconds, even as you walk down a flight of stairs or across campus.* We can tell you from personal experience that this technique works, especially when you combine it with visualization and affirmation techniques.

Visualize Your Success

The human mind is incredibly powerful. *What you see in your mind and how you talk to yourself can determine your success or your failure.* It really is up to you. For some people, "seeing" is the most effective; for others, talking is.[35] A person whose fear is very powerful may need to see a professional who can find the best way to help,[36] but for most folks, visualization and verbal affirmation make the difference.

Creating Successful Images   In **visualization,** you create a specific mental image of your successful performance to use as a kind of mental practice for the event ahead of you. Athletes have been using visualization for years. Dick Fosbury, Olympic gold medalist in the high jump, says, "I developed a thought process in order to repeat a successful jump: I would 'psyche' myself up; create

---

I couldn't wait for success . . . so I went ahead without it.

Jonathan Winters, comedian

Visualization Creation of mental image of a successful performance

a picture; 'feel' a successful jump—the perfect jump; and develop a positive attitude to make the jump. My success came from the visualization and imaging process."[37] What he did in his mind, he did with his body. Fosbury revolutionized the way athletes approach the high jump and broke through previously imagined limits of possibility. When you watch the Olympics today, you see high jumpers using both visualization and a version of the "Fosbury Flop."

When an individual goes through a *mental* rehearsal for a physical action, the muscles prepare to perform that action. In a sense, they practice silently what they are to do. In the same way, your mind can rehearse the image of what you want to do as a communicator. To create visualizations for your communication, follow these steps:

1 See yourself in a specific communication setting, such as an interview, a speech, or a conversation. Picture yourself as confident and in charge.

2 Picture clearly what you would be doing in a perfect performance. See and hear yourself as you communicate in the situation. Create a complete mental picture of the entire event, as if you're watching yourself on a videotape replay.

3 Imagine your emotional response to the experience. Sense how you would feel in context of the transaction. Suppose you're preparing to confront a friend about her drinking problem. You'd feel confident you're doing the right thing—concerned, caring, serious, determined, focused on her and her problem. If you're preparing to make a speech, however, you might feel confident and well prepared, excited about your information, involved, eager to inform your audience, physically coordinated, and dynamic.

Self-talk Messages to yourself to improve your approach or performance

---

Affirming Successful Interactions   Here we're talking about **self-talk.** Far from meaning you're crazy, talking to yourself to improve your approach or your performance is smart. "As a learning strategy it promotes the learner's selective attention to appropriate features of a skill."[38] Some people call this process "managing your mind" or "inner leadership."[39] Your words affirm in your thinking the things you've visualized yourself doing and feeling. Combining images with words makes a greater impact on your performance.[40]

As you change your actions, you also can change how you think about yourself. For example, improving your grades improves your self-esteem. But the opposite is also true—changing how you think about yourself can change the way you do things. Seeing yourself as a better student can affect your performance—and your grades. Using self-talk and visualization, then, allows you literally to practice and train mentally to reach your goals.

Affirmation Positive, present-tense description of a desired achievement

---

You can guide your self-talk by writing out an **affirmation,** a statement that is a personal, positive, present-tense description of achievement using words depicting actions and feelings.[41] Let's consider each element:

■ *Personal.* Affirm what *you* visualize yourself as doing, describing the act precisely as it is to your senses: "I am walking confidently in to my interview appointment. I'm excited about the interview. I'm smiling and holding out my hand. I shake hands firmly and wait to be invited to sit down."

- *Positive*. Keep the affirmation positive. "My words are flowing fluently; I know exactly what to say; I'm expressing my ideas clearly," affirms the image. If you said, "I'm not using a lot of 'uhs,' or 'you knows,'" you'd be focusing on what you *don't* want.

- *Present-tense achievement*. Use terms to describe your actions as if they are happening now instead of in the future tense. For example, saying, "I *am* confident and at ease," makes you feel the image in the here and now.

- *Action words*. Include specific sensory details; words describing movement and responses are easy to visualize—for example, "I am keeping direct eye contact with my audience," or "My gestures are strong. They emphasize my important points."

- *Feeling words*. Use words that describe your emotional reactions to involve the feeling dimension of your thinking-feeling-doing relationships. You might say, "I am energized and eager to tell my listeners . . ."

An affirmation statement for a public speech might go: "I am well prepared, speaking fluently and energetically, moving comfortably, gesturing dynamically. My audience is attentive and supportive. I care about my listeners, and I enjoy watching and listening to them to make sure they understand my ideas. This is enjoyable, and I do it well."

Practice Your Skills

Nothing substitutes for good practice, but practice does *not* necessarily make perfect; repetition of any behavior simply makes it habitual. Only *perfect practice makes perfect*.

"I absolutely will *not* mispronounce 'cinnamon' this time," the television cooking show host promises himself. And he mispronounces it again. "Okay," he says to himself, "cimmanon, cimmanon, cimmanon. I've got it." No, the speaker has ci*mm*anon, not cinnamon. Or, "I *will* use eye contact when I speak," the political candidate declares. So she practices her speech looking at chairs, gets up to deliver the speech, and looks straight at the listeners' chests, not their eyes. How embarrassing! These people practiced, but they practiced the wrong things.

Many people's experiences, and a lot of research, suggest that training, knowing what you're talking about, and good practice reduces apprehension and improves the quality of your communication.[42] Practicing correctly calls for knowing what your goals are.

Setting Goals   You've got the visualization and affirmation. You've done some preparation for your communication event. Now you analyze that vision to select a few attainable goals for yourself. You will do best with *two or three* goals to work on at a time rather than a lot all at once. Begin with those that will provide you with the greatest progress in your development and those you know are *attainable*. Set realistic practice goals. If you were lifting weights, you wouldn't set 500 pounds as a practice goal, would you? You'd start lighter, with challenging but attainable weights for each practice session. So it is with communication goals. Perhaps you're comfortable talking one to one, but uncomfortable in a group. Then a first goal might be to speak up more at your project group meeting. After some success, you would set a new goal, perhaps to ask questions or to express an opposing opinion.

Achieving Goals   Now you can use specific visualization affirmations for each goal, practice mentally, and put it into action with physical practice. Here are some steps:

1   Prepare for your actual practice (that could mean content preparation such as research or planning or physical preparation such as setting up a tape recorder or notes).

2   Review your visualization and affirmation.

3   Practice your behavior in the situation you've selected. As you experience some success, go back over the *successful* behaviors; practice them in your mind.

4   Disregard unsuccessful behaviors; just identify what you want to do better and rehearse the *right* way to do it.

5   Set new, slightly more difficult practice goals.

6   Repeat the process with the new challenge.

Suppose you want to speak out in class more confidently. Your first goal could be "Ask a question in class." Visualize yourself doing that, fulfilling an affirmation statement something like this: "I am listening carefully. I'm curious about a related idea. I raise my hand and the teacher calls on me. I speak up clearly and organize my question so the professor and the class understand me. The exchange makes the class more interesting, and I enjoy learning as I listen and question."

You could have practice sessions with a friend, working to make your questions clear, direct, and confident. Then choose a class in which the teacher encourages participation so you *can* ask questions. Do your homework so you're prepared. Then go to that class, listen, review your affirmation statement in your mind, and ask a question, as clearly and confidently as you can. This, too, is practice. Pretty soon it becomes easier, and you actually *do* enjoy the transactions with the professor and your classmates. You're involved, and you like it. You're achieving a communication goal. You're on the way.

If the first attempt falls flat, use it as a learning experience. "Trial-and-error learning" cannot occur if you never have errors. When you make a mistake, focus on it only as a means for identifying what will work better next time. Then forget the mistake and start to visualize yourself using the new, improved behavior in your next opportunity. Write and rehearse your affirmation and, at the first chance, practice it perfectly.

Summary

Your credibility and your confidence influence the success of your personal life and your career. Credibility is how others perceive your competence, objectivity, trustworthiness, coorientation, and dynamism; credibility is also affected by the situation and by individual constructions of what a credible person is. To become a credible communicator, you need to make each of these attributes part of your life and practice communicating them to others in your interactions. When you know others find you credible because of qualities you genuinely have, then you can feel more confident in yourself and your message.

Confidence results when you feel you can meet the challenge in a communication situation. Your culture, gender, status, family, and other background experiences have contributed to your feelings about yourself as a communicator. Some people are more willing than others to communicate, and some suffer from more apprehension than others. Everyone feels some anxiety about communicating in one context or another; the key is how you manage it. If you react to your physiological symptoms negatively, your fears will increase the symptoms, and you will feel even less confident. If you interpret them positively, you can use them to "fuel" an energetic and dynamic delivery—and thus increase your confidence.

Assess your skills and build on them as a foundation for developing greater confidence. Your confidence will grow as you learn to use relaxation techniques and to visualize and affirm your performance. With appropriate practice, you can attain your goals as a credible, confident communicator.

Exercises

1   Complete Form 2.1 at the end of this chapter. Instructions for scoring are included on the form. What do you think this self-assessment reveals about your willingness to communicate with others? When do you feel perfectly comfortable? When do you begin to get a little anxious about a situation? What factors have influenced your feelings? Think about your background experiences, family, culture, role models, and so on. How have they affected you? How can you now change any of your behaviors that may have weakened your confidence in the past?

2   Think back over your experiences, and identify an occasion when you felt you communicated very well. Perhaps you created a new understanding out of an argument with a friend? Maybe you persuaded someone to listen to your point of view? You might have taught someone how to do something?

Now write a brief description of the situation and identify as precisely as possible the following:

- Which of the five factors of credibility do you think you brought to the situation? How do you think the other participant(s) saw your credibility? How did that affect your interaction?

- How did you communicate your credibility? What did you say and do that made the other person(s) feel you were credible?

- How confident did you feel in that situation? Why? If you were apprehensive, what was it like? How did you manage it? How did your confidence level affect the way you communicated?

3 Make a list of communication goals you would like to achieve. Make them as precise as you can, and identify a situation in which you could practice some skill toward achieving that goal. Now, use the "Visualize Your Success" section of this chapter to help you visualize yourself communicating exactly the way you want to in that situation. Write an affirmation statement for the goal. Remember to phrase it in the present tense and to make it descriptive of your specific behaviors, your positive feelings, and the positive responses you get from others.

4 With a small group, share the goal and affirmation statement you created in Exercise 3. Make sure each person's goal is in present tense, positive in tone, and descriptive of specific behaviors and others' responses. Now, do the following:

   a With your group, design a short practice situation for each person's affirmation. Make it something you can do with members of the group role-playing the person or group in which you want to develop your skill.
   b Close your eyes and relax. Have a group member read your affirmation aloud to you while you visualize the situation clearly.
   c With the group helping you, practice your goal behavior.
   d Have your group give you feedback. Start with what you did well, and talk about how you can make it even better. You might consider rewriting your affirmation to make it stronger.
   e Repeat this process so every member of the group can practice his or her affirmation.

5 Listen carefully to a speaker, either on television or in a public performance (this could be a politician, a preacher, a lecturer, and so on). As you listen, analyze the speaker's credibility. Consider the factors of objectivity, competence, trustworthiness, coorientation, and dynamism. Also consider the situation and your personal opinion about what you think increases a speaker's credibility.

   Now prepare a 2-minute report on the speaker's credibility. Explain briefly who you heard, where they spoke, the topic, and the context. Then describe how much (or little) credibility you saw in the speaker. Be as specific as possible in describing the speaker's behaviors and quote the speaker's words to demonstrate your point. Present the report to the class.

Cyberpoints

The following Cyberpoints can be easily accessed from the Student Companion website for this text at http://academic.cengage.com/communication/lumsdenccc3. Click on *Student Book Companion Site* and select this chapter from the pull-down menu at the top of the page that says "Select a chapter. . . ." Click on *Cyperpoints* under *Chapter Resources* and you will find links for the exercises following.

1 Are you interested in women's body images and how they affect self-confidence? Use InfoTrac College Edition to locate the article "Body Feelings Sink Women's Self-Image" from *USA Today*, v128, i2656 (Jan 2000), p7, or Julia Savacool's "Women's Ideal Bodies Then & Now," from *Marie Claire*, v11, i4 (April 2004), p102. What have you learned about the influence of body image on self-confidence? Summarize your discoveries.

2 Want to know more about how people use visualization to improve their performances? Use InfoTrac College Edition to search on the keywords *visualization*, *imagery*, and *self-talk*. You'll find several articles there. Identify the article(s) you read. What did you discover? How can you use what you learned in your own communication?

3 If you're interested in what makes folks credible, use InfoTrac College Edition to search on the keywords *credibility* and *charisma*. Access at least three different articles from your search. Is the concept of credibility presented differently than it is in this chapter? Based on the articles you reviewed, what are some reasons it is important to improve your credibility with others?

4 For an example of a speech analyzed for the credibility it conveys, go to the *Communicating with Credibility and Confidence* website at http://academic.cengage.com/communication/lumsdenccc3, and select Chapter 2 from the pull-down menu. What aspects of credibility presented in this chapter were present in the analysis? Were additional aspects used? If so, do you believe they will help you develop your credibility?

5 Go to the *Communicating with Credibility and Confidence* website at http://academic.cengage.com/communication/lumsdenccc3, select Chapter 2 from the pull-down menu, and click on *Willingness to Communicate* and *Communication Apprehension Surveys* to find out how different people (cultures, genders) respond. Do you think humor might be related to communication confidence? Use InfoTrac College Edition to locate Nathan Miczo's "Humor

Ability, Unwillingness to Communicate, Loneliness, and Perceived Stress: Testing a Security Theory," *Communication Studies* v55 i2 (Summer 2004), p209. What are two ways you can use the findings of this article to improve your communication?

6   For a wonderful insight into self-concept and self-confidence, take a moment to meet Maya Angelou. Visit the BBC's website at http://www.bbc .co.uk/ and search for Maya Angelou. Read four facts, watch two talks, listen to links, maybe even visit her homepage. Did you capture where she came from? Did you experience who she is today? How does your meeting of Maya Angelou inform the responsibility you must take for your own self-concept and self-confidence?

Form 2.1

Self-Assessment of Willingness to Communicate

Following are 20 situations in which a person might choose to communicate or not to communicate. Assume you have *completely free choice*. Indicate in the space at the left what percentage of the time you would choose to communicate (0 = never, 100 = always).

_90___ 1. Talk with a service station attendant

_100__ 2. Talk with a physician

_99___ 3. Present a talk to a group of strangers

_85___ 4. Talk with an acquaintance while standing in line

_100__ 5. Talk with a salesperson in a store

_100__ 6. Talk in a large meeting of friends

_100__ 7. Talk with a police officer

_80___ 8. Talk in a small group of strangers

_100__ 9. Talk with a friend while standing in line

_100__ 10. Talk with a server in a restaurant

_80___ 11. Talk in a large meeting of acquaintances

_60___ 12. Talk with a stranger while standing in line

_80___ 13. Talk with a secretary

_99___ 14. Present a talk to a group of friends

_50___ 15. Talk in a small group of acquaintances

_20___ 16. Talk with a garbage collector

_100__ 17. Talk in a large meeting of strangers

_100__ 18. Talk with a spouse (or girl/boyfriend)

_100__ 19. Talk in a small group of friends

_20___ 20. Present a talk to a group of acquaintances

Summarize your scores on the Scoring Form on the following page.

Scoring for Form 2.1, Self-Assessment of Willingness to Communicate

Subscores

Group Discussion
Add scores for items 8, 15, and 19; divide by 3 ___76.6___

Meetings
Add scores for items 6, 11, and 17; divide by 3 ___93.3___

Interpersonal conversations
Add scores for items 4, 9, and 12; divide by 3 ___81.6___

Public speaking
Add scores for items 3, 14, and 20; divide by 3 ___72.6___

Stranger
Add scores for items 3, 8, 12, and 17; divide by 4 ___81.75___

Acquaintance
Add scores for items 4, 11, 15, and 20; divide by 4 ___58.75___

Friend
Add scores for items 6, 9, 14, and 19; divide by 4 ___99.75___

Total Willingness to Communicate Score

Total subscores for stranger, acquaintance, and friend
Divide by 3 ___81___

McCroskey, J. C. (1992). Reliability and validity of the willingness to communicate scale. *Communication Quarterly* 40, 16–25.a. Reprinted by permission of Eastern Communication Association.

Chapter 3

Perception and Thought: Making Sense

Tony Freeman/PhotoEdit

Objectives for This Chapter

Knowledge

- Understand how people perceive and interpret stimuli
- Know what factors affect the process of perception
- Understand how critical thinking works
- Understand how to analyze an argument for validity and truth

Feelings and Approaches

- Be aware of how factors of perception affect your own and others' messages and interpretation
- Be confident in using critical thinking to receive and plan communication
- Enjoy examining factors of perception and reasoning in messages

Communication Abilities

- Use critical analysis to understand perception and messages
- Develop valid arguments through critical thinking
- Develop messages that aid others' perception and understanding
- Attend to others' messages perceptively and analytically

Key Terms

perception

sensory fatigue

selective attention

shaping

culture

gender

hierarchy of needs

social exchange theory

consistency needs

critical thinking

inductive reasoning

deductive reasoning

cause-and-effect reasoning

ome years ago, in London, we were watching a production of the musical *Cats* when a bomb scare halted the show. The audience was quickly ushered outside, where the actors proceeded to continue their performance. When a van carrying the bomb squad drove up, an actor waved it through the crowd with a gallant bow. After the officials checked the theater and pronounced it clear, most of the audience trooped back in for the finish of a marvelous performance. When Don tells the tale, the van is white. When Gay tells it, the van is black. We both saw the same van—we both even remember the "cat" actor who directed it through the crowd. And we're equally sure of its color. Who is right? We'll never know. Each of us has a different reality about that van.

That's okay, because we know that *each person creates his or her own reality*. No matter what "really" happens, the reality you *believe* in is the one you *perceive*. That's the event you remember and discuss with others. Communication is about bringing human realities closer together. Sometimes, the gap between what two people perceive or think is so enormous that each must use great energy and discipline to understand the other.

Fortunately, if you know a bit about how people perceive and think you can more accurately perceive messages from others and from your environment. You can think more openly about what these messages mean; and you can communicate your thoughts more clearly so your receivers respond to them the way you intend.

With all that in mind, this chapter examines how people perceive their "reality" and how to use critical thinking to understand and respond to that reality more effectively.

The Process of Perception

Perception Process of becoming aware of and interpreting stimuli

Perception is the process of becoming aware of and interpreting stimuli, an absolutely fascinating part of communication because what and how you perceive is the unseen foundation for creating and responding to ideas within yourself and between you and others. All at one time, you listen to others, notice things, and talk to yourself (usually silently), using an intrapersonal, ongoing internal monologue to process information you perceive. Take a look at Figure 3.1 for a glimpse of the perception process.

First you *sense* (see, smell, taste, touch, hear) stimuli. Then you unconsciously *select* one of those stimuli to attend to (for example, there are millions of light rays that bend to allow for numberless shades of colors, but what do you see?

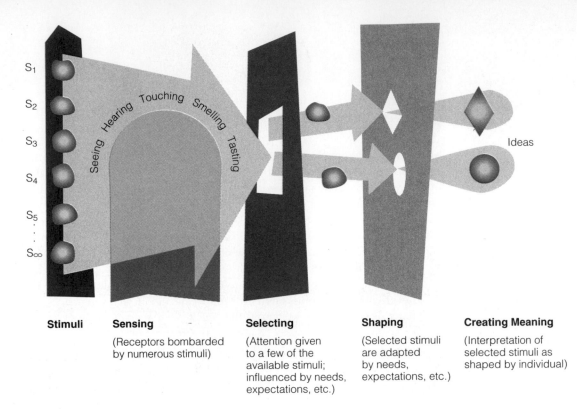

Stimuli	Sensing	Selecting	Shaping	Creating Meaning
	(Receptors bombarded by numerous stimuli)	(Attention given to a few of the available stimuli; influenced by needs, expectations, etc.)	(Selected stimuli are adapted by needs, expectations, etc.)	(Interpretation of selected stimuli as shaped by individual)

Figure 3.1 *A basic perception model*

That bright red shirt over yonder). Having unconsciously acknowledged a stimulus, your mind starts to *shape* it into something you can understand and, finally, to see some *meaning* in your perception.

Let's examine each step separately and identify ways you can verify the accuracy of your perceptions as a communicator.

Sensing

Humans experience the external world through their five senses. Our senses are essential to communication because they serve as the receptors for cues available within the environment. Yet people often miss important cues (such as chunks of a professor's fascinating lecture!). Why? They're experiencing **sensory fatigue;** that is, the senses tire quickly from too many or too much repetition of stimuli. When that happens, attention wanes.

Figure 3.2 demonstrates sensory fatigue. Stare directly at the heart's center for 20 seconds. Then look at a plain white background until an image appears. What do you see? Has the heart appeared on the plain white field? What color is it?

Sensory fatigue State in which senses become tired while processing stimuli

Figure 3.2 *A demonstration of sensory fatigue*

After staring for just 20 seconds at the heart against its white background, sight receptors have fatigued. When you shift your gaze to the plain white background, you see that the heart's color has changed. You perceive the new shade because your sensitivity has been dulled to the original color. Because white reflects all colors, you now see only what is left after the original heart's color is removed.

The same fatigue happens to your other senses. Have you ever walked into a room that had a strong odor but found, to your relief, that the smell disappeared quickly? The odor did not diminish; rather, your sensitivity to it decreased. The same phenomenon occurs with other senses. You hear a faint whine from fluorescent lights, but after awhile, the sound is gone. Even a word, which spoken once has meaning, becomes meaningless if it's repeated over and over.

Why does a communicator need to know that? Because in communication, too, a repetitive stimulus loses the listener. Isn't it true that a speaker who drones on in a monotone, and/or stands motionless and expressionless, simply loses you? Message senders, then, need to find ways to keep listeners' senses acute, and listeners need to find ways to offset their sensory fatigue.

Selecting

You cannot respond to every stimulus that reaches your sensory receptors—you would be so overloaded you might go berserk. At any given time, your senses are bombarded with an infinite number of external stimuli. What you do, therefore, is pay **selective attention,** focusing on "one detail so much you do not notice other events."[1] Look at Figure 3.3, for example.

Selective attention
Process of focusing on one detail and not noticing others

Do you see a dog? Bird? Rabbit? Bell? They're all there. Knowing that, can you see them all now? Can you see them all at once? Really, your eyes shift quickly back and forth, focusing on one and then on the other, excluding the others for that moment. Selecting a stimulus is like tuning a radio; when you set it for one station, you don't receive what's being transmitted on all the others. To be confident of your perceptions, you need to "tune in" or select essential message cues.

Figure 3.3 *What do you see?*

Shaping

Shaping Perceiving a stimulus through personal filters or screens

Once you focus on a specific stimulus, you may shape the cue to suit yourself. That is, an incoming stimulus goes through personal filters or screens you have developed from your individual experiences. With personal **shaping,** you may perceive a stimulus very differently than it actually is.

Shaping a perception in your mind is something like the Play-doh you probably played with as a kid. You put the stuff (stimulus) into the Play-doh Factory, and pushed it through a template to make the shape of a crescent, a star (or a thought). That's a simplified form of what you do when you receive verbal and nonverbal cues; you reshape them through the "templates" that you have created from your background and experience. Another example of perception is in Figure 3.4.

Look at Figure 3.4 and read the message aloud. Look at it again. Most people see only one *the* when they look at this for the first time, but it really says *the* twice: "Faces in the *the* Crowd." That's because people expect to see only one *the*—rarely does English include two *the*'s in a row. You (or anyone else) may shape stimuli to conform to what you expect, need, or want to perceive.

Creating Meaning

After you select and shape stimuli, your knowledge and experiences affect how you decode the message and what it means to you. Unconsciously, you sort through memories to find how they relate to the present stimulus. What you find could lead you to understand something close to what the sender intended, or to believe the message means something you can't identify, or even to have a meaning almost opposite to the speaker's intent.

Someone says to you, for instance, "That's a great new haircut!" Depending on your past experience with that person, his or her nonverbal cues, and how

Figure 3.4 *What do you read?*

Faces
in the
the Crowd

you happen to feel about your appearance at the moment, you might think that's a nice compliment—or an implication that anything's better than your last haircut, which looked like a haystack.

One of our favorite cartoons is the *Peanuts* on page 58. Linus decodes significantly different meanings in the clouds from Charlie Brown's. Linus could not perceive Thomas Eakins or the stoning of Stephen if he had never learned about them. (That's why you have to take those general education courses, to learn broader frames of reference from which to interpret your world, and to understand others' worlds.)

The meaning you draw from any stimulus, then, is directed by your experiences. Consider three different baseball umpires' points of view. Miguel says, "Some are balls and some are strikes, and I call 'em the way they are." He believes his perception and reality are one and the same. Yoshi says, "Some are balls and some are strikes, and I call 'em the way I see 'em." He knows perception and reality do not always match. But the legendary umpire Bill Clem showed the best understanding of perception when he said, "Some are balls and some are strikes, but they ain't nothin' 'til I call 'em."

Nobody sees a flower— really—it is so small we haven't time—and to see takes time like to have a friend takes time.

Georgia O'Keeffe, 20th-century U.S. artist

Factors Affecting Perception

You see somebody as friendly; your friend Peggy perceives her as hostile. You both think you're right because each of you is influenced by a wide range of personal characteristics. How you "see" something may result from your physical and psychological states; your beliefs, attitudes, and values; your culture and gender; your motivations; and/or your goals and expectations.

Physical and Psychological States

Lots of things may just block perception. Maybe the problem is physical. Your senses are dulled temporarily, perhaps by exhaustion from studying all night or from a severe cold. Do you then have trouble separating and recognizing concepts or perceiving stimuli accurately? Or maybe a physical condition such as hearing or vision loss limits one sense or another. That can lead to using other senses more efficiently. A person with hearing impairment may read lips, interpret

Peanuts © by Charles Schultz. Reprinted by permission of United Feature Syndicate, Inc.

nonverbal cues, and communicate in sign language, or someone who is vision impaired may listen intently for nuances of meaning.

Psychological factors, of course, can skew or block perception, too. If you are terribly anxious you may be unable to listen and comprehend,[2] fearing, perhaps, that new information will be too difficult to understand. In fact, people who are apprehensive about listening often perceive themselves as incompetent and messages as too complicated and difficult. This leads them to process poorly what they hear.[3]

Beliefs, Attitudes, and Values

Your beliefs, attitudes, and values—which are closely related, but quite distinct—form screens that shape your perceptions and influence interpretations:

- A *belief* is something we think is true because of our experience or learning.[4] Beliefs may be about any object (Asia is the world's largest continent), past event (World War II ended in 1945), and/or future occurrence (the Chicago Cubs will win another World Series).

- An *attitude* is a way you evaluate or act toward something.[5] These positive or negative responses affect your interpretations of new objects and ideas.

- A *value* is part of a cluster of related attitudes and beliefs, priorities for your choices on the basis of what you think is good or bad, right or wrong, worse or better.[6] Values dwell in a person's deepest self, a core of important concepts that deeply influence his or her perceptions and judgments.

Beliefs, attitudes, and values are closely related, but they may also be different. A student may *value* education very highly, but *believe* herself to be incompetent, a belief that would make her perceive classes as too difficult. That might be reflected in a negative *attitude* toward attending class. Her professors might interpret her behavior as meaning she doesn't value her education. But, if her belief about herself changes through some good experiences, her perception of (and attitude toward) her classes might also change, so that belief, attitude, and value would converge to make her perceive her educational experience favorably.

Culture and Gender

Culture Systems of beliefs, values, customs, behaviors, and artifacts shared within a society

Gender How one sees oneself in relation to society, sex, and roles

What is a culture, anyway? From hundreds of definitions, some experts boil **culture** down to "a system of shared beliefs, values, customs, behaviors and artifacts that the members of a society use to cope with their world and with one another."[7] Essentially, your culture structures how you see things.

So does your gender; but gender doesn't just mean whether you are male or female. **Gender** is a "social, symbolic creation," one acquired through experience, time, and cultural development.[8] Gender, therefore, is the way you see yourself and others in relation to society, sex, and roles.

It is even suggested that gender is a culture in itself: "If adults learn their ways of speaking as children growing up in separate social worlds of peers, then conversation between women and men is cross-cultural communication. Although each style is valid on its own terms, misunderstandings arise because the styles are different."[9] That men and women experience this problem is evidenced by scores of self-help books that claim to help them communicate better between their respective planets.

Certainly, deeply held values often come from cultural and gender experiences. Cultural anthropologist Edward Hall tells us, "One of the functions of culture is to provide a highly selective screen . . . [that] designates what we pay attention to and what we ignore."[10] The greater the diversity of those involved in the communication, the more complex are the transactions among their screens and memories as they shape stimuli and create meanings.

Language

If you know a word for an idea or object, you might perceive it, accurately or inaccurately. If you don't have a word for it, you might not perceive it at all. *If the word you have for an object is slanted or loaded in some way, you might perceive the object in a distorted or prejudiced manner.* Just think of the implications of that statement. If you grew up in a household where members of another race were referred to with a nasty term, you might perceive every member of that race negatively—only because of the attitude conveyed through that language.

It's also interesting, we think, that words available in a person's language may affect his or her ability to perceive distinctions among items. There have long been theories that within a culture people develop words to make fine distinctions among concepts that are important to them.[11]

The way people perceive time, for instance, is one way language and perception interact. Many tribal languages depict time differently from English, reflecting a difference in how people actually respond to the passage of time. The Sioux, for example, do not have words for expressing past and future tense,[12] while the Hopi view time as a psychological concept, not as an external period of hours or days.[13]

A student from Uganda explained to us that in his tribal culture that had no concept of hours, friends might agree to meet at a path into the village "the next day," with no set time appointment. Both individuals would get there, and neither would be late or early. How could that be? He finally got us time-obsessive North Americans to see that without a set hour, the friends had no basis to *perceive* "early" or "late." The one who got there first simply waited until the other arrived.

Motivation

"I'm just not motivated," your little sister says as she stares blankly at her textbook, unable to perceive anything she needs to learn for her exam. You shake your head and keep on studying, knowing you would be humiliated if you flunked the test in your class. Why are you motivated and she is not?

Perhaps you have different motives. A *motive* is a reason, a drive, perhaps a need, that spurs individuals to move in some direction or factors into their perceptions and actions. To communicate successfully means appealing to others' motives as well as understanding your own.

There are a multitude of theories about what motivates people. Some useful ones for understanding perception in communication include:

Hierarchy of needs
Ascending levels of need, each of which must be fulfilled before next level can be achieved

- A *hierarchy of needs*. Maslow's **hierarchy of needs** theory is old,[14] but very useful because it shows why and how individuals' needs and motivations vary. Figure 3.5 shows ascending levels of needs, suggesting that people must fulfill each step comfortably before they can be concerned with the next level. Only when your basic physiological needs are met can you

Figure 3.5 *Maslow's hierarchy of needs*

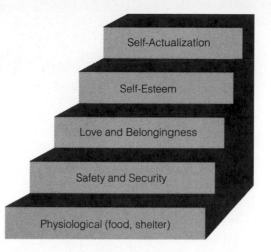

Self-Actualization

Self-Esteem

Love and Belongingness

Safety and Security

Physiological (food, shelter)

worry about safety and security; once safe, you are free to yearn for love and social belongingness. Then you can feel and meet your self-esteem needs. Once there, you can climb toward what Maslow called "self-actualization," seeking fulfillment in personal intellectual, artistic, or spiritual growth. Understanding how your own and others' needs may link to where one is in life can provide insight into how best to communicate. For example, you might think that simply offering to tutor your younger sister in math will appeal to her—after all, you can help her improve her grades. Ah, but if all she is motivated to do is serve her social needs, studying comes in a poor second to going out with her friends. In her place, you'd jump at a tutoring offer, but she might perceive it as another interference with what she really wants to do. Your suggestion might appeal more if you present tutoring as a way to free her for more social time in the future.

Social exchange theory
Choosing an action based on the weighing of rewards and costs

- *Social exchange needs*. Kelley and Thibaut's **social exchange theory**[15] explains how people perceive communication as an opportunity to reap rewards or to avoid costs or punishment. That is, people weigh their options, predict results of a choice, and consider whether rewards will outweigh the costs. They then compare results to what they minimally will accept, and how the result would compare to other possible choices. Think of it this way: Little sister compares spending evenings being tutored to being with friends and finds tutoring unattractive. But if she then weighs this decision against the probability she won't be allowed to go out at all if she doesn't improve her grades—well, then, her motivation still is social, but the cost-benefit analysis begins to make your tutoring offer look pretty good.

Consistency needs
Striving to maintain balance among attitudes, beliefs, values, and behaviors that motivates people to choose among conflicting information

- *Consistency needs*. A powerful motivation to accept or reject an idea is one's **consistency needs**. Festinger's cognitive dissonance theory[16] suggests that people need to feel consistency among their attitudes, beliefs, values, and/or behaviors. When people are conscious of inconsistencies,

*S*omeone asks:

Would you like to do so-and-so? A picture forms in my mind and as I look at it, it is either appealing or unappealing and I say yes I would or no I wouldn't. But this picture is not precognitive, it is a composite of past experiences that will be more or less *unlike* the coming event.

From Hugh Prather, *Notes to Myself* (New York: Bantam, 1990).

they feel a dissonance—a kind of tension—between two items of information (*cognitions*). When tension becomes great, they are motivated to reduce it in some way. For example, Grandpa is in a nursing home and he's lonely. His grandkids love him (Cognition 1), but they don't visit him often (Cognition 2). These two cognitions are dissonant, and that dissonance makes the grandchildren feel uncomfortable, perhaps guilty. According to the theory, they will be motivated to choose among these options: Change Cognition 1 and stop loving Grandpa—not likely; change Cognition 2 and go see Grandpa more often. If they actually do it, fine. If they don't, their choices are to avoid negative information (being reminded that he's lonely) or seek positive information (eagerly listening for reports that other people are giving Grandpa plenty of company). These are unconscious ways of rationalizing or manipulating one's own perceptions to relieve that feeling of dissonance.

Ways to Check Perceptions

Like everyone else, you only "see in part," so it's necessary to check your perceptions and interpretations. There are several ways to do this:

- *Ask other people*. Compare your observations and interpretations with others. Look for similarities and differences.

- *Rely on multiple senses*. Does what you see support what you hear? Are there contradictions? You may see a sweater that looks soft, for example, only to touch it and find it's scratchy.

- *Repeat observations*. If possible, you can review a scene, watch a video replay, or observe the situation from a different angle. Good science tries to reproduce research results to ensure accurate conclusions; this is a good habit for everyday life, too.

- *Consider possible misinterpretations*. How might your perceptions have led you astray? Did something in your background, expectations, environment or someone else's slanted comment influence your interpretations?

- *Consider possible changes*. Because something *was* true doesn't mean it *is* now. Perceptions can be made more accurate by "dating" events; if you say, for example, "When we went to Grant Park in 2003, it was great," your statement doesn't set up a perception that it's still great today. Maybe, maybe not.

- *Examine generalizations*. Avoid generalizations. You can "index" thoughts with relevant qualities, such as, "*As a teacher*, John is outstanding." John may be a dolt as an auto mechanic, so indexing leaves John's other abilities unevaluated.

- *Assume there's more*. Consider your perceptions and your statements about them to be incomplete. Mentally or orally add "etc." to acknowledge the probable existence of other unnoticed or unstated attributes.

The Process of Critical Thinking

We've heard students (and others) moan, "I'm just not logical!" "I hate analysis!" "Please—I'm all heart and no brain." Almost always, they're wrong about themselves. They just haven't learned how to think critically. We fondly remember the outright glee of a student who had once declared himself to hate analysis and, after getting the hang of it, loped into our office declaring that he loved critical thinking. As it turned out, he was very, very good at it. What a terrific feeling that was.

Critical thinking is essential, to life, to careers, to citizenship. To success. Think about this: "Americans can now expect to change jobs as many as a half-dozen times in their lives—a feat requiring considerable mental agility. The ability to sift, analyze, and reflect upon large amounts of data is crucial in today's information age."[17] Or this: "Critical thinking skills—the ability to think logically and make smart decisions" are the most important skills an interviewer should look for when you apply for a job.[18] Or this: The National Education Goals Panel declared the prime objective for colleges is to increase the proportion of graduates "who demonstrate an advanced ability to think critically, communicate effectively, and solve problems."[19]

Critical thinking
Deliberate analysis of data, reasoning, and conclusions

Whether you're discussing an issue, deciding who to vote for, planning your career, preparing for a speech, or arguing a case before a judge, you need to think critically. **Critical thinking** is deliberately analyzing data, reasoning, and conclusions. It is thinking about thinking, examining ideas and to what extent their connections to data and to one another are valid. Such thinking involves more judgment, analysis, and synthesis than the memorized or mechanical approach you might use for a simple task.[20] For example, you can remember and repeat a joke without much thought, but if you analyze it to see if it might offend a specific audience, or if you give it a new twist to amuse yet another audience, you're using higher-order skills of critical thinking.

Unfortunately, people can be smart yet make poor decisions just because they are not *disposed* to think critically. It takes a disposition—the inclination, willingness, or motivation—to think critically. For example, basic skill in analysis is looking at more than one side of an argument, yet most people who have this ability don't use it unless specifically asked to do so.[21]

Fortunately, we believe you can develop both disposition and ability, but you must want to think, and then to think well. Good thinking includes:

Thinking in a broad and adventurous way; Sustaining intellectual curiosity; Thinking across multiple contexts and perspectives; Building knowledge and understandings; Being intellectually careful and clear; Seeking truth and evidence; Being analytical and strategic.[22]

You can develop your skills day by day in every life and communication situation by consciously thinking in these ways:

- *Solving a problem?* Think of ways to plan approaches, achieve communication goals, and monitor your progress and your communication.

- *Making a decision?* Think of alternative approaches, review them objectively, and wisely choose the way you phrase and support messages for specific listeners and situations.

- *Justifying a position?* Think of multiple viewpoints, distinguish between different frames of reference, and use good evidence and arguments to present and analyze ideas objectively and competently.

- *Explaining an idea?* Think of interpretations and ideas, use supporting evidence, build and adapt explanations, and logically connect reasons to conclusions.

- *Designing a message?* Think of ways to structure messages that adapt to goals, organize parts strategically in relation to one another, and consider alternative approaches.

You can sharpen your critical thinking abilities, and thereby both your credibility and your confidence, by examining data, reasoning, and conclusions for their validity and logic. It's actually fun. No, really, it is! Read on.

Idea Logic

We—Don and Gay—have always enjoyed critical thinking because it's like playing with ideas or doing a puzzle, examining what goes into ideas, what makes them good, what makes them bad. Critical thinking analyzes the data, reasoning, and validity of a conclusion. When you learn to use these analytical tools, you become more astute and credible both as a listener and as a communicator.

Starting with Data   A professor of ours once explained his exams (they were fiendishly specific) this way: "You all think you can think—but you can't think without *facts*. So I want you to tell me facts." He had it exactly right. Thinking starts with data.

Poor information leads to poor conclusions, so the first step is to evaluate a source of information by asking:

- *Is the source primary or secondary?* A primary source is the newspaper, book, article, speech, or person that originally presented the statement. Getting information directly from the original source doesn't guarantee truthfulness or accuracy of data, but it does tell you the information is precisely as it was originally stated. In a secondary source, someone has summarized, paraphrased, or quoted material from other sources. Thus, a secondary interpretation may be quite different from the intention of the original source.

- *Is the source qualified?* Consider the individual's expertise, relevant academic credentials, experience, and affiliations with reliable and relevant organizations. Heed the warning that "well-known or highly honored people are often asked to comment on subjects outside their own field of expertise."[23]

- *Is the source's communication logical and consistent?* Examine a source's information for good critical thinking, evidence, valid conclusions.

- *Is the source reputable?* Find out if the person is acknowledged and respected by other experts in the field, if published work has been reviewed by respected peers, and if other experts rely on the source.

- *Is the source ethical?* Examine the source's actions and communication for honesty, objectivity, and fair-mindedness. Does the source have the best interests of the audience in mind?

If sources don't live up to these standards, you should be skeptical of their credibility. As a source yourself, applying these criteria to your *own* habits will tell you how credibly and ethically you are handling information you give to others.

Understanding Reasoning   Have you ever "leaped to a conclusion" and been embarrassed about how wrong you were? It's easy to do. Between perceiving something and drawing some conclusion, you make an inference, truly a mental leap. Critical thinking helps you determine if your "leaps" will land you on solid ground.

To test your reasoning, you have to examine each part of the process. We have diagrammed this process in Figure 3.6. As the figure shows, reasoning starts with *data*. Data may be anything that stimulates an inference—a personal observation, a statistic, a quotation. Often, data are evidence with which you prove your point to a receiver. From that data, you make an *inference*. An inference often is unconscious, so we have used a dotted arrow to link the data to the claim/conclusion. This means that you need to figure out the unstated (and perhaps unaware) inference connecting data and claim. The inference is backed up by a *warrant* or reason for drawing the conclusion.[24]

For example, Sarita says ice cream is good for people, so you decide to have ice cream for lunch. Your data is ice cream is good for people—your inference is it's good for *you*—or maybe you just want ice cream and Sarita has given

Figure 3.6 *Diagram of an argument from data through reason/ inference to conclusion*

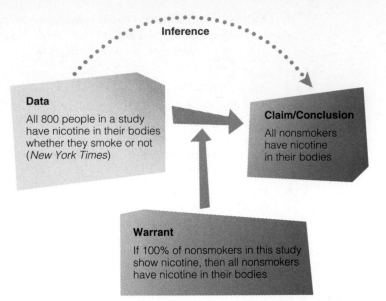

Inference

Data

All 800 people in a study have nicotine in their bodies whether they smoke or not (*New York Times*)

Claim/Conclusion

All nonsmokers have nicotine in their bodies

Warrant

If 100% of nonsmokers in this study show nicotine, then all nonsmokers have nicotine in their bodies

you an excuse. Your warrant is Sarita said so. Is Sarita credible? Is she correct? And if that wonderful food is good for people in general, is it good for you in particular? And if it is, are there other issues in making this decision that you haven't considered?

When you draw a conclusion based on reasoning from data or evidence, you've created an argument for your conclusion. But is it a *good* argument? Good arguments are solid building blocks that structure credible messages; poor arguments are sand, shifting away to leave your message tottering and weak. It might be hard to tell at first glance, but it's not too hard to evaluate your own and others' arguments by analyzing data, warrant, connections, and the conclusion to an argument.

You can identify and analyze an argument partly by its type. Here, we'll examine how inductive, deductive, and cause-and-effect reasoning, as well as combinations of these types, function in an argument. We will start with the following data reported in the *New York Times*:[25]

> *The first 800 people in a federal study of exposure to tobacco smoke had signs of nicotine in their bodies whether they smoked or not.*

Inductive reasoning
Drawing a general conclusion from specific cases

Inductive Reasoning   You're using **inductive reasoning** when you draw a general conclusion from specific cases. In this instance, from the 800 specific cases of people who showed signs of nicotine you *might* draw the general conclusion that all people must have signs of nicotine in their bodies. Would that conclusion be valid? To find out, you can ask:

■   *Are there enough cases in the sample to justify a conclusion?* Are 800 cases sufficient to generalize to all people? Probably not.

- *Do the cases represent the same population as that to which the generalization will apply?* Or, did all 800 come from one region? Were they similar in terms of age, sex, race, socioeconomic status, and so on? If so, they were not representative of "all people."

- *Are there exceptions to the general conclusion?* Have any people been found without nicotine traces? In this case, earlier studies did show some people without nicotine traces.

- *Can exceptions be accounted for without weakening the conclusion?* Maybe. Perhaps the earlier studies were done so long ago that conditions have changed.

Analyzing these questions may lead you to reject the generalized conclusion as improbable or to qualify it as "possibly" true for people in the region of the study or for people similar to them rather than for "all" people.

Without asking such questions, you can't know whether statistics mean a thing. When advocates on both sides of an issue use statistics to support contradicting generalizations, look carefully at their sources for their statistics, whether they actually support the speakers' generalizations, and whether one outweighs evidence for the other side.

Deductive Reasoning   What if you start with a generalization and move to a conclusion about a specific instance? That's **deductive reasoning.** For example:

All 800 people in the study have nicotine in their systems.

Paul was examined in that study.

Therefore, Paul has nicotine in his system.

To test deductive reasoning, you would ask such questions as:

- *Is the generalization accurate?* Yes, because it limits the generalization to those who were examined.

- *Is this specific case the same as the ones encompassed by the generalization?* Yes, Paul was one of the 800.

- *Is this specific case different in some way that makes it unlikely to fit the generalization?* No, Paul was part of the tested group.

That reasoning is okay. But what if the generalization is changed?

Most people living in the northeastern United States have nicotine in their bodies.

Paul lives in the United States.

Therefore, Paul has nicotine in his body.

Now apply the questions for examining deductive reasoning. Do you have good evidence that *most* people have nicotine traces? Does Paul live in the Northeast? Even if you can answer yes to both these questions, do you know whether Paul falls into the "most people" category, or is he one of the minority who does not have nicotine traces?

Deductive reasoning
Drawing a conclusion about a specific case from a generalization

---

It's easy for deductive reasoning to sound good when it is not. People often blindly accept a general statement as true, or overlook exceptions, so they fall for an invalid assertion. Much advertising counts on automatic acceptance of questionable generalizations that may not even be stated. For example, a commercial tells you Tantalizing Toothpaste will make your smile brighter and shows a sad-faced loner transformed into the life of the party after brushing. There are two unspoken generalizations: The product will make any user's smile brighter, and all people with bright smiles have exciting social lives. Both generalizations are untrue, so the reasoning is both invalid and untrue. But it may still sell toothpaste.

Combined Reasoning   Usually, the reasoning people use combines deductive and inductive reasoning, often incorporating other types of reasoning as well. One of the most common is **cause-and-effect reasoning,** in which people believe one event caused another because one event occurred after the other one.

Cause-and-effect reasoning Drawing the conclusion that one event is responsible for the occurrence of another

Look at the combination of reasoning methods you might use to conclude that you will take a communication class. A friend tells you her communication class helped her make better grades in other classes. She's using cause-and-effect reasoning. The class was the cause for her improvement. Then other friends tell you the communication class was interesting. You generalize from those cases that communication is always a good class. That's inductive reasoning, generalizing from specific instances. Because you believe communication is a good class, you conclude that you, specifically, will like the class, too. That's deductive reasoning, drawing a specific conclusion from a generalization..

Is your combined reasoning valid? To find out, you can ask:

- *Do you have sufficient examples?* Your friend is just one example of improved grades, and only a few friends said they liked the class.

- *Has the "effect" been preceded by the same suggested "cause" every time, or are there exceptions?* Did other students like the class? Every single one?

- *Did the suggested "cause" happen concurrently with other events that could be alternative "causes"?* Could your friend just like the teacher a lot? Have worked harder?

- *Do other "causes" or multiple causes seem more probable?* Did she like the teacher, like the subject, win prizes at speech competitions, admire good speakers?

Qualifying Conclusions   Because few conclusions are absolutely certain, you look for how *probable* the claim is. If the source has left parts of the argument unstated or exaggerated the conclusions, you may have to guess what is not stated as well as to analyze what is said.

As you examine a source's argument, you may doubt some of the data, rationale, or claim. As a speaker, you are ethically obliged to qualify any areas of which you are unsure, perhaps by explaining or supporting the source, data, or rationale, and by using terms such as *perhaps, possibly, probably,* or *almost certainly* to indicate how probable the conclusion is. As you see, each qualifier implies a different degree of certainty. If there is a lot of credible evidence and the reasoning is strong, you may be justified in saying the claim is "almost certainly" or "very probably" true. If evidence is slight or the reasoning is shaky, your claim just might be "possibly" true.

The Process of Planning Messages

Your messages start in your own perceptions, true, but they take shape as you use critical thinking to analyze your audience and plan messages so that they will reach listeners and connect with their perceptions and their sense of logic. Here we'll give you a start on creating transactions such as we described in Chapter 1, with principles that apply whether you're giving someone directions to get to your house, reporting research findings to a work team, or planning a public presentation. (We talk a lot more specifically about organizing speeches in Chapter 13.)

Consider Audience Perceptions

If you want others to hear and understand you, you have to engage their personal perceptions. You need to adapt to your listeners, stimulate their attention, choose the best language to express your thoughts, and organize ideas to help them understand.

Adapt to Receivers   A message misses the mark if it isn't adapted to the listeners, so you need to know everything you can about them. What do they know about the topic, and how much detail do you need to provide? If listeners are highly informed, you can enter the dialogue at a different point than if they have little or no information.

Besides knowledge, however, you need to examine what goes into your listeners' perceptions; motivations, attitudes, values, beliefs, needs that drive them; ways their culture and gender affect them. That is, everything we talked about as part of perception will affect how your audience hears and responds to your message. Given these insights into your audience, you can make intelligent choices in planning what you say and how you say it.

Choose Appropriate Language   A long time ago, Aristotle observed that language choices should fit the speaker, the situation, and the listener. That means:

- *Use understandable language.* Don't talk down, don't talk up—just talk *with* people. Consider their age, education, and experience as well as their personal values, beliefs, attitudes. If you must use words new to your listeners—specialized terms or jargon, perhaps—then define them, possibly with examples and explanations.

- *Use inclusive language.* Words people can connect to will bring them into your message. Sexist language excludes people, so, unless you're truly talking about a group of men (no women at all included), avoid using masculine pronouns (*he, him, his*), which imply the subject is male. Some people refuse to believe this affects female listeners' perception of how messages relate to them, but it does. Similarly, words you use may imply a judgment or stereotype of a person. Even though most of our students tell us there is little difference between the words *lady* and *woman*, when we ask who is most likely to become manager of a major corporation, a "lady" or a "woman," the same students say a "woman." These responses are based on unconscious stereotypes, so it's best to avoid even seemingly innocuous sexism.

- *Create word pictures.* Use a storyteller's technique; use words to create mental pictures that intensify listeners' perception. You can rouse sensations of seeing, feeling, hearing, smelling, or tasting by describing vividly what an object or an experience is or how it functions. "The child looked sad" is not as vivid as "The little girl's huge, dark eyes welled with tears, and one ran slowly down her cheek."

- *Tell stories.* Stories can be marvelously personal and real to listeners, whether it's from your own or someone else's experience, from literature, or from your imagination. To craft a story into a tool for enhancing your messages, use this advice from a professional storyteller.[26] First, identify what's most important about your topic. Then find internal conflicts that create drama (good versus evil, poor versus rich, strong versus weak, ideal versus real). Now organize the content to develop with a feeling of drama. Select a conclusion that resolves conflict and punches home the point. Finally, find a way to get feedback that shows you if listeners understood. The most indifferent audience will suddenly become entranced!

Even with the best language use, perception being what it is, listeners need help to follow logical connections and to remember information. It's called organization.

Organize Ideas Clearly Here's a useful hint that will show up over and over again in this book: *Use clear, logical categories.* It's long been known[26] that people can process only five to nine ideas at a time, with seven being the "magic number,"[27] so lists of ideas just don't work. To illustrate, read the following line; then cover it up and repeat it out loud:

dog, red, four, two, blue, one, cat, horse, yellow, bird, green, three

Could you remember it all after one reading? The list has more than seven items, so most people would not recall all of them on the first try. Now look at them this way:

dog, cat, bird, horse

red, blue, yellow, green

one, two, three, four

It's easier to remember when similar items are grouped together. Miller calls this process *"chunking"* information,[28] dividing it into logical, memorable chunks. In the example, you have only three major chunks to remember; within each chunk, you have only four related items. Even though the list totals 12 items, it's easier to remember in chunks of related concepts.

Your message will be easier to understand if you organize it this way:

1   Chunk your ideas in groups of related items.

2   Create no more than five major chunks in each message.

3   Include no more than five subgroupings or items in each major chunk.

4   Maintain a clear, identifiable, and logical relationship *among* all major chunks.

5   Maintain a clear, identifiable, and logical relationship among all items within any major chunk.

Provide a Framework Just letting your listeners know where you're going and where you've been is amazingly helpful. All this takes is three simple steps: (1) *Preview* what you are going to talk about and maybe even state what you are not going to talk about. (2) Use *transitions*; connect each aspect of the message to other parts with a word bridge (for example, "But not only do we need to do this for others; we also need to do it for ourselves"). And (3) *summarize* what you have said. A quick review of the key aspects of a message helps ensure a clear understanding.

For example, you might say to a salesperson, "I have two major concerns about a new car—price and safety [preview]. I absolutely cannot pay more than $20,000, but safety features are just as important [transition]; I want air bags, antilock brakes, childproof locks, and a security alarm. So, let's see what you have available for less than $20,000, with those safety features [summary]."

Keep Their Attention A very old joke has it that a farmer explained to a visitor that you have to train a mule with tender, loving care—but then he hit the mule with a stick. When the visitor looked puzzled at this contradiction, the farmer explained, "You have to get his attention first." Groan. Since, as a communicator, you can't hit your audience with a stick, you need more subtle ways to get and keep attention. These work well:

- *Movement, change, and contrast.* Audiences snap to attention when ideas, language, voice, body, and visual images juxtapose in contrasting ways. It may be in words and ideas, such as with John F. Kennedy's oft-quoted call, "Ask not what your country can do for you, but what you can do for your country." But contrast also is essential in varying voice, tone, pace, and inflection, and physical movement.

- *Intensity.* Intensity may be emotional, conveyed by a moving story or language that touches receivers' passions. Intensity may also be in loudness, brightness, or sometimes repetitive impact of a message. In his stirring 1963 speech, Martin Luther King Jr.'s reiteration of the phrase "I have a dream" created a repetitive vocal intensity that combined with the emotional intensity of each dream he expressed.

- *Familiarity.* Listeners attend to examples related to their experiences; for example, viewers are likely to be drawn in by television coverage of their school, town, or immediate neighborhood. Many speakers, entertainers, and politicians arrive at communities in advance, or send people ahead, to capture local tidbits to include in their presentations.

- *Humor.* Humor—when appropriate to you, to your listeners, and to your point—helps keep listeners focused on your message. Your humor should boost your credibility as an outgoing, friendly, enthusiastic, positive, and open person who is sensitive to others' feelings.[29] You might use humorous short stories, exaggeration, facial expressions and body movements, quick responses to the unexpected, absurdity or irony, generalizations with obvious humorous intent, wordplay and puns—all these can be effective. It's absolutely essential, however, that your humor focus on what you want to accomplish in your message—irrelevant jokes can destroy your credibility and undermine your objectives.

These concepts for getting attention apply in all communication contexts—even in one-to-one communication, sensory receptors begin to fade fast. The person who sits like a lump and drones on soon is left alone. Someone who is energetic and enthusiastic draws others' attention by making the conversation a lively, vivid experience.

Consider Audience Reasoning

"I'm no rocket scientist," someone may say, "but I know when something makes sense." People do have a sense of logic, and they like to have their intellect respected. It makes sense to make sense with logical messages.

Think of it this way. Imagine a map that shows a town in the northeast corner and another town in the middle of the map, but indicates no roads between them. How do you get from one town to the other? Ideas are like that—they need "roads" to connect them. Your listeners may miss your reasoning because your message doesn't connect ideas. When that happens, your receiver may be confused and fill in gaps with incorrect assumptions.

Suppose you are interviewing for a job as an accountant. You want to communicate your competence to the interviewer, so you say, "I have excellent qualifications for this position." That's a claim. You sound confident, which is good, but you need to provide data as evidence for your excellent qualifications.

You state your data—accounting courses, relevant extracurricular activities, and previous job experience. Now the message becomes more complete, logical connections develop, and your credibility begins to emerge.

To be sure your interviewer sees exactly why your qualifications are good, you add the third element, warrant or rationale, to explain why and how the data lead to the conclusion: "My courses, my activities, and my previous work experience [your data] have made me a very competent accountant. The position I'm applying for demands the kind of skills I have [your warrant], and I believe this makes me an ideal candidate for the job [your conclusion]." Hearing the three parts of your reasoning connected makes it easier for the interviewer to understand and accept your ideas.

Whatever the situation, imagine yourself as the uninformed or skeptical receiver of your message. What does that receiver need in order to form a reasoned, accurate judgment? Then plan a message that provides that rationale.

Creating messages in this way ensures you are logical, thorough, and ethical in your approach to your receivers and they have a chance to truly understand— and accept—your ideas. This increases your confidence in your communication because you know you have a clear plan. Finally, it increases the listener's sense that you are credible, because you have demonstrated your competence, objectivity, and trustworthiness in creating a message that is complete and comprehensible.

Summary

When you receive or give a message, you start from an intrapersonal process of perception that unconsciously selects one stimulus from multitudes of available stimuli in your environment. You then attend to that stimulus and shape it into something you can recognize. From this mentally shaped stimulus, you create some meaning. The process is influenced by your physical and psychological states; beliefs, attitudes, and values; culture and gender; language; and motivations, including needs, beliefs, attitudes, and values. With all of these influences, your perception may be incomplete or inaccurate, so it's important to check perceptions carefully.

Just as people can be shaky in their perceptions, so can they be shaky in their logic. It is vital for a communicator to be a good critical thinker, evaluating the source and the data from which an argument is drawn, analyzing the rationale for a conclusion by looking at the type of reasoning (deductive, inductive, or cause-and-effect) that is used, and examining connections among these parts and to the claim that is drawn from them.

Often arguments are incomplete, leaving out the rationale or the connections, and you must hypothesize what connections might be, analyzing their potential validity or invalidity for the claim. Because most arguments are based on the probability, not absolute certainty, of a claim, analysis should recognize and state the degree of probability for a claim, using terms such as *possibly*, or *probably*, or *certainly* to indicate that probability.

Awareness of perceptual factors and skill in understanding and creating logical arguments are part of planning effective messages. You consider first the audience's perceptions, including the degree of knowledge they have about the topic, and then adapt to those receivers, choosing appropriate language, organizing ideas into a limited number of clearly related chunks of five or fewer ideas, using variety and stimulation to gain and keep attention, and developing arguments that use good data, clear rationales, and reasonable qualifiers to draw valid and ethical claims.

Exercises

1 Observe a situation for a brief period of time (perhaps at the mall, the student center on campus, or at home). Then write three paragraphs about your observation. In the first paragraph, write only statements of observable fact. In the second paragraph, write only inferences that *could be* concluded from the fact. In the third paragraph, write only judgmental statements that *could be* made about what you observed and the inferences.

2 Can critical thinking improve your perception? In this exercise, your goal is to apply the tools of critical thinking to your perception process throughout the day. Reread the section in this chapter about critical thinking. Select one aspect of critical thinking you will apply for the day. For example, you could focus on inductive reasoning. Keep a log of four to six times during the day you remembered to apply your selected aspect of critical thinking. (Focus on receiving messages for this activity. You may need to continue the log for a second day to get four entries.) Remember, what you enter in the log could apply to any time that you are aware of your perception: alone, with others, driving, reading, talking, watching TV, online, at work, and so on. In a small group, discuss how you think the use of critical thinking affected your perception. How could it also affect your communication?

3 Recall an occasion that resulted in two people misperceiving each other's messages. With a classmate, do the following:

a Analyze the factors—personal and/or message—that caused the misperceptions.

b Make notes about your analysis so you can refer back to them.

c Quickly work out a brief skit in which you demonstrate that misunderstanding.

d Present the skit to the class.

e Ask the class to identify what factors might have caused the misperceptions in your experience.

Compare your analysis with the other student analyses you heard. Explain what you and your partner thought were perception issues; did your classmates see the same thing? Or were other students' perceptions also influenced by factors that caused yet another set of perceptions? If so, what were they?

4 Select an abstract idea or concept from recent work in any class you are taking (such as democracy, socialism, existentialism, romanticism, probability, truth, and so on). Work out a way of defining and explaining that concept to the class, using suggestions in this chapter for organizing and facilitating message perception with context, attention-getting approaches, and adaptation to your receivers. Time your definition to be no longer than 2 minutes, practice it, and present it to the class.

5 Select an advertisement or an editorial from a magazine or newspaper. Analyze the argument, examining the source and data that are used, the rationale and type of reasoning it involves, qualifiers that are (or ought to be) used, and the claim it makes (see the "Idea Logic" section of this chapter). Identify areas where a part of the argument is not stated, and hypothesize what it seems to be on the basis of the appeal made to audience perceptions. In what ways do you think the argument is valid? In what ways do you think it is invalid?

Now, rewrite the argument so it would be valid. Do you have to add qualifiers? Suggest more data? Write or rewrite the rationale? Rewrite the claim?

Cyberpoints

The following Cyberpoints can be easily accessed from the Student Companion website for this text at http://academic.cengage.com/communication/lumsdenccc3. Click on *Student Book Companion Site* and select this chapter from the pull-down menu at the top of the page that says "Select a Chapter." Click on *Cyperpoints* under *Chapter Resources* and you will find links for the exercises following.

1 Do you wonder how your brain works to create perception and do other wonderful things? Go to the *Communicating with Credibility and Confidence* website following the instructions in the previous paragraph and click on *Brainworks*. You might be fascinated with what goes on up there and how you can improve your use of your brain. What are three things you found interesting?

2 There's a whole other area of thinking that you can use: creative thinking. Go to the *Communicating with Credibility and Confidence* website and click on *Creativity* for ways to understand and improve your creativity. In what ways can you increase your creative thinking? How could creative thinking improve your communication?

3 Do you want to improve your creative and critical thinking? Go to the *Communicating with Credibility and Confidence* website; click on *Teasers* and try a few to stir up your brain. What part of this experience used critical thinking? What is an example of how you used creative thinking while doing this exercise?

4 There is a wealth of recent literature about perception and its implications for how you communicate with others. Use InfoTrac College Edition and the keyword *perception* to find the following articles:

Schmitt, M., Gollwitzer, M., Forster, N., & Montada, L. (2004, Oct.) "Effects of Objective and Subjective Account Components on Forgiving." *The Journal of Social Psychology*, v144 i5 p465.

Markey, C. N., Markey, P. M., & Birch, L. L. (2004, Aug.) "Understanding Women's Body Satisfaction: The Role of Husbands." *Sex Roles: A Journal of Research*, v51 i3–4 p209.

Jeffries, N. (2004, Aug) "Sensory Evaluation: Science, Mystery and the Perception of Benefit." *Global Cosmetic Industry*, v172 i8 p36.

(2004, July, 26) "The Outdoors of Perception." *Brandweek*, v45 i28 p18.

Blakeslee, S. (2004, July 13) "When the Brain Says, 'Don't Get Too Close.'" *The New York Times*, pF2 col 02.

Review at least three of the articles. What did you learn about perception? How can the aspect of perception touched on in the articles influence your communication as a sender and/or a receiver?

Chapter 4

Listening and Questioning: Negotiating Meanings

Jose Luis-Pelaez, Inc./CORBIS

Objectives for This Chapter

Knowledge

- Understand why and how listening and questioning are important to communication
- Identify barriers to good listening and questioning
- Recognize the qualities of good questions for various situations
- Understand goals and approaches for different types of listening and questioning

Feelings and Approaches

- Have confidence in using listening and questioning skills in various communication contexts
- Sense another's satisfaction in being listened to
- Value opportunities to be an empathic listener
- Feel credible in listening and questioning roles

Communication Abilities

- Convey credibility as a listener and questioner in interactions
- Overcome barriers to listening
- Listen actively in one-way communication situations
- Use listening and questioning interactively
- Use empathic listening and questioning in appropriate situations
- Listen and question collaboratively in dialogue

Key Terms

confirming

information overload

active listening

thought speed

interactive listening and questioning

empathy

empathic listening

collaborative listening and questioning

H

ave you ever heard a conversation like this one?

"Are you *listening to me*?"

"Of course I am. . . ."

"What did I say, then?"

"Uh . . . you said . . . uh . . ."

"You see? You *weren't* listening!"

"Well, I've heard it all before."

Is this relationship in trouble?

Here's another conversation you may have heard—or had:

"I covered that," says the professor, "on Wednesday."

"Well," says the student, "I was here Wednesday."

"Then you must have heard my 40-minute lecture on that subject," says the professor.

"Yeah, but I didn't get it," says the student.

Is this student in trouble?

In the first conversation, two people may be torpedoing their relationship by failing to listen to each other. In the second, the professor assumes "covering" the lecture material meant it was "heard." That isn't necessarily so. Researchers learned long ago most people forget 50% of a speaker's information immediately, and half of the remaining information within 8 hours.[1] Therefore, by evening, this student would have been lucky to remember 25% of what the lecturer said that morning. There goes the student's grade, not to mention credibility with the professor, just because of poor listening.

In this chapter, we examine how listening and appropriate questioning affect success in all aspects of your life, from your career to your personal relationships. We identify barriers that block effective dialogue; examine listening and questioning for different contexts; and explore ways to increase your effectiveness.

Listening and Questioning for Your Future

Your success in life depends largely on your ability to communicate, which in turn relies greatly on your ability to listen and to ask good questions effectively. Consider the purposes for which you listen to another, either silently and attentively or interacting with appropriate questions.

You listen to *expand or deepen knowledge* or to help you *analyze and evaluate* information. Listening and questioning perceptively also serves to *build your credibility* with others, showing your coorientation with others, perhaps indicating you are trustworthy, objective, and competent. And you listen to help *build relationships*, both to learn what the other feels and to share what you feel; or you might listen quietly to *help and support a friend* who is trying to make a decision or is suffering through a crisis.

In each case, your ability to listen is important to you—to your success in college, in your career, and in your relationships.

Listening and Questioning for Academic and Career Success

What do you do to succeed in classes? You read, of course, and do assignments—but from 55% to 70% of your classroom time is spent in listening,[2] using "academic listening skills" that research shows are crucial to your success.[3] As you listen to a professor, you might ask questions for clarification or expansion of what you hear. You certainly listen and inquire in student groups; you make presentations, then listen to and answer questions; and, of course, you listen to others' presentations and ask questions. It's no surprise that students who listen well are more successful academically than those who do not, often even exceeding the level their standardized intelligence quotients would predict.[4]

In the workplace, these skills are equally crucial. If you don't believe it, key in *listening* on any search engine on the web. You will get thousands of responses. Scan the first several pages quickly, and you will find dozens of articles and websites for corporations—market advisors—sales groups—business and consultants, etc., etc., etc., saying such things as, "Make the connection: Only by listening carefully to what clients have to say will advisers truly understand their needs."[5] Or, "Learn to listen: Closing the mouth and opening the ears facilitates effective communication."[6] And corporate gurus Austin and Peters write that excellence in corporations is "built upon a bedrock of listening, trust and respect for the dignity *and* the creative potential of each person in the organization."[7]

Communication research backs up these experienced opinions, finding most North American employees spend about 60% of their time listening to others, and the higher they rise the more they listen.[8] Eighty percent of executives responding to one survey rated listening as the most important skill in the workforce,[9] and the majority of Fortune 500 corporations in another survey consider listening so crucial they provide special training in it for their employees.[10] "Effective leaders," a business researcher concludes, "prove they are more than managers by willingly honing their listening skills."[11]

Don't assume that any career will insulate you from listening. John, a former student of ours, is a graphic artist. John works at a computer, with the client watching over his shoulder and describing what she wants. John must listen attentively and ask precisely the right questions to transform his client's thoughts into graphic form. John's listening is the conduit through which a client's ideas and his own creativity can flow together; his questions direct and

Listening Makes a Difference

Donna Shalala, President of University of Miami, says that "the most important thing I would say is that I learned to listen." Shalala's impressive career spans 30 years of leadership and public service in the Carter and Clinton administrations and as president of Hunter College, University of Wisconsin at Madison, and University of Miami. Here a reporter describes a time at the University of Miami when Shalala's listening skills made a difference.

Parking was a problem, and she suggested prohibiting freshmen from parking on campus, but she postponed a decision because staff members told her parking privileges were important to freshmen. At the president's brunch she found out why these privileges were important. "As the parents came through the line to meet me," Shalala said, "there would be a grandparent who would say to me how their grandchild would be able to come visit them," she said. "The freshmen needed the cars to visit their grandparents who stayed in South Florida. If I hadn't slowed down and listened, I would have missed a recruiting edge."

Juana Jordan, "University of Miami President Donna Shalala Extols Art of Listening," *Tallahassee* (Florida) *Democrat*, Knight Ridder/Tribune News, February 11, 2004.

---

alter the process to achieve results they both want. Because he is good at this process, John's credibility is so strong—both with his company and his clients—that the most difficult and important accounts often are assigned to him.

Importance to Your Relationships

Who wants a dentist to drill a tooth before listening and confirming which one hurts and how much? Ouch. And that's a professional relationship. In more personal relationships, dialogue is that much more important. People can make or break their relationships with the way they listen and question each other; such transactions are important in:

> *Everything has been said before, but since nobody listens, we have to keep going back and beginning all over again.*
>
> Andre Gide, French Nobel Prizewinner for Literature

Confirming In dialogue, one person listens and asks questions that value the speaker and the message

- *Confirming one another's worth.* When someone listens carefully and openly and shows acceptance of you and your feeling, that's **confirming.** You feel valued. When you confirm another as well, the two of you begin to build a dialogue that includes both ideas and feelings.
- *Reducing risks.* A person who listens to you attentively and asks appropriate questions helps you to make yourself understood. You tend to trust that person, and trust reduces your risk in communicating openly.
- *Building mutual support.* As you and another person listen carefully to each other and exchange understanding, you weave a web of mutual support, encouraging both of you to share more of your thoughts and feelings.

- *Developing shared meanings.* Through dialogue and mutual support, you two explore new and uncharted realms, learning more from each other and negotiating new meanings in your relationship.

Sadly, we all have seen relationships in which this kind of dialogue never happens. Sometimes, even people who have been married for years seem not to listen to or to know very little about each other. Their relationship is built on a shallow foundation and bounded tightly by windowless walls.

Listening Barriers

A very old but very good line goes, "I know you believe you understand what you think I said, but I am not sure you realize that what you heard is not what I meant." Sure, there may be problems with the speaker's message, with transmission, or with a receiver's hearing loss, but most often listening fails because of inadequate skill and/or mental blocks to listening.

Inadequate Skills

"Hearing and listening," says one consultant, "are two very distinct activities. We hear with our ears. We listen with our head, eyes, heart and gut."[12] She has that right. Even if you hear the stimulus, you have to *process* information to listen. Sometimes, people don't listen well because they have not learned how—or they have learned the wrong way.

Elgin notes that some people have had "nonlistening habits for so long that they are almost *incapable* of listening—if they had a listening gland, it would be atrophied from disuse."[13] Children, far from being taught to listen and question, may be trained only to obey. ("Just do as I say!") Or to turn off listening to avoid difficult situations. Parents may say, "We don't listen to those things in our family," or, "Don't pay any attention to him," or, "Pretend you don't notice."[14] As a result, many adults have established nonlistening habits that protect against risks from challenges, threats, or responsibilities. It's as if they believe that covering up their ears and humming will make bad things go away, but instead the bad things just remain and grow.

Few people have actually had formal training in listening. Although listening is the most used communication skill, it ranks last, after writing, reading, and speaking, in amount of time spent on it in formal schooling. It's assumed that people "just know" how to listen. Not so.

True, everyone listens poorly sometimes. You've probably had moments when it was virtually impossible to concentrate on what a speaker was saying or something blocked your ability to perceive clearly. The causes may rest in an inability to focus, in inadequate responses to the message content, or in emotional barriers. Let's look at some of these.

Focusing Problems   "I just can't *concentrate!*" Or, "I can feel my eyes glazing over!" Sometimes we all feel that when we need to listen; reasons for loss of concentration include:

- *Disinterest in the topic.* If your self-talk says, "This is boring—uninteresting—irrelevant," or "I couldn't care less," you won't find a point of interest, and won't hear a word.

- *Distractions.* Somebody whispers to you, or your stomach growls, or you're worried about your upcoming speech—and you miss the speaker's most important point.

- *Fake listening.* As speakers, we love the "wide-asleep listener," who nods brightly, looks directly at us, and dreams on. Unfortunately, fake listening may make a speaker assume the point is clear, thus failing to ask for feedback—and everyone loses.

Content Responses   Sometimes *what* you hear can block your listening. For example:

- *Listening only to details* can actually obscure the crucial concepts the speaker's trying to get across. Think of details as support or explanations that help to understand the bigger picture.

- *Taking copious notes* can obscure key ideas of a speaker's statement. Note big points and fill in supporting details later, if necessary.

- *Assuming,* or "filling in" what the person didn't say or what you didn't hear can lead you to exactly the wrong conclusion; listen openly, then ask for clarification.

- *Zeroing in on one idea* keeps you mentally running circles around an idea, so you don't hear the rest. Listen to everything openly, then deal with the bit that might have obsessed you.

- *Rehearsing responses*—mentally phrasing what you'll say in response, scoring imaginary points—keeps you from hearing remarks that might answer everything you're planning to say.

Emotional Blocks   Everyone, no matter how good-willed, has some established beliefs and limits. It takes conscious effort to avoid setting up certain barriers to listening.

- *Stereotyping or labeling.* "I know her type," you think. "I know what she'll say." You already have a wall up against listening. If you open the gate, you might be surprised at what you'll hear.

- *Judging the messenger.* "Yuck. What a loser," you think, or, "I can't stand that voice!" If you're busy with personal judgment, you might miss information that matters.

- *Loaded words.* The speaker uses words ("god" or "devil" terms) that trigger religious or political or emotional issues for you, and you can't focus on what she's really trying to say.

To be an ally to a homeless person is very simple: Approach him with an open mind and listen to his story. Don't listen with the idea that he's a typical Terry the Tramp—listen to him as a person. And don't go to a bureaucrat for answers, ask a homeless person what he needs, and what he can do with your help.

Doug Castle, a homeless man in Seattle

- *Anxiety.* You're thinking, "This is too difficult for me;" you're anxious about "getting it," so your anxiety blocks your ability to listen to and comprehend new material.[15]

- *Information overload.* "I've got too much on my mind to listen," you say. If your brain feels overstuffed with too much data to process and remember, you probably have **information overload** and need a break before you try to take in more.

- *Exhaustion and stress.* You're so worn out your eyes glaze over when you try to listen. You might need to sleep, meditate, pray, and/or solve a problem before you can listen to someone else.

Information overload
State in which listener has received more data than can be processed and remembered

Listening and Questioning Approaches

Once you're aware of the issues we've just discussed, you can become a more effective listener, whether you're listening actively, or interactively, or empathically, or collaboratively.

Listening Actively

Listening, though you may be silent, takes your commitment to understanding and your active involvement mentally. **Active listening,** a mental as well as a physical process in which you are "tuned in," engaged with the speaker, involved in shaping your understanding of the speaker's meaning, is easier when you do the following:

Active listening Process in which listener focuses on and silently questions speaker's ideas to shape and understand the speaker's meaning

1   *Get set physically for listening.* One consultant suggests assuming "an uncomfortable position" to stay attentive.[16] At least, sit where you can maintain eye contact, keep your posture alert, and show the speaker your support with nonverbal feedback.

2   *Screen out distractions.* Ignore interfering stimuli, or, if you are distracted by a compelling thought, make a quick mental note to follow it up later. This will free you to get back to full listening.

3   *Set aside stereotypes and assumptions.* Say to yourself, "It doesn't matter if I don't like (him/her/that subject)—I want to know what this speaker has to say." Opening your mind will not change your core values, but it may expand your information and understanding.

4   *Focus on main points, concepts, and evidence.* Listen to understand ideas, not to memorize small details. Note the speaker's evidence and reasoning, and make connections among ideas. If a detail worries you, again, make a quick mental note to clarify it later; then listen to what comes next.

Thought speed Time between the rate of human speech and rate of listener's ability to process information

5   *Use your thought speed.* **Thought speed** is the open time between the rate of human speech (125–175 words per minute) and the rate of your *processing* of information (500–600 words per minute). Since you can think faster than a

speaker can talk, you can drift into daydreams or, far preferable, use thought speed to process and analyze what you're hearing.

6   *Organize information while you're listening.* Listeners can recall 70–90% of well-organized messages, but lose a lot of data if a speaker is disorganized.[17] Try mentally connecting ideas and "chunking" points into a logical structure, or creating analogies to connect the speaker's ideas to information familiar to you, to enable your listening and remembering.

Listening and Questioning Interactively

You might use active listening exclusively in some context—perhaps in a lecture audience—but most often, you need to use **interactive listening and questioning.** This develops dialogue, cooperatively analyzing ideas, and asking and answering questions, usually to serve these four purposes:

1   *Clarify information.* You might ask, "Can we go over that point again, please? It's not clear to me," or, "Could you provide an example of how that would work?" or, "How would you define that concept?"

2   *Further develop information.* Perhaps you'd ask, "How often does that happen?" or, "What is the effect of that?" or, "Can you tell me more about that?"

3   *Foster critical thinking.* You might inquire, "How should that information be interpreted?" or, "How does this information square with other data on the same subject?" or, "What is the rationale for this?" or, "What is the evidence for that?" or, "Is this ethically defensible?"

4   *Examine communication processes.* Especially in a group, you often need to ask, "Does anybody else have anything to say?" "How can we manage this conflict?" "Is this fair to everyone?"

Asking questions is an art, requiring a genuine commitment to making communication a two-way dialogue and to arriving at good insights and conclusions. You can ask good questions if you:

- *Listen to questions others ask.* Someone else may very well ask your questions. Don't repeat a question that has already been answered satisfactorily, but, if you have a follow-up question, state its connection so the speaker understands what you want to know.

- *Ask questions ethically.* Seek to learn the truth, to understand, and to clarify. Ask questions that support the communication process, rather than using questions to manipulate others, to distort information, or to score points. Ask hard questions in relation to information and issues, not to the speaker as a person.

- *Ask one question at a time.* Or, if it's unavoidably two points, preview: "I have a two-part question. Part one is . . . part two is . . ." This helps the speaker to answer, and it keeps issues clear so you know if and how your question has been answered.

- *Be clear and specific.* Describe briefly what you're uncertain about and ask for clarification. You might ask for examples or definitions, or paraphrase what you think the idea was, or give examples or analogies and ask if they represent what the speaker said.

- *Probe for analysis.* In the spirit of dialogue—not of competition—inquire about evidence, assumptions, ethical, or controversial issues directly related to the speaker's ideas. Phrase questions that get to a statement's logic, rationale, evidence, and validity of relationships among data, warrant, and claim.

- *Don't make speeches that pretend to be questions.* If you have a point to make, say so: "I don't have a question, but I do have something to say. . . ." Then say it. Briefly!

These guidelines will help you get information and insights you need from an interaction. Furthermore, your questions will support your own credibility by showing clearly your goodwill toward persons and their ideas.

We regret to note that sometimes communicators use questions manipulatively, to lead someone to say or do something against his or her better judgment or wishes. Twenty-five hundred years ago, the Greeks distinguished between two kinds of questioning. One was *dialectic,* designed to lead participants to truth through questioning, listening to, and answering one another. The second was *eristic,* using questions to win a point by leading the receiver to reveal a weakness or concede a dispute.

You often see eristic questioning used to put people on the defensive or to win a point. There's the television image of the attorney, for example, badgering and haranguing a witness in order to trick the individual into appearing guilty or to diminish the credibility of testimony. This questioning approach does not lead to understanding, clarity, or truth; rather, it subverts the process. An ethical questioner listens carefully and asks questions in such a way as to arrive at the truth and to develop genuine dialogue.

Listening and Questioning Empathically

Imagine that you are telling a good friend about a problem. Your friend says, "Oh, I'm so sorry, I feel so sorry for you. . . ." And you cry together. That's sympathy. And it's pretty sweet. But then, nothing has changed, has it? Instead of that, perhaps, your friend listens intently, asking just the right questions, and gains a genuine understanding of your feelings, communicating this to you in such a way that you can see more clearly what you feel and make your own decision about what to do. Which is better?

The first alternative is sympathy—kind, but insubstantial. The second is **empathy,** which helps a person understand the ideas and feelings of another With **empathic listening,** the listener centers on understanding and reflecting the speaker's feelings.

The beginning listener needs to learn the value of silence in freeing the speaker to think, feel, and express himself.

Robert Bolton, author and president of a communication consulting firm

Empathy Understanding ideas and feelings of another person

Empathic listening Listening that focuses on the speaker's feelings

Listening with Your Eyes

Barbara Bocci, one of our students, shared this experience with us:

When my oldest son was just a toddler, he scolded me because I was busy making dinner while he was telling me about an incident at school. I assured him I *was* listening to him, but he argued, "You're not listening with your eyes."

A three-year-old taught me that each person wants to feel that he or she has our undivided attention. I began to set aside a few minutes before bedtime to spend personal one-on-one time with each child. Twenty years later they still remember our special sharing times.

If you are listening empathically, your questions are limited, serving only to clarify your understanding. From your empathy, then, you can give responses that hold up a mirror for the speaker to see his or her own feelings and thoughts more clearly, finding personal insights from your reflection of what you hear and see.

You would listen empathically to a friend who has a heartache, or to a child who has something important to share, but you might also use empathic listening in a work situation. Even in management, "actively listening to and empathizing with what other people have to say are two of the important qualities of leaders. . . . Leaders who possess these qualities have the potential to promote positive work relations, inspire trust and bolster their companies' bottom line."[18]

In our own experience—in teams, in consulting, in teaching and administrative work—empathic listening has helped us detect and correct problems that have hurt individuals and rendered them ineffective. Sometimes, for example, one person's use of insensitive language or humor isolates another. In a work team, a woman expresses concern about a policy change on single parents with children. A man—not known for his sensitivity—scoffs, "Oh, you women— you're too emotional. It's just the difference—women are emotional, men are logical." That's one way to silence a person, isn't it? But another member shows empathy with the woman (eye contact, a smile), and drawls, "Well, it seems logical to connect day care needs of the 70% of our employees who are women to the bottom-line aims of the policy, doesn't it? If they have to miss work, we all lose, right?" With empathy and good communication, everybody wins.

When you sense that a person could use some empathy from you, *commit fully* to giving your whole attention to listening with full, undivided attention, eye contact, involved body posture, responsive face and voice, appropriate touching. And listen, listen, listen.

Empathic listening is often silent, except for encouraging noises. As you begin to feel you have some insight, you can question and communicate your empathy verbally, but with great care. Keep in mind these bits of advice:

- *Tune in to the speaker,* being very aware of nonverbal and verbal cues, body posture, facial expressions, gestures, and voice conveying emotion. Be sensitive to how the other person phrases ideas and to cues that indicate an emotional response. When you think you understand what another person is feeling, give feedback to mirror those feelings.

- *Describe the speaker's nonverbal cues,* encouraging a response with something like, "You seem a little glum (or pretty happy) today!" If your friend says, "Yeah, I am really discouraged about my grades," invite her to continue, with a question such as, "What's happening there?" or the classic, "Care to talk about it?"[19]

- *Question carefully to develop understanding,* using open, supportive questions and leaving room for the other person to choose whether and how to respond. If your friend with the grade problem answers your "What's happening there?" with "I just don't know—I'm just too busy to do all the stuff I need to do," you could say something like, "Yeah, you do seem to be so busy and tired. What's that about?" You've allowed her to reveal as much as she wants to, and your empathy can help her to get her own, clearer picture of her problem.

- *Reflect back your understanding with empathic language* that helps the other see more clearly. She will feel supported by your empathy if it focuses on her and her concerns. You can do this by *paraphrasing,* in your own words, what you think the other person is saying and feeling. A paraphrase can be very simple: "So you're saying you're too exhausted to do the work?" Or, it can be a metaphor or image, such as, "Sounds like you're trying to juggle six balls and dance on a hot griddle at the same time!" Such responses allow the other to see more about her responses, which can lead her to her own insights as she explains them to you.

- *Avoid slipping from giving empathy into advising.* It is so gratifying to solve someone's problem, and most of us find that easier than just listening. Very often, however, people don't need or want you to find the solution; in fact, they may already know what they have to do. They just need you to listen. Let the speaker ask you for advice if it's wanted. Otherwise, stay clear of it!

- *Be tentative with your empathy.* There are three absolute no-no's in listening empathically:

  1   Never say, "I know just how you feel." You really don't, because you are a different person with different experiences.

  2   Never launch into telling your own story: "The exact same thing happened to me. . . ." It may be helpful to share an experience, but keep the focus on listening to the other. That's the whole point.

3   Never try to analyze psychological reasons behind the other person's responses. If you think someone needs professional guidance, suggest that—but listen empathically first.

Listening and Questioning Collaboratively

At its best, communication is a collaborative process—the **collaborative listening and questioning** process is developed when speaker and listener work as a team to develop a shared understanding. Collaborative listening and questioning draw on all skills of active, interactive, and empathic listening—and more.

Stewart and Thomas talk about a similar concept as "dialogic listening," a process of building new meanings and insights through dialogue.[20] The concepts of dialogue, dialogic ethics, and dialogic listening all rest on the belief that humans can communicate with respect for one another and for themselves, with the objective of mutually seeking truth and justice.

Here's the difference among the types of listening and questioning: Active and interactive listening and questioning focus on *gaining information*; empathic listening and questioning focus on *the other person's feelings*; collaborative listening and questioning focus on intensive dialogue in which participants work to shape their ideas. It is as if two or more people had an uncut piece of marble and, together, they chipped and shaped away at it until they created a three-dimensional "sculpture of meaning." Stewart and Thomas identify four distinct features of this kind of collaborative dialogue:[21]

1   *Mutuality.* The entire process focuses not on individual interests but on *all* participants' interests.

2   *Open-ended playfulness.* This allows participants to develop their thoughts creatively, opening paths to new ideas and insights.

3   *Presentness.* The process is centered in *now* more than in the past or the future.

4   *Issue-oriented.* The focus is on ideas and issues that are *in front of* participants, not on motivations for responses. It is not, in other words, psychotherapy.

Listening and questioning together in this way can be a playful process, but it also is focused and intense; it is genuine teamwork in developing ideas. Admittedly, collaborating takes time and effort—but the result is worth it. Stewart and Thomas identify four techniques that can help people build a dialogical listening process:[22]

1   *"Say more"* is a response to encourage the speaker to develop thoughts and suggestions, think more deeply, and identify more possibilities. You might repeat "Say more" several times in a dialogue to keep your partner talking to clarify and expand ideas.

2   *"Run with the metaphor"* suggests that when one person creates a metaphor, participants carry it further, play with it, and use it for deeper

As we look at the picture, we get the feeling that something special is happening. What kind of listening seems to be going on? How do you think the father and daughter feel? What about the picture shows you that feeling?

analysis. A couple is discussing their relationship, for example. It might go like this:

"Our relationship is just a dance on ice."

"What kind of a dance?"

"Ballroom—dipping and gliding . . ."

"That's nice . . . kind of sweet."

"Yes, and I like it sometimes, but it seems as if it's all on the surface—maybe more like skating without knowing what's underneath the ice. . . ."

Here, the couple develops the metaphor and, if they run with it, they may find out what's really at issue in their lives.

3   *"Paraphrase plus"* describes the give and take of reflecting and adding information. You put another person's statement in your own words and *then* develop ideas further; your partner paraphrases what *you* have just developed, adding a response. As you do this together, you begin to discover new ideas or sculpt a deeper meaning. Let's continue with our couple as they use paraphrase plus:

"You mean we might have some problems we haven't recognized? [paraphrase]. That may be true—like maybe we don't listen to each other enough, or we don't deal with problems with our parents [plus]."

"You believe lack of listening is undermining our relationship and so are our parents [paraphrase]. Maybe so—in fact, maybe if we really listened to each other we could deal with the parent problem better. Like, for example, I feel you don't really listen when I tell you what your mother does . . . [plus]."

Working together this way, these two people can truly create some understanding and improve their relationship together.

4   *"Context building"* refers to explaining your frame of reference for your statements and encouraging your dialogue partner to explain his or her context. In our example, the dialogue might continue with context building like this:

"When do you feel that way? Is it all the time, or are there particular circumstances?"

"Well, it seems as if you ignore me especially when I'm upset about how she handles the kids. . . ."

Now, they are beginning to build a context that will help to reveal important issues they need to resolve.

In our example, the couple is listening interactively for information, empathically for feelings, and dialogically to build new meanings. Dialogic listening gives them the tools of "say more," "run with the metaphor," "paraphrase plus," and "context building" to reach new levels of understanding.

Don't think, however, that a collaborative dialogue is only for solving personal problems. Do you need to develop a special team project? Do you need to better understand a philosophical view in one of your courses? Collaborating with someone through dialogue, listening, and questioning can help you create a new idea or better understand an old one.

It's true that "sculpting" meaning takes time and commitment. Furthermore, people must learn to do them together because each technique is cooperative. "Say more" can get tiresome if you don't understand your partner is deliberately pushing you to think more deeply. Suggesting you "run with the metaphor" sounds silly if you don't know it means to continue developing the metaphor until you have a new insight from it. This type of listening and questioning is a skill that people learn, develop, and use together because they are motivated to search for more complete, more mutual interpretations, and because they want to build effective interpersonal or work relationships.

As Figure 4.1 shows, each type of listening serves a different purpose, but often within the same dialogue. You listen actively, taking notes, as your study partner tells you about a class you missed; you move into interactive listening and questioning, asking questions to clarify, confirm, or expand your understandings. Then the two of you might start discussing your anxiety about your team project, using empathic listening and questioning to support and reflect each other's feelings—and then develop a collaborative dialogue to create a good plan for the project.

Listening and Questioning Skill Development

When we say in class, "Let's start working on listening skills," some student always cracks, "Huh? What did you say?" The joke still makes us—and other students—laugh. We all know most people don't listen particularly well. But there are ways to improve these skills. It's worth the effort, because being a good listener and questioner contributes to your credibility with others and your confidence in yourself. All it takes is commitment, preparation, and practice.

Figure 4.1 *Relationships among active, interactive, empathic, and dialogic listening*

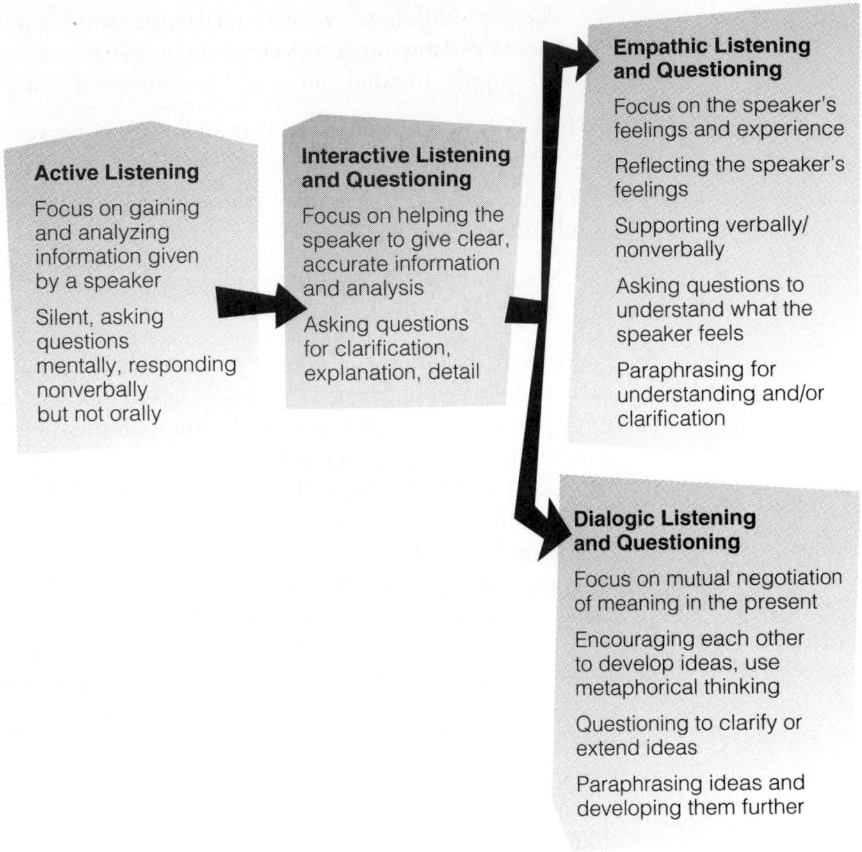

Active Listening

Focus on gaining and analyzing information given by a speaker

Silent, asking questions mentally, responding nonverbally but not orally

Interactive Listening and Questioning

Focus on helping the speaker to give clear, accurate information and analysis

Asking questions for clarification, explanation, detail

Empathic Listening and Questioning

Focus on the speaker's feelings and experience

Reflecting the speaker's feelings

Supporting verbally/nonverbally

Asking questions to understand what the speaker feels

Paraphrasing for understanding and/or clarification

Dialogic Listening and Questioning

Focus on mutual negotiation of meaning in the present

Encouraging each other to develop ideas, use metaphorical thinking

Questioning to clarify or extend ideas

Paraphrasing ideas and developing them further

Commitment

Although a long day of really listening to others takes little obvious physical effort, it can leave you feeling as if you'd moved a truckload of furniture. Commitment to listening means a willingness to work hard, to put everything else aside, and to concentrate on the other person and the ideas.

Preparation

To develop your listening skills, start by examining how you listen and how you question, and then select specific areas in which you'd like to improve. Visualize yourself listening or questioning in ways that perfectly fulfill that image, then write an affirmation statement (see guidelines on pages 42–43 in Chapter 2): an affirmation should be phrased positively, in present tense, and should describe your feelings and behaviors as well as the speaker's response to you.

The second preparation step takes place when you are in a situation that requires careful listening. Try doing the following:

1   *Relax.* One simple way to relax so you can focus on listening is to breathe deeply. Take several slow, deep breaths; feel oxygen circulating through your body and brain. As you breathe, think of being calm and centered on the other person. Then, as you listen, if your mind begins to wander or you begin to feel stress, repeat deep breathing.

2   *Set your mind for listening.* Make a mental commitment to intense listening; block out distractions, and focus your eyes and your mind on the speaker.

3   *Identify your goals in listening.* Know why you're listening to this person: to get information, to deepen or expand your knowledge, to establish your credibility, to support or help, to develop a relationship. Identifying your goals will help you center your attention on the person and the message.

Practice

In listening, as in other skills, the key is to set some small practice goals—very specific, very clear skills you want to develop. Review your affirmations as you visualize your successful behavior. Select a context for practice—a classroom, a dialogue with a friend or family member, or an interaction at work. Then practice your listening and questioning in that context. After you've practiced, assess your success. When you feel you've listened well or asked questions effectively, review what you did. Keep rehearsing and practicing what works well. Then look for opportunities to practice again. Soon, your confidence will grow as you become comfortable with these skills and as you enjoy your experiences more. Furthermore, feedback from others will show you they find you credible and appreciate your ability to listen and ask intelligent, useful questions.

Summary

Abilities to listen and to question well are essential to get information, to build your own credibility and confidence, to support or help another person, and to build relationships. These skills are also essential to success in your school, career, and personal life. Unfortunately, hearing impairments and environmental conditions can hinder good listening, as can inadequate skills, focusing problems, poor content responses, emotional blocks, information overload, and anxiety.

Active listening involves silently processing and interpreting information; interactive questioning and listening involves asking questions to clarify, confirm, or develop information. In empathic listening and questioning, the listener focuses entirely on understanding and reflecting back the speaker; feelings, using questions and paraphrasing to help the speaker understand his or her own feelings. Collaborative listening and questioning uses dialogue to focus on a mutual process of "sculpting" new or deeper meanings together by centering on the present, helping each other build context for ideas, and developing understanding through "paraphrasing plus," "running with the metaphor," and "saying more."

Developing skill in listening and questioning demands commitment to hard work and preparation through relaxation, visualization, and focus on listening. This requires centering your attention on the speaker and your objectives for listening and questioning. Finally, you can develop your abilities by setting goals and by practicing each type of speaking in appropriate contexts and situations.

Exercises

1   How good are your listening and questioning skills? Use Form 4.1 to find out. First, complete the assessment on your own. Then ask a friend and your boss or your teacher each to complete the form on how she or he would rate your abilities. Now compare the three ratings. Where are ratings the same? Different? Why? In what ways do you think you listen well? In what ways do you think you need to improve as a listener?

2   With a small group, observe a televised, taped, or live dialogue between two people. Identify what barriers blocked participants' dialogue and what listening and questioning skills they used to arrive at understanding. What would you suggest to the participants to improve their listening and questioning? Then develop a group report on your observations.

3   Think of a time you experienced or observed either very good or very bad listening and questioning. This could be something that happened to you, a friend, or a family member; it could be something you saw in a public place; it could be something you saw on television or in a play. Analyze what you observed in terms of the following questions:

What were the circumstances or context of the interaction?

Who were the participants?

What were participants' individual purposes in the dialogue?

What types of listening and questioning did you observe?

What barriers did you observe?

What worked effectively in the transaction?

Now, briefly describe the experience and your analysis of it to the class.

4   After each member of the class has given his or her report for Exercise 3, meet in small groups and do the following:

a   Identify what most experiences/observations had in common. What general principles can you derive?

b Identify what seemed unique among the observations. How can you account for the differences?

c Create a list of 10–15 rules for good listening and questioning, based on what you've read and what the reports have revealed.

d Share your list with the class.

Cyberpoints

The following Cyberpoints can be easily accessed from the Student Companion website for this text at http://academic.cengage.com/communication/lumsdenccc3. Click on *Student Book Companion Site* and select this chapter from the pull-down menu at the top of the page that says "Select a chapter." Click on *Cyperpoints* under *Chapter Resources* and you will find links for the exercises following.

1 Want to see what trainers are doing to help folks in the workplace to listen better? With InfoTrac College Edition, use the keyword *listening*, and limit your search to the journal *Training and Development*. Read Richard M. Harris, "Turn Listening into a Powerful Presence." How can improved listening make a difference for you in the workplace or for your career?

2 Have you noticed that people of different cultures seem to have different styles of listening? You can find out more by using InfoTrac College Edition and the keyword *listening*, by limiting your search to the journal *International Journal of Public Opinion Research*. Read the article, "Cultural Differences in Listening Style Preferences: A Comparison of Young Adults in Germany, Israel, and the United States," by Christian Kiewitz, James B. Weaver III, Hans-Bernd Brosius, and Gabriel Weimann. What did you discover that can help you improve your listening as you communicate cross-culturally?

3 Are you curious about how the physical process of hearing works? Go to the *Communicating with Credibility and Confidence* website at http://academic.cengage.com/communication/lumsdenccc3 and click on *listening*. Summarize what you discovered.

4 How is listening important in your life? Go to the International Listening Association's website at http://www.listen.org/ and select one of the articles listed on the homepage. Look for one of the articles by Purdy or McKay. Identify discoveries you made reading the article. Based on the article you read, how are you doing as a listener? Explain.

Form 4.1

Assessment of Listening and Questioning Skills

For each of the following statements, check the response that best describes the listening/questioning skill.

I/You:	Usually	Sometimes	Rarely
1. Am/are motivated to listen and question well	___	___	___
2. Am/are interested when others speak	___	___	___
3. Manage distractions well	___	___	___
4. Pay attention well	___	___	___
5. Get major ideas	___	___	___
6. Take only necessary notes	___	___	___
7. Don't jump ahead and make premature judgments	___	___	___
8. Don't stereotype the speaker	___	___	___
9. Don't jump on an idea and focus only on it	___	___	___
10. Don't think only about what I/you want to say	___	___	___
11. Control emotional reactions to loaded words	___	___	___
12. Give positive nonverbal support to the speaker	___	___	___
13. Keep mental attention on the speaker's ideas	___	___	___
14. Approach dialogue as a mutual process of sharing ideas	___	___	___
15. Encourage the speaker to extend ideas	___	___	___
16. Paraphrase others' ideas to confirm or extend meanings	___	___	___
17. Show empathy for the speaker appropriately	___	___	___
18. Ask questions to clarify information	___	___	___
19. Ask questions to help develop and analyze information	___	___	___
20. Know what I/you want to ask	___	___	___
21. Ask specific questions	___	___	___
22. Ask questions clearly	___	___	___
23. Ask for information with examples, definitions, and analogies	___	___	___
24. Use open-ended questions to allow the speaker to elaborate	___	___	___
25. Use probing questions to get at specific information	___	___	___
26. Build on questions others ask	___	___	___
27. Ask questions ethically	___	___	___
28. Do not use questions to manipulate the speaker	___	___	___

Chapter 5

Nonverbal Communication: More Than Words Can Say

Objectives for This Chapter

Knowledge

- Understand the types and functions of nonverbal cues
- Know how culture, gender, and individual variables affect nonverbal communication
- Identify ways in which nonverbal cues contribute to developing credibility
- Know how nonverbal interactions affect confidence

Feelings and Approaches

- Be sensitive to others' uses and interpretations of nonverbal cues
- Approach nonverbal communication as a way of enhancing verbal messages
- Feel confident in using nonverbal communication effectively and credibly

Communication Abilities

- Decode others' nonverbal cues accurately
- Use nonverbal communication confidently
- Use eyes, face, and body to convey messages clearly
- Use voice and speech dynamically, clearly, appropriately, credibly
- Adapt nonverbal communication to individuals and settings appropriately

Key Terms

nonverbal communication

vocalics

detractors

communication accommodation

kinesic

synchronous messages

proxemics

territory

personal space

haptics

artifacts

monochronic cultures

polychronic cultures

"**Y**our actions speak so loudly I can't hear a word you say!"

Funny, but true: Even brilliant words mean little without meaning given them by the right nonverbal cues. One researcher says, "Nonverbal behavior, in particular, determines the persuasive impact of a message."[1]

Nonverbal communication Communication that accompanies, replaces, or carries verbal messages

Nonverbal communication is communication that accompanies, replaces, or carries verbal messages, such as your vocal or facial expressions, your posture, your movements, or even the ring you wear on your finger to symbolize your commitment to another person.

What you convey nonverbally affects others' perceptions of your credibility as well as your own confidence. Suppose you're making a speech. Intrapersonally, you are monitoring and responding to your own cues. You're pretty anxious, making your hands shake and your mouth feel dry, which undermines your confidence. This causes you to hesitate and talk too slowly or too quickly—and this causes your listeners to believe you're unsure, unprepared, or even untruthful. In contrast, being in control of your nonverbal cues helps you feel more confident, and your listeners get a better impression of your message and your credibility. Of course, your listeners' positive response, in turn, boosts your confidence. For example, teachers are more satisfied in their jobs and feel better about themselves when students show verbal and, even more so, nonverbal responsiveness.[2]

That's why we want this chapter to help you develop your own credibility and confidence through understanding how nonverbal communication functions and by sharpening your ability to encode and decode nonverbal messages effectively.

Communication: More Than Words

People trust their ears less than their eyes.

Herodotus, fifth-century BC Greek historian

Whatever your words, your nonverbal cues affect how you are understood. You may, in fact, perceive 60–70% of a person's meaning from nonverbal rather than verbal cues.[3] Adults especially use nonverbal cues more for judging a speaker's emotions and attitudes than for recalling and analyzing information,[4] but young children may believe words more than nonverbal cues.[5] Maybe this is why adults are confused when children take a teasing comment as a serious rebuke; adults mean to signal "just kidding" nonverbally, but children don't recognize those signals. By adulthood, however, people automatically use nonverbal cues to accomplish several functions in shaping their transactions—and decode those cues with mixed success.

Nonverbal Cues Shape Transactions

Try this: Quietly watch a couple of people as they talk to each other. Don't listen, just watch. You'll see a quiet dance of adaptation, with each using nonverbal cues that mesh with cues of the other. Burgoon, Stern, and Dillman explain, "People may adapt their communication behavior to one another in a variety of ways. These adaptation patterns undergird human interactions and relationships."[6] In guiding conversational adaptation, nonverbal cues accomplish the following:[7]

- *Repeat.* You confirm the words "I'm very pleased" with a warm smile, eye contact, and a touch.

- *Emphasize.* You might accompany "I'm very pleased" with a raised or lowered voice or with tears of joy or gratitude.

- *Complement.* You could accompany "I'm very pleased" with a hug and kiss that add an unspoken "and I love you very much."

- *Substitute for words.* Eye contact and a warm smile can communicate "I'm very pleased" without a word being said.

- *Contradict the verbal message.* A sarcastic tone and rolled eyes might turn "I'm very pleased" into "I am not at all pleased."

- *Regulate conversation.* Nonverbal cues signal who can talk, when, to whom, and for how long. If you say, "I'm very pleased," and the other person smiles silently and waits, you may feel the need to say more, or if she or he smiles and then looks at someone else, you probably will be silent.

Of course, the shape of the transaction depends on participants' ability to decode nonverbal cues they perceive. And accurate decoding can be very, very difficult. People tend to believe nonverbal cues more readily than verbal cues, and they interpret them through personal and cultural screens.

Nonverbal Cues Are More Believable Than Verbal Cues   Why would you believe a person's nonverbal cues more than their words? Perhaps because you know intuitively, first, *nonverbal cues are harder to control.* When muscles in your jaw clench with anger, for example, you may have trouble relaxing them enough to sound believable when saying, "No, really, it's fine." Second, *nonverbal cues come from many sources at one time,* so they may outweigh the words. Our friend Mike cannot hide his irrepressible humor. He may make a serious comment, but if he sees an underlying joke, his eyes twinkle, his voice rises, the corners of his mouth turn up—and we know there's something funny in the back of his mind. Third, *nonverbal cues are more unconscious than verbal statements.* You may be unaware of looking at your watch, twitching your foot, folding your arms, and tapping your fingers—but an observer might interpret those behaviors to mean that you're rushed or nervous.

Nonverbal Cues Are Harder to Decode Than Verbal Cues   Even so-called experts in lie detection have trouble. In one study of 509 experts (psychiatrists, court judges, police detectives, polygraphers, and Secret Service officers), only the Secret Service officers did better than chance at detecting lies from nonverbal cues.[8] Research "in behavioral lie detection has yielded one consistent finding: humans are not very skilled at detecting when deception is present."[9]

Some individuals do seem to decode nonverbal cues more accurately than do others. For example, women may be better attuned to nonverbal cues,[10] and middle-aged people seem more perceptive about nonverbal cues than young or old observers (although contextual and situational cues, as well as knowing the individual, make decoding easier for anyone).[11]

Certainly, an individual's culture affects nonverbal communication, so you can never assume others' nonverbal behaviors will mean the same as yours. Andersen says, "The primary level of culture is communicated implicitly, without awareness, chiefly by nonverbal means."[12] Nonverbal communication is deeply rooted, often unconscious, reflections of a group's understandings about one another and how life should be. In a recent trip to Bali, for example, we (your authors) were struck by two things: People spoke very softly, and they invariably responded to a smile with a brilliant, warm, open smile of their own. We found ourselves speaking more softly than we do in the United States and enjoying the feeling of openness and peace that emerged from this smiling culture.

A good communicator is aware of how unconscious and culturally shaped nonverbal cues can be, and is careful both in giving and interpreting nonverbal cues. This awareness can help you to be a more sensitive nonverbal communicator in any context.

Voice and Speech: Instruments of Communication

"It's not *what* you say but *how* you say it." In this class, your voice and speech are the instruments you use to make people understand you for every oral assignment, and in your life, they carry your meaning every time you speak to someone.

Using Voice and Speech

Vocalics The sound of your voice and the way you speak, which affect how you are perceived

The sound of your voice and the way you speak are powerful influences on how a listener perceives you and your message. The technical term usually used for voice and speech communication is **vocalics,** which include such nonverbal cues as pitch, tone, volume, range, and quality of voice, and even detractors such as "um" and "you know." These vocalic characteristics make you want to listen (or not), help you understand messages (or not), and affect how much you like the speaker (or not). And, they affect how listeners respond to you when you speak.

You need an open vocal quality and vocal variety to keep your listeners' attention and emphasize your meaning. That means you can vary your *inflection*—variety in pitch, volume, and rate—to give meaning to your words:

- *Pitch* is the high or low tone of a sound. Everyone has an individual natural pitch, with a possible range of low to high pitches. Varying your pitch emphasizes meaning and keeps listeners interested—and increases your credibility as well.[13]

- *Volume* is the softness and loudness of speech. You can increase or drop volume to intensify or dramatize meanings and to increase your impact. Speaking louder may increase your credibility, for example, while speaking softly at an intimate level may make the audience see you as warmer and friendlier.[14]

- *Rate* is the tempo or speed of speech. People may be most favorably impressed when your rate is close to or slightly faster than their own[15] and consider you competent, intelligent, and objective if you use a quick tempo.[16] A slower tempo, however, may make a speaker seem more thoughtful and trustworthy.[17]

To illustrate the relationship between inflection and meaning, say these seven words: *Yvonne said Karriem gave a great speech.* Try varying your rate, pitch, and volume the way each of these speakers would make the statement:

Someone expressing surprise Yvonne would have made that statement

Someone expressing surprise Karriem could have done so well

Karriem talking about Yvonne's speech

Yvonne implying she really thinks Karriem's speech wasn't that effective

With each change in inflection, you change what those seven words mean. Changes may be subtle, but they provide entirely different interpretations.

Clear articulation and fluency in your speech also affects a listener's response to you and your message. That is,

- *Articulation* is how you speak words, pronouncing them correctly and clearly. When you speak articulately, your listeners feel you are confident and composed. If understanding you is difficult, listeners may become impatient or dismiss you with some stereotype.

- *Fluency* is speaking smoothly, without **detractors** (sounds and words interjected instead of pauses between words and sentences, as speakers often do when they are nervous). Two types of detractors are most common: *vocalized pauses,* such as "um" and "er," and *verbalized pauses,* fillers such as "you know," "like," "and," and "and so forth." (Like, um, y'know what we mean?) Everyone "ums" and "ers" and "y'knows" occasionally, but habitual use gets in the way of your effectiveness.

Detractors Sounds and words interjected between words and sentences

Adapting Voice and Speech

As with all communication, you can self-monitor and adapt your use of voice and speech to communicate more effectively and increase your credibility. Stereotypes and negative judgments are not fair, but they exist. Saying "goin'" instead of "going" or "dem" instead of "them," or even speaking with a regional dialect can cause listeners to jump to conclusions about the speaker's education, class, status, personality, character, mood, race, age, gender orientation, and even body type.[18]

This does *not* mean that if you speak with a dialect or an accent you must "get rid of it." It does, however, make sense to know how to communicate most clearly for a given situation. If you were in France, it would be an advantage to speak French; yet when you returned to North America, you would return to using English. Similarly, if you and your family and friends speak an informal dialect, why give it up? The point is to be able to switch when you meet with others who are not part of your in-group.

By using **communication accommodation,** "individuals adapt to each other's communicative behaviors."[19] In other words, they learn to switch codes for their listeners, as some U.S. senators do after being taught "how to drop their regional accents when they are in Washington, and how to pick them up again on the campaign trail."[20]

Communication accommodation Methods used by people to adapt to others' communication behaviors

If you'd like to improve your use of voice and/or your speech, take a look at the *Communicating with Confidence and Credibility* website—there are some good ideas there.

Body Movements Large and Small

Your brain stays busy constantly, processing messages from your body and mind and the environment. Then your responses to those messages show up as **kinesic** communication—eyes, face, and body movements that others then interpret as meaningful messages.

Kinesic Movements of the eyes, face, and body people perceive as meaningful

The Mathematical Marriage Predictor

You might not think that mathematicians have anything particularly relevant to say about your love life. But you'd be wrong—if we're talking about James Murray, a mathematician at the University of Washington in Seattle who teamed up with psychologist John Gottman to explore the rocky road of romance. Here's what the two did. They videotaped hundreds of volunteer couples discussing such things as sex and money. You know—the sorts of things on which everybody always agrees, right? . . .

Then they broke down behavioral responses to these high-pressure discussions. . . . A set of equations was drawn up that represented the interactions . . . leading to . . . Ding! . . . a prediction as to whether this marriage would last.

Sound like a stretch? Think you can't possibly tell that much about a couple from a single interview and some calculations? Four years later Murray and Gottman did a follow-up to see whether the equation had made the right prediction. It sure had—their Mathematical Marriage Predictor was right an astonishing ninety-four percent of the time.

Some conspicuous findings included the fact that, in marriages that lasted, laughing occurred five times more frequently than in couples destined for break-up. . . . The one behavior that most consistently predicted divorce was the appearance of a contemptuous or mocking facial expression on one partner's face when the other one spoke. According to the Mathematical Marriage Predictor, it's "roll your eyes and say goodbyes."

From William Orem, retrieved September 13, 2004, from http://amos.indiana.edu/library/scripts/marriage.html

Eyes and Face

Usually, people get their first impression from your eyes and face. How can you use them well?

Communicating with the eyes (known as *oculesics*) accomplishes two important functions. First, eye contact *signals attention and/or intimacy*. For example, it is in your favor when eye contact shows your professor you're paying attention. First, it's still good advice to *use eye contact when you speak*, at least for North Americans. Eye contact increases your credibility; you are more dynamic, and listeners find you more believable, likable, and persuasive.[21] If you're in an interview, sustaining eye contact with the interviewer makes you more likely to be hired than a person who looks away or down.[22] Or, when some couples gaze at each other steadily, they increase intimacy and feel more liking and passion for each other.[23]

Second, eye contact helps *establish and maintain power and control*. In Western cultures, people who maintain eye contact while *talking* seem dominant,[24] and people who maintain eye contact while *listening* to a person of higher status appear subordinate, perhaps explaining why women (who historically have been subordinate) tend to show interest and involvement by sustaining eye contact in conversations. Men, however, usually use sustained eye contact only as a challenge to others. A professor says, "Men in my classes tell me that they lose face and come across as wimps if they don't return a stare."[25] Yet in Japan, listening *without* eye contact is courteous, especially to people of higher status.[26] Imagine the cultural misunderstanding when a Western employer talks to a Japanese employee who, being polite, averts his eyes—and the supervisor interprets this as insolence or indifference.

Though eyes make contact, the face speaks first and loudest. Early research found people interpret *how* others feel mainly from their facial expressions and the *intensity* of their feelings from their body cues.[27] From the face, people judge a person's attractiveness,[28] dominance,[29] and kindness and warmth.[30] They even watch when and how people smile to judge their credibility.[31] A smile that is genuine and appropriate to the situation powerfully communicates your trustworthiness and your confidence.[32] In return, a person who seems pleasant and involved in dialogue draws more smiling, nodding, and pleasantness from others.[33] The effect of a smile goes even further, sometimes influencing a person who received a smile from one stranger on the street to help another stranger pick up objects she or he had dropped.[34] (Interestingly, this study was done in France where, we have been told, people don't respond to a smile. A cultural myth? Perhaps so, since French persons who received a smile helped others—and since, in our own experience, the French were as responsive to a smile as anybody else we ever met!)

As varied as nonverbal communication is across cultures, at least people across the world seem to express basic emotions with the same facial movements. In various studies, Japanese, Americans, English, Spanish, French, Germans, Swiss, Greeks, and South Pacific Islanders recognized happiness, surprise, fear, anger, sadness, disgust, contempt, interest, bewilderment, and determination in photographed faces of people from other cultures.[35]

More finely tuned expressions, however, may be controlled by your cultural background, your gender, or your social status. In Japan, for example, disgust traditionally is not shown in public,[36] so this feeling may be covered with an opposite expression, such as smiling. How confusing to a Westerner!

Posture and Gestures

The intensity of your feelings and your personal power communicate through your body. The way you stand or sit, gesture, or even move your shoulders carries meaning.

Posture   Parents and teachers preach, "Stand up straight!" and, "Don't sprawl!" That's because it's long been known that *good* posture—straight but relaxed—increases others' perceptions of an individual's competence and confidence.[37]

The face is the mirror of the mind, and eyes without speaking confess the secrets of the heart.

Jerome, fourth-century CE Christian saint

This woman who has just won an Olympic Gold Medal and this Bosnian woman who just learned that her husband has been killed in Sarajevo have very different emotions. Some of their nonverbal cues show these differences, yet some aspects of their behavior are much alike. What is it that shows you the emotions they are really feeling? Look at their supporters— what is different and yet the same with them?

Your body posture conveys information about how you see yourself, and how you feel about a topic through three aspects of your relationship to someone else: immediacy and involvement, rapport, and dominance and control:

- *Immediacy and warmth* are "actions that signal closeness, intimacy, and availability for communication rather than avoidance and greater psychological distance."[38] In North American conversation, immediacy relates to eye contact and close conversational distance, facing each other directly, leaning forward, maintaining an open body position, and free gesturing, all of which show interest, indicate that you are responsive to others, and encourage conversation.[39] On the job, people who show immediacy (physical involvement in the person and the moment) "generate reciprocity and accommodation leading to a more positive work environment and more desirable outcomes."[40]

- *Rapport* is a feeling of connection, perhaps of coorientation, and develops when people feel some mutual empathy, coorientation, trust, and concern. Immediacy and involvement behaviors help to build these feelings, which are essential to cooperation and intimacy in a relationship. So does *mirroring,* an interaction adaptation where one person reflects another's body posture, facial expressions, and voice with the same behavior. Mirroring

"Ignore him. He just walks that way to bug his parents."

may be unconscious behavior, stemming from a person's empathy for another; it is most effective in connecting with someone you're close to or someone who is discussing a problem with you as a friend or counselor. In more casual conversation, mirroring can strain communication;[41] perhaps the mirrorer seems to be trying too hard or even to be mocking the other person.

■ *Dominance and control* are bodily positions showing power and status; they vary by culture, situation, and gender. High-status Japanese bow to be polite—but low-status Japanese bow lower to show deference.[42] North Americans are seen as powerful when they sit or stand in an erect, but relaxed and open, posture—and North American men often show dominance by leaning or tipping their chairs back, whereas women often avoid dominance by adapting their positions to conversational partners. This may make women's partners more comfortable than men's, because women's behavior appears more accommodating and interested.[43]

Gestures   Members of a culture clearly understand some gestures and use them deliberately (some not so nice!), but most gestures are unconscious expressions of a feeling or an idea. Either conscious or unconscious gestures are of four main types:[44]

1   *Emblems* have well-defined meanings within a culture or an identity group. Watch people using emblems; observe umpires, coaches, pitchers, and catchers at a baseball game, or lovers signaling across a room, or signers using American Sign Language, or irate drivers. You use emblems yourself, all the time—but you have to be aware that people not in your culture or in-group may not share your understanding. In the United States, for example, your raised hand with

the palm inward and fingers wagging means "Come here." In Italy, it means "Good-bye." Or you may innocently point to an object with your left hand and deeply offend a person from Thailand, where that's an obscene gesture. In the United States, your hand held up with the palm outward means "Stop!" In Greece, it means something we can't print here. It's a real insult.

2   *Illustrators* "show" what your words mean, adding clarity, dynamism, and emphasis. Often, an illustrator emerges for a specific point. You might say, "Teamwork is interdependent, interwoven, cooperative," for instance, and weave your fingers together to illustrate what you mean. Sometimes, too, an emblem and an illustrator can be the same, as with shouting, "Stop right there!" and raising your hand, palm out, as if to block action.

3   *Regulators* control turn-taking in conversations. Regulators will encourage people to talk—nodding to acknowledge a speaker's point, perhaps, or giving a thumbs-up sign—or to switch speakers, with signs such as impatient head nodding ("Yeah, yeah, it's my turn"), looking at watches, fiddling with objects, moving into closed-off body positions, or, perhaps, moving as if to leave.

4   *Adaptors* are habitual actions that in some way help to manage a person's needs, emotions, or relationships. They are unconscious shorthand moves directed toward the self (head scratching, neck rubbing, ear pulling) or toward someone else (pointing, shrugging, nodding). An object, such as a pencil, can be used as an adaptor, too. Listeners often interpret adaptors negatively.[45] For example, you may fuss at your hair because you hate your new haircut, but others may think this adaptor means you're nervous. In general, it's better to avoid adaptors except for those that serve a practical purpose—such as using a pointer to show a spot on the map.

Students often worry that "I talk with my hands too much!" That is very rarely the case; gestures can add interest, clarity, and energy to communication. There are two major guidelines for effective gestures: First, try to use **synchronous messages**—that is, hand, body, and head movements that coordinate with your words, reinforcing rather than contradicting what you say. With such consistent messages, listeners are more likely to see you as competent, composed, trustworthy, extroverted, and sociable.[46]

Second, keep your body movements in proportion to the number of people you're speaking to and amount of available space. In an intimate conversation, keep gestures close to you. In a speech, use gestures big enough for everyone to see them, and strong enough that people believe that *you* believe what you're saying.

Space and Touch

You can make someone very comfortable or very uncomfortable by how close you position yourself to them or how you touch. The use of space and touching express and influence people's perceptions of their relationships as well as issues of power and control.

Synchronous messages Hand, body, and head movements coordinating with spoken words

Proxemics The perception, use, and restructuring of space as communication

Territory A specific place you feel is yours

Personal space Space surrounding an individual actively maintained to protect against threats

Space When you choose a seat, back off because someone's "in your face," or stand up to give your report, you're using and reacting to **proxemics,** the "perception, use, and structuring of space as communication."[47]

You've no doubt seen people (or animals) passionately defend their "territory" or "personal space." A **territory** is a specific place you feel is yours, whereas your **personal space** is your invisible, adjustable bubble, a "three-dimensional zone" within which you can regulate your interactions with the outside world.[48]

Consciously or unconsciously, people often use space to get what they want. Sometimes the goal is positive, as when an individual moves closer or farther away to accommodate someone else's comfort zone. Although a leader may sit at the head of the table because Western expectations typically are the person of highest status takes that position, today's leaders often deliberately sit elsewhere to open discussion and empower others.

More negatively, people sometimes use space to control or manipulate others' responses by crowding them, standing threateningly over them, or keeping them at an extreme distance. Some executives sit behind enormous desks at the far end of a large room, with a visitor's chair placed some distance away, to manipulate the visitor into feeling powerless and keep control in the hands of the executive.

What happens when someone invades your personal space or territory? You probably show increased physiological stress[49] and signs of anxiety and defensiveness. People mark their territories with fences and graffiti; they glare when someone approaches their desks; they get to class early so they can claim "their" seats.

How much space does a person need? Early research by Hall identified four social contexts for unconscious distances people set as boundaries for interaction: intimate, personal, social, and public.[50] Specific distances vary according to culture and gender (the ones indicated following were determined in research with white, North American, males), but these categories seem generally to cross cultures as comfort zones for individuals:

1 *Intimate distance* (to about 18 inches): A zone for comforting, loving, maintaining intimacy, and playing contact sports.

2 *Personal distance* (18 inches to 4 feet): A comfortable conversational distance. If you get closer than 18 inches, you're "inside the bubble" and you make the person uncomfortable; if you move past 4 feet, the other may feel an urge to close the gap.

3 *Social distance* (4 to 12 feet): About right for interacting with strangers, business contacts, store clerks, and so on. Often, space is set by a desk, a counter, or some other barrier that implies, "This close, no closer."

4 *Public distance* (12 to about 25 feet): Average distance for addressing groups or getting someone's attention from a distance. It's too far away for confidentiality but far enough away to spread a message to a number of people.

Cultures vary, certainly within the range of each context. A recent study found that in an interview "Anglo Saxons positioned themselves furthest away from the interviewer, followed by Caucasians (Central and Eastern Europeans), and then Latinos."[51]

Cultural influences. Just how much space a person needs swells or shrinks with the type of activity and participants' ages, relationship, and racial or cultural homogeneity or heterogeneity.[52] You might be comfortable in closer proximity to someone like you than to a person whose background or culture are different from yours. Even the language you're using may affect distance choices. In one study, when speaking in their own languages, Japanese stayed the greatest distance away from each other, North Americans were closer, and Venezuelans were closer still. When all spoke in English, however, both Japanese and Venezuelans conversed in about the same space range as North Americans.[53]

Gender influences. Similarly, gender roles affect space requirements within any culture. A number of research studies indicate "women are perceived to be more social, more affiliative, and of lower status; as a result, space surrounding women is considered more public and accessible than space surrounding men."[54] So, people are more likely to crowd into a woman's space than a man's, and, furthermore, if a woman actually takes more space, she may be violating others' expectations and making them uncomfortable.

Haptics Communication by touching

Touch Touching and being touched, technically called **haptics,** is a deep biological and psychological need. Lack of tactile stimulation actually relates to higher infant mortality and to later health problems, a tragedy seen in the historical health records of infants deprived of touch in orphanages and hospital incubators.

What does touching communicate? Experts suggest the following:

- *Support.* Touch can convey warmth, reassurance, or comfort,[55] with a hand on a friend's shoulder or a hug just when it's needed. Touch may even help to heal body and mind. Leathers comments, "Given the therapeutic power of touch, it is a sad fact that many individuals who most need touch are the least likely to receive it."[56] The ill, the lonely, the old—they are most likely to be untouched and to feel unloved.

- *Power.* In Western cultures, individuals of higher status and greater power are allowed to touch those of lower status and power, and he or she is more likely to touch.[57] Even if you're well intentioned, your status may make your touch intimidating or insulting. One manager patted his subordinates on the arm or back—thinking to motivate them—and so offended his Asian employees that some asked for transfers.[58]

- *Affiliation.* Touching is a clear clue to people's liking and affection for each other.[59] It also signals development of interpersonal relationships according to cultural norms for what kind of touching is acceptable at which stage.

- *Ritual.* Rituals define large and small beginnings, transitions, and endings in people's lives, and touching helps to mark those moments, as in handshakes or kisses for greetings and farewells, or in major events, such as a wedding, when guests kiss the bride. In a sense, these touches remind us transitions are part of life and add security and importance to such moments.

Touching, so vital to living creatures, also is incredibly enmeshed in matters of culture and gender, status and power. To be effective as a communicator in a diverse society takes sensitivity and observation, because generalizations don't give you much footing. To give you a small sample of research learnings about touch: In casual conversation Italians and Greeks touch more than the English, French, or Dutch,[60] and African American men touch each other more than white men do; African American women touch each other more often than white women do; and both sexes touched others of their own race more than they did people of another race.[61]

But then, even within a culture men and women may touch differently. Western women distinguish between affiliative touching (for warmth and affection) and sexual touching—but Western men don't see the differences.[62] Or, women touch each other more than men touch each other, and women touch children more than men do—but men touch women more than women touch men.[63] And it appears that hand touches, at least with Czechs, Italians, and North Americans, are connected with dominance, but non-hand touches are not.[64]

All that (and much more) probably means that a wise communicator watches to see how touching is used in any culture or context before making physical contact with another. Even in your own culture, touching intended to be casual may appear to be sexual, and in an organizational setting—business, professional, academic—a person who has been touched in a sexually suggestive or aggressive way has a right to state objections and then to bring sexual harassment charges. (If you want to know more about this issue, to go to the *Communicating with Credibility and Confidence* website.)

Personal Symbols: Subtle Influences

It may not be fair, or even reasonable, but many personal, subtle, nonverbal messages influence others' impressions of you—and when they are favorably impressed, people see you as credible, give you positive feedback, and that contributes to your self-esteem. People with high self-esteem are less likely to fear communication,[65] so the personal nonverbal cues that impress others can increase your confidence as well. Your appearance, use of objects, and attitude toward time all symbolize something about you to others.

- *Appearance*. Physical attractiveness is nice, but it doesn't amount to credibility. In light of these findings, and since the way you dress and style your hair can also affect how others see your credibility, likeability, attractiveness, and dominance,[66] our best advice is to be on the safe side: *Select clothes and grooming appropriate to the situation and in which you feel self-confident.* Picture the setting, the participants, and yourself in relation to your goals—then choose your costume.

- *Objects*. Like pottery that tells the story of ancient peoples, contemporary people tell about themselves with **artifacts**—all they wear, carry, leave behind, or spread around: clothing, buttons, and perfume, tote bags and

Artifacts Things living people use to symbolize themselves

backpacks, pictures, posters, flowers decorating your room. You can be stereotyped or not, liked or loathed, and trusted or suspected on the basis of these symbols. For example, in a recent study both managers and students rated male interviewees' credibility and hirability higher if they wore no jewelry, lower if they wore jewelry, lower still if they wore an earring, and lowest yet with a nose ring.[67] True, the type of job, location, and biases of the interviewer might change that result, but still, it's wiser to leave piercings unadorned for an interview.

Time: A Cultural Concept

Not only do artifacts impress people positively or negatively. How you manage time can be at least as big. Think of how many English language phrases reflect an obsession about time: "Time is money," "Don't be late," "Don't waste my time." An individual who is late for an appointment in the United States may be viewed as irresponsible, incompetent, rebellious, or manipulative.

Some other cultures, however, see it differently. In the Hopi tradition, for example, each person, plant, or animal has its own time system, and you can't impose one's deadline on another.[68] In the Maasai culture, wisdom of the past guides life, but present and future are irrelevant. In Kenya, public transportation has no schedule. A Kenyan who tells a nervous American the bus will leave "just now," means "when the bus is full, of course," and not before.[69]

Monochronic cultures
Cultures in which people attend to one thing at a time, with focus on deadlines and schedules

Polychronic cultures
Cultures in which people do many things at once, with focus on relationships and immediacy

Attitude toward time permeates cultures in a variety of ways. Hall labels cultures as monochronic or polychronic.[70] In **monochronic cultures** (meaning single-time)—such as are found in most of North America—people generally attend to one thing at a time. In **polychronic cultures** (meaning multi-time)— such as are found in most of Latin America—people do many things at once. In a business meeting, monochronic individuals might be prompt and stick to the agenda so they can finish on time. The polychronic persons might be late because a previous engagement took longer than planned, and they would willingly override the agenda to deal with other concerns and social relationships in addition to explicit meeting goals.

"Even within the dominant mainstream of American culture," say Porter and Samovar, "we find groups that have learned to perceive time in ways that appear strange to many outsiders. Hispanics frequently refer to Mexican or Latino time when their timing differs from the predominant Anglo concept, and African Americans often use what is referred to as BPT (black people's time) or hang-loose time—maintaining that priority belongs to what is happening at that instant."[71]

In today's diverse world, communicators must be sensitive to differing concepts of time. If your culture is monochronic and you're in a polychronic meeting, relax and go with the flow. You'll learn and enjoy a lot you would otherwise miss. If your culture is polychronic and you're meeting with people who are monochronic, be sensitive to their need for deadlines and schedules. If you're working with a diverse group, discuss norms and work out compromises. Not only is your credibility at stake, but your communication is more effective and more pleasant when you adjust to people and circumstances.

Settings: Structures and Environments

Would you rather make a speech in a dark, dingy, overcrowded room or a well-lit, ventilated, comfortable space? Would you rather say "I love you" in a subway station or on a romantic carriage ride? Of course, you would choose surroundings that fit your purposes best; you're already aware that environment exerts its own nonverbal effect. The environment can affect these three human responses:

1   *Emotions* are influenced through form, shape, line, space, color, sound, smell, and more. Color, for instance, can affect interpersonal communication by calming or inciting people. An old story has it that legendary football coaches Amos Alonzo Stagg and Knute Rockne gave their teams pep talks in locker rooms painted an arousing red but housed visiting teams in rooms painted a soothing blue.

2   *Power and control* can be symbolized and exerted through arrangements of space, sound, and aesthetic elements in a room. We saw that in presidential debates of 2000, which used three different arrangements to equalize power and control factors. The first debate posed each candidate at a lectern in a traditional arrangement, facing Tom Lehrer, their questioner, and the audience. The second used a discussion arrangement, each man seated and facing Mr. Lehrer. And the third pitted the candidates against each other, "extemporaneously" answering people's questions in a town-hall meeting arrangement. The candidates needed to prove their credibility, be confident under pressure, and respond flexibly to varied situations that directly affected the power they could show as candidates and amount of control they could take.

3   *Communication conditions.* Both layout and conditions of a room and use of electronic media can affect communication immeasurably. There's a reason theater seats "partially obstructed" by a column are cheaper—the experience isn't the same if you can't see all the action. Or if a room is overcrowded and people are buzzing, it's hard to hear and respond to messages. Similarly, electronic media affect communication transactions. As you give a speech with a camera watching you, you could be more nervous (even though that tape definitely helps speakers develop skills). At work, audio- or videotape, computer databases, e-mail, virtual teams, or teleconference facilities serve to share information, diagrams, or notes with electronic blackboards, telewriting, or remote slides. Each electronic medium not only structures how you send and receive messages, but also limits the types of interactions you can have. Then again, you might telecommute, working in your kitchen and wearing your bunny slippers. In each case, room environment and media influence how you communicate and to what effect.

You cannot have a proud and chivalrous spirit if your conduct is mean and paltry; for whatever a man's actions are, must be his spirit.

Demosthenes, fourth-century BCE Athenian statesman and orator

Nonverbal Development: Credibility and Confidence

Yes, nonverbal communication is cultural, complex, and often unconscious. Even so, you can use it and interpret it effectively. Here are some hints for becoming more effective on both fronts.

Receiving Nonverbal Cues

You can't "read people like a book." Anyone who thinks that's possible probably is nonverbally illiterate. You can, however, interpret messages much more effectively if you do the following:

1   *Don't jump to conclusions* about others' nonverbal behavior on the basis of what you or people you know would do. Recognize that variables such as culture, age, gender, status, and context may influence nonverbal cues, but don't assume you know how those influences may be manifested in an individual's behavior. Be careful to avoid stereotyping. Keep an open mind, observe, and listen.

2   *Observe nonverbal cues in clusters and over time.* One nonverbal cue on one occasion won't tell you much, but as you observe a person, you may see patterns in the same individual over time. If Kailyn always smiles, it doesn't necessarily mean she's happy; if she smiles, her eyes wrinkle up, her posture straightens, her gestures widen, and her laughter tumbles out, then you have more evidence of her joy. If you get to know her and see these cues frequently when she has reason to be happy, you can use this pattern as a basis for knowing when she is, in fact, happy.

3   *Look for consistency and inconsistency.* What nonverbal cues are consistent with each other and with verbal cues? When do nonverbal cues contradict one another or the verbal message? If Kailyn says, "I'm happy," and she smiles—but her eyes, other facial features, and body don't move—then there's a contradiction that makes you wonder what's really going on.

4   *Be tentative.* Formulate hypotheses carefully, and watch to see if they seem to be supported. Often, a person's nonverbal cues reflect many internal thoughts and feelings or are responses to multiple cues from several other people. Suppose, in a group, you express an opinion, and Stan scowls. Is he responding to you, or to a sarcastic remark from someone else, or to a thought about his job? Notice cues, but be careful in interpreting them.

5   *Ask for clarification.* If verbal and nonverbal cues are contradictory, or if you are puzzled by a nonverbal response, you may be able to inquire about a person's feelings. When you observe Stan's scowl, you might say, "Stan, maybe you disagree? I noticed you didn't look too happy when I said . . ."

Sending Nonverbal Cues

You've been developing verbal and nonverbal habits since you were born, and improving them is a lifelong challenge. Good actors, however, learn to use nonverbal communication so it is expressive and appropriate to the verbal message—and so can you. Here are some techniques:

1   *Get good feedback.* Ask friends and family to observe and tell you what they see and hear when you talk. You may want to do Exercise 3 in Cyberpoints at the end of this chapter to help you get the most specific information you can.

2   *See and hear yourself.* Use videotaping and audiotaping. Yes, being videotaped is awful, but it helps. Look first for what you do well and keep it up; then look for inconsistencies, contradictions, and bad habits you can improve.

3   *Visualize yourself using effective nonverbal cues.* Visualize yourself communicating consistent and dynamic nonverbal messages, write out affirmations of how you want to be, and use them in your self-talk to help you visualize your ideal nonverbal communication. See yourself as credible, dynamic, confident. Hear your voice and speech as supporting your message, audience, situation, and yourself. Visualize your nonverbal cues supporting and reinforcing your verbal message, so you are comfortably communicating ideas unambiguously, clearly, and interestingly.

4   *Be sensitive to listeners.* Be aware of both your nonverbal communication and other people's reaction to and interpretation of it. As you interact with others, adapt to listeners whose first language is different, or who have hearing or vision disabilities, so they can pick up your cues. Think of how your cues might affect others' cultural or social norms, and avoid doing things that might dominate or offend others or cause them to stereotype you.

5   *Practice for clarity and impact.* Use voice, speech, body, and face to make your message clear and effective. Consider conditions of the environment; if acoustics are poor, for example, raise your volume; or if the room is small, lower your volume and shrink your gestures to fit the space.

Finally, remember two things: (1) Reading another's nonverbal cues requires you to observe, to be sensitive, to avoid making assumptions. (2) For every word you use, you give your listeners untold numbers of nonverbal cues. The clearer and more engaging your nonverbal communication, the higher your credibility with others and the greater your confidence will become.

Summary

Nonverbal communication consists of cues other than words, cues that often overlap one another and verbal messages they accompany. Nonverbal cues may repeat, emphasize, complement, substitute for, or even contradict a person's verbal message. They are used to regulate turn-taking and topic-changing in conversation, and they indicate and develop dimensions in relationships among participants.

Nonverbal cues are more unconscious, harder to control, and much more numerous than verbal messages they accompany, so people often trust them more. Adults rely on nonverbal cues for 60–70% of their interpretation of a message and derive much of their impression of others' credibility from nonverbal behaviors. Even so, people often inaccurately interpret nonverbal cues, because those cues are influenced by the situation as well as the culture, gender, and status of participants.

Nonverbal communication includes voice and speech (vocalics); eyes, face, and body, including gestures and posture (kinesics); touch (haptics); space, including territory and personal space (proxemics); and personal communicators such as objects (artifacts) and time. Setting, too, contributes to mood, flow, and stimulation of communication through sensory characteristics and electronic media.

You can become a better interpreter of others' nonverbal cues by drawing conclusions with great care and being sensitive to multiple influences that might cause particular behaviors. Becoming an effective sender of nonverbal cues requires both interpersonal and taped feedback, taping and analyzing messages, using good models, and practicing both privately and in interpersonal transactions so you can observe and adapt to others' responses.

Exercises

1   Think about how your family uses nonverbal communication. What are the family norms for space and territory? For touching? How do family members use facial expressions, gestures, eye contact? Where do you think the family norms come from? Are there cultural or social factors that influence them? How do you think these norms affect you and your own nonverbal communication? To what extent are you satisfied with your own use of nonverbal communication? What if anything would you like to change, and how do you think you could do that? Write an essay describing your responses to these questions.

2   With one other person, carry on a conversation about any topic that interests you. As you speak, try to mirror your partner's nonverbal communication—posture, eyes, facial expressions, gestures, use of space and touch, and voice and speech. Do this for 3 minutes, and then switch roles so your partner is mirroring you. Now, discuss what effect the mirroring had on your communication. It probably seemed silly and embarrassing at first, but as you practiced it, what happened? Now, monitor your behavior as you talk with people you are very close to. Do you naturally mirror others' behaviors? Is this mirroring different from mirroring a casual acquaintance? How?

3 With a small group of students, view a foreign film—one from a culture different from your own. Watch the way the actors use territory, personal space, and touching. Now compare your observations to the norms for using space and touch among the people you know. Where are there similarities? Where are there differences? Speculate as to how those differences might affect communication between the two cultures. As a group, present a short report to the class on what you have observed.

4 Select a piece of literature to read aloud to the class. It could be a poem you like, an editorial, or a very short story. Children's stories are excellent for this purpose. On your own, read your piece aloud and time it. Then cut it, if necessary, to be no longer than 3 minutes. Now practice it aloud on audio- or videotape. Observe yourself, and practice repeatedly. Work on getting the maximum expression from your vocal quality, volume, pitch, tempo, and speech. Practice making eye contact, facial gestures, and body movements so that your listeners will want to hear you. Then read the story for the class.

Cyberpoints

The following Cyberpoints can be easily accessed from the Student Companion website for this text at http://academic.cengage.com/communication/lumsdenccc3. Click on *Student Book Companion Site* and select this chapter from the pull-down menu at the top of the page that says "Select a chapter." Click on *Cyperpoints* under *Chapter Resources* and you will find links for the exercises following.

1 Want to improve your voice and speech? Go to the *Communicating with Credibility and Confidence* website at http://academic.cengage.com/communication/lumsdenccc3 for suggestions, exercises, and resources to help you do just that. What did you learn that can help you improve your voice and speech?

2 Are you concerned about inappropriate touching or sexual harassment? Go to the *Communicating with Credibility and Confidence* website for information on how to avoid either being an unintentional harasser or the victim of harassment. What are precautions you can take to reduce inappropriate touching or sexual harassment? What are ways you can respond to inappropriate touching or sexual harassment?

3 How good are your nonverbal communication skills? Go to the *Communicating with Credibility and Confidence* website and click on *Form 5.1, Personal Nonverbal Communication Assessment.* Print out and make two copies of the form. First, complete the assessment on your own. Then ask a friend or family member to complete the form based on how she or he would rate your abilities. Now compare your responses. When you are not sure why you or your helper chose an answer, discuss it. What specific behaviors are involved? Are they strengths? Do you need to improve them? How can you strengthen your nonverbal communication?

4 For more information on some interesting aspects of nonverbal communication, use InfoTrac College Edition to search on the keyword, *nonverbal*. Take a look at:

Charski, M. (2004, May 10) "Body of Evidence: Watch What You Say—with Your Eyes, Hands and Posture." *ADWEEK*, v45 i19 p54.

Flora, C. (2004, May-June) "The Once-Over Can You Trust First Impressions?" *Psychology Today*, v37 i3 p60.

Tierney, J. (2004, Feb. 22) "Mr. Likable vs. Mr. Electable." *The New York Times*, pWK1 col 01.

Floyd; K., Erbert, L. A. (2003, Oct) "Relational Message Interpretations of Nonverbal Matching Behavior: An Application of the Social Meaning Model." *The Journal of Social Psychology*, v143 i5 p581.

Write a summary of what you read. How can you use these ideas to build your credibility and/or confidence?

Chapter 6

Verbal Communication: Connecting with Language

Objectives for This Chapter

Knowledge

- Understand the importance of language in human communication
- Identify linguistic elements in messages
- Know factors that influence how individuals use language
- Understand how language contributes to credibility and confidence

Feelings and Approaches

- Be aware of and sensitive to uses of language
- Develop confidence in using language effectively
- Feel credible in using language

Communication Abilities

- Consider others' backgrounds in interpreting and in phrasing messages
- Use language that communicates ideas clearly and vividly
- Use language styles that increase credibility and confidence

Key Terms

verbal communication	denotative meanings	high-context society
strategic ambiguity	connotative meanings	low-context society
euphemisms	syntactics	metaphors
redefinition	style	images
DELs	standard language	
semantics	nonstandard language	

Τhe minute a baby says his or her first word, Mom or Dad gleefully telephones or e-mails the family to announce the event. They are sure their baby's grasp of language signals genius. Maybe, maybe not, but a child's picture of the world, identity (and, yes, self-confidence and credibility) develop largely through **verbal communication,** using language, written or oral, as a symbolic code to communicate ideas. The perfect example of someone for whom words revealed a world is Helen Keller. She was blind and deaf, but the moment she understood that the symbols Annie Sullivan signed into her hand meant water, she discovered language. And language released her brilliant mind from an intellectual prison—even though her body remained in its biological prison of darkness and soundlessness.

In this chapter, we look at how people use language to create meanings and how people use language to do harm. We examine how language styles reflect and affect status and power—and, finally, we find ways that skillful use of language can develop your credibility and confidence in communicating.

What Words "Mean"

Death and life are in the power of the tongue.

Proverbs 18:21, Old Testament of the Bible

Did a word mean what you thought? Or did you say what you mean? Or did meaning follow what you said? That's likely the best guess. "The language forms we use to describe a specific event . . . will distinctly affect our memory of the original event, in a way that makes it consistent with our linguistic expressions."[1]

Words Clarify Ideas

It's strange, but true, that as people communicate about their perceptions, their words also shape perceptions by clarifying ideas in these ways:

- *Description.* Your eyes see images, your mind thinks thoughts—but describing them with words makes them "real," limiting or expanding your perceptions. When you use one set of words, you exclude others and the images they might have created. Consider: "A red shirt" or "A soft, flowing shirt of deep scarlet washed silk." Are they the same shirt? Perhaps, perhaps not. Certainly images formed from each description are different in the minds of both speaker and listener.

- *Categorization.* Words label specific categories and exclude others: "Ms. Whalen is a corporate attorney" tells us something about her education,

La Llama, El Habla/Flame, Speech

.... **W**e talk because we are mortal:
words are not signs, they are years.
Saying what they say,
the words we are saying
say time; they name us.
We are time's names

The dead are mute
But they also say
what we are saying
Language is the house
of all, hanging over
the edge of the abyss.
To talk is human.

.... **H**ablamos porque somos mortales:
las palabras no son signos, son anos.
Al decir lo que dicen
los nombres que decimos
dicen tiempo: nos dicen.
Somos nombres del tiempo.

Mudos, tambien los muertos
pronuncian las palabras
que decimos los vivos.
El lenguaje es la casa
de odos en el flanco
del abismo colgada.
Conversar es humano.

From Octavio Paz, A *Draft of Shadows*. Copyright © 1979 by Octavio Paz and Eliot Weinberger,
Reprinted by permission of New Directions Publishing Corporation.

her profession, and her status, but also excludes many elements of her personality and her life.

- *Distinction*. Language discriminates among ideas, drawing attention to differences and away from similarities. In the language of politics, for example, "He's a liberal and she's a conservative" implies great differences, when, in reality, the two individuals' political beliefs may be more alike than they are different.

- *Evaluation*. Words often imply value judgments about events, objects, and people. An executive says, "I'll have my girl get back to your girl," betraying an unconscious attitude that a secretary is a female possession who is less than adult.

Words Develop and Change

Old words fall into disuse or acquire new meanings, and new words are created. Once, a neighbor rushed over to our house, indignantly proclaiming, "Do you know what they're going to do? They're going to change the dictionary! Now, nobody'll know what anything means!" She got it backward. A dictionary doesn't dictate the meanings of words; it simply reports what people think a word means at the moment. New words emerge from many sources, and they develop to meet many changing needs for expression.

Basic Sources of Words   Trying to trace the source of a word can be both fun and challenging. Etymologists actually spend their lives as word detectives, tracking the development of words and meanings.

One way words enter a language is *onomatopoeia,* words that imitate sounds. *Bark,* for example, sounds like a dog's expression. Or words enter a language as *derivatives,* borrowed freely from other languages, weaving and tangling through cultures and throughout history. English is infused with Latin, for example: *Mater* long ago became *mother.* Or *finite* in Latin (something measurable, defined, limited) also is *finite* in English; *finito* in Spanish; *fini* in French; *definito* in Italian. These, like many words, are *cognates;* that is, they sound similar and carry similar (not identical!) definitions because they derive from a common root. You may hear cognates you're sure you understand, such as the Spanish *simpatico.* The English cognate, *sympathetic,* might convey compassion, but to a Latino, *simpatico* might mean a person's special ability to comprehend, to get along with people, to relate to them. Perhaps it's like coorientation?

Adoption is a common source for a new word, too. Listen to a foreign language radio station and see how many familiar words you notice. *Radar,* for instance, will sound and mean the same in any language, although it started with English. Word adoptions may occur for new ideas, too, as when science and technology terms move directly into the major languages of the world. Then, too, adoptions frequently reflect social changes and mores. Victorian English adopted French terms to express ideas that weren't quite—uh—proper, as in *enceinte.* They couldn't say "pregnant" in polite company!

Adaptive Sources of Words   The world is changing almost blindingly fast, and people need new words for new ideas, so they often shorten phrases or create words for specific needs. Common shortcut symbols include jargon, acronyms, and slang.

- *Jargon* is language specific to an in-group or profession. It might be inner-city slang, military talk ("grunttalk" for noncommissioned personnel), academic or technological talk, or the language of the "digitally hip," whose dictionaries of digital idioms are obsolete by their first printing.

- *Acronyms* are words formed by combining the first letters of a phrase, perhaps with an extra vowel for easy English pronunciation. We mentioned *radar,* an international acronym for "RAdio Detecting And Ranging"—an electronic device that spots and locates an object by measuring the time it takes for the echo of a radio wave to return from it and the direction from which it returns.

- *Slang* is nonstandard, informal, lively, innovative language reflecting and defining a group and its members by encoding in-group jokes and information. Dictionaries of student slang, for example, mostly contain words or

Simon and Garfunkel sang, "The words of the prophets are written on the subway walls and tenement halls." What gives language its power? How do verbal and nonverbal cues interact in signs and graffiti? What do you suppose motivates people to express their views in public places?

phrases related to drunkenness, throwing up, and sex. Some slang, such as "tossing your cookies," goes back generations.[2] Newer slang, often derived from metaphors, puns, or abbreviations for ideas, is personal, carries inside jokes and meanings, and avoids more prolonged explanations and descriptions. Of course, some slang, which we ought not quote, may offend listeners, give the impression the speaker has a warped sense of being cool, or diminish the speaker's credibility with others who are not part of the in-group.

Words Manipulate Feelings

Within any language structure, people choose their words and their syntax with goals in mind. Whether conscious or unconscious, ethical or unethical, strategies to manipulate others' feelings or positions use words to obscure, to redefine, and, at times, to hurt.

Words to Obscure   Ambiguity—words that could have different interpretations—can be due to carelessness or lack of vocabulary or may be deliberate, a "message which is constructed to allow for multiple interpretations in order to mask or deviate from a privately represented belief, attitude, fact, or feeling." This **strategic ambiguity** might be a kind way to protect another person from an unpleasant truth or a subtle way to influence another person, a way to avoid an issue, to control the flow of communication, to influence how another perceives you, or to manage a potential conflict.[3]

For instance, "I really have to think about your sermon today," might mean you didn't understand a word your religious leader said. Or, "I'd really like to

Strategic ambiguity
The deliberate use of words that may have more than one possible interpretation

drive my car tonight," could mean, "I know *I'll* stay sober, so I'll be the designated driver."

Similarly, **euphemisms** are words or phrases that deliberately gloss over hard or potentially offensive aspects of a message. A favorite corporate euphemism, for example, is the *golden handshake,* symbolizing retirement incentives to unload older employees and hire younger ones at lower wages. Or the goal may be to *downsize* the organization, a euphemism for cutting personnel. After *downsize* became negative, a new euphemism, *rightsize,* was substituted. That makes it much better for the person who's been fired, right?

Euphemisms and strategic ambiguity are not always bad, but they may be used unethically to manipulate, control, and/or oppress people. Laws containing loopholes from which certain groups benefit, contracts that are vague and easily interpreted to cheat another, language that glosses over injustice—all use strategic ambiguity for unethical purposes.

Words to Redefine   **Redefinition** uses language to change a perception of persons or events, sometimes, for positive purposes. Efforts to change sexist or racist language, for example, redefine terms to reduce stereotyping. Retitling the head of a department as the "chairperson" rather than "chairman," for example, is a small step toward recognizing that women can be leaders, too. Referring to "people of color" instead of "minorities," redefines the subject as people, not objects, and acknowledges that "people of color" are not necessarily in the minority (indeed, worldwide, they are by far the majority). Redefinition, therefore, can use language to connect rather than divide people. A side benefit is that when your language elevates others, rather than stereotyping them, you also gain greater credibility.[4]

Unfortunately, redefinition can also play a major negative role in *propaganda,* "mass 'suggestion' or influence through the manipulation of symbols and the psychology of the individual."[5] Propaganda relies on vagueness, ambiguity, euphemisms, or redefinitions to manipulate the receiver.

In Nazi Germany, dictionaries and encyclopedias were rewritten, changing definitions to make actions of the fascist regime seem acceptable. The term *Abstammungsnachweis,* for example, had previously been defined in terms of cattle breeding but was redefined as a "genealogical certificate of Aryan origin."[6] Nazi propaganda then used the term to justify selective breeding of "desirable" humans and extermination of those considered undesirable—Jews, Gypsies, homosexuals, people with low intelligence or disabilities, the aged and infirm. More recently, men, women, and children have died by the millions under the force of "ethnic cleansing," a euphemistic redefinition of genocide to justify rape and murder of populations in Bosnia, the Sudan, Somalia, and many others.

As a *communicator,* you can watch your own language for strategic ambiguity, euphemisms, and redefinitions for both good and evil so you can make ethical choices about what you say. As a *receiver* of communication, particularly through the mass media, you can detect—and resist—others' efforts to manipulate and control your responses. Analysis of language can be the key to making decisions and controlling your own destiny.

Euphemisms Words or phrases that gloss over offensive aspects of a message

Redefinition The use of language to change perceptions by changing the words used

DELs Derogatory ethnic labels; names that attribute negative characteristics to a person or group

Words to Hurt   Some words are meant to hurt. That includes obscenities and **DELs,** or derogatory ethnic labels that attribute negative characteristics to individuals and groups. DELs, toxic labels based on race, color, gender, sexual orientation, age, and abilities, are name-calling that members of an in-group use to distance and devalue members of an out-group. More than 1,000 DELs have been documented in the United States.[7]

In his *Letter from a Birmingham Jail,* Martin Luther King Jr. describes how DELs can feel: "You are humiliated day in and day out by nagging signs reading 'white' and 'colored'; when your first name becomes 'nigger,' your middle name becomes 'boy' (however old you are) and your last name becomes 'John,' and your wife and mother are never given the respected title 'Mrs.'"[8]

It isn't true that "sticks and stones may break my bones but words will never hurt me." Words can break hearts. DELs diminish the humanity of the targets by associating their group with subhuman categories. Even calling a woman a "chick" casts her into the role of a ditzy, fluffy, incompetent baby fowl. She's cute but relatively worthless. She's not much good when you call her a "hen," either.

Furthermore, DELs may influence so-labeled members of an out-group to "develop resentment and distrust for the majority group, and, consequently, [lead to] rejection of many of the values of the majority culture."[9] This, again, pits groups against one another. "Why can't they just be more like *we* are?" an in-grouper says of an out-group. But why would you want to emulate someone who so labels you?

DELs categorize people so that neither the labeler nor the labeled may see the real person. Language so defines and limits what people perceive, labels may obscure what lies beyond them.

There are two cautions it's wise to remember. First, groups often absorb into their vocabularies and humor the very DELs that hurt them. In so doing, they diffuse the effect, and the DEL becomes an inside joke. From an outsider—even an outsider who is a good friend—a DEL takes on a different meaning. A person outside of the group should never try to usurp an inside joke; it's much better to avoid DELs entirely. They carry poison. Second, avoid dismissing the thoughtful use of language as "politically correct." Rejecting "political correctness" can be nothing more than another euphemism for "I don't care if I hurt people."

Thoughtfulness creates better communication *and* higher credibility.

How Language Maps Meaning

Did you ever make a three-dimensional model of a territory for a grade school project? Besides sticky hands, what did you get? By modeling that territory, you learned it. We hope. That's how language is—it means nothing until it's related to ideas like maps relate to territories. Out of words, people create maps to represent the territory of their experiences. A map is *not* the territory itself, and a word is not the "thing," but the symbolic representation of the idea.[10]

People create meanings from their word maps by using and interpreting words within the structure of sentences. Let's look at how two concepts—semantics and syntactics—function in creating and communicating meaning.

Semantics

Semantics The study of how people use words as signs or symbols for ideas and perceptions

Denotative meanings Meanings of words that are shared by speakers of the language

Connotative meanings Meanings of words that are based on an individual's personal experiences

Semantics is the study of how people use words as signs or symbols for their ideas and perceptions. Signs—like "Stop!"—are clear, concrete representations of one idea that require little mental processing. Symbols are less precise abstractions of experience, either denoting the character of a thing or connoting a feeling about it. **Denotative meanings,** compiled in dictionaries, are those you share with other speakers of your language. **Connotative meanings** are much less likely to be shared. They are personal, drawn from individual experience, background, values, and needs, existing in one person alone. For example, we once asked a class what *freedom* meant. Several white, middle-class North Americans said freedom was doing what they chose; two Cuban refugees felt freedom was escaping from oppression and poverty; some African American students saw in freedom opportunity and self-esteem. For one battered wife, just then rebuilding her life, freedom was not living in fear. We try to paraphrase these students' connotative meanings, but we know that each was so personal and so deeply held that we can only approximate the distinctions among their meanings.

Syntactics

Syntactics The way languages arrange and order words to convey meaning

Every language has its own **syntactics,** or ways of combining and arranging words, creating routes and relationships that help to convey meaning. For example, visualize a country road. Along that road, you see white houses. There are 20 of them. All of them are small. Now, arrange that information into one standard English sentence. Most English speakers, even young children, would say, "There are 20 small, white houses along the road." That's syntactics.

It can be hard for someone learning a second language to order thoughts in the expected way. In Spanish, for example, you don't put ownership first; you put the object first. "I'm going to John's house" translates to Spanish as *"Voy a la casa de Juan"* or, back to English, as "I'm going to the house of John." A small difference, yes—but both the words and the order must be correct, because the syntax *creates and communicates the logic and emphasis of the statement.* In the English version, John gets the emphasis; in the Spanish version, the house takes precedence.

Language of Social Identity

People define themselves and their society by their language, not a minor thing. In fact, this is a very, very big thing. "Cultural premises and rules about speaking are intricately tied up with cultural conceptions of persons, agency, and social relations. . . . In this sense a code of speaking is a code of personhood and society as well."[11]

That means language can become a volatile issue. Not long ago, the United States was seized in an intellectual and emotional spasm over the Oakland, California, school board's decision to teach *Ebonics,* which some call "Black English or Black English Vernacular—a language . . . slang . . . dialect . . . bad English . . . sloppy . . . illegitimate . . . wrong. . . . Others have said explicitly that Ebonics is a descendant of the language that was forced upon slaves, who were prevented from learning to speak as their white masters did."[12]

Fox concludes Ebonics "is a dialect of American English, [but it's best to teach standard English in North American schools for the pragmatic reason that students need it] in looking for jobs in the future."[13] Simply put, the power structure in North America uses standard English.

Throughout history, conquerors have tried to stamp out cultural identities by eliminating the language of the conquered and substituting their own. India, Africa, the Indies, Ireland, Native America—for a few—underwent a conqueror's language imposition. Oppressors argue that homogeneity—of culture, language, thinking—makes people and society easier to control and manage.

When Puerto Rico passed from Spanish to U.S. control in 1898, for example, the U.S.-appointed Board of Education mandated English in schools. The board president explained, "If the schools are made American, and teachers and pupils are inspired with the American spirit, . . . the island will become in its sympathies, views, and attitude toward life and toward government essentially American. The great mass of Puerto Ricans are as yet passive and plastic. . . . Their ideals are in our hands to create and mold."[14]

Issues of moral arrogance aside, is it even possible to convert a people's identity this way? After almost a hundred years of English language policy, "the Spanish language . . . is the fundamental tool used by most Puerto Ricans for most communication. But in this context it also serves as a symbolic marker for Puerto Rican identity, in direct opposition to the English-speaking United States."[15] Puerto Ricans may speak English, but Spanish still represents *who they are.*

So it has been in other lands. In Ireland, the English made it illegal to speak Gaelic, but "hedgerow teachers" secretly met at the edges of fields with little groups of students to impart the Irish language and culture. Today, Gaelic is taught in Irish schools along with English, and many Irish speak both comfortably. In Ottowa, Canada, billboards (often with tongue-in-cheek wit) and official signs are in both French and English, bridging the uneasy divide between the two languages. The language battle rages in the United States, where many people hope eliminating translations of public signs and documents into immigrant languages will create a homogenous culture.

Cultures in power consistently have underestimated how vital language is to a people's concept of themselves. As well, they have overlooked the richness of thought that diversity of language can bring to society. Recognizing that fact, the European Union's worry that Internet communication will blend European languages and cultures led to a 3-year Multilingual Information Society program "to preserve the cultural crucial languages in all their diversity," including an effort to provide translation services and dictionaries over data networks.[16]

Of course, Switzerland manages with four official languages.

Language Styles Affect Meaning

Style In communication, the way a person uses language

You use semantics, word order, grammar, and idiosyncrasies (of your own, your family, or your in-group) that come out as your language **style.** Style reveals a person's status and power, and reinforces differences of gender and culture.

Status and Power

In-groups in society are those who have power or dominance—and out-groups are those who have different cultures, norms, and/or social positions and are excluded from the social world of the in-group. On a broad scale, higher-status (socioeconomically, professionally, racially) people will be the major in-group, while folks of lower status will be identified with out-groups. (Of course, out-groups may create in-groups that also keep others out. Really. For example, the Ladies' League of Center City would be an in-group to which an inner-city gang is an out-group; but that gang may have greater status than other gangs, which are out-groups to them.) It's complicated, but real.

Standard language Language associated with power and status within a community

Nonstandard language A dialect or style that differs from the standard language within a community

Naturally, people are comfortable communicating with their own groups, but they may feel alienated by the way other groups communicate. Typically, **standard language** is a style "most often associated with high socioeconomic status, power and media usage in a particular community," and **nonstandard language** is a style, or dialect, that uses some qualities of vocabulary, grammar, syntax, and/or usage that distinguish it from "standard" language.[17]

Often, standard and nonstandard languages also use high-prestige or low-prestige speech patterns. Standard American English, for example, is distinguished by "correct" grammar and vocabulary usage as well as pronunciation typical of the Midwest. Most broadcasters, actors, and high-level power brokers speak standard American English. By these criteria, most North Americans probably speak a version of a nonstandard style or dialect.

Unfair though it is, those who speak a standard style are seen as more credible, competent, intelligent, confident, and ambitious than people who use regional dialects or minority ethnic styles.[18] Teachers, too, sometimes judge students' personalities, social backgrounds, and academic abilities negatively when students use nonstandard language. Even nonstandard speakers *themselves* evaluate standard speakers as more competent than members of their own group, although they still are more attracted to members of their own group.[19]

Kimo, for example, speaks "pidgin" with his Hawaiian coworkers. In school, teachers once scolded, "You'll never get anywhere speaking pidgin." But pidgin was quick, colorful, and expressive, and Kimo could "talk story" with his friends, who shared so much with their special language. Now, though, a new worker arrives speaking standard English. Kimo and his friends feel uncomfortable with her. They fear she might be promoted over them, even though they have more experience, because she speaks standard English. For Kimo's group, pidgin provides solidarity and identity, but it also separates them from others and, possibly, hinders their career advancement.

The language style a person speaks often reveals her or his degree of power in the society. People who have not shared metaphors and symbols of the power group are not much heard in larger arenas of power. They are, essentially, a *muted group*.[20] Typically, muted groups are women, members of ethnic minorities or out-groups, people who have disabilities, the elderly, and the poor. Their styles have their own strengths, but mark them as less powerful in society at large.

Again, as with speech patterns described in Chapter 5, the most effective strategy is to learn how to be fluent in various situations. As African American women explained their own talk in one study, they use "style-switching to accommodate the demands of African American and dominant cultural settings."[21]

Gender

Julia Wood points out that "in addition to expressing cultural views of gender, language reflects our own gendered identities."[22] For the most part, even though today's little girls may play Little League, and little boys may have grown accustomed to girls in their world, each sex really grows up in its own speech community, learning their culture's socialization and language of their sex.

Each culture has its own male and female speech communities within it. In one, Malagasy, characteristics of powerful/male and powerless/female talk are the opposite of most cultures. "In Malagasy society women have lower status than men, but they use our stereotypical 'powerful' language; they do the confronting and reprimanding . . . in direct opposition to society's nonconfrontational, conversational norms. . . . Their constant violation of societal norms is seen as confirmation of their inferiority." So, despite reversal of the language traits of each gender, males remain the powerful and dominant group in Malagasy.[23]

In North America, however, Tannen classifies the language of white males and females into *report-talk* and *rapport-talk*.[24] She notes that men generally use a "report" style similar to public speaking: they lecture, inform, and correct others. By contrast, women's "rapport" style builds relationships by questioning, encouraging, affirming, and supporting others in conversation. You know the jokes about women talking too much? Actually, men talk more overall, but at home, women talk and question to get men to open up to them. "Again and again," Tannen says, "women complain, 'He seems to have everything to say to everyone else, and nothing to say to me.'"[25]

Investigations of status and gender styles have found subordinate and/or female communicators tend to be more *tentative, hesitant, polite, correct, and colorful* in their rapport-talk; higher-status people, often male, are more *certain, commanding, confident, less polite, and more colloquial* in report-talk. Keep in

Sisters with a Language

Jiangyong, China—Stooped over like a wilted rose, 95-year old Yang Huanyi hobbles out of her tiny, spartan home to receive guests who come calling from around the world.

In her gnarled hands she clutches a rough-hewn notebook. It is the reason so many foreigners journey to this bucolic corner of southern China to visit her.

On its pages Yang has written the woeful story of a girl trapped in an unhappy marriage, a common lot among women in rural China. But the tale is not what attracts attention. It is how Yang recorded it: in a unique form of writing invented and passed down through generations by the women of Jiangyong—and kept apart from their fathers, husbands, and sons. . . .

Using their special form of communication—called *nushu*, or women's script, in Chinese, they carved out their own private linguistic space in a world dominated by men. . . .

The language, mainly written but sometimes spoken or sung, enabled its users to share thoughts, spread gossip and swap experiences at a time when most of their sex in China were illiterate and often denied identities apart from their menfolk. . . .

"Beside a well, one does not thirst," a popular *nushu* saying holds. "Beside a sister, one does not despair."

From Henry Chu, "China's Mother Tongue Is Dying," *Los Angeles Times*, April 15, 2002, pp. A1 and A12.

When a scholar discovered the existence of nushu *in the 1950s, the Chinese government tried to stamp it out, but the old women secretly kept it alive. Although almost gone as a living language,* nushu *will be preserved by scholars who see in it a testament to the power of language and of the human spirit.*

We wonder: How many other secret languages were created and used by oppressed peoples around the world and throughout history?

mind, however, that generalizations about male and female language styles are useful only up to a certain point.

Furthermore, individual cases often contradict traditional expectations. You may know "high-status" men who build close rapport and "low-status" women who assume command. Then, too, these days people more often understand that both men and women can be executive powerhouses and tender parents, at work or at home respectively.[26]

The best style to use—for men and women—is the one that works for understanding and credibility. The choice depends on the situation (adaptation or code switching yet again). Report-talk may be better for business meetings, and rapport-talk may be essential for sharing feelings with a friend or growing a relationship. Ideally, men and woman should be able to adapt their styles to the listener and their communication goals.

Culture

Just as your family's communication affects your own style, so does culture affect a family's style. The influence of culture is explained by Edward Hall's theory, which places cultures along a continuum of high-context (people know all about one another and their affairs) to low-context (people know little about one another and their affairs).[27]

High-context society A society with close family and community groupings, in which people share the same knowledge about each other and their environment

A **high-context society** (such as many Asian cultures or tribal cultures) is likely to be agrarian with close families and communities. If you and your neighbors know all about one another and share common experiences, you do not need a lot of explanation and detail in talking. You can fill in gaps easily. You do, however, need to maintain harmony because you share so much. So high-context people often (but not always) are indirect and work to maintain *face,* or respect for self and others. Japanese children, for example, learn early neither to call attention to themselves nor to hurt the feelings of others; their mothers teach them "the subtleties of face-giving and face-threatening behaviors through modeling their mothers' behaviors."[28]

Contrast this subtlety, self-effacement, and concern for harmony with that of a **low-context society.** As in North America, the culture is more likely to be industrialized and diverse, with scattered family, community, and socioeconomic groupings. People cannot all have the same knowledge of one another and their environment, so they have less context in common for their communication. There is little motivation to sacrifice individual wants for group harmony, because there is less closeness among people. U.S. cities exemplify low-context cultures, and you can easily see how this affects communication. North Americans are more likely to be direct, explicit, and focused on individual goals of the communication.

Low-context society A society with scattered family, community, and socioeconomic groupings, in which people do not share the same knowledge about each other and their environment

A friend of ours experienced what can happen when people from each culture type interact. Peter was in the People's Republic of China on a business trip, and his host interpreter told him they would be meeting with an important state official that evening. The dialogue went like this:

Peter: Should I wear a tie?

Interpreter: You may wear whatever you wish; he is a very important person.

Peter: Then I should wear a tie?

Interpreter: Oh, you may wear anything that's comfortable for you. It will be a special evening.

Peter: So a sweater would be okay?

Interpreter: Whatever you would like to wear will be fine. He's an important person. It will be a very nice occasion.

Finally, after many of these ambiguous messages, Peter asked the right question:

"Will *you* be wearing a tie?"

"Oh, yes," replied the interpreter. "He's a *very* important person."

The high-context, face-saving Chinese culture made it impossible for the host to tell his guest what he should wear. The interpreter kept the issue open until our friend asked the right question in order to elicit a polite answer that guided, but didn't demand, Peter's dress choice. Peter wore a jacket and tie.

How Your Language Communicates Meaning

When you know you use language well, you're more likely to feel confident of what you say *and* of your credibility. The way to develop language skills is by developing vocabulary, language choice, clarity, and using language that stimulates listeners and makes messages vivid.

Building a Vocabulary

The difference between the right word and the almost-right word is really a large matter—it's the difference between the lightning bug and the lightning.

Mark Twain, 19th–20th-century humorist, novelist, essayist

We've heard students say, "I have a lousy vocabulary." That may not be true, but it is true that most of us can improve our active vocabularies. Admittedly, there are a lot of English words. The average high school graduate knows about 80,000 words[29] out of the million or so words in English, including specialized fields.[30] If you want to embark on a vigorous effort to expand your vocabulary, many excellent programs are available, but you also can improve your vocabulary without a commercial program by using these guidelines:

1   *Cultivate curiosity.* Become conscious of words—their nuances, their sources, their uses. Words give color, emotion, and impact to ideas. Look on new words as puzzles to solve and potential tools to make your own.

2   *Read extensively.* Experts say the real secret to building vocabulary is reading.[31] Think of your textbooks as vocabulary sources and read a variety of well-written literature or news magazines from which you can learn new words and phrases. Then start using some of the new words they teach you.

3   *Listen for language.* Tune in to words that most effectively and clearly communicate concepts. Listen to lectures, sermons, broadcasts, and friends, and notice words that work. Make new words your own, not just by looking it up in the dictionary but also by doing the following:

- *Look at context* for a hint of the meaning. If someone says, "Of *course* he didn't contribute. . . . He's a parsimonious jerk." You could infer that *parsimonious* means stingy and money-grubbing.

- *Ask an expert* such as a professor or instructor who can give you the definition, possible contextual interpretations, and history of a term. The more you learn about a term, the easier it is to remember and to use.

- *Dissect the word,* by looking for familiar roots (usually from Latin or Greek), prefixes, and suffixes that tip you off to part of the meaning, and for parts of the word similar to other words you know. Take the wonderful *antidisestablishmentarianism.* You know that *anti* means "against"; *dis* also means "opposition" (as in to "*dis*believe"); an *establishment* is a permanent institution; *arian* is a suffix indicating that a person subscribes to the concept (such as "vegetarian"); and *ism* is a suffix indicating a philosophical position. When you take the pieces apart, you can get a hint that *antidisestablishmentarianism* refers to opposing the position of withdrawing support from institutions.

Communicating with Clarity

Ideally your message is clear to listeners, using concrete language and minimizing ambiguities. You can eliminate ambiguities by paying attention to words, phrases, and sentence structures that might be misconstrued. Look out for the following:

- *A single word can be interpreted with more than one meaning.* Does "She's such a perfect model" mean she's a great person to emulate, or that she models for *Vogue* magazine?

- *A phrase may be interpreted with more than one meaning.* Does "That teacher really has high standards" mean he's a tough grader, extremely ethical, or works very hard?

- *The syntax, or arrangement, of a sentence may suggest more than one meaning.* One form (called "amphibole") goes like this: "The board solved the problem with money." Was the problem financial, and the board solved it? Or, did the board use money to solve some other problem?

To eliminate ambiguity, consider possible interpretations of your message from your listeners' point of view and pay attention to their nonverbal and verbal feedback. If you're preparing a report or speech, ask someone to listen to your rehearsal and let you know when parts are ambiguous.

It also helps you to avoid ambiguity and make listeners understand when you use *concrete terms*. As symbols, words range from concrete to abstract. A concrete term is specific and simple, dealing with just one idea. Words that embrace broader sets of ideas are more abstract, as they have less specific detail about the meaning. You might represent abstraction levels as a sphere, with layers or levels of abstraction that move out from the center, as shown in Figure 6.1.

At the center, you have a concrete core of specific meaning about one idea. As you move outward through successive rings, each term provides more room for other ideas or things to be included in the category. Words become more abstract and more general. Although the core term is still part of a broader category, the specific individual would be hard to identify. Consider how both denotative and connotative meanings may change at each layer.

At the core, Sarah is a unique individual. Her family can see Sarah clearly in their minds when they say her name. For them, "Sarah" is filled with personal feelings and understandings. The next layers become more abstract. At Layer 2,

Figure 6.1 *Abstraction circles*

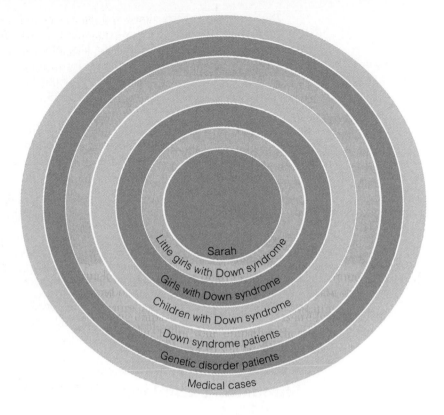

Sarah

Little girls with Down syndrome

Girls with Down syndrome

Children with Down syndrome

Down syndrome patients

Genetic disorder patients

Medical cases

Whoever would love life and see good days must keep the tongue from evil and the lips from speaking deceit.

1 Peter 3:8–11, New Testament of the Bible

Sarah is no longer Sarah; she could be any little girl with Down syndrome. In Layer 3, Sarah may be among girls of all ages and sizes, and at Layer 4, Sarah is one of all children without reference to gender or age or character.

Then, to the medical establishment, at Layer 5, Sarah is even more abstract—just a Down syndrome patient. At Layer 6, she isn't even a person, she's a genetic disorder. How impersonal, how unreal—but yet, how handy an abstraction for conveying a wealth of information about Sarah's condition among medical experts. At this level, connotations revolve around medical questions rather than individual ones about the girl herself. Finally, at Layer 7, Sarah is a medical "case." She has lost personality, gender, age, character, even her specific condition. She is simply a file folder full of records to be discussed at health care team meetings.

Only if members of her health care team can get back to talking about Sarah—the concrete, real, person—can that group of professionals begin to understand subtleties and connotations of the human being as well as medical facts and implications of the case. Abstractions are essential to discussing complex and specialized ideas—but concrete language is crucial to understanding individual and specific issues.

Sometimes, an abstraction *is* the perfect word for what you want to say and for the listener. A good rule, however, is to go down through those layers of abstraction in your mind and choose the least abstract term that will express what you mean. If you were Sarah's doctor, for example, you might say to another doctor, "That Down case I talked to you about last week." To Sarah's parents, it's far better to say, "In reviewing Sarah's situation," instead of, "In reviewing the case."

When you must use an abstraction, define the term for anyone who might not know it. At times a dictionary or expert definition will do. Other times, such as personal conversation, subtlety is better. Here are some ways you can define words in context of your conversation:

- *Build definitions into your discussion* with clarifying phrases or examples, for instance, "It seems to me the problem with attrition—that is, when someone leaves—is that. . . ."

- *Clarify an idea with comparisons and contrasts* to other ideas, as in, "This is a global plan: it doesn't focus only on national problems, it addresses more general worldwide problems."

- *Use analogies* to show how a more familiar concept resembles the one you want to clarify, for example, "Feeling empathy for another is like walking in that person's boots."

Stimulating Thinking and Senses

The very best moment in communication is the "Aha!", when listeners grasp the idea at a personal level. When you use metaphors and images, you can provoke others' thinking processes and make them truly "see" the ideas.

Metaphor The comparison of two things by calling one the other

A **metaphor** compares two things by calling one the other, providing a powerful way to connect ideas in the listener's mind. One management writer suggests, "A CEO proposing a joint venture may frame the opportunity by using the metaphor of 'a train leaving the station.' To fail to jump on board is to be left behind. A manager opposing the venture may frame it as 'hopping on the bandwagon,' highlighting the foolishness of joining without the benefit of careful analysis."[32]

The insight a metaphor brings to you becomes your own, taking on power and dimensions that you would never see without the help of the metaphor. To develop skill at making metaphors, practice by comparing two concepts in your mind and then develop a metaphor to express it. For instance, a counselor referred to a desperately needy, impossible-to-satisfy client as an "energy vampire." With these two words, she conveyed the idea that her energy was being sucked from her by her voracious client.

Images Vivid "pictures" drawn with words

Images are vivid "pictures" drawn with words, often including metaphors, which arouse the receivers' senses and make the picture real in their minds. Once again, the listeners "own" the ideas. This is, in part, because people have sensory memories that can be triggered by smells, sounds, tastes, feelings—or your descriptions of them. "The evening was cold" is a flat bit of information. But with "I could feel ice daggers cutting through my forehead, my fingers were too stiff to bend, and I trembled like a tuning fork in that 50-mile-an-hour wind," the listener can conjure up his or her own similar experiences and *feel* what you were feeling.

The importance of metaphor and imagery in language cannot be exaggerated. Often, they work together and even can trigger a redefinition of old ideas. Sometimes, a new metaphor helps people to see ideas and people in an entirely different light.

To develop skill at creating images, practice identifying and describing all the sensory elements in an experience. Brainstorm every sight, sound, smell, taste, and feeling in an experience, and then combine them into a description. Talk it out loud, so you can hear and feel the flow of ideas. As you work to express ideas, refer back to Chapter 3, where we talk about using language to aid listeners' perception. These learnings are basic to communicating in any context. As you begin to prepare presentations, you also will find both verbal and visual ways to aid understanding in Chapters 12 through 15.

Summary

Language develops a person's sense of identity and shapes his or her perception of the world. People create their own meanings for words; the study of this process is called "semantics." Humans locate the meanings of ideas on mental maps of their thoughts and perceptions. They connect these words through specific arrangements dictated by the language. The study of how words are ordered and arranged is called "syntactics."

The language of a people reflects their understandings of life and determines their sense of identity and pride. Language connects or divides people on the basis of similarities and differences of social status, gender, power, and culture. In-groups and out-groups within society influence how people use language. Each language has standard and nonstandard styles that reinforce stereotypes and expectations based on position and power. In most societies, social positions create powerful groups and less powerful groups, called "muted groups," who do not know and use the language of power and are therefore kept in subordinated positions. In the United States, powerful, high-status, and "masculine" communication generally is competitive, assertive, direct, and report-style. Less powerful, lower-status, and "feminine" communication often is cooperative, less direct, and rapport-style. This may be because girls and boys are conditioned as if they lived in different cultures, even within the same society.

Across the world, low-context cultures, such as the United States, rely on direct, assertive communication because little information is universally shared among people and individual effort and goals are highly prized. High-context cultures, such as those of Asia, use indirect, tactful, face-saving communication to preserve harmony because people hold much information about one another in common and rely on cooperation and harmony to get along.

Language changes constantly, with new words being generated and old ones changing to provide ways for obscuring or softening ideas through strategic ambiguity, for setting others apart through derogatory ethnic labels, for redefining concepts in the minds of others—for good ends or bad—and for shortcutting ideas to present them conveniently and quickly.

The effective use of language increases a person's credibility and confidence. A successful communicator builds vocabulary (through reading and becoming conscious of words); communicates with clear, unambiguous, concrete terms; and stimulates listeners' thought processes with such language strategies as metaphors and images.

Exercises

1 Select five advertisements from magazines or videotape five television commercials. Analyze the language used in the messages by answering the following questions:

What words are used that are concrete or very specific?

What words are used that are abstract and ambiguous?

In what ways is the language adapted to the specific audience?

What words are intended to stimulate thinking and imagery?

2 With another classmate, talk about ways in which derogatory ethnic labels (DELs) affect communicators. Analyze the impact DELs have on individuals. Consider these questions:

In what ways might DELs affect members of the target group?

What do DELs reflect about those who use them?

How does the use of DELs relate to a dialogic ethic of communication?

In what ways do DELs affect each of you at a personal level?

3 With a small group of classmates, create a vocabulary game from terminology used in this textbook. You might consider a board game, a quiz format, or any other approach your group creates. First, write the rules for your game in clear, concrete, nonambiguous language, and select the terms to be used. Then arrange for each group to play at least one other group's game. Analyze this activity by considering the following questions. Were your game rules specific enough to cover all issues that arose while playing your game? Did creating your game or playing that of another group actually increase your vocabulary? What did you learn about language during this exercise? How can you apply your learning to your day-to-day communication?

4   Prepare a one-minute presentation in which you talk about a special occasion in your life, such as a social event, a trip you have taken, or a surprise encounter. Develop the presentation relying extensively on imagery and metaphors to express your ideas and feelings (see the section in this chapter called "Stimulating Thinking and Senses").

Cyberpoints

The following Cyberpoints can be easily accessed from the Student Companion website for this text at http://academic.cengage.com/communication/lumsdenccc3. Click on *Student Book Companion Site* and select this chapter from the pull-down menu at the top of the page that says "Select a chapter." Click on *Cyperpoints* under *Chapter Resources* and you will find links for the exercises following.

1   Are you interested in how technology is affecting language use? Use InfoTrac College Edition to locate the following articles:

McCrory, A. (1997, Dec. 15). "When E-mail Greetings Shouldn't Be Warm." *Computerworld*, 31 (50), 33.

Revah, S. (1998, April). "The Language of the Digitally Hip." *American Journalism Review*, 20 (3), 12–14.

Do you feel the principles presented in the articles still hold true? Are problems the same? Would you suggest something different? Why?

2   Many people are too lazy or just don't know how to make their language nonsexist and nonracist, that is, inclusive of all rather than exclusive of gender or groups. For some hints on how to make your language inclusive (in speech or in writing), go to the *Communicating with Credibility and Confidence* website at http://academic.cengage.com/communication/lumsdenccc3. Look in Chapter 6 for "How to Be Inclusive in Communication."

3   Taking responsibility for your own ideas and perceptions with your language can build your credibility and confidence. One way of taking responsibility is by using "I" language. Read the article on "I" messages at http://mentalhelp.net/psyhelp/chap13/chap13g.htm. Think through how you can carry out the three steps identified in the article. Identify three situations in the past week when you could have improved the communication, and perhaps the outcome of the transaction, by using "I" messages. Review the section in the article on problems. List the problem you most expect to come up as you try using this change in language choice.

Chapter 7

Relationship Climates: Creating Communication Environments

Getty Images

Objectives for This Chapter

Knowledge

- Understand communication climates, causes, and effects
- Identify supportive and defensive communication behaviors
- Know how communication game playing affects relationships
- Understand causes, effects, and strategies for managing conflict

Feelings and Approaches

- Be confident and motivated to create and maintain positive communication climates
- Feel comfortable in using assertive communication
- Have confidence in managing conflicts and game-playing situations
- Be confident in building relationships and solving problems

Communication Abilities

- Self-monitor and adapt communication to build good communication climates
- Be supportive and assertive as appropriate
- Use appropriate communication to manage game playing or conflicts
- Develop credibility through positive communication

Key Terms

Our student, Dashawn, says her office is awful. Management is secretive and unpredictable. Workers don't dare speak about a problem because neither managers nor workers trust one another. The climate feels heavy and threatening, like a tornado is about to hit. In contrast, Dashawn describes her grandparents' home as "warm and breezy," like the gentle, playful relationship they've had for 46 years. The warm climate reflects how confident Dashawn's grandparents are in themselves, in each other, and in their relationship. Each is credible, open, and trusting with the other.

In each case, people's words and actions have created a **communication climate**—a set of conditions affecting the quality of communication and relationships. This chapter explores what supportive and defensive communication climates are like, how people create them, and how you can improve climates even when they involve conflict or game playing.

Communication climate A set of conditions that affect the quality of communication and relationships

Developing Supportive Communication Climates

What if you walk into a terrible climate in your new job, say, or you see a bad climate developing in your campus club? Do you have to just grit your teeth and bear it? Not necessarily; you might be able to alter the climate if you have self-confidence, credibility with others, and skill in self-monitoring and adapting.[1] You would need to understand what the climate could be, observe what it is, and communicate in ways that help to alter it.

When indeed shall we learn that we are all related one to the other, that we are all members of one body?

Helen Keller,
20th-century
American author

Characteristics of Supportive and Defensive Climates

If you know others respect your ideas and feelings so you are free to communicate about them, you are in a **supportive climate,** what philosopher Martin Buber[2] called an "I-Thou" relationship, in which people **humanify** each other—they see themselves and others as people, not as objects. Someone who humanifies you acknowledges your uniqueness, value, and rights. This reduces your defenses, enabling you to "concentrate upon the structure, the content, and the cognitive meanings of the message."[3] When you and others support one another, then, you are better able to negotiate genuinely shared meanings.

Supportive climate A communication environment in which listeners respect a speaker's ideas and feelings, allowing for open communication

Humanify View as a person with feelings, rights, values

In a **defensive climate,** people are likely to **objectify** one another; perhaps fearing criticism of some flaw they see in themselves.[4] When someone treats you as an "it," you've been objectified, treated as a thing that can be owned, meas-ured, or manipulated; a thing without feelings and importance.[5] People behave self-protectively when they feel threatened, of course, and this feeds into a circu-lar, progressively more defensive set of interactions.

Figure 7.1 shows how communication behaviors develop a supportive or defensive climate.

The figure begins with risk—as does just about any effort to communicate. Even asking a clerk for help risks a rude "Whaddayawant?" In a conversation, your first risk is in sharing something about yourself. That is **self-disclosure.** If the other responds supportively (see the list of supportive behaviors in Figure 7.1), you are free to build a positive climate together. If the other responds negatively (again, see Figure 7.1) you are put on the defensive. When the climate is sup-portive, it is open, trust increases, and people are able to share more of them-selves and create more trust. When it is defensive, people may simply withdraw or escalate their transaction into conflict.

At first, you may disclose no more than your name and, perhaps, your occu-pation. As you develop a relationship of any kind, you each learn more from the other as you match bits of information. Suppose you're introduced to a stranger and you say, "I'm a college student." That's a low-risk disclosure, but if the stranger snipes, "Another know-it-all college student, huh?" you might defend yourself with your own sarcasm or walk away. However, if the person responds, "Really? That's great. I never went to college, but I'm thinking about starting," each of you has contributed equally, and you have reason to trust each other with more information that can develop a good climate.

Self-Disclosure

Used sensibly, mutual self-disclosure helps to increase both credibility and con-fidence. Used unwisely, self-disclosure risks responses that can damage your self-concept and your effectiveness. It's important to understand what self-disclosure can accomplish, what influences it, and when and how you should use it in your transactions.

Effects of Self-Disclosure   Your self-disclosure surely affects how others re-spond to you. First, disclosing something about yourself tends to make other people like you more,[6] and, second, information you share helps people per-ceive you more accurately. They get a first impression from observing you, from which they attribute to you beliefs, motivations, and values. From attributions, they predict how and why you will act.[7] They could be wrong. But if you tell them about yourself, they can draw a more accurate understanding of you.

That's just from sharing yourself. But when you and another reciprocate equally with self-disclosure, you begin to see one another as competent and socially attractive,[8] and you build together a reciprocal sense of each other's coorientation and credibility. You start developing trust gradually, as each of

Figure 7.1 *Communication behaviors and cycles of supportive versus defensive communication*

Person A takes **risk** and **trusts** Person B with a **self-disclosure**

Person B responds:

If response is **SUPPORTIVE** it shows:

Empathy—caring about A's goals, feelings, ideas

Description/problem orientation—identifying, focusing on the issue, not on the person

Equality—showing respect, equal footing with the other person

Spontaneity and openness—freedom to hear and express ideas, feelings

Provisionalism—being objective, seeing possible alternatives, leaving room for another's ideas and feelings

leads to

Supportive climate

Increasing trust and willingness to take risks and self-disclose, continuing cycle of building support and empathy

If response is **DEFENSIVE** it shows:

Neutrality—indifference to A's goals, feelings, ideas

Evaluation/blame—judgmental statements focusing on the person, not on the issue

Superiority—implying the other person is inferior, less important

Strategy and control—manipulative behaviors to force the other person to respond in a predetermined way

Certainty—being absolute, seeing no alternative interpretations, closing off to another's ideas and feelings

leads to

Defensive climate

Conflict

Withdrawal

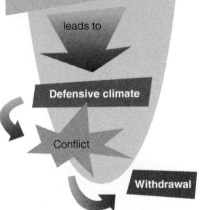
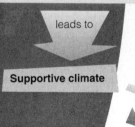

Figure 7.2 *The Johari Window*

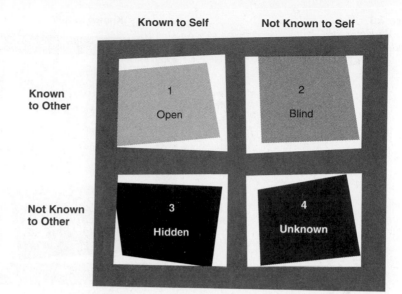

From J. Luft, *Of Human Interaction* (Palo Alto, CA: Mayfield, 1969). Used by permission of the publisher.

you disclose some of your vulnerabilities and show you are trustworthy in protecting the other's vulnerability.[9]

There's another benefit in self-disclosure. Saying something aloud to someone else can open up a window to your *own* feelings and ideas. A way of visualizing that effect is Figure 7.2, called the Johari Window (named for Joe Luft and Harry Ingram, who designed it).[10]

1   Quadrant 1 represents *shared information*—things you know about yourself and tell or demonstrate to others. The larger Quadrant 1 is, the more open your life is to you as well as to others.

2   Quadrant 2 represents *information about you that you're unaware of, but that others have observed.* You may be unaware of some of your own attributes (perhaps good, perhaps bad) but your disclosure and others' responses can give you insights. A student of ours once disclosed she hated her voice. When other students disclosed *they* thought her voice was beautiful, she jettisoned that negative self-concept. Her confidence rose, because she now knew she had a great vocal instrument with which to work.

3   Quadrant 3 represents *things you know about yourself but haven't shared with others.* For example, a friend of ours recently came out of the closet. Hiding his homosexuality has been agonizing, but he felt it would be enormously risky to disclose this information. Would his family reject him? Would his friends abandon him? Fortunately this man's family and friends are supporting him; he's able to share his life more openly with others, and he's drawing closer to his family.

Figure 7.3 *The Johari Window with expanded "open" area*

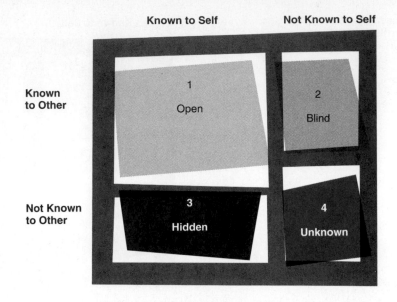

Known to Self   **Not Known to Self**

Known to Other

1
Open

2
Blind

Not Known to Other

3
Hidden

4
Unknown

4   Quadrant 4 represents *secluded things that no one—including yourself—realizes about you.* Everyone has some unrecognized issues or talents or desires residing behind the cloudy pane of Quadrant 4. Disclosure can illuminate those unknowns. When a student disclosed she was unhappy in her major, for example, she suddenly saw *why* she was dissatisfied. A creative woman, she had buried her creativity because "artsy stuff" wasn't valued in her family. When she disclosed what she did *not* want, this student gained insight into what she *did* want; a simple conversation helped her decide to change her major to the right one for her. (In other cases, a counselor, a support group, and/or a psychotherapist may be needed to help uncover an unrecognized issue).

Your self-perceptions, therefore, can broaden through self-disclosure. Figure 7.3 shows how the Johari Window "open" quadrant might open up through self-disclosure and feedback. As you discuss previously hidden areas and receive feedback, your self-disclosure helps you understand previously blind sections. With supportive transactions, you also begin to gain insight into previously unknown areas. These insights can chase away negative perceptions or fears that may have shadowed your concept of yourself. As you know yourself better, and as you discover your own strengths, you gain confidence in yourself and your ability to express your ideas.

Personal Influences on Self-Disclosure   "People assume that your self-disclosure style represents your emotional state and needs," say Demarasis and White, "and that it predicts how you will behave in a friendship or relationship."[11]

That makes your self-disclosure pretty important. But it is risky. What determines how you use it? How much you self-disclose and to whom, when, and where depend on several factors, including your culture or identity group.

Deborah Tannen, linguist, says,

I challenge the assumption that talking in an indirect way necessarily reveals powerlessness, lack of self-confidence, or anything else about the character of the speaker. Indirectness is a fundamental element in human communication. . . . For speakers raised in most of the world's cultures, varieties of indirectness are the norm in communication. . . .

From Deborah Tannen, *Talking from 9 to 5* (New York: Morrow, 1994), pp. 75–85, 96.

Amy Tan, Chinese American novelist, says,

There was nothing discreet about the Chinese language I grew up with. My parents made everything abundantly clear. Nothing wishy-washy in their demands, no compromises accepted: "Of course you will become a famous neurosurgeon," they told me. And yes, a concert pianist on the side.

In fact, now that I remember, it seems that the more emphatic outbursts always spilled over into Chinese: "Not that way! You must wash rice so not a single grain spills out."

From Amy Tan, "The Language of Discretion" (1990); reprinted in John Stewart, *Bridges Not Walls*, 7th ed. (1999), pp. 11–104.

In one study, people in the United States disclosed the most, Japanese the least, and French somewhere in the middle.[12] This is consistent with the idea that information sharing is lowest in very high-context cultures and highest in very low-context cultures. Remember that discussion in Chapter 6? So people in the United States, a low-context culture, generally want and give a lot of information, whereas people in high-context cultures such as Japan expect to know more from intuition and less from being told. In France, a middle-context culture, people might use some self-disclosure and expect others to intuit the rest.

Similarly, gender roles can influence your self-disclosure habits. From early childhood, females tend to disclose more in forming intimate friendships. Males, whose groups tend to be more competitive and less intimate, share interests and reciprocate favors but reveal vulnerabilities less than women do.[13] This might be why, when they *need* someone to talk to, both men and women tend to look for women as listeners.[14]

Many people, however, are *androgynous*, meaning men or women who adapt their communication, using "masculine" *or* "feminine" styles as befits the situation. Androgynous male and female high school students, for example, disclosed more to others and were less lonely than stereotypically feminine or masculine students.[15] Perhaps someone who shares openly makes friends more easily than a person who hesitates to share—and, perhaps, an individual of either sex who can be tender or tough according to the circumstances may be more likable and interesting than one who always acts as either a "dainty girl" or "macho boy" stereotype.

Guidelines for Self-Disclosure   This may seem odd, but most conversations between friends, and even between intimates, don't contain a lot of self-disclosure.[16] Maybe they've already shared the most important information, or maybe it's because self-disclosure *is* risky. Following are some things to consider in choosing whether or not to self-disclose:

- *What are the situation and the issues?* In most transactions, self-disclosure is superficial—about jobs, basic interests, general likes and dislikes. To go deeper, you need a context and foundation for matching your disclosures equally, for building trust.

- *To what extent has the other person disclosed information to you?* If you've just met, neither of you has a basis for deep disclosures. A new acquaintance, in fact, won't be prone to pursue interaction with you if you immediately spill something negative about yourself.[17] If you've built a base of shared disclosure, then you can feel freer to share more.

- *What is your relationship to the other person, and how has she or he treated disclosures before?* It should be that the more intimate the relationship, the more you can self-disclose safely. That is not always the case, however. Sometimes, families or spouses are quickest to judge and slowest to understand. Before making intimate disclosures, consider the other person's track record.

Assertiveness

It isn't *always* good to say what you think or want, but sometimes it's very good. In Western cultures, at least, assertiveness is credible. **Assertive communication** means openly communicating, with awareness of yourself and concern for others, what you need or want other people to know or do. With assertiveness, you can argue for your position without infringing on the positions of others. You can disagree without being disagreeable. You can focus on the issue without judging the person because you are humanifying, not objectifying, the individual.

Assertiveness is radically different from aggressiveness. Suppose your boss has given you more work than you can do. If you're assertive, you might open the discussion with, "Can we talk about my work? I'm sure I can't complete it all by the deadline." That's fine, but a person who isn't skilled in assertiveness might use **aggressive communication,** a "me first" position that disregards others' feelings or needs. Aggressors actively seek to control another's feelings and behavior, whether with a punch in the nose or, more likely, words that inflict psychological pain by attacking a person's self-concept.[18] An aggressive approach to the excessive workload might be the comment, "Well, I see that, as usual, you've made yourself look good by loading me up with work so I'll look

Figure 7.4 *The communication climate/assertiveness grid*

	Self-Disclosing (Influencing others)	Self-Protective (Influenced by others)
High Concern for Rights of Others	Assertive Open climate	Passive Closed climate
Low Concern for Rights of Others	Aggressive Hostile climate	Passive-aggressive Anxious/hostile climate

bad." Spoken loudly, this sarcastic attack strengthens the listener's feeling of being dominated.[19] Not surprisingly, people don't much like people who are verbally aggressive.[20]

Of course, there are styles between aggressiveness and assertiveness. People might care about their own rights but fear the other's response if they speak up, so they use **passive communication.** Passive responses hide behind silence or false agreement, appeasing others yet building up resentment or frustration. A passive response to the ever-increasing workload might be to huddle behind the stack of work, silently grinding away, knowing that the issue will come to a head when the work isn't done on time.

Finally, people may be anxious about what they want but too fearful of a negative response to ask directly; this dilemma can lead to **passive-aggressive communication**. Passive-aggression finds ways to block other people, halt progress, or punish someone without being caught at it. It is passive-aggression when the worker, faced with a mountain of work, "loses" part of the boss's data in the computer or "just mentions" to other workers how the boss has been padding the expense account.

Figure 7.4 shows how these four communication behaviors work. When you are *assertive* (upper left-hand corner of the grid), you are open and self-disclosing, you try to influence others, *and* you are very concerned for their rights. This behavior fosters an open climate. By contrast, the other three communication responses contribute to closed and hostile climates. When you are *aggressive* (lower left-hand corner), your concern for others is slight, even though you are open, self-disclosing, and willing to influence. This behavior contributes to a defensive climate. When you are *passive* (upper right-hand corner), you allow others to control the interaction and are too concerned about how others react. This behavior fosters a closed climate. When you are *passive-aggressive* (lower right-hand corner), you won't try to express feelings or influence others directly, but you may be hostile and find ways to punish others. This behavior contributes to a hostile and/or anxious climate.

It's probably obvious that people who use aggressive, passive, or passive-aggressive communication feel defensive themselves and make others defensive,

Passive communication Using silence or false agreement to appease others while building up resentment or frustration

Passive-aggressive communication Acting like one agrees and accepts, but seeking to undermine the process with later behavior

too. People who can express themselves assertively, with empathy for others, can help to create an open and supportive climate for communication.

Empathy and Confirmation

Your assertiveness may be excellent, and your self-disclosure may be well-chosen to create supportiveness. In addition, however, you need empathy and skill in confirming others.

You remember our Chapter 4 discussion of empathy in listening and questioning. When you communicate your **empathy,** your understanding of "the other's values, meanings, symbols, intentions,"[21] you truly humanify another person. They know that you feel *with* them in their joys or sorrows. Empathy develops as you focus directly on individuals, absorbing a sense of what they are feeling as you watch and listen and question, looking to understand, not just what they feel, but their personal context. How do background and experiences, culture and identity groups, and wants and needs affect the person? Through your understanding, your empathy grows.[22] So does the supportive climate.

Supportive climates grow when people know others empathize with them and when others confirm them. A **confirming response** makes you feel recognized as a worthwhile person, with worthwhile ideas and feelings. A confirming response may be nonverbal and/or verbal, with warm eye contact, an accepting body posture, nodding, or perhaps touching to indicate understanding—with or without words such as "That's a good idea" or, "You've earned the right" or, "You said that so well."

The opposite of confirmation is a **rejection response,** a lack of confirmation or even an aggressive reaction that discards you or your ideas. Rejection may be a direct superior, sarcastic, or know-it-all refutation of what you say; or the person may simply walk away without a word or may interrupt you in midsentence. Rejection could be pseudoconfirmation ("That's great, now let's eat") or an irrelevant statement that has nothing to do with what you said. Rejection isn't necessarily *meant* to be that; a person may just be distracted or absent-minded or be defensive or aggressive for reasons unrelated to you. Even so, rejection may leave you standing alone and wounded.

Similarly, a **disconfirming response** makes you feel almost invisible or, worse, undesirable. A disconfirming response may be impervious, revealing the listener's indifference to what you have said—for example, "That's not my problem." An impersonal response also disconfirms you through detachment—for example, "Those are the rules and I just follow them." Or there's the incongruous response, revealing contradiction between the words themselves and the nonverbal cues.[23]

When people feel acknowledged and confirmed, they usually feel free to communicate. When they believe that another person is rejecting them—even if their perception is inaccurate—people become defensive. Confirming others demonstrates your coorientation with them and your interest in what they have to say. It increases your credibility and it opens up communication. Even when you disagree with the message, you can confirm the person.

The older man is looking at a square of the Names Project quilt—a square that has been handmade by friends and family to memorialize someone who has died of AIDS. The project assistant seems to be comforting him. What is it about this picture that shows the empathy one man brings to the other?

R._crd/The Image Works

Identifying Defensive Communication Climates

Did you ever hear yourself thinking, "If I say this . . . I'll make her do that," or, "Fight, fight, fight—why can't we work this out?"? You could be trapped in a struggle for control that becomes a game of many innings. Surely competition and conflict are a part of life, but when the need to "win" shapes a communication climate, the game playing and conflict that result can injure or destroy relationships.

Game Playing

Ruth and Mel are talking about the dance they just left:

Mel: Raoul was his usual suave and debonair self tonight, wasn't he?

Ruth: Yeah, he's fun to be around.

Mel: Well, he's got more money and education than I have.

Competitive Game Playing	Cooperative Communication
Win-lose goals	Win-win goals
Not trusting	Trusting
Defensive strategies	Supportive climate
Manipulative	Open

Ruth: Oh, Mel, that's not important. Anyway, Raoul isn't all that terrific.

Mel: Tell the truth. You'd rather be with him than me.

Ruth: No, Mel, I love *you*. Raoul's not my type. Actually, I think he's kind of fake . . . you know, like . . . you're much more *real*. . . .

Mel: Yeah, right.

Mel wants Ruth's reassurance, and Ruth keeps on trying. Ruth and Mel have played this scene before and will again. They are trapped in **game playing,** a competitive, win-lose manipulation so one partner can achieve some personal goal. Game playing can be disastrous for relationships because it hinders participants' ability to relate on an intimate level.

There are such things as cooperative games, but *competitive* games assume that if there's a winner, there also must be a loser, so each participant has two alternatives: *win* or *lose*. Figure 7.5 shows the strategies and consequences of competitive versus cooperative communication.

In *competitive* interpersonal games, each person's goal is to win. Defensiveness results, because participants try to manipulate each other's vulnerabilities. Trust is impossible. Each knows the other is anticipating moves, taking calculated risks, and choosing moves to counteract or defeat the other's moves. A win-lose orientation is fine in games such as team sports, boxing, and chess. Similarly, a debate pits well-prepared advocates against each other so a judge can determine the winner based on arguments and evidence. Competition is fine when victory is the objective. Competition, however, is damaging in interpersonal and professional relationships.

In *cooperative* communication, the goal is for everyone to win, so people must take a risk, trust one another, and work together. In this supportive climate people can share control and develop mutual understanding through open communication because it is unnecessary to worry about protecting themselves. Obviously, cooperative behaviors are essential to develop relationships and achieve everyone's objectives.

When people try to "win points" by manipulating others when cooperation is called for—say, in a marriage—competition kills cooperation. Neither person wins; the outcome is *lose-lose,* and the climate is seriously damaged. Yet, many relationships are trapped in competitive games.

Game playing A competitive manipulation of communication so that one player can achieve a personal goal

They are playing a game. They are playing at not playing a game. If I show them I see they are, I shall break their rules and they will punish me. I must play their game, of not seeing I see the game.

R. D. Laing,
20th-century
psychologist and poet

There are several clues, besides your generally reliable gut feeling, that some-body's playing a game. These include the gimmick, the repeated script, and the payoff.[24]

- *Gimmicks* are a game player's predictable approach or phrasing that gets others to respond in a particular way. Suppose you hear a supervisor say sarcastically to the secretary, "Didn't you go to secretarial school?" Hav-ing witnessed this situation before, you know that this statement starts a series of snide remarks to make the secretary defensive. The secretary "loses points" (self-esteem and increased subservience), and the supervi-sor "wins" by intimidating the secretary into working overtime or doing personal favors.

- *Scripts* are consistent ways the game plays out. The script may not be word-for-word every time the gimmick starts it, but it has an observable structure. Like the script for a play, a game-playing script may include victims and vil-lains and heroes in some plot, action, and climax. We once knew a woman who played a game that could have been called "Poor Me." She would open a conversation with "You'll never believe what he did *this* time." If we fell for this gimmick and asked, "What?" she would spin a tale of woe describing her husband's transgressions, repeatedly stating, "I just don't know what to do." If you fell into the trap and made a suggestion, she would tell you why your idea wouldn't work. As the game continued, you realized that she was victim, her husband was villain, the plot involved her travails, and she was looking for a hero to rescue her. The climax of the game was her tearful acceptance of her lot in life.

- *Payoffs* are rewards a player hopes to get from the game. To someone else, the payoff may be negative, but to the game player it is something she or he needs, wants, expects, and/or can handle emotionally. The payoff may be something tangible; Jared pretends not to understand instructions until, in desperation, his boss gives the job to someone else to do. Or the payoff may be intangible; little Sirah quietly pinches her baby sister, Dottie, until Dottie screams in church and gets yelled at for disturbing the sermon. Sirah smiles because that little stinker who gets all the love has landed in trouble. Even if Sirah is punished later for having caused Dottie's outburst, that, too, may be a payoff in confirming Sirah's belief that she is unloved and rejected. Payoffs, even painful ones, are predictable and therefore secure for the game player; they are individual, complex, and powerful motivators for playing games.

Conflict

Conflict Tension people feel in a relationship when they perceive that they have differing goals or feelings

Conflict is tension people feel between them over mutually exclusive goals or feelings. Conflict isn't an argument; you can argue once about an issue and resolve it. Conflict continues through a series of events, sometimes changing over time, often having "little to do with the behaviors occurring in any single interaction, but, rather, may be strongly associated with previous relational experiences."[25]

Nonviolent Solutions

onviolence is the answer to the crucial political and moral questions of our time; the need . . . to overcome oppression and violence without resorting to oppression and violence . . . a method which rejects revenge, aggression and retaliation. The foundation of such a method is love.

From the Rev. Martin Luther King Jr., in his speech accepting the Nobel Peace Prize, December 11, 1964.

At home, with friends, or in the workplace, people often clash over one or a combination of these issues:

- *Information* may be lacking, or people may interpret what they have differently. A clash over data can be resolved by getting data and carefully analyzing the issue together.

- *Resources* such as time, money, materials, or support may be limited, so people struggle over who gets what for what purpose. From company departments to families, people fight over money or time.[26]

- *Expectations* about roles or behaviors can clash, from couples over household roles to supervisors versus workers who don't meet their conscious or unconscious expectations.

- *Needs that are unmet* can cause defensiveness and anxiety in people. For example, an individual who needs reassurance may conflict with one who constantly uses put-down humor.

- *Power and control* conflicts are over who controls whom, although it often takes the *form* of conflict over issues such as personality, expectations, resources, information, or needs.

- *Values and ethics*, which undergird personal responses to issues of good and bad, or right and wrong. Value-laden issues are deep, long lasting, and sometimes irreconcilable.

- *Personality* clashes, when people irritate one another, can occur in any context and can infuse all of the other sources of conflict.

Conflicts can be caused by multiple issues. You can't stand your coworker (personality), and she resents that your office budget is higher (resources); you feel she withholds information you need (data; power and control; unmet needs) so the two of you build up stress and anger. Conflict rules and the climate is defensive. What can be done? Anything?

Changing Defensive Communication Climates and Ending Games

There *are* approaches to changing climates, altering game playing, and managing (if not resolving) conflicts. They take full commitment and personal restraint, but they can save some bad situations.

Approaches

How do you handle a conflict or a game? Do you *always* react the same way? Perhaps not; an individual's approach varies according to the situation and personal influences such as age, gender, culture, and self-concept.

Take age, for example: In one study, young couples were direct and expressive in alternatively fighting, analyzing, and joking about conflicts. Middle-aged couples avoided conflict if possible; if they couldn't avoid it and the issue was important, they went at it as younger couples did. If they couldn't avoid conflict on an unimportant issue, they did as older couples do—gave it as little energy expenditure and expression as possible.[27]

Once again, gender also has its influence: Julia Wood says, "Research on marriages consistently finds that both partners perceive that husbands' preferences count more than those of wives on everything from how often to have sex to who does the housework."[28] Interestingly, either men or women who tend to be masculine tend to downplay issues or walk away from them, and people who tend to be more feminine are more likely to try to work them out.

The influence of both gender and culture is complex. A person from a high-context culture (remember Chapter 6?) tends to be more collectivistic and self-effacing, to maintain harmony and save face, whereas a person from a low-context culture would be more assertive and direct.[29] Individuals' *self-construals* (how they see themselves), however, are more important than cultures. It seems people who see themselves as independent tend to dominate, and people whose self-construal is interdependent with others are more likely to avoid and compromise.[30]

Still, even within cultures, conflict management styles depend on context. We have seen some assertive Asians working out conflicts in very direct ways—and some shrinking North Americans avoiding it at all costs. Culture has its effects—but they aren't always so generalized as theory or research might imply.

Whatever your age, gender, culture, or preference for dealing with a defensive climate, game, or conflict, the best thing you can do is choose an approach that's best for the situation. Here are some alternatives:

- *Postponing* an issue until time, place, or situation is better—or until someone has cooled down. You don't want to ignore a conflict or game for long, however, if you value the person or issue. Anger or frustration can contribute to stress diseases and/or interpersonal disaster.

- *Indirectly influencing participants* can "save face" or avoid retribution. A coworker says, "The boss was griping because *we* aren't working hard enough," when what she really means is, *"You're* not carrying your weight." Many families and cultures are indirect. A western Apache, for instance, might bring a child into line by saying to another adult, "Girls are butterflies." Little girls who hear the comment know it is an indirect rebuke for chasing "around after each other, like they had no work to do."[31] Or often Asian families might have an intermediary speak privately to each participant in a conflict and work out face-saving resolutions.[32]

- *Reversing the trend* is possible by not buying into the conflict—by being open and supportive no matter how someone else behaves. Or, in a game-playing situation, you could try reversing the predicted script.[33] Your friend repeatedly digs for reassurance with the gimmick, "I can't believe how stupid I am"; you're supposed to respond, "You're not stupid; in fact, you're really smart. . . ." You might reverse the pattern with "Sometimes I really feel stupid, too." That eliminates the payoff and surprises the game player into thinking about your response instead of automatically following the usual script.

- *Directly confronting and negotiating the issues* can be the only real option, but you must prepare carefully and communicate with keen awareness of both the other person and yourself. A small point may seem big because your adrenaline is pumping, yet compromise seems reasonable when you calm down. Sometimes, however, compromise might betray your ethics or values in a way you'd regret. Cool assessment of those issues can give you a more realistic position from which to start a complex process. Confrontation takes dedication and effort.

- *Withdrawing from interaction* may be the best choice; sometimes you have to separate yourself from a conflict situation. Ending a relationship or quitting a job to avoid conflict should never be the easy route; withdrawal can bring its own problems. Sometimes, however, you analyze all alternative options and conclude that none of them offers the potential of a positive solution.

- *Seeking professional help* can be the best way to manage a problem. There's no guarantee, but private and public counselors for individuals and families really can help, and organizations today frequently employ counselors to work with individuals, departments, or teams in managing conflicts and building cooperation. Additionally, professional negotiators and mediators are available to help work out organizational or political struggle.

Communication for Managing Games and Conflicts

You have to build a new climate to alter a conflict or a game, and this demands an expectation that you can, in fact, make this situation work for everyone—a truly win-win attitude.

As you work through the issue, you need to examine what each person wants and needs, to look at the sources and symptoms of the problem, and to work out satisfactory compromises. "A compromise is one type of win-win solution, although it requires that both parties give up something in order to solve the problem."[34]

You have to state what you want, think, and/or feel in assertive ways that respect your own character without impugning someone else's. Use language that takes responsibility for your own feelings, and resist the all-too-human temptation to hang responsibility around the neck of the other person. For example:[35]

- *Use "I" statements* such as "I think," "I feel," "I want." Avoid "you do," "you think," or "you feel." Using "I" acknowledges that your position and feelings are your own and avoids blame or judgment, certainty, or manipulation of the other.

- *Avoid "all" statements* and absolute, know-it-all language. Saying "I believe" or "probably" leaves room for people to disagree and still communicate. Saying "always," "never," or "impossible!" undermines the negotiation process.

- *Use specific language;* that is, if you mean yes, say yes; if you mean no, say no. Don't fog over meaning out of politeness or dread. "I'm sorry, but I won't do that" is clear, whereas "I am very hesitant to take such an action" is ambiguous (and annoying!).

- *Use definite pronouns* and avoid indefinite ones such as "it" and "they." *"It* seems to be a problem." What does? *"They* said we had to." Who did? People may feel defensive because they simply don't understand the point.

- *Use words that "own"* your feelings or choices: "I feel. . . I think," not "You do . . . You are . . ."

- *Avoid the language of guilt or helplessness.* "Ought" and "should" may imply guilt and induce resistance, so substitute *can, want, will,* or *might;* or *won't, don't,* or *refuse to.* If you say, "I don't want to" or "I will," you assume responsibility.

- *Use the active voice.* Say, "I believe," rather than "It is believed"; say, "I have decided," instead of "It has been decided."

It's extraordinarily liberating to use language that follows these guidelines; it allows you to express your feelings and to encourage others to express theirs. As you focus on exchanging ideas in this way, stay calm and controlled, monitor your nonverbal cues, and use positive self-talk. Is your heart beating too fast? Are you becoming flushed and angry? Then take deep breaths, focus on the issues rather than your anger at the other person, and tell yourself, "I'm cool, I'm okay, I'm dealing with this."

Monitoring your own responses and watching feedback is crucial. What you say or do might seem like aggression to others, even if you don't mean it that way. Make sure your words or actions don't attack others' competence, character, background, and/or appearance or threaten them in some way. Even teasing can be an aggressive attack on an individual's weak points and sense of self-worth. Nonverbal cues, too, such as crowding another's space or using threatening postures or gestures, can be construed as aggressive. And aggression makes people feel embarrassed, inadequate, humiliated, hopeless, desperate, and/or depressed. It can even damage an individual's self-concept.[36]

What's worse, verbal aggression can escalate to physical violence, compounding psychological with physical abuse.[37] Aggression can backlash, too, by lowering your self-esteem, increasing your frustration, making you feel inadequate, and reducing your credibility with others. Observers tend to see an aggressor as lacking credibility, character, and competence, and a person who has been attacked as all the more credible.[38]

As you monitor your own responses, also watch others' nonverbal and verbal cues. So much depends upon the sequence and interaction; for example, conflict might escalate if you give someone unsolicited advice, but the same advice that responds to another person's request for it may be seen as your positive regard for that individual's face.[39]

In fact, creating a better climate, reversing a game-playing situation, or managing a conflict may all come down to your regard for others as well as yourself.

Summary

The climate in which people communicate and the way they communicate interact continuously. A climate may be supportive, freeing people to communicate openly, or it may be defensive, causing people to clam up or to escalate tensions into hostility and conflict. In a supportive climate, communicators are able to disclose information about themselves, which helps develop trust and empathy. This makes the climate increasingly supportive. Transactions can be assertive and, at the same time, confirm the worth of others and their ideas.

In a defensive climate, lack of self-disclosure, empathy, and trust are often related to poor management of conflict and competitive communication patterns. Relationships may develop conflicts involving what participants perceive as mutually exclusive goals, creating ongoing problems in the relationship. Although conflict is inevitable and sometimes can be constructive, it often becomes a continuing condition that needs to be managed. Game playing, related to conflict, occurs when participants play out predictable scripts involving some gimmick at the start and a payoff at the end. Communicating to reverse games and to manage conflict requires people to work cooperatively, good-humoredly, and supportively, using assertive, nonthreatening behavior and descriptive, responsible, and nonevaluative language.

Exercises

1   Compare and contrast the climate in two situations you have experienced (in a relationship, your family, your workplace, your school, an organization, and so on). Describe what the climate is like (stormy, cloudy, sunny, balmy . . .), and identify the communication behaviors you have observed participants using in each climate. Try to pin down specific examples of supportive

and/or defensive communication, and trace the way such a communication choice has contributed to the climate.

2 Recall an occasion when you have had a defensive response to something another person has said. With a partner, do the following:

a Work out a short skit that uses defensive communication to show what that experience was like and how you reacted.

b Work out a revised skit that shows how the climate could have been changed to a supportive one with different communication behavior.

c Play the first skit for the class (you can play yourself and your partner can play the other person in your experience).

d Ask the members of the class to identify which behaviors were defensive.

e Now, play the revised skit for the class.

f Ask the class to identify which behaviors were supportive.

3 In a group, use Figure 7.1 to identify what kinds of defensive communication behavior are exemplified by the statements following. Speculate on why a receiver might feel defensive or react defensively upon hearing each statement. As a group, write a more supportive way of expressing the idea for each one, and share your ideas with the class.

"Well, when you've lived as long as I have, dear, you'll know how important your education is."

"You're always late, and it's because you just don't care about me."

"Yeah, yeah, I know. So you had a bad day. Didn't we all?"

"Well, of course you'd think that—people like you always do, don't they?"

"I'm sure you'll want to contribute for the party, since you didn't for the last one, even though everybody else did."

"Why do you always do that? You know how you make me feel when you talk about my parents that way. You just hate them, that's all."

4 Find an example of defensive or supportive communication; it could be a short scene from a play, a poem, an excerpt from a story or a novel, an editorial, even a comic strip. In a 2-minute speech, share the piece you've found with the class and explain how it exemplifies supportive or defensive communication. Relate the analysis to Figure 7.1 to specifically identify what kinds of statements are involved.

Cyberpoints

The following Cyberpoints can be easily accessed from the Student Companion website for this text at http://academic.cengage.com/communication/lumsdenccc3. Click on *Student Book Companion Site* and select this chapter from the pull-down menu at the top of the page that says "Select a chapter." Click on *Cyperpoints* under *Chapter Resources* and you will find links for the exercises following.

1   For a range of articles on conflict, including some interesting case studies, use InfoTrac College Edition and the keywords *conflict management*. Here are three articles to get you started:

Lubit, R. (2004, March-April) "The Tyranny of Toxic Managers: Applying Emotional Intelligence to Deal with Difficult Personalities." *Ivey Business Journal Online*, v68 i4 p1.

Olson, L. N., & Braithwaite, D. O. (2004, Summer) "'If you hit me again, I'll hit you back': Conflict Management Strategies of Individuals Experiencing Aggression during Conflicts." *Communication Studies*, v55 i2 p271.

Solomon, D. H., Knobloch, L. K., & Fitzpatrick, M. A.. (2004, Spring) "Relational Power, Marital Schema, and Decisions to Withhold Complaints: An Investigation of the Chilling Effect on Confrontation in Marriage." *Communication Studies*, v55 i1 p146.

Read each article (or three others of your choosing). What are three things you learned that can improve your communication in future conflict situations?

2   Are you curious about how negotiation works in the "real world"? Go to the *Communicating with Credibility and Confidence* website at http:// academic.cengage.com/communication/lumsdenccc3 and select Chapter 7 from the pull-down menu to learn strategies for negotiating issues in business and professions and to find out something about negotiation as a career. What did you find that you can use now or in the future?

3   Do you think you see a game going on in your life? Go to the *Communicating with Credibility and Confidence* website following the instructions in Cyberpoint 2 for more information about game playing and how to cope with and/or change it. What is a game-playing situation you have been in recently? What have you learned reviewing these links that can help you to cope or change?

Chapter 8

Personal Relationships: Growing with Another

Lawrence Migdale/Photo Researchers, Inc.

Objectives for This Chapter

Knowledge

- Know the factors that influence initial conversation
- Identify issues that affect developing relationships
- Understand communication in families
- Know how conversational skills reflect credibility and confidence

Feelings and Approaches

- Feel confident in conversing with strangers and others
- Feel positive about developing and maintaining personal relationships

Communication Abilities

- Self-monitor, adapt, and achieve goals in communicating interpersonally
- Develop trust and empathy in intimate relationships
- Communicate effectively in relationship systems
- Enhance credibility in conversations with others

Key Terms

affinity seeking

person-centered messages

social penetration

interpersonal bonding

intimate relationships

turning point

depenetration

relational "rules"

relational themes

family

dysfunctional relationship

codependency

Human beings are social creatures. Even as you stand alone, awed by a blazing sunset, you might wish for someone to share that aesthetic high. Through communicating interpersonally, humans share themselves, and, sometimes, develop deep bonds that last a lifetime.

In Chapter 1, we defined *interpersonal communication* as a dynamic process that touches people emotionally and psychologically.[1] This process, of course, may stay at the social level, or it may develop further into a deeper relationship—perhaps from acquaintanceship to friendship to courtship to commitment to rearing families. That's what this chapter talks about—interpersonal communication in all those stages of interhuman relationships.

We'll start at the beginning—getting to know people—and move through conversation to developing relationships to couple and family communication.

Getting to Know People

Many kids and most puppies "never know a stranger." Few adults can be that open; still, any stranger *could* be a potential best friend. You might meet someone in a class, at church, or, like a couple we know, through an electronic newsletter. (Several years and a baby later, their relationship seems to be going along quite well. But they did, at some point, meet face to face.)

What draws you to someone—or someone to you? And what influences your conversations?

Attraction

Of course, the context of meeting influences your impression and structures your transactions.[2] A person in her professional role as lawyer, for instance, might seem very different when she's on the ski slope.

"A first impression is like a filter," say communication consultants Demarais and White. "People take in initial information—they notice your body language, what you say and how you respond. Based on this initial information, they form an impression and make decisions about what you are like and how they expect you to behave in the future. They then see you through this filter. . . . They seek information that is consistent with their first impression and will not look for, or even will ignore, behavior that doesn't fit their impression of you."[3]

> *Why this need to divide up, classify and neatly package every new acquaintance? . . . A judgment of another person is an abstraction that adds qualities that are not there and leaves out what is unique.*
>
> Hugh Prather, American philosopher

Just watch people trying to make an impression in a club. Some researchers have observed that initiating romance is like a dance of courtship. One person uses appearance, talk, and/or movement to attract the other person's attention while "looking good." There is much back-and-forth, ambivalent, "Maybe I like you, maybe I don't" nonverbal behavior—drop eyes, glance back—move closer, pull away—smile, go blank. Each person signals interest—pulls in the tummy, straightens the shoulders, makes eye contact, smiles, grooms, primps. An interested couple position themselves face to face, closing themselves in and others out. They lean forward, make eye contact, and may exaggerate laughing and gesturing, showing invitation and sexual arousal. They often act like parent and child, touching, stroking, nuzzling, and cooing, all to communicate potential physical intimacy and availability. A flirtation might not end in a sexual liaison, but it is a consistently implied goal of a courtship dance.[4]

Changing social norms and cultural mores deeply affect this dance. In the 1950s, for example, society approved the come-hither bits, but scowled at anything that suggested sexual invitation. Today, some people fall right into bed despite the threat of AIDS; in those days "going all the way" (resolution or sexual intercourse) was (theoretically) acceptable only on the wedding night. Even today, many individuals, cultures, and identity groups stringently limit opportunities to flirt, let alone to make sexual contact; some societies still arrange marriages and stone people to death for premarital or extramarital sex.

Whether in finding romance or simply finding friends, attraction probably starts with a person's physical characteristics and/or a sense of similarity; in fact, a major part of being drawn to someone is **affinity seeking,** as people look for ways to feel similar and close.[5] They try to present themselves well, show their credibility, and engage with the other person by looking for common interests, being polite, and getting involved.[6] Yet affinity isn't quite enough to motivate a relationship— nor do differences necessarily keep people apart once they get a chance to interact.[7] You might initially regard someone as unattractive and strange, but conversation may start a wonderful friendship when you discover how bright and funny he or she is. And that conversation may be influenced by many things.

Personal Influences   As you already know, many influences shape a person's communication. Awareness of these influences can make you a better, and more comfortable, conversationalist. You recall from Chapter 2, for example, that the degree to which people are willing to communicate is influenced by their culture, and the degree of apprehension they feel may be a product of their family and school experiences. You also recall from Chapter 7 that people from high-context cultures might consider less information to be sufficient, while people from low-context cultures might require more,[8] so, for instance, a Japanese person might give you less information than a North American would. Don't overgeneralize, however. Within "low-context" North America are, for example, traditional Apache and Navajo high-context cultures. Those who grew up in these cultures avoid conversation with strangers, getting to know them only by being in the same place and observing them for awhile within that context.[9]

Affinity seeking Communication behavior in which participants look for ways to feel similar and close

Randy Faris/CORBIS

Sometimes, too, men and women use different styles, with men conversing for direct information exchange, not so much for harmony and feelings,[10] whereas "women's speech tends to display identifiable features that foster connections, support, closeness, and understanding."[11] He, therefore, may think she's "off topic" in creating those connections and giving support—and she may think he's unfeeling or indifferent when he's just trying to share the information. These differences in style can be frustrating for both sexes. A woman may talk about a problem, expecting a man to empathize; the man may give suggestions, expecting that she wants concrete help with solving the problem. Both are contributing from their own perspectives; neither understands the other. Still, it's probably women's "rapport-talk" that makes both men and women often prefer a woman as a conversational partner,[12] finding women to be better conversationalists than men.[13]

Conversation Building

Some communication events aren't really conversations. If you say, "Hi, how ya doin?" you might not be looking for more than "Okay—you?" These bits are *Phatic* communication, just brief acknowledgements that allow people to connect for a moment.

Other communication events fulfill a range of social and relational needs for human beings. Think about how you have experienced these three types of events:

1   *Ritual* communications are symbolic structures of tradition, and your credibility can rise or fall on your sensitivity to others' rituals. When our friends went

to China on business, they discovered how essential it is to share a tea ritual before conducting a conference. A factory in a very poor district had no money for tea, but they seated their guests at a table and graciously shared a traditional tea with their hosts—except that *unflavored hot water* was poured as if it were served with the finest tea; not a word was said about the water. Without serving "tea," the hosts would have lost face—and their guests would not have been able to move on to their conference.

2 *Exchange* conversations share information, ideas, and, sometimes, feelings. An exchange can be essential to the goals of participants. For example, a couple plans their day—"Can you pick up the cleaning?" "Okay, if you'll you walk the dog." "Fine—then we'll go visit Ralph in the hospital before dinner." Exchange talk is essential to daily life or business but engages participants at a relatively superficial level.

3 *Bonding* conversations may go deeper, to develop relational processes and feelings between persons. You bond with someone as you disclose, support, and adapt to each other. For instance, your friend is sad, so you listen empathically and share your own feelings. As you do, you strengthen the emotional glue that holds you and your friend together.

You might find yourself in a conversation that meets several of these descriptions at once, or in sequence. Whatever the context, conversations follow a structure to develop topics and maintain interest.

Structure There's a reason for the phrase "the art of conversation." Like a painting or a novel, conversation follows a structure to develop themes or topics.

Good conversationalists understand how to open a conversation, how to feel the flow of talk and keep it moving along, and how to end it.

Opening a conversation usually works this way:

1   Introduce or show recognition: "I'm so glad to meet you," or (hailing a friend) a wave, a smile, or a "Hi, how ya doin?"

2   Indicate accessibility by showing you're open to conversation with eye contact, smiling, turning toward the other, perhaps asking, "What are you doing these days?"

3   Initiate or respond to a topic with a question or observation, such as "I haven't been to a movie in so long. What's worth seeing?"

Developing a conversation involves:

Exploring topics at a safe level and moving gradually from basic information and situational topics (the place, time, weather, and so on) to questions and observations. (We talk more about topics soon.)

Closing a conversation takes three steps:

1   Give and recognize cues that it's time to move on, such as looking at a watch or saying, "I didn't know it was this late."

2   Make summary statements that highlight the most important points of the conversation ("Well, I really am glad to hear about your award . . .").

3   Express positive closures. Languages the world over use some variation of "Go with God," or "Good fortune," or "See ya!" or, on e-mail, a happy face emoticon.

Topics   If you worry about finding topics for conversation, do some homework. Think about how you can share information from your life—classes, talents, hobbies. Cultivate curiosity; reading and observing, drawing from magazines, newspapers, television, radio, movies, lectures all give you information that will make you more interesting and credible. Besides, your confidence increases when you know you can discuss events and issues.

The first rule of good conversation is to be genuinely interested in your conversational partner and think about how to engage him or her in your conversation. The second rule is to be interesting yourself. And, yes, you can be interesting:

Disclose a bit about yourself, encouraging your partner to respond with some self-disclosure, so each exchange builds on the previous one.

Ask good questions that help identify interesting ideas and encourage your partner to talk. Open-ended questions such as, "What do you think about . . . ?" or "How would you . . . ?" are good starters.

Listen a lot; offer opinions after you hear some from the other person, or if you're asked.

Use free information, that is, pick up ideas from people's verbal or nonverbal cues.[14] Someone's wearing a button that says, "It takes 100 dumb animals to make a fur coat, and only one to wear it," so you open with a friendly, "Great button! I guess you're opposed to wearing fur?"

Conversation Flow

"Imagine conversations as the erector set of human relationships: They not only create the foundation and frame on which relationships are built but supply the mortar that binds people together."[15] It is through mutual adaptation that two people build a conversation that goes somewhere. Monitoring both your own talk and the give and take helps to make adaptation work.

Self-Monitoring "Did I really say that?" you groan. Or, "I did all the talking!" To avoid such forehead-slapping regrets, keep in mind these guidelines:

- *Quantity of information.* Talk enough but not too much; cues from your partner will help you know to elaborate or abbreviate your comments. Are you shy or quiet? Then practice developing ideas with description and detail. Are you outgoing? Ask yourself how much you really need to share—and watch for signs of boredom or overload in your listener.

- *Quality of information.* Communicate ethically, credibly, truthfully—and be sensitive to the situation and your listener. Quality information doesn't mean blunt or tactless disclosure of every feeling you have. Stay open-minded, and free others to express their own opinions.

- *Relevance.* Stay on topic; avoid distracting, irrelevant comments, but allow topics to develop and evolve as you talk. Sometimes, you have to give up something you really wanted to say in order to keep the conversation moving smoothly.

- *Clarity.* Communicate coherently. Think about what you are saying from the viewpoint of the listener. Take time to express your ideas so they are organized, clear, and specific.

Give and Take A conversation may be an adventure, or it may be an agony. It's more of an adventure if it flows smoothly, evenly, and interestingly. To make your conversation do that, you need to:

- *Reciprocate and cooperate.* Try to balance talking and listening. Even in talkative North America, people are more attracted to and satisfied in communicating with people who listen to them and who don't dominate the conversation.[16]

- *Use **person-centered messages,** statements and questions that focus on the other person, that show you recognize that person's uniqueness and worth. Doing so enables partners to feel equal, keeps others involved in the conversation, and increases your credibility.[17]

- *Demonstrate interpersonal involvement.* Show interest in your partner and the conversation with nonverbal closeness, attentiveness, alertness, animation, and concentration on the other person.

- *Use humor appropriately.* Humor is superb for making points, reducing stress, and connecting with people. Unfortunately, funny people sometimes

> *Conversation is the socializing instrument par excellence, and in its style one can see reflected the capacities of a race.*
>
> José Ortega y Gasset, late 19th–early 20th-century Spanish writer

Person-centered messages Conversational behavior that recognizes each participant's worth

find humor in something that leaves others unamused,[18] so choose humor to fit your relationship and the situation.

Relationships

Friends can love one another, and lovers can be friends—yet, love and friendship are not entirely the same. Both are privately negotiated personal relationships requiring a "considerable investment of emotional energy"[19] in loyalty, fidelity, trust, affection, and commitment. Trading self-disclosures and learning to see the other person's point of view is important to developing friendships, and to being satisfied with romantic relationships.[20] As they grow closer, people take more risks, disclose more, and begin to build empathy and trust. Does this sound familiar? It should be, because it's part of the positive climate building we discussed in Chapter 7. You can see this process represented in Figure 8.1.

Figure 8.1 *Process of interpersonal relationship development and bonding*

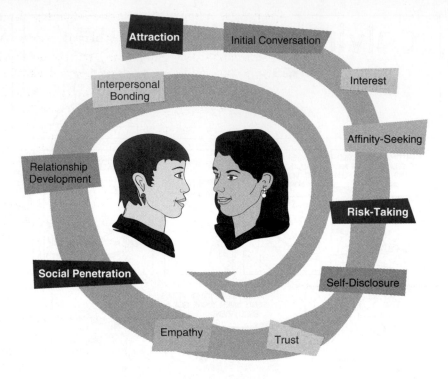

Each friend represents a world in us, a world possibly not born until they arrive, and it is only by this meeting that a new world is born.

Anaïs Nin, 20th-century French writer

Social penetration The process of gradual widening and deepening of a relationship as two people develop mutual trust and empathy

Interpersonal bonding The process of forming individual relationships

Intimate relationships Mutually supportive, trusting, enduring associations between partners

---

One analysis of relationship development is called **social penetration,** the gradual widening and deepening of a relationship as two people trade self-disclosures and develop mutual trust and empathy.[21] We see the process as something like peeling an artichoke. People start with exchanging information, move to exchanging understandings of emotion, and progress to exchanging and sharing activities in their lives. As they peel off more of the outer, tougher leaves, they make deeper disclosures about themselves to each other, exposing more of their inner selves, which leads to **interpersonal bonding.** Each person's personality becomes better known to the other as, through self-disclosure, they peel away layer after layer until they reach the heart.

Building and Bonding

True friendship and genuine love are rare and wondrous bonds between people. Bochner defines interpersonal bonding as "the process of forming individualized relationships, affinities that are close, deep, personal, and intimate."[22] **Intimate relationships** are not necessarily sexual, but they *are* interdependent. Friends or lovers may not have peeled off all those tough outer leaves, but partners know and care about each other and talk about things they would not share with other people.

The process of developing a close relationship may go through stages:

1   *Initiating:* Introduction and start of conversation

2   *Experimenting:* Asking questions, volunteering small disclosures, getting to know one another, and sharing information and activities

3   *Intensifying:* Becoming emotionally aware of and committed to each other, giving, sharing feelings, seeking deeper closeness[23]

4   *Integrating:* Feeling more like one person than two, confirming the relationship; becoming more deeply connected, closer, and interdependent

5   *Bonding:* Feeling fully committed to each other and to the relationship in the present and the future[24]

Knowing about these stages can provide some insight into your relationship development, but you also need to know it might not follow such clear stages as this implies. Many friendships remain very casual without going through stages at all.

You can also profit from knowing that a relationship will develop and change through dialectic—the tension partners generate and the process of resolving it—between needs for *stability or change,*[25] or between the relationship's *development versus deterioration.*[26] People experience natural tensions between opposite wants or needs, such as *openness versus closedness; predictability versus novelty;* and *autonomy versus connection.* In a relationship, partners work out that dialectic between them in an ongoing process that may not fall into a clear series of stages.[27] Here's an example of the dialectic of stability versus change experienced by two people. Tory and Kim have been dating for awhile; Tory really wants to move in together, but her messages about it are contradictory because she doesn't want to give up independence. Kim's cues also are confusing—she's afraid of moving in together because her last relationship was a disaster, but she's also afraid to lose her relationship with Tory. Their own internal tensions over these needs then create a tension between them. Together they must find a way to resolve that tension and make a mutually satisfactory decision. Perhaps they can reassure each other about fear of change and make new living arrangements feel stable; then they might move in together. They will have negotiated a new aspect of their relationship that may open up the path to deeper commitment and bonding—or not.

Growing and Dissolving

Turning point Moment when a relationship undergoes an incremental change

Do you remember experiences that seemed to turn a relationship in a new direction? People often can identify **turning points,** specific moments at which something has caused an incremental change in their relationship for better or, if there are too many turning points, for worse.[28] Both romantic relationships and friendships are affected by self-disclosing, doing things together, and distance, but some turning points are likely to be negative for casual friends.[29]

Turning points seem to occur in certain contexts, such as in *early dating and time together—or times of physical separation and reunion—or periods of*

Will Schutz, psychologist, says that these three elements are necessary for successful interpersonal relationships:

1 Self-regard—to understand, respect, and like myself

2 Truth—the great simplifier of personal and interpersonal difficulties

3 Choice—I empower myself when I take responsibility for myself.

From Will Schutz, *The Truth Option: A Practical Technology for Human Affairs* (Berkeley, CA: Ten-Speed Press, 1984).

---

psychological separation through conflict or avoidance and reconciliation. Other turning points may be occasions of *intense positive or negative experiences,* or when *some external competition motivates a couple who chooses to see each other exclusively.* A relationship may experience a turning point, too, when a partner *sacrifices individual interests or needs to provide support, help, or gifts to the other.*[30]

Turning points may improve the quality and depth of a relationship or quite the opposite.[31] The term **depenetration** describes how partners find less reward in their relationship and start closing off to each other.[32] Casual friendships may develop and degenerate along a straighter line than romantic relationships, reaching maximum closeness earlier, and terminating same-sex friendships over such things as activities for men and conflict for women.[33]

In depenetration, deeper relationships go through a process of *differentiating,* as partners perceive negative differences between themselves; *circumscribing,* when they limit communication to safe, impersonal topics; *stagnating,* when the two have little to say and care less; this leads to *avoiding* each other; and, finally, *terminating,* when one or both partners call it quits.

Consider, for example, Malachy and Francis. They are extremely close and caring, but one day, Malachy begins to see Fran's neatness as "compulsive," compared to Malachy's "healthier" casual style (differentiating). Irritated by Malachy's "mess," Fran closes off communication on all issues related to lifestyle (circumscribing). Gradually, Malachy and Fran stop talking, and Malachy becomes too busy to spend time with Fran (stagnating). Fran begins to develop a new relationship that provides excuses for staying away (avoiding). Finally, inevitably, Malachy and Fran end their relationship (terminating). Later, each of them might identify particular turning points at these stages. Perhaps Malachy's response to Fran's "compulsive neatness" peaked when Fran disposed of family pictures, or maybe Fran gave up and made a date with another friend when Malachy forgot their anniversary.

Depenetration
The process through which partners end a relationship

Being a Couple

As you and a partner develop a long-term relationship, you begin to build a kind of emotional house within which you'll live. Making that house strong takes caring, commitment, communication—not to mention a lot of giving, sharing, and forbearance. And often forgiveness.

Consciously or unconsciously, any couple creates a relationship structure of unwritten rules and communication themes. **Relational "rules"** are expectations of how couples should relate to each other, negotiated between each person's expectations of how a relationship should be.[34] Some rules are common to the society, such as the traditional Chinese norm that a wife does as her husband's mother tells her. Other rules are idiosyncratic, for example, "We never call each other at work." A third set of rules are implicit or explicit agreements, some mutually set ("We take turns doing the dishes") and some consciously understood but not discussed ("We don't talk about our mothers"). Still others are unconscious or unacknowledged, even though an observer might see them ("She always makes the decisions; that's how they operate").

Relational themes emerge from what the couple talks about—the weather, work, the news—their gossip, playing, fighting. You'll see a close corollary to dialectics, or relational tensions, in the seven general themes that often weave through couples' discussions:[35]

1   *Dominance/submission,* when partners jockey for control

2   *Emotional arousal,* when they express feelings about the context of the discussion

3   *Composure,* when they talk about stress in a relationship

4   *Similarity/difference,* as they talk about their commonality or difference

5   *Formality,* when they expect to follow guidelines for their behavior and style

6   *Task/social orientation,* as they address the focus of the relationship

7   *Intimacy,* which addresses relational issues between them

Here's an example of one statement that brings all of these themes together in a troubled period in a couple's life: "You're trying to force your point of view again [dominance/submission], and I feel so frustrated [emotional arousal]—I know we're both working too hard [composure], and I know I just get upset and you just work harder [similarity/difference], but we've got to make a rule that we take time off [formality]; pay more attention to each other [task/social orientation]— we've got to find each other again [intimacy]."

All couples have problems, small or large. It isn't a big deal, perhaps, if people disagree over taking out the garbage, but it can be serious if they conflict over intimacy or loss of trust or when they resort to aggression to feel powerful in the relationship.

Relational "rules"
Expectations of how couples should relate to each other

Relational themes Aspects of their relationship that emerge from couples' conversations

---

Lee Anne Knight and Scott Bukofsky exchanged these vows at their wedding.

Presider: Hello. Welcome. Thank you for coming. We are gathered here tonight to celebrate the marriage of Scott and Lee Anne. They have come here tonight to express their love for one another. It is fitting that you are all here to share this moment with them since you are the ones who have helped shape their lives. All that you have taught them and every experience you have shared with them have in some way led them to this moment. I will now ask them to state their intentions.

Vows: (In turn) I [Scott/Lee] take you [Lee/Scott] to be my [wife/husband]: to love, honor, and cherish all the days of my life. I will be considerate of your wishes and desires, and respect your integrity and intentions. I will support your dreams and aspirations and strive to keep our lives full of laughter and joy. I do this at peace with myself and the world, secure in my decision, aware of your uniqueness, yet strong in the conviction that it is only together that we can achieve our fullest potential.

Expectations of Intimacy

"I can't believe you! You didn't . . . You never . . ." Fulfill my expectations, that is. When one person's expectations are unmet, a couple may go into a cycle of one person demanding change and the other withdrawing.[36] And men and women differ in what and how they communicate about important intimacy issues:[37]

Self-perceptions. Men, seeing themselves as independent and rational, may pull back from women, who think of themselves as cooperative, nurturing, and emotional. So she tries to get closer, and he backs off—and intimacy breaks down.

Self-disclosure. A man will tell you what he thinks, a woman will tell you what she feels. So she believes that he fears the intimacy she wants—and he feels she just talks too much about personal issues.

Meaning of personal relationships. Each expects the other to understand his or her fears, yet women may not understand men's unease with close personal affiliation and intimacy, nor men to respond to women's fear in impersonal and competitive situations.[38]

Expression of intimacy. Once again, women are frustrated because men share information and ideas but express less emotion than women—and men because they take such expressions for granted.

People in any committed relationship, whether it is friendship or romantic, heterosexual or homosexual, need to work hard at understanding and adapting to each other. Maybe that's the most important part of all—communicating with care.

Hold faithfulness and sincerity as first principles.

Confucius, fifth-century BC Chinese philosopher

Loss of Trust

Trust: The mortar holding a relationship together, confidence developing bit by bit as two people make choices that show their trustworthiness. Once trust is lost, it's well-nigh impossible to regain. Oh, people do succeed in rebuilding relationships, but it's a long, hard road to get back from such trust-busters as infidelity, deception, and suspicion.

Infidelity is prevalent and deadly, and "without the expectation of fidelity, intimacy becomes awkward and marriage adversarial. People who expect their partner to betray them are likely to beat them to the draw, and to make both of them miserable in the meantime."[39]

Deception isn't limited to infidelity, of course; deception can also be a strategy for avoiding conflict. Suppose Cassie's worried because Kurt didn't show up last evening, and she asks, "What happened? Was something wrong? You didn't even call." If Kurt is fully honest he might say, "I know; I meant to, but . . . well, the truth is, I was hanging out with Leah and Rudy, and we decided to get something to eat and we got to talking and the evening just got away from me."

Okay, Kurt's only crime is thoughtlessness. Ah, but if Kurt can't cope with disagreement he might deceive Cassie in one of these four ways:[40]

1   *Quantity deception.* "Well, gosh, I just got busy. . . ." A quantity deception is a "half-truth," deception by omission.

2   *Quality deception.* "Yeah, Pete I had to go to the hospital with Ali." A quality deception is, in other words, a lie.

3   *Relevance deception.* "How about we go out to dinner tonight?" Kurt diverts attention, so he needn't tell the truth.

4   *Clarity deception.* "Yeah, like, y'gotta help a friend, right, and . . . uh . . ." A clarity deception is equivocation, which Kurt hopes will confuse and deceive Cassie.

Deceiving a partner is a no-win move. First, *deception hurts credibility*. It's worst as a violation of quality—the lie—but all deception is damaging,[41] and deception creates and feeds on suspicion. Deceivers' nonverbal cues arouse their partners' suspicions, and suspicious partners respond by being more dominant, assertive, formal, and manipulative. The deceivers react by increasing their deception cues, and the problem escalates.[42] That, of course, feeds suspicion, and the relationship spirals down into a morass of distrust.

Of course, when the lie is about important information, and/or when the deceived person considers lying to be immoral, and/or when she or he already is suspicious because of previous experiences, the lie may destroy trust entirely—and the deceived partner is likely to end the relationship.[43]

Physical Aggression

Why do people get violent in relationships? It's so destructive, but sometimes people don't know how to communicate frustration, so they boil over.[44] And they may be predisposed to violence because they suffer from low self-esteem, repressed shame, and anger[45]—and often because they grew up in violent families. Then there's substance abuse, which often feeds violent responses to frustration and anger; alcohol is involved in 80% of murders, 70% of serious assaults, and 50% of family conflicts requiring police intervention.[46]

When someone uses violence to control a partner, the result may be rape. Rape is not about sex, it's about power and control, and when a person forces sex on an unwilling partner, it's rape, whether the two are strangers, dating partners, or spouses. Sadly, as aggression and violence increase, so does rape. And so does its "acceptability." Surveys reveal some alarming findings. For example, 33% of college males say they would rape a woman if they thought no one would find out, and 50% admit they have gotten a woman drunk and/or coerced, manipulated, or pressured her to have sex.[47] Moreover, up to 66% of women have been sexually abused before they are 18, and up to 75% of college women have been coerced into having sex one or more times.

Wood observes that "rape is most common in societies that embrace ideologies of male toughness and that disrespect women. . . ." Noting that in many societies rape is almost unknown, she concludes, "Violence against women is not innate in male sexuality and acceptance of violence is not inevitable."[48]

Communication plays a serious role in preventing date, acquaintance, and spousal rape. "No" has got to mean "no," and the aggressor has to understand that. One problem is that men tend to perceive more sexuality in interactions than women do,[49] and to interpret a woman's friendliness as invitation.[50] Rapists, in particular, seem unable to differentiate a woman's nonverbal cues. Seducers and rapists have assumed that a woman's "no" means "maybe" and her "maybe" means "yes." Wrong.

Violent partners and victims can get help to stop the cycle and alter their communication patterns. Hotlines can refer individuals to family service and support groups that help batterers, rapists, and their victims, and most communities have organizations to help both batterers and their partners. Alcoholics Anonymous and Narcotics Anonymous groups provide assistance for alcohol and drug problems. And colleges, religious organizations, communities, and police departments offer programs to help battered and abused women, children, and men. Often, safe houses provide a person who is afraid a place to stay until an alternative living situation can be arranged. Violence can be stopped and people can be helped before all involved are both physically and emotionally damaged.

Being a Family

"Well, in *our* family, we . . . " (do it this way; don't do that . . .). Ever hear that? Every family exists within a culture and has a culture of its own, made up of the ways the family is structured and the rules and images that make it work.

Take a child born in India, who "perceives many people living together in one house and is learning about extended families. By being in the same house with elderly people, the child is also learning to value the aged. In most of Africa the entire village raises a child, and the child thus learns about the extended family."[51]

Family An interdependent couple or group that creates its own structure within a larger culture

Within a larger culture, then, a **family** is an interdependent couple or group whose communication organizes its existence. Family members depend on one another to meet both physiological and psychological needs, from doing the laundry to supporting one another in times of grief. Family members might include spouses, cohabiting couples of the same or opposite sex, parents and children, a single parent and children, and/or siblings or even friends sharing a home.[52] Many contemporary families are "blended," as parents have brought their children into new relationships from previous families.

Each family creates itself in its own unique way. Members bring previous experiences to a new relationship, and this history shapes the way members communicate and patterns they develop in an optimal or dysfunctional family existence.

Family Development

People sometimes wail, "I'm becoming my mother!" or, "I heard my father's voice coming out of my mouth!" In lamentation or celebration, people see threads of childhood in the fabric of adult existence. Each family is unique, but is affected by these factors:

Time brings changes in jobs and homes; children are born, grow, and leave; parents age and die. Each change influences family communication and development.

Relational prototypes based on previous experiences and social stereotypes shape new families as members go out on their own. A man who expects a warm dinner on the table every night because it was that way in his family may be disappointed when his wife works long hours.

Irrationality may also be logical in a family, with emotion and reason being "implicit collaborators" in determining communication behavior.[53]

For example, a teenager regularly prefaces her exits with a smart remark that precipitates a fight with her mother. Daughter marches out, and Mom throws up her hands in angry defeat. Irrational, yes, but the confrontation has an internal logic. The teenager insults her mother to assert independence; time brings changes. The mother must learn to accept her daughter's independence but feels guilty about losing control, consistent with her relational prototypes. When it's clear that the teenager will no longer accept parental control, her mother has a logical reason to "give up."[54]

Every family has *role expectations* for each member, who identify their roles with comments such as "Mom's the disciplinarian" or "Dad keeps the books,"[55] describing many roles necessary to members' welfare and the family's stability. Members may share some roles, or a specific person may fill a given role exclusively, but if no one meets these needs, individual members or the family as a whole may suffer. As families develop, roles often need to be changed, too, and this may contribute to family conflict.

Roles are changing as society changes. In the United States, fathers once had little to do with their children; parenting was the mother's role. Today, while mothers still are responsible for most of a child's care, North American fathers are spending an average of 2.5 hours per weekday and 6.2 per weekend day with their children.[56]

Families, like couples, develop their own *rules and themes,* as well as *images* of the family that all members recognize. For example:

- *Rules.* Members know who can talk to whom about what topics, when, and under what circumstances. Perhaps sex is an acceptable subject of conversation with your grandparents, for example, but you don't dare mention it in front of Aunt Harriet.

- *Images.* Families share mental pictures, concepts, feelings, metaphors, and myths of the family: "My family is a circus," or, "My family is a safe haven." An image both reflects and defines roles and rules for family communication.

Family rules and images can provide a sense of cohesion and uniqueness for the family as a whole, but it's not so easy when one member takes previous experiences into creating a new home with someone who has experienced different family rules and images. The new family won't be like each of the partners' old ones, so they have to negotiate a compromise that will be healthy for all the members.

Optimal Family Functioning

Becoming a father, that is no achievement. Being one is, though.

Less Murray, 20th-century Australian poet

We would like to tell you exactly how to create a "happy" or "normal" family, but we can't. It's impossible to define a "normal family," because definitions are so culture- and value-laden. Certain factors, however, are characteristic of families that function at optimal level:[57]

- *Members support one another.* They are not oppositional, hurtful, manipulating, or defensive.

- *Members enjoy themselves and one another.* They are spontaneous, playful, humorous, and witty. They do not take life too seriously.

- *Members are directed toward one another.* They are not self-involved and do not focus excessively on analyzing problems and motivations.

- *Members maintain conventional boundaries.* Children are respected and nurtured but not treated as peers to their parents. That is, family roles allow children to develop at a normal pace, guided by boundaries that protect the process.

Dysfunctional Family Relationships

Dysfunctional relationship Interactions in which participants play games and manipulate one another, which breaks down the optimal relationship

Codependency Patterns of behavior that "enable" participants to behave in dysfunctional ways

In a **dysfunctional relationship,** members may play games, manipulate one another, and enable one another's self-destructive behavior. Instead of interdependency, they may act with **codependency,** when members enable one another

Survey Links Drug Use, Relationship with Father

According to a new survey released last week by the National Center on Addiction and Substance Abuse (CASA) at Columbia University, the quality of a teenager's relationship with his or her father directly affects the likelihood of the teen's using drugs or alcohol.

In its first analysis of family structure and substance abuse risk, CASA found that children living in two-parent families who have only a fair or poor relationship with their father are at a 68 percent higher risk of smoking, drinking and using drugs than are all teens living in two-parent households. They are at higher risk than teens living in a household headed by a single mother, who are at a 30 percent higher risk of substance use compared to all teens in a two-parent household.

The safest teens, according to CASA's analysis of its fifth annual CASA National Survey of American Attitudes on Substance Abuse, Teens and Their Parents, are those living in two-parent homes who:

- Have a positive relationship with both parents
- Go to both parents equally when they have important decisions to make
- Have discussed illegal drugs with parents
- Report that both parents are equally demanding in terms of grades, homework and personal behavior.

From *Alcoholism & Drug Abuse Weekly*, September 6, 1999, p. 5.

---

to behave in dysfunctional ways. The family hangs together because no one knows what it is like to be otherwise. With codependent partners, for example, the husband of an alcoholic may rant and rave but clean up her mess and lie to the boss to cover her absence, then make up, take the blame, and set the stage for the next episode. A codependent family member is characterized by "an overdeveloped sense of responsibility, a fear of personal criticism, a fear of abandonment, and a need for control."[61]

If you've known a dysfunctional family (most of us have), you may recognize the roles members play to enable others to avoid issues. For example:

- *The identified patient.* The person with a problem who takes all the family's attention, drawing attention away from others and from facing issues. Suppose a father is an alcoholic. Everyone focuses on his problem and covering for him so the neighbors won't know. In the process, they ignore a child's increasing depression or chaos in the household.

- *The scapegoat.* The "bad" person on whom all misfortunes are blamed so the family won't have to take responsibility for itself. Perhaps the eldest son constantly is told he is a "bad boy," and he fulfills that prophecy by regularly getting into trouble at school. His parents are always rushing off to see the principal and figure out ways to discipline their son—and they don't have time to figure out why their relationship is deteriorating or why they can't pay the bills. By attending to the scapegoat, the family avoids taking responsibility for any other problems.

- *The hero.* The "good" person who does everything right. The hero often is the child who cooks dinner, gets good grades, wins awards, is amiable and kind, and covers up for others' bad behavior. This child is a miniature adult who must keep the family together, no matter what. Despite all her or his successes, this "hero" child can never feel adequate because no one can be all things, and no child is an adult.

An adult child of an alcoholic writes, "There are approximately 28 million of us in the United States alone—probably more, because one of our characteristics is that we try to deny there was ever anything wrong with our parents. Yet we were shaped by their alcoholic way of life."[62] As a child, this woman's task was to care for her father and mother when they were drunk, to keep the secret, to cover the guilt. She was reared to be a codependent, an enabler, playing "the hero" to her parents' roles as patients. As an adult, she had to let go of those roles and learn new ones for a healthy relationship.

Sadly, people who grew up in dysfunctional families often bring codependent patterns into new relationships, but *dysfunctional family patterns do not have to be repeated*. Self-help programs, books, and counselors can guide grown-up children of dysfunctional homes to relinquish these patterns and create healthier ones. People can find assistance or referrals in most college counseling centers and groups such as ACOA (Adult Children of Alcoholics). For many people, breaking dysfunctional patterns is the first step to building good relationships and healthy families for the future. It's worth the effort.

As families develop, they face opposing forces that members must find a way of managing. Consider how the following issues might have affected your own family experiences:

- *Stability and change.* Change is certain, but people are uncertain when they face change. A healthy family helps members to maintain their sense of family and, at the same time, to adjust to the stress of changing circumstances.[58] A dysfunctional family may teeter constantly on the brink of crisis, unable to achieve stability nor to embrace change.

- *Integration and separation.* A family needs to integrate members' roles, interests, and needs into the family system. When someone leaves home or a member dies, a strong family can help members integrate and deal with separation without losing the sense of family and support.[59] A dysfunctional family may fail to integrate members, responding to one another with fear, jealousy, or competition; yet, members may be unable to adjust relationships when a member leaves home.

- *Power and control issues.* Power in families normally is asymmetrical, and adults control family functioning as children develop. That's a secure situation. If, however, adults fear they are controlled by the children, there's a problem. Physically abusive parents often "attribute high levels of power to children, and children are themselves placed in a parenting role."[60] The consequence can be a violent and dysfunctional family, as parents who think their own power is threatened try to control their children.

Summary

Interpersonal communication ranges from a relatively superficial level of social relations to the much deeper level of interhuman relations at which people are touched emotionally and psychologically, influencing changes in individuals and their relationship over time. Getting to know people starts with attraction and opportunity. The conversation process starts with casual talk and exploratory communication to develop commonalities between participants. Keeping a conversation moving requires going beyond topics related to the setting and into topics of interest to the participants.

When you start developing friendships, you explore more about one another in a gradual process of interpersonal bonding in which you form deep and personal affinities. This may lead to friendships, which may become enduring intimate relationships in which friends support, trust, and care for each other. Romantic relationships may start with a courtship ritual that moves from attention-getting strategies to sexual invitation and activity. As the romance develops, the couple may go through a number of turning points that define their relationship and its stages.

As two individuals become a couple, they develop a mutual identity with unwritten rules that govern communication and conversational themes that define their relationship. Problems may arise due to gender expectations and role barriers that affect the openness of communication between the partners. Worse problems may arise if partners deceive one another, destroy trust, and/or resort to violence.

Families evolve from members' previous family experiences and relationships. Families establish roles to serve functions of the family, rules to structure communication among members, and images that portray the nature of the unique family. In optimally functioning families, members are mutually supportive, enjoy one another's company, are directed toward one another rather than self-involved, and maintain appropriate boundaries and structure in which children can develop.

When families become dysfunctional, members may be codependent, enabling one another to act in ways that are destructive to themselves and/or the family. People can turn around dysfunctional behaviors—and create healthier families—with assistance from a wide variety of sources such as books, self-help and support groups, counseling groups, and agencies.

Exercises

1 Think back to a relationship you have had (this could be a good friendship or a romantic relationship). Do the following:

   a Analyze the stages your relationship went through.

   b Identify the turning points in your relationship.

   c Apply the diagram in Figure 8.1 to your relationship. How were—or were not—the levels of communication described in that diagram reflected in your relationship?

2 With another student, do the following:

   a Make up a description of a situation for a blind date. Write the roles for two characters; explain what their characteristics are, and what the setting is for the date.

   b Each of you take one role, and role-play for your class the opening conversation for your date.

   c With the class, discuss how the conversation developed.

3 Browse through anthologies, magazines, or song lyrics to find a poem or short essay that expresses your beliefs and values about friendship, romantic relationships, or families. Practice reading the piece aloud until you can read it with excellent eye contact and feeling for the words. Then read it to the class.

   In a small group, discuss the selections your classmates read. What did they have in common? What important ideas did they share? From this discussion, create a list of "principles of interpersonal communication in prose and poetry" with your group. Report your list to the class.

   Together, integrate the lists into one, eliminating any repetitions.

4 With a small group, observe a play or television show that portrays a family. Do the following:

   a Identify the image you think members might have of their family.

   b Identify the roles each member plays.

   c Identify how rules seem to work in this family.

   d As a group, present your observations to the class.

Cyberpoints

The following Cyberpoints can be easily accessed from the Student Companion website for this text at http://academic.cengage.com/communication/lumsdenccc3. Click on *Student Book Companion Site* and select this chapter from the pull-down menu at the top of the page that says "Select a chapter." Click on *Cyperpoints* under *Chapter Resources* and you will find links for the exercises following.

1   For further information to help with family communication problems, go to the *Communicating with Credibility and Confidence* website at http:// academic.cengage.com/communication/lumsdenccc3 and choose Chapter 8 from the pull-down menu.

2   Are you interested in families in a variety of cultures? Use InfoTrac College Edition and the keywords *family* and *culture*.

3   Use InfoTrac College Edition to locate and read the article by Stacy L. Norris and Richard L. Zweitenhoft, "Self-Monitoring, Trust, and Commitment in Romantic Relationships."

Chapter 9

Professional Relationships: Transacting for Success

Objectives for This Chapter

Knowledge

- Understand how to communicate professionally in organizations
- Know how roles, stereotypes, and expectations affect workplace communication
- Identify ways to manage workplace harassment
- Recognize elements of intercultural communication competence
- Identify the types, functions, and goals of interviews
- Know how to prepare for and conduct interviews

Feelings and Approaches

- Approach college and career communication professionally
- Be aware of stereotyping and expectations in college and the workplace
- Feel comfortable in communicating with colleagues of diverse cultures
- Have confidence as an interviewer and interviewee

Communication Abilities

- Communicate appropriately with people in different organizational roles
- Develop intercultural communication competence
- Communicate credibly in professional situations
- Prepare and conduct interviews credibly

Key Terms

professionalism

organizational culture

goal conflicts

stereotypes

interview

primary question

secondary question

open-ended question

closed question

leading question

job-qualification question

behavioral question

situational question

simulation

Why are you investing all this time, energy, and money into college? Our guess is you are preparing for a satisfying, productive, and successful career. To reach your goals, you need credibility and confidence in your **professionalism,** that is, communication showing involvement, competence, pride, and ethical standards in what you do. Being professional helps you move from promising student to effective employee and leader.

Professionalism Communication that shows involvement, competence, pride, and ethical standards in one's work

At this moment, you are in at least one organization—your college—and probably others. In the future, you will communicate within many organizations, often at the same time. That's why this chapter examines organizational life and ways to communicate professionally within it, as well as ways to develop your professional communication skills so your interviews will help you reach your goals.

Communicating in Organizational Cultures

When you enter a new organization—college, social, or corporate—you may feel as if you're a stranger in a strange land. In a way, you are. There are new people, new ways of doing things, new expectations. No matter how excellent your academic or technical qualifications, you can rise or fall on understanding the system and communicating within it.

Organizational culture The way things are done within a specific organization

Wherever you are, you will see an **organizational culture,** in which, "as in all cultures, all facts, truths, realities, beliefs and values are what the members agree they are—they are perceptions."[1] Members of organizations develop norms and expectations that both reflect and reinforce their ways of communicating,[2] using communication as "'means' to create, maintain, and facilitate change in the culture of an organization."[3]

Really, large organizations have multiple cultures:

- *"Official" culture* is leadership's ideal, often published as a "mission" or "vision" statement of organizational goals and values that provides a rationale for policies and actions. If a college mission statement commits to serving a diverse population, for instance, then the college should develop recruitment and retention policies to encourage enrollment and success of a diverse student body.

- *"Unofficial" culture* develops over time through members' interactions. Stories about past events, teachers, students, and athletes and interactions, together with your own experiences, quickly teach you the unofficial culture and how people relate to one another at different levels in the hierarchy as well.

- *Subcultures* grow within a larger culture in teams, offices, and departments. Perhaps faculty in one college department work well together and are helpful to students, whereas in another department professors squabble internally and give students little attention. Such norms reveal departmental subcultures, reflecting individual personalities as well as experiences and attitudes they have built as a separate group within the larger organization.

It has been said that "as organizational environments become more complex and turbulent, and as diverse institutional forms merge and emerge, organization and their members are pulled or are purposefully moving in different, often competing directions."[4] New types of cultures are emerging in *dispersed-network organizations*, and *virtual organizations*, and *boundaryless organizations*.[5] You could work in one of several dispersed offices or externally to one as, for example, a telecommuter, a temp (a subcontracted temporary worker), or a professional in the field (medical professional, auditor, therapist, creative consultant, designer, investigator—or almost anything else). This situation provides new privileges and challenges both for workers and organizations. People can feel unconnected to the organization and uninformed about policies affecting them and their work. Some organizations are using "all hands" meetings, say once a month, to provide information and develop some identity,[6] but this is impractical for organizations whose workers are widely dispersed.

Your ability to build positive relationships and show commitment as an active part of the communication network will contribute to your success and tenure in the job.[7] As well, professional behavior will help you cope with difficulties such as conflicts, pressures to comply, and/or stereotyping, bias, and harassment. Let's look at those issues here.

Goal Conflicts and Compliance Pressures

Ideally, what you want from your work and what your boss wants from you will match up nicely. But as you try to achieve your *personal* and *career* goals, your boss is trying to fulfill *management* goals, and these differing objectives can create **goal conflicts.** Here's an example: Ali, a physical therapist, asks for time off to attend a two-week skills workshop. Meanwhile, management has ordered Ali's supervisor, Jan, to increase patient load without hiring more therapists. She can't spare Ali for two weeks. Ali is an outstanding therapist, and Jan has supported him in the past, yet this time she turns him down. Ali is perfectly justified in feeling this is unfair, but it's management's call.

A manager's success in meeting organization goals relies on the effectiveness of subordinates, so their compliance with procedures, rules, orders, goals, and so on is essential. A manager may try to get compliance by explaining what is wanted in a friendly but persuasive way, or perhaps hint indirectly, get someone else to talk to the person, or even use coercion or threats.

Most supervisors say they prefer a positive, friendly approach[8] and a direct, cooperative strategy of reasoning and friendliness to gain compliance from their subordinates. Current research suggests that at first, both women and men tend

Goal conflicts When your personal and career goals differ from each other or from your management's objectives

Professional Speech

Three months after she joined an infomercial company in January 2002, 23 year-old Kristy Pinand moved up to a producer from production assistant.

The promotion was, like, so cool. But Ms. Pinand's routine use of such "teen speak" bothered her boss. "She sounded very young," potentially hurting her ability to win clients' respect, recalls Collette Liantonio, president of Concepts TV Productions in Boonton, N.J. She urged the youthful-looking staffer to watch her words.

Ms. Pinand . . . now rehearses her remarks aloud before she calls a client. "How you talk should not be how you're judged, but of course it is," she observes. . . .

Humphrey S. Tyler, president of National Trade Publications in Latham N.Y., frequently rejects sales and editorial candidates because they exhibit grammatically incorrect speech. "It's as if they pulled out a baseball cap and put it on backward," the publisher complains. "It simply reflects a low level of professionalism."

The well-educated controller of a Chicago company has long aspired to become a chief financial officer elsewhere. But recruiter Laurie Kahn refuses to recommend him because he often says "me and so-and-so," followed by the wrong verb form. "I don't know how much he'll be able to advance," says Ms. Kahn. . . .

A General Electric unit hesitated to elevate a Massachusetts plant manager to a higher-paid corporate spot five years ago because "every other word he said in the plant was the f-word," recalls Laurie Schloff, director of executive coaching at Speech Improvement Co. in Boston. GE warned that he wouldn't get his promotion unless he cleaned up his foul mouth, then tapped her to assist him for eight weeks. . . . She taught the manager to avoid slang and employ more formal language during meetings. He won the coveted transfer.

to use positive strategies, but when those don't work, women are more likely to continue in a positive vein and men are more likely to use negative sanctions.[9]

Facework plays a role in choice of compliance strategies, as the persuader uses "a variety of communication devices available to interactants for preventing face loss (both their own and others'), restoring face if lost, and facilitating the maintenance of poise in the advent of disrupted interactions."[10] Facework seeks to avoid embarrassment and find an equitable rationale for complying. Research indicates people concerned primarily with their own face use dominating and emotionally expressive approaches, but people concerned with the other's face or with mutual face try to integrate interests, be obliging, and to compromise.[11]

It appears that when the supervisor and subordinate build a relationship of similar, cooperative communication behaviors, and when the supervisor uses positive facework in a compliance or reproach situation, subordinates view the interaction as being more fair and the supervisor as more credible and competent than when negative approaches are used.[12]

Let's go back to Ali and his supervisor, Jan. If she's aware that Ali needs to save face just as much as she does, she might say, "I'm so disappointed that I can't

A growing number of businesses retain speech coaches for rising stars with speech flaws. . . . A coach analyzes an individual's discourse, pinpoints shortcomings and videotapes each session. Clients take the tapes home and do daily drills in front of a mirror. . . .

A senior project manager at a major financial-services company was surprised when his supervisor blamed his stalled career trajectory partly on his thick Brooklyn accent. Despite his M.B.A., he was speaking too fast and skipping many consonants; his "deez" and "doze" made him sound uneducated and inarticulate.

"Some words didn't come out the way they should," the 46-year-old Brooklyn native admits. "People will draw conclusions about your leadership abilities based on how things are expressed."

The man's employer covered the $5,000 tab for 14 sessions ending in March 2003 with New York [speech] coach Laura Darius. . . . The project manager later assumed a wider role that requires constant interaction with senior executives. He believes his communication ability has improved so much that he will soon become a managing director.

What should you do if you suspect your speaking habits are retarding your professional progress—but management doesn't offer a speech coach?

Seek frequent feedback about your communication competency from your boss, both informally and during performance reviews. . . .

Feedback helped cure Ms. Pinand, the infomercial producer. When she slipped into teen speak during shoots, Ms. Liantonio "would give me a look that said, 'There, you are doing it again.'" In July, the young woman became the company's production director.

From Joann S. Lubin, "To Win Advancement, You Need to Clean Up Any Bad Speech Habits," *Wall Street Journal*, October 5, 2004, B1. Used with permission.

clear you for two weeks, Ali. You do such incredibly good work and you deserve to take this workshop. And, besides, I know it would be a good experience. . . . Let's keep an eye open for other opportunities. Maybe management will see how much we need more therapists." If management has allowed her any discretion in rewarding people, she might talk with Ali about other ways to recognize his great work.

Stereotypes, Bias, and Harassment

Stereotypes Screens of expectations and judgments through which people filter their perceptions

In organizations, just like in neighborhoods or schools, people filter their perceptions of a "new kid on the block" through a screen of expectations and **stereotypes** to infer "additional 'knowledge' of what else is likely to be true of the individual."[13] One of our students, a registered nurse in an urban hospital, writes, "I am frequently asked, 'Do you have many foreign doctors?' The person who asks this question usually uses a certain tone as if to say, 'Are they qualified and as skilled as American doctors?' I think it is unfortunate that these prejudices exist. It is even more disturbing that people are unaware of these preconceptions."[14]

Stereotypes can trigger biased judgments—a fine doctor might be rejected for his race; an excellent prospect for leadership might be overlooked because of her sex. Bias is unfair and illegal, *and* self-defeating, because it deprives organizations of talents a diverse workforce can contribute.

That's why many U.S. organizations have been working to recruit and retain people who have suffered from such bias in the past. DuPont uses ombudsmen to track the careers of women and people of color; Xerox and AT&T actively seek advice and critiques from groups who traditionally experience bias; and many organizations have instituted training to diminish bias in the workplace.[15]

Sometimes, stereotyping by sex or race, combined with competition for power and control, is expressed in harassment that hurts the victim and costs the organization. A few years ago, Denny's Restaurant chain was "making amends to the black community. And every employee, especially managers, must attend sessions on the advantages of a multiracial clientele." Why? Because Denny's was slow in noticing a de facto policy of systematically ignoring and embarrassing African American customers until the company had to pay a $54 million class action settlement.[16] And in 1998, there were 15,618 sexual harassment complaints to the Equal Employment Opportunity Commission (EEOC). In the same year, Mitsubishi paid $34 million to 500 women workers to atone for sexual harassment; in 1999 Astra Inc. paid $10 million in a settlement for 120 women.[17] Organizations are trying to face the issues, but there's a long way to go.

We hope you never have to deal with these issues, but if you do, you can find out how. The EEOC has published guidelines, and just about every organization has published policies and procedures to follow if you need to get help or bring charges. Yet again, a professional attitude can help to prevent problems but, if they arise, can also help you to solve them.

Communication Connections

These days, a prime necessity in personal and career life is to build bridges to others whose goals and cultures may be different from yours.

Bridging Goals and Needs   If you can understand where someone is coming from, you're halfway there. If your communication gains cooperation, you're all the way there. It helps to:

> *Get to know the other person.* Talk, listen, learn to understand others. Even professors are just people who loved school, and/or their disciplines, so much that they never left. Or a supervisor was so good at doing what you're doing now that she or he was promoted. The more you learn, the more you can become credible and confident in communicating.

> *Identify the other person's goals.* Teachers, supervisors, administrators— all have goals for you, so review syllabi, job descriptions, or mission statements. How can your good work help to fulfill management's goals? Consultants stress that helping your boss achieve management goals makes your boss look good, and that usually also advances your objectives.[18]

Identify your own goals and needs. If there's a problem getting a job done, talk about it. As professors, we can tell you we like to be kept informed. Whether you're talking to a professor or a supervisor, you don't have to publicize your private life, but you do need to discuss barriers to your effectiveness. Together, you may find ways to surmount them.

Work within the structure of the organization. As soon as you enter a new system, even a new class, learn where and whom to consult for help, know your goals, and learn the organizational processes. Then when you need help, you know what to do.

Find out how you're doing. You need to know if you're on the right path, so ask for feedback on your work. Suspend ego, shelve defensiveness, communicate cooperation. Keep your eye on the goal. Explain carefully, ask precise questions, paraphrase back—and keep an open attitude. Then you can find ways to solidify your successes and correct any problems.

Establish relationships for the future. Every communication transaction can be important to your résumé, letters of recommendation, future interviews, and, perhaps, to finding a *mentor*: someone in a position to encourage, guide, and serve as a model for you—someone who finds you credible and takes an interest in your future. Many successful people credit a mentor for their college and career success. *Your* mentor could be any one of your professors or supervisors.

Bridging Cultures   Your success often depends ultimately on your credibility and confidence in building professional connections between you and other people—sometimes people from different cultures and backgrounds. Start by putting yourself in their shoes. Stephan and Stephan note that "individuals often experience intergroup anxiety before interacting with people from a different culture. [Intergroup anxiety] is also common within cultures, for example, in contacts between members of different racial and ethnic groups, and between members of nonstigmatized and stigmatized groups,"[19] such as people who are old, who are gay or lesbian, or who have disabilities.

The prospect of interacting with someone "different" can be scary; people may fear they will embarrass themselves, or feel incompetent or frustrated or even threatened by the other person's evaluation, rejection, and perhaps aggression. They might also fear their own identity group's sanctions against interacting with an individual from that other group.[20]

It takes a supportive, open climate and intercultural communication competence, self-monitoring, and adaptability to reduce the anxiety of intergroup communication. Research has found that when Anglo Americans apply this principle by giving social support to immigrant Hispanic workers, for example, praising them or helping them with personal problems, it helps to reduce acculturative stress for these newer workers.[21] Remember in Chapter 3 we discussed the important perception differences among observing, inferring, and judging. Applying that to intergroup communication, Gudykunst and Kim note that when you observe and listen to someone from another group, it helps to

	Bill	Muhammed
Description	He stands close to me.	He backs off from me.
Interpretation	Maybe he's pushy.	Maybe he's prejudiced.
	Maybe he's friendly.	Maybe he's cold.
	Maybe he's trying too hard.	Maybe he's thinking about something else.
	Maybe Arabs get closer than North Americans.	Maybe North Americans don't get as close as Arabs do.
Evaluation	I'm uncomfortable, but I'll try to understand.	I need to be close, but I'll try to back off a little.

Figure 9.1 *Steps in achieving intercultural understanding*

"differentiate among a description of what we observed, how we interpreted it, and our evaluations":[22]

- *Description* recognizes specific actions without qualifying them in any way.
- *Interpretation* includes hypothesizing a series of possible explanations for the described act but not reaching a hasty conclusion about what it means.
- *Evaluations* should be withheld until sufficient information is available to weigh quality and meaning of the person's behavior.

Suppose Bill (North American) is talking with Muhammad (Saudi Arabian). Muhammad gets very close, face to face, and gestures broadly. Bill becomes uncomfortable and backs off. If Bill jumps straight to evaluation—as people often do—he may think, "This guy is pushy." Muhammad is concerned because Bill backs off; if he also leaps straight to evaluation, he may think, "This guy is cold and he doesn't like me." If each can separate his description from interpretation and evaluation, however, the thinking might go as shown in Figure 9.1.

If Muhammad and Bill can keep their thinking and responses clear in this way, they can reduce intergroup anxiety and open up intercultural communication. Good advice for adapting to people from other cultures and interests is to use "an unconditionally constructive strategy" in which you behave with rationality, understanding, consultation, reliability, noncoercion, openness, and acceptance to create a situation that is good for both parties *and* good for the relationship.[23]

Communicating in Interviews

Interview A goal-oriented conversation in which participants follow a question-and-answer structure

First you have to get the job—and that requires successful interviews. An **interview** is goal oriented, a structured process of questioning and answering to achieve a purpose. As interviewee you may do 70% of the talking,[24] usually as answerer but also as questioner to learn more about the job.

How to Talk to a Bureaucrat

A bureaucrat is just someone who works in a bureaucracy—a person who is tired, frequently abused, often lacks real authority, and has "heard it all." The beleaguered bureaucrat may hide behind "Write a memo," or "It isn't in my job description," or "See so-and-so," or "It's time for my break."

How do you dissolve the bureaucratic wall?

- *Be friendly.* Make eye contact, smile, talk person to person, show that you aren't on the attack. A brief personal comment, such as, "You folks are really busy today, aren't you?" or "I really appreciate you taking time with me," or "I like your poster up there," can put both of you at ease.

- *Expect to cooperate in solving a problem.* Look to the person behind the desk as a source of information and help. Show you are taking a win-win approach to the discussion. But remember that the client before you may have been rude, so your bureaucrat may already be defensive. Your cooperative attitude may come as a surprise. Keep a problem-solving, win-win attitude, and she or he will come around.

- *Prepare and organize your approach.* Know exactly what you want and whom you're supposed to see. Take everything you might need with you, arranged so you can put your hand promptly on exactly what you need. And carefully plan how you will explain what you want.

- *Stay focused.* Keep your attention on the goal, not on reacting to the other person's tone or style. Explain carefully, ask precise questions, confirm your understanding by paraphrasing what you heard.

- *Be persistent.* If you're not clear on what you have to do, or you're not satisfied with the answer, keep after it. Rephrase, ask for explanation, make sure it's right. If you have to go to another source or a higher authority, be nice about it, but be assertive and clear in explaining what you need.

- *Show appreciation.* Even if the encounter's been a bit hairy, try to wind it up with appreciation. Bureaucrats don't get many "Thank you's," or "You've really been a big help" comments. Your appreciation will make both of you feel good—and your bureaucrat will have a better attitude toward the next client to come along!

Interviews occur in various contexts, are directed to specific objectives, have a structure, and rely on effective communication. Needless to say, your success is more likely if you understand interview processes and carefully plan and prepare for the transaction.

Interview Types

Not all interviews are job interviews. You may be interviewee *or* interviewer to reach goals necessary to develop a career, resolve issues in your life, or influence other people to act in ways that meet your objectives.

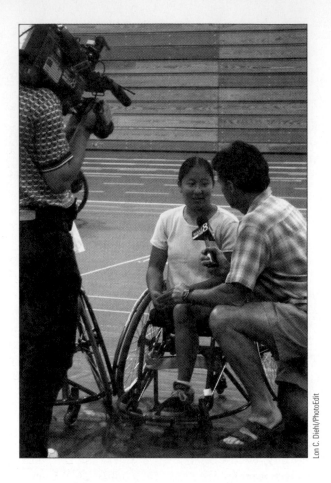

A television broad-caster interviews an athlete about her game

Lon C. Diehl/PhotoEdit

- *Information interviews* seek data for purposes of problem solving, research, news, or entertainment. You might interview experts for your speech or subjects for a research project in your job.

- *Selection interviews* determine who best fits a particular position. As interviewer, you question to see which candidate is best; as interviewee, you give information showing how you meet requirements—and ask questions to learn if this is right place for you.

- *Performance appraisal interviews* evaluate your work and set objectives for future performance; they may influence grades, promotions, raises, transfers, or training opportunities. Sometimes, performance appraisal is disciplinary—to document, clarify, and correct problems. It sounds intimidating, but a well-conducted discipline interview can be a fair way to clarify goals and help a person do a better job.

- *Exit interviews*, conducted when an individual is leaving an organization, can help both organization and employee. The interviewer's purpose is to find out why the employee is leaving and what she or he found positive and/or negative in working there. Some organizations also help the interviewee identify alternative options for the future.

- *Needs analysis interviews* help organizations to increase satisfaction, productivity, and quality by revealing "employee feelings, causes of problems, and expectations and anticipated difficulties."[25] With this information, changes and interventions can be made.

- *Persuasion interviews* really are one-on-one efforts by an interviewer to influence an interviewee to comply, cooperate, change an attitude, or take some action. Even sales presentations might interview a customer to identify needs and show products or services that may meet those needs.

- *Helping interviews* assist an interviewer to help the interviewee solve or cope with a problem through listening and questioning, diagnosing, advising, and counseling. The interviewer may be a health care worker, counselor, advisor, teacher, or someone in a personal relationship who tries to help another by listening and questioning empathically.

Interview Homework

Picture this: You're in an interview. You clearly understand the other participant, the goals, and the issues surrounding the interview. You're ready. You did some homework and you're prepared.

The big question is, *What does each of us want as the major outcome of the interview?* Questions and responses should lead directly or indirectly to these ends. An employment interviewer might ask, "What can you do for my organization? Why are you a better bet than other candidates?" If you want that job, you'll demonstrate how your training, background, experience, and talents are just what they need. To get the data you need to answer this question, do the following:

1   *Collect information* you may want to show, quote, or document, and organize it for easy access. In an employment interview, for example, the interviewee needs a résumé and, perhaps, a portfolio of work. The interviewer should have studied any previously submitted materials and have brochures, job descriptions, and procedural guidelines to show the candidate.

2   *Review everything you can learn about the other person and/or organization.* If you are interviewing for a job, find out how economically sound and socially responsible the organization is. The library or the net provides sources such as *Dun and Bradstreet's Book of Corporation Management, Standard and Poor's Register of Corporations*, and many business-oriented newspapers and magazines. It's always a good idea to review the company's website and to look at the latest annual report to corporate stockholders (or to donors if for a position with a not-for-profit charitable organization). Your information about the organization impresses the interviewer and informs your decisions. Think about how the organization's reputation and policies mesh with *your* career and life criteria.

3 *Understand policies and procedures.* Before the interview, the interviewer should know policies and procedures for conducting and following up the interview, follow these steps, and inform the interviewee about them. Equally, the interviewee can and should ask about such things as qualifications, follow-up interviews, decision dates, and so on.

It doesn't hurt to recognize that either interviewer or interviewee could have a secondary goal. You might interview a professor for information that will help you earn an A on your project; secondarily, you might hope to develop a contact for a future letter of recommendation or even a mentor. Your interviewee wants to help you with your project, but also might like to recruit you as a major.

Interview Planning

Each step of an interview affects how you impress the other person and how effectively you accomplish what you want to do. You really want to plan carefully.

Arrangements Your very first impression is before the interview, when you set it up. So you need to be organized, professional, and cooperative. The interviewer may initiate a meeting or the interviewee may request it. In either case, follow these steps to arrange an interview:

1 *Request the interview* with a letter or a call, and remember your first impression matters, even if your first contact is with a secretary or assistant. In one survey, 91% of executives considered their assistant's opinion important in selecting an employee.[26] Your letter or call should courteously and confidently explain who you are and why you want the interview. If you're the interviewer, you need also to indicate about how long the interview will take.

2 *Set up the interview* as conveniently as possible for the other person. If meeting in person is impossible, ask for a telephone interview. In either case, set a specific time that is convenient for both of you so the interview can proceed without interruptions.

3 *Confirm the arrangements* before the interview with a note thanking the interviewer in advance, restating your purposes in the interview, and confirming the time and place. Then, the day before the interview, call to confirm your appointment. This prevents embarrassing errors and shows your consideration and competence—both vital to your credibility.

If you don't get your interview on the first try, don't give up. A New York radio station manager made this point: On the day a DJ quit, an applicant happened to call. The résumé he had sent in happened to be on top of the manager's file. She noticed it, listened to the applicant's audition tape, accepted his call, gave him his interview, and awarded him the job. Was it luck? Lucky that this applicant *had sent in a fresh résumé and made follow-up calls once a month for two years*! The station manager said, "He put himself at the right place at the right time with the right qualifications for what I needed." This wasn't luck. It was organization, persistence, and determination.

Strategy and Structure   Good interviews develop a carefully outlined strategy to cover important points and still have room to pursue ideas. Interviewers usually choose one of the following strategies:

1   *Exploratory strategy interviews* allow participants to identify and examine a range of ideas by starting with one or two questions that allow the interviewee to expand on ideas, then probing responses more deeply. Exploratory strategies work well for helping or information interviews, but not necessarily when a list of issues must be addressed or a judgment must be made.

2   *Objective strategy* or *structured interviews* are useful for selection or research. The same structure is used for all applicants or subjects, asking a series of carefully prepared job- or goal-related questions for which predetermined rating scales evaluate answers. Interviewers must "stay on script" yet be able to formulate probing follow-up questions, to listen, and to assess nonverbal cues.[27] In selection interviews, these steps lead to more reliable decisions[28] by ensuring that the interviewee can present essential information on specific criteria.[29]

If you're the interviewee, understanding each type of interview aids you in preparing responses for whichever one you meet. If you're the interviewer, outlining your strategy will keep you on track. Perhaps you're writing a newspaper article about a political issue and you interview your state senator about it. You might have an outline like the one shown on the *Communicating with Credibility and Confidence* website at http://academic.cengage.com/communication/lumsdenccc3. With this outline, you build a personal rapport, you guide the exploratory interview, and you leave room to follow up on ideas.

Any type of interview should include at least the following information:

■   What procedures your interview will follow

■   How information from the interviewee will be used

■   What next steps are necessary

■   What procedures are to be followed in the next steps

For example, in selection interviews, the introduction should include a precise description of the organization, the job, and the steps the hiring procedure will follow. The conclusion should outline exactly what the next steps are. If an interviewer does not provide this information, the interviewee should ask for it.

Question Functions and Forms   As interviewer, you need questions that find what you need to know. As interviewee, you need to anticipate what your interviewer might want and be ready to provide it.

In both roles, questions serve two functions: to get *objective information*, which "includes unbiased and testable facts . . . names, dates, locations, and circumstances," and to find *subjective information*, which "includes personal feelings, attitudes, and beliefs."[30]

It is better to know some of the questions than all of the answers.

James Thurber, 20th-century American humorist and novelist

A common questioning strategy is to start with a **primary question,** one that the interviewer has planned in advance. Often, you can anticipate some of these and plan answers. "What was your most important experience in college?" as a primary question might allow you to talk about something that indirectly shows how you could fit the organization's needs.

A primary question frequently leads to a **secondary question** that probes your answers for more in-depth information. If you answered our sample primary question with "Being president of my major department's club," secondary questions might be, "What was it about that experience that was important to you?" or, "What did you learn from doing that?" Although you can't be sure what secondary questions will be asked, you can think about what the interviewer is looking for, what kinds of probes might reveal that information, and how you might answer them.

Unfortunately, interviewers may miss important information because they don't know how to formulate primary or secondary questions or because they don't use the best question *form.* Here are two good basic question forms and one bad one:

- An **open-ended question** allows for a variety of answers. They often start out with "What," "How," or "Why." "How did you become interested in this field?" for example, lets the interviewee develop an answer from almost any starting point. An interviewee who has really thought about how previous experience fits what the interviewer is looking for can formulate an answer so it demonstrates these qualities.

- A **closed question** asks for yes/no, either/or, or multiple choice answers. They should be used only when there really are limited choices. "Did you graduate from college?" is a legitimate yes/no question. "Did you go to college or straight to work out of high school?" however, excludes the possibility you went to a technical school, or an art or drama academy, or into the military. If there is some other option to a closed question, the interviewee can respond with something like, "Well, neither one. Actually, I . . ."

- A **leading question**—also known as a "loaded" question—can be misleading, manipulative, and unethical. Leading questions make people defensive because the wording sets up an answer that invites judgment. An interviewee can avoid this question trap by analyzing the question and choosing an answer carefully. Suppose you've said you were active in a service group that helped the homeless. If the interviewer then asks, "What political bias was behind your decision to join that group?" you would recognize a leading question. Instead of defending your politics—a losing proposition—you could *confront the implication tactfully*: "I don't think I had a political bias. I got into it because I saw people needed help. . . ." Or, you could *sidestep the implication* entirely and simply explain your unbiased motivation for participating in this group, for instance, "My friend was involved and she asked me to help."

Questions for Selection and Performance   Selection and performance interviewers question to learn your qualifications and personality. Interviewers need to phrase questions carefully. Interviewees can plan ahead to answer these types of questions credibly:

- A **job-qualifications** question probes beyond the résumé to find out how you meet criteria for the job. Use examples from your experience to show how you meet the organization's needs—and make clear your ability and willingness to learn.

- A **behavioral question** asks you to recount ways you've acted in previous situations. These can be powerful predictors of future success or failure.[31] An interviewer who wants to know how you handle defensive people might ask, "Describe a time you had to deal with someone who was nasty. How did you feel? How did you handle it?" You'll be ready to answer if, in preparing for your interview, you've analyzed both job and related experiences. When you're asked such questions, you'll have a reservoir of ideas. Answer with a specific description of the situation and your responses to it, and show how it relates to your qualifications for this job.

- A **situational question** asks about a hypothetical situation and how the candidate would handle it, for example, "As a supervisor, what would you do if you discovered someone was punching in for another employee to cover up chronic tardiness?" As with behavioral questions, prepare by reviewing your real experiences in your mind; then answer by describing what you would do so it shows your confidence and ability to solve the hypothetical problem. You might say, "I would talk to both workers privately to see what was going on. When I was sure of the facts, I would choose a disciplinary action consistent with company policy."

- In a **simulation,** interviewees role-play a situation so the interviewer can assess leadership, problem-solving, people management, and presentational skills. In fact, some of your instructors may have presented a classroom lecture when they interviewed at the college. To prepare for simulations, review what you know about the skills important to the job, and conduct some role-playing practice sessions with friends. Videotape, analyze, and improve your performance so you're comfortable with role-playing when you're asked to do it.

An interview should serve the needs both of the interviewer and the interviewee, but there is a line into a person's private life no interviewer should cross. The Equal Employment Opportunity Commission (EEOC) requires that selection procedures and questions be relevant to important job qualifications; interviewers are barred from asking questions about marital and family status, age, race, religion, sex, ethnic background, credit rating, and arrest records unless they can prove that the information has a direct bearing on job qualifications.[32]

It happens, unfortunately, that some interviewers don't know or don't care about the law. Some do ask questions not to assess the applicants' qualifications, but to eliminate them from consideration because of their nationality, race, religion, gender, or sexual orientation.

This can create a dilemma. If you answer even though the question is unlawful, you might lose the job opportunity. If you confront the issue, you might also lose the job opportunity. You might not want to work for an organization that uses such tactics—but what if you do want the job, anyway? Start by assuming that the question is based in ignorance rather than malice, and choose a response that allows the interviewer to leave the issue gracefully. Your options are to:

- *Bridge the question by moving from it to something else.* An interviewer who asks, "What church do you go to?" might just be curious—or might want to screen out people with certain religious beliefs. A bridging response might be, "That brings up a great experience that taught me the leadership skills I need for this position. For 2 years I was a youth counselor . . . ," thus ignoring the specific religious question but speaking to your experience.

- *Confront the issue tactfully.* You might respond, "Is that relevant to my job qualifications? Could we go over the criteria?"

- *Confront the issue bluntly.* Simply say, "I never answer this question in an interview because the EEOC lists it as unlawful." If you have to use this response and it costs you the job, you're probably better off without it.

Interview Confidence and Credibility

Good interviews are good because you are confident, you know what you're doing, and you demonstrate your credibility as you talk. When you've prepared thoroughly, you can build your confidence by training like an athlete—that is, both mentally and physically. Use visualization and affirmation to see the interview and your behavior exactly as you want it to be. Get a friend to role-play the interview with you, preferably with videotape. Discuss the goals and situation of the interview and then practice both asking and answering questions. This will help you not only improve your fluency and verbal presentation but also identify question areas for which you need more information or analysis.

Here are a few guidelines for managing a credible interview:

1   *Dress appropriately*, that is, just a bit more dressy than you would for the job. Your dress and grooming should boost credibility and confidence. One consultant says applicants "need to wear the uniform of the team they want to be a part of. . . . Initially people are more comfortable with people who look like they do."[33]

2   *Communicate nondefensively and cooperatively.* Assume that you both mean well, and strive to make the other person comfortable. You may both feel awkward and on the spot, but an open attitude, smiling, direct eye contact, and a firm handshake all help to ease the tension.

3   *Stay on top of your own stress.* Take slow, deep breaths to reduce defensive responses, and recognize that an interviewer might make you uncomfortable because of his or her own inexperience—or that interviewers sometimes structure selection interviews to put the interviewee under stress. An interviewer in a

I'm a great believer in luck, and I find the harder I work, the more I have of it.

Thomas Jefferson,
Founding Father of the
United States of America

second or third meeting may play "bad cop" to see how you handle pressure. Here, again, if you understand the interviewer's purposes, you have a better opportunity to maintain a positive approach and control your responses.

4   *Be honest and direct.* An interview, although brief, is a relationship. As soon as deception enters into it, trust and credibility are lost. Goldhaber says, "Do not try to be what you are not. If you know the answers, give them. If you do not know the answers to some of the questions, be smart enough to say so."[34]

5   *Listen actively to questions and answers.* Ensure that you know what you are being asked or told; listen interactively, asking for clarification or definition when you need it, with responses such as, "Could you give me an example of what you mean?" or, "Are you referring to . . . ?"

6   *Ask your own questions.* Consultants say that asking good questions not only gives you information about the job, but gives a better impression of *you*. More jobs are offered to interviewees that show interest in the interviewer and in the company than to those who simply answer questions.[35]

7   *Monitor your own and the other's nonverbal communication.* The eyes, face, body, voice, and use of space indicate a lot in an interview. Adapt your communication to the interviewer's. In the United States, it's generally true that people establish rapport, openness, and credibility with direct eye contact; a warm, firm handshake and forward-leaning posture; relaxed gestures; and a strong, confident voice, but if you're doing all that and your interviewer stiffens up a bit, adapt by being a bit more formal.

Finally, winding up and following up an interview can make or break your credibility. Be sure you do these three things:

1   *Summarize and confirm what you have learned.* Ensure the other person is comfortable with your conclusions.

2   *Ask permission to call if you have further questions or need to confirm information.*

3   *Follow up appropriately.* Write a thank-you note for the interview and, if your next step involves a phone call or sending information, be sure to follow through promptly.

Summary

A professional attitude that reflects involvement, competence, pride, and high ethical standards is the foundation for your communication in college and in your career. In any type of organization, people must learn to understand organizational cultures with their unique norms and roles and to communicate with people such as faculty members, supervisors, and bureaucrats who have their own goals and pressures.

Workplace tensions can result from differences among organizational goals, workers' goals, and managers' needs to motivate and direct subordinates to comply with management preferences. Unfortunately, people's expectations and stereotypes can result in bias based on an individual's gender, race, or identity group, or in harassment. People can avoid being harassers by screening their own messages and may be able to stop others' harassment with carefully selected communication strategies. A professional attitude allows all members of an organization to communicate freely and integrates strangers into the organization. A professional attitude includes intercultural competence, whereby individuals are adaptable and seek to understand and work with people from other cultures.

Both in college and in careers, skill in interviewing involves understanding requirements that vary according to the specific goals—information, selection, performance, persuasion, or helping. Building confidence and credibility in interviewing depends on identifying goals, researching, arranging, and planning the strategy and structure of the interview. Interview questions may be open-ended or closed and may probe more deeply into responses to previous questions. Often, questions are behavioral or situational, and sometimes they are simulated situations so the interviewer can observe the interviewee. Interviewers should avoid questions that are loaded or that make unlawful inquiries into the interviewee's personal lives.

You can become more confident in interviews if you train for them through preparation, stress management relaxation and visualization, and role-playing. Your credibility is enhanced by your preparation and interaction.

Exercises

1   Go to the student center and strike up a conversation with a stranger who differs from you in culture or ethnicity. Try to talk for awhile. Then reflect on these questions:

   a   How did it feel to approach a stranger?

   b   Did you experience anxiety based on your cultural or ethnic differences? If so, what was it like?

   c   What did you do differently than you might in talking with an acquaintance or a stranger who appeared to be from your own identity group?

   d   What did you learn from the encounter?

   e   How can you use it in your future communication?

2   Most organizations, including your college, should have an office that deals with issues of bias and harassment in the institution. Choose a partner from class and set up an appointment and interview an officer in such a department. Find out what the legal issues are in preventing or correcting bias and harassment problems and how the office goes about ensuring

that the organization complies with their obligations. Report your findings to the class.

3 With a small group, do the following:

a Decide on one topic about which you want to get information.

b Together, design an interview outline for your topic.

c For each person in your group, identify someone as an expert on the subject to interview. (These could be anyone from professors to local politicians to members of organizations dedicated to your topic.)

d Decide which one of you will interview which expert.

Separately, do the following:

a Do your background homework, revise your outlines as necessary, and arrange an interview.

b Conduct your interview. Use a tape recorder if possible, and take good notes.

c Write a thank-you note to your interviewee.

Together, do the following:

a Compare and contrast the information each of you obtained and the process each of you went through in the interview. Where are they similar? How are they different?

b Discuss what factors may have created differences between your interviews. Consider your preparation, organization, and questions, as well as the way you and your interviewee approached and interacted in the interview.

c As a panel, report to the class what you found out about your topic and about interviewing from this experience.

4 Search through the classified ad section in a major newspaper to find an advertisement for a job in a field that interests you. Imagine that you are going to apply for the position and do the following:

a Identify the interviewer's goals. What criteria do you think an interviewer would use to judge an applicant?

b Consider what would contribute to an appropriate background for an applicant. Think about courses, extracurricular experiences, attitudes, abilities, and so on.

c Research the background of the organization and consider how what you have learned might affect an applicant's interview.

d Consider what objective questions an interviewer might ask.

e Consider some subjective questions an interviewer might ask.

f Make a 3-minute presentation to the class explaining your findings.

Cyberpoints

The following Cyberpoints can be easily accessed from the Student Companion website for this text at http://academic.cengage.com/communication/lumsdenccc3. Click on *Student Book Companion Site* and select this chapter from the pull-down menu at the top of the page that says "Select a chapter." Click on *Cyperpoints* under *Chapter Resources* and you will find links for the exercises following.

1   Do you want more information on dealing with racial or sexual harassment? Go to the *Communicating with Credibility and Confidence* website at http://academic.cengage.com/communication/lumsdenccc3 and follow the instructions in the previous paragraph. Summarize what you learned about dealing with racial or sexual harassment.

2   For a sample interview outline, go to the *Communicating with Credibility and Confidence* website and follow the instructions in Cyberpoint 1. What are two things in the outline that you have used in interviews before, or already knew about? What are two things in the outline you want to be sure to remember the next time you interview?

3   You can get sources on interviewing from Quintessential Careers at http://www.quintcareers.com/intvres.html and browse the list of Interviewing Resources. Explore at least three of the links. Write a brief summary comparing what you learned about interviewing from these cyber-resources with what you learned from the text.

4   To get insights on how employment interviewers approach the selection interview, go to http://job-interview.net. Browse and explore three or more links on this interview resource page. Write a brief summary of what you learned that can help you improve your communication for your next interview.

5   Do you have some interviews coming up? Use InfoTrac College Edition and the keyword *employment*—you'll find current articles written by personnel professionals that will help you prepare. Review three articles and summarize what you found helpful for future interviews.

Chapter 10

Groups and Teams: Communication and Leadership

Rob Lewine/CORBIS

Objectives for This Chapter

Knowledge

- Understand the role of working groups and teams in contemporary society
- Identify elements that transform a group into a team and a superteam
- Distinguish among task, group-building, and individual roles and processes
- Know what makes leaders credible
- Describe leadership roles in groups
- Understand styles and approaches to leading groups
- Know how to prepare and lead group meetings

Feelings and Approaches

- Feel comfortable working in groups and teams
- Develop confidence and credibility in fulfilling leadership functions
- Enjoy helping a group develop and succeed
- Be confident when exercising principled leadership

Communication Abilities

- Communicate effectively in group-building and task roles
- Help other members to communicate in a group setting
- Work with others in developing goals and strategies for solving problems and making decisions
- Serve leadership functions in groups and teams

Key Terms

Groups can be lots of fun. Groups can be productive. Groups can be frustrating. In your career, community, church—in your life—your personal skills in teamwork and leadership can make or break the experience.

The sure thing is you will *work* in groups and teams, sometimes even in virtual teams, where your collaboration is primarily electronic. These days, teamwork is critical in just about any career. Why? Because "two heads are better than one"? That's one reason. In one study, groups outperformed even their best individual members 97% of the time.[1] Each member of the group brings a unique background, set of experiences, and viewpoint; when members interact, they draw new insights from one another and develop new approaches no one of them could have generated alone. Such diversity creates a rich field of ideas and knowledge for solving a problem or achieving a goal.

This chapter examines why teamwork is so important and how your group can become a team and even a superteam, preparing you to share leadership or to be the designated leader in groups, and it gives you methods to get a specific group or team started on its work.

Groups, Teams, and Your Future

At this time, in this century, it is essential to work well with groups and teams, because, first, in all venues they are used extensively in creating, problem solving, and decision making. Second, because teamwork enhances your own success.

Members Work Together to Attain Goals

What do you want in your career? And what does your organization (or organizations you're associated with) want? Organizational goals and personal goals often work together, but for clarity we will look at them one at a time.

Organizational Goals   Why do contemporary organizations emphasize small group and teamwork so heavily? We've noted one reason: A diverse group achieves better ideas and solutions. In addition, *participants are involved in their own learning and decision making—and that leads to greater satisfaction and agreement with the group's decision. This means people are more committed to a decision they themselves have made.*[2]

Not only do organizations bring together people from a wide range of backgrounds to serve on teams, but employers now actively seek managers and workers who have teamwork skills. Managers' jobs are shifting rapidly from the traditional functions of organizing work and increasing individual production to focusing on "team motivation and output . . . [and] the functions of coaching and facilitating."[3]

Of course, group work takes time, effort, and ability. And it's true that some problems don't need teamwork: if you have a sophisticated math problem and one mathematical genius, let the genius solve it. If there's a fire in a wastebasket, go ahead and put it out—don't wait for a committee. But anytime you want diverse insights and talents, a group is best.

Personal Goals   In school, on the job, in your community, in your religious organization—working in a group can help you, personally. For example:

Leadership development. Groups provide opportunities to develop and demonstrate your leadership abilities to employers.

Career advancement. One General Foods employee stated her subcommittee work "exposed more people to my past and present skills and led to my being called in on some new product development projects."[4]

Personal satisfaction. Studies and experience show that high-performance team members see "their teams as special and their experiences as having participated 'in something bigger than myself.'"[5]

One of our students described the satisfaction he and his teammates felt after a very successful class project. They stood in the college parking lot for an hour, he reported, basking in the knowledge that they had accomplished more together than any one of them could have done alone.

Such satisfaction results, in part, from what one theorist calls "flow" or "optimal experience," when collaboration is so involving it blocks out any other interest.[6] Cohen and Mankin explain that "effective collaborations . . . are the wellsprings of knowledge and creativity, key strategic resources for performance success in all modern organizations, but particularly in the virtual organization."[7]

In all groups, not just in work teams, communication uses knowledge and skills developed throughout this book, including abilities to speak, listen, question, and adapt to nonverbal cues. When you master these abilities, you can enjoy teamwork—and nothing gains credibility and respect more than managing group communication successfully.

Members Adapt Formats to Attain Goals

Although we focus on problem solving and managing work or study in small groups, it's important to recognize some ways groups are used in public or media communication. For example:

■ **A panel:** A group, often with a moderator, that exchanges information among members who share ideas and dialogue in a relatively informal manner

Panel Group that presents information to an audience through members who share ideas and ask and answer questions informally

Virtual Teams

Many organizations use virtual teams who communicate primarily through the Internet, e-mail, or specially designed software programs. Wally Bock, consultant, author and keynote speaker, says this about virtual teams.

Virtual teams are a great way to bring together people with varying expertise who may be scattered across geography, or maybe separated by the times that they work, or maybe hard to bring together in physical meetings for other reasons.

You can use virtual teams for problem solving, quality assurance, product development, information sharing, and a variety of team-oriented activities—just like in the physical world. We also know that virtual teams can be more innovative than their physical counterparts. But there are some rules you need to follow.

1. There should be a clear purpose and focus. . . .

2. Unless all the participants have worked together before, you'll have to allow for a time when they get to know each other . . . in a physical meeting or virtual ones. . . .

3. Participants on a virtual team need to be aware that there are different kinds of communication rules when communicating online. . . .

With those rules in mind, here are a couple of tools to use with your virtual teams.

Physical meetings—On any kind of long-term project, physical meetings, especially in the early stages, are important to help the team work better.

Virtual meetings are ways to handle specific, narrowly focused issues quickly when folks are separated by geography.

Virtual conferences are effective ways to bring in an expert or to allow one team member to make a presentation to others without having to put them all in the same place. . . .

Copyright 2003 by Wally Bock. Retrieved September 15, 2004 from Wally Bock's extensive Resource Website along with many other articles and resources: http://www.bockinfo.com/

Symposium Formal group session in which each participant gives a speech to an audience, without interaction among group members

Forum Open meeting in which audience makes comments and asks questions

- A **symposium:** A more formal group session in which each participant gives a speech without direct interaction among members, often followed by a panel discussion

- A **forum:** An open meeting where the audience may interact with the group, often following a panel, symposium, or speech

Such group formats are relatively brief events, but the planning group may meet over weeks or months. Whatever a group's goals—to plan an event, develop a product, publicize an idea, build a new church, elect a senator—small work groups and teams *can* become superteams with excellent communication and leadership skills.

Groups, Teams, and Superteams

Group Two or more persons interacting to influence and be influenced by each other

Team Group of people who share an identity and have a mutually defined goal

You're in a **group** if it's two or more people interacting and mutually influencing one another and, if your group is highly motivated, it can become a team. Maybe a great team.

A **team** is more than a group. It is "a diverse group of people who share leadership responsibilities for creating a group identity . . . to achieve a mutually defined goal."[8] A team's identity can depend on its task. An Indianapolis 500 pit crew, for instance, changes tires, fills gas tanks, and makes adjustments on cars with little talk but with split-second timing and accuracy. A creative team at an advertising agency, however, might talk for hours to bring radically different concepts together into one idea that will satisfy the client and appeal to the public. Many factors contribute to the level of development a group might achieve:[9]

1   *Working groups:* Short-term groups (although they may be called "teams" by their organization)

2   *Pseudoteams:* Groups that *could* become teams but are weaker than working groups because their interactions are ineffective and they haven't tried to excel

3   *Potential teams:* Pseudoteams that are trying to improve but need clarity about goals, discipline in working together, and a sense of collective accountability

4   *Real teams:* Teams whose members share commitment and responsibility for their goals and transactions as a team

5   *High-performance teams:* Real teams that *also* share a common concern for one another's personal growth and success

As you see, not every group becomes a team—or needs to—but "every work group can become a work team . . . every work team can become a superior work team,"[10] which some call a **superteam.**[11]

Superteam High-performance team that achieves exceptional results

Effective Team Characteristics

Effective groups and teams develop a unique character and ways of working that are most highly honed when the team becomes a superteam.

Unique Character   Sometimes a group's character is so strong members reflect it even when apart. You can see this in these attributes:

Syntality Personality of the group

- **Syntality:** To a group, what personality is to an individual, but it is far more than the sum of individual members.[12] A given group might reveal a dynamic, aggressive syntality in interaction even though individual

Many tasks are more successful when you use teamwork.

Paul Barton/corbisstockmarket.com

personalities range from pale to vivid. Superteam syntality is strong, unique, and focused.

- *Synergy:* A combination of energy, drives, needs, motives, and vitality of the members. If synergy is low, either little is accomplished or motivated *individuals* do all the work. A superteam has high synergy and members work intensively together, multiplying their effectiveness and reaching their goals with mutual effort.

- *Vision:* A sense of purpose and direction, a "clear and elevating" inspirational quality[13] that expresses deep aspiration and meaningful and memorable themes members find important, if not exciting.[14]

- *Goal orientation:* Members' ability to describe goals they have established in the same terms and keep team focus on the target. Without clear, commonly held goals, members won't continue to devote time and effort to the group. Superteam members commit to team goals, even if they differ from their original preferences, working together to keep on track by continuously asking, "What are we trying to achieve?"

- *Culture and image:* Shared values, beliefs, and a strong identifying self-image; influenced by society, the organization, and members' backgrounds, team culture and image are the group's own. The image may be represented in a name, logo, or symbols, such as "Fly-by-Nites," a Xerox Corporation team that had responsibility for improving the overall quality of overnight air shipments. Their name communicated both their humor and their togetherness as a team.[15]

- **Cohesiveness:** Members' commitment and perception of the group as important, often called "esprit de corps," "groupness," or "team pride." It's a

Cohesiveness The degree to which group members are attracted toward each other and the group

glue holding members together, creating a "one for all and all for one" feeling. Superteams are strongly cohesive and know they're good. In fact, superteams must avoid becoming arrogant or overconfident. It's unbecoming.

Working Relationships   It's in collaborating that a team becomes a superteam, creating relationships that show the following qualities:

- *Commitment* to one another and the team shows in working *with* others rather than for or against them, sharing a "win-win" attitude that achievement of one is to the credit of all. Members respect knowledge, competence, and contributions over status and position, have high expectations of themselves and others, and constantly look for better ways to do things.

- *Diversity seeking*, recruiting and respecting members who vary in gender, ethnicity, background, and expertise, enriches the team with greater insight and better problem-solving strategies and solutions.[16]

- *Communicating openly*, listening and sharing without prejudging or holding back. Superteam members are quick to respond, positive, and optimistic even when things are not going well. They are able to confront people and issues, eliminate roadblocks, and build formal and informal relationships that include people who can be helpful to them.

- *Accountability* is every member's responsibility; it keeps members contributing to the team whether members are apart or together and seeking feedback as a desirable, shared, helpful process for improving their team.

- *Creative and critical thinking*, in distinguishing priorities and choosing flexible, creative, or routine approaches, and taking legitimate risks to achieve significant gains (but carefully analyzing options and potential outcomes before taking action), leads to creative and practical solutions.

Effective Team Developmental Phases

Early observations found that some groups develop through the following five general stages:

1   *Forming.* Members organize and orient themselves to one another and the group.

2   *Storming.* Conflicts—perhaps minor, possibly major—arise.

3   *Norming.* Members develop norms for communication and conflict management.

4   *Performing.* Members complete work, feeling a sense of satisfaction.

5   *Adjourning.* Members end their work and say good-bye.[17]

Midpoint crisis Moment when team members realize that time is half-gone but work is less than half-finished

Groups may vary in these stages, but work groups seem to share one critical turning point: a **midpoint crisis** (also called a "sophomore slump"[18]) when members suddenly realize their time is half-gone but the work isn't half-finished.

Some immediately reassess and refocus their work; some panic, then settle down and get on with it. And some groups even break up but then return, motivated and committed to their goal.[19]

Leaders and Leadership

Must every group have a formally designated leader? No. Does every group need leader*ship* to succeed? Yes. There is an important difference between "leader" and "leadership."

Leadership Verbal and nonverbal communication behavior that influences team processes to achieve goals

Leader Person holding a designated title or position in a group

- **Leadership** is verbal and nonverbal communication behavior that influences a team's processes to achieve members' and the team's needs and goals.[20] Whether there is a designated leader or not, members with leadership skills influence the group because others respect their credibility and responsibility.

- A **leader** is a person holding a designated position. An individual may be elected or appointed as president, chairperson, or department head. These titles imply status and expectation that the person will fulfill specific functions, including providing leadership.

You've often heard people complain because their workplace or government "lacks leadership"—even when there clearly is a manager or an elected official. *"Leader," therefore, describes a title; "leadership" describes behaviors that help the group*. It would be wonderful if all leaders knew how to lead. Leaders are not, however, always the best-qualified individuals. People outside the group or group members themselves may select leaders because of high rank or status, political influence, popularity, or cultural expectations. Japanese, for example, consider age seniority primary for selecting a negotiation team leader.[21]

Emergent leader Person who becomes a leader by helping groups develop effective processes

Frequently, a leader is not appointed or elected, but becomes an **emergent leader** by providing information and leadership that help groups develop effective task and group-building processes. Unfortunately, groups may overlook a good prospect if they judge leader potential by stereotypes of socioeconomic status, education, class, race, culture, age, gender, or special abilities or disabilities. Nye and Forsyth, for example, found that "despite identical performance information for the male and female . . . leaders, some subjects exhibited less liking and expressed less desire to work for female leaders."[22]

Shared Leadership

Shared leadership Group situation in which all members take leadership responsibility

With or without a designated leader, groups are most effective with **shared leadership,** when *all* members take responsibility for leadership. Katzenbach and Smith state that in *every* high-performance team they investigated, "leadership is shared. . . . The leader's role remains, but is mostly ceremonial or for the benefit of outsiders."[23] Gouran points out that many individuals must provide leadership to counteract problems as a group works toward its goal.

When such leadership is absent, groups often make bad decisions and take harmful actions.[24]

When you work in a team, therefore, you can't ignore leadership needs by saying, "Well, *I'm* not the leader." With these obligations in mind, let's examine how you might provide leadership roles in your groups.

Leadership Roles

"She took the role of leader," you might say of someone at a meeting. Or, "He was the secretary," or, "He just had to play the clown."

In groups, as in life, people play roles that help or hinder the transactional processes of building the group and completing its task. You might play several roles in one meeting, depending upon your purposes; experts traditionally divide roles into three categories: group-building, task, and self-interest/blocking.

Group-Building Roles   When you help to manage feelings and create harmony, you're playing **group-building roles** that encourage a sense of groupness, an open climate, and a mutually supportive and cooperative attitude. These roles make members comfortable in offering creative ideas or arguing a point without fear of being judged. Group-building roles help members to think and work together; they empower individuals and, in so doing, empower the team. As you provide group-building leadership, you also demonstrate coorientation and trustworthiness and build your credibility. Here are ways to help build your group:[25]

- *Suggest and encourage positive norms.* Set an expectation of openness, mutual concern, cooperation, and responsibility. Openly state your preference for a supportive climate, and ask for other members' agreement.

- *Encourage each member's involvement.* Ask for information, ideas, opinions, and feelings; support others through agreement or open-ended questions, attentive listening, and verbal and nonverbal confirmation.

- *Encourage trust and openness.* Take a few risks and disclose a little about yourself. Suggest group norms for confidentiality, expect it, and protect others' disclosures.

- *Help manage conflicts.* When conflicts arise, remind the team that conflict is normal and can be helpful; stay objective and find ways to support negotiation and compromise.

- *Make connections.* Help people to support one another; look for things in common and state your appreciation for others' contributions. Encourage open-mindedness and interest in others' points of view.

- *Create a sense of teamness.* Orient discussion toward mutual goals; support team processes, encourage analysis of teamwork, comment on what's working well, and suggest positive improvements.

- *Work actively to deal with team stress.* Acknowledge stressful situations, help diagnose causes of stress, and find ways to relieve it; use humor, "time-out," and negotiation to ease tensions.

Leaders empower others by making them feel significant, helping them to feel their learning and competence are important, making them feel a part of a community, and instilling them with a sense of excitement about their work.

Warren Bennis, a leading American theorist and writer on leadership

---

Group-building roles
Functions that help manage members' feelings and create harmony in the group

---

People in a hurry may feel that group-building roles take time away from getting the task done. Actually, group-building roles make it possible to reach the goal by creating a positive communication climate.

Task Roles   When you help a group agree on its structure, develop flexibility and adaptability, and set clear goals and objectives, you are fulfilling **task roles.** In working through a process of achieving a task, a good team researches and shares information and cooperates in open and creative critical analysis, problem solving, decision making, and task achievement.

Managing group building *and* task achievement can be a bit of a juggling act—but an exciting one to perform. Further, your credibility increases in the eyes of your teammates as they see your competency and objectivity. You will help to achieve task goals if you contribute the following:[26]

Task roles Functions that help a group establish structure, develop flexibility, and set goals and objectives

- *Be sure meetings are organized.* Suggest and confirm meeting arrangements, agendas, records, and assignments. Remind group members when the discussion gets too far off track.

- *Discuss and confirm team goals.* State goals for the team and ask for confirmation that everyone agrees with them.

- *Identify what the team needs for its work.* Ask people to brainstorm needs for information and resources. Help decide how to get what's needed through discussing individual expertise and interests; suggest ways to divide up research and other outside work.

- *Orient the team toward task processes.* Keep discussion on track, summarize what's been done, suggest next steps, and check to see if people agree before moving on.

- *Make sure information is shared.* Ask for, summarize, review, and analyze information. Ask for others' analyses and opinions and bring previously absent members up to date.

- *Provide information and ideas.* Take it on yourself to get good information and explain it clearly to the team.

- *Contribute creativity and critical thinking.* Give ideas and analysis and encourage others to do so, too. Ask questions and make suggestions. Cooperate with others to analyze logic, reasoning, and proposed solutions.

- *Test conclusions for ethicality.* Ask questions that stimulate thinking about how ethically members treat one another. Examine the value and acceptability of all suggestions, decisions, and possible actions.

Whew! No one should be doing all of these all the time—but everyone should be sharing in the leadership by being sure all these roles are fulfilled as the group needs them.

Individual Interest/Blocking Roles   Even in the best of teams, there will be the *aggressor, blocker, recognition seeker, self-confessor, fun seeker, dominator, help seeker, and/or special interest pleader.*[27] You'll know it when you see it.

These **individual interest/blocking roles** can destroy a meeting when a member draws attention away from task or group-building processes to serve his or her own wants or needs.

Of course, there are times to express anger, to be humorous, or to be playful. Something is needed, sometimes, to manage a conflict or relieve tension. Someone who persistently shifts focus away from the issues, however, loses credibility and blocks both group-building and task processes.

Group, task, and individual interest/blocking roles can interact, even within one simple transaction. Darren says, "I'm really tired," and Malia snaps, "Who cares? We've got work to do," a response related to the task, all right, but really an aggressive attack. Of course, the victim will react defensively. This interaction will impede both group building and task performance. Someone must exercise leadership to harmonize the tension and move the task forward.

Principled Leadership

As effective as groups can be, they have their drawbacks. One danger is a group of people may forget to consider what is right or wrong, simply swept away by the desire to conform or by the anonymity of being "just one of the group." It is imperative that each member provides **principled leadership,** asking, "Is this right? Is it ethical?" Not only are there ethical issues about decisions the group might make, but also about your relationships with one another. If it is against your principles to manipulate others to do something that clashes with their values, you might apply that ethic by not allowing yourself or others to manipulate a member of your team.

Larson and LaFasto identify principled leadership as a critical component of outstanding teams,[28] helping members use principled reasoning that raises the quality of members' thinking and potential for better decisions. After working with someone who has provided principled leadership, members tend to use more principled reasoning for themselves.[29] And lest you think ethics are irrelevant to teams in the workplace in this day of disenchanted competition, think again. Some hiring personnel "now are more likely to scrutinize a candidate's reputation and actions through the lens of ethical ideals."[30]

It may take courage to apply your principles, to encourage ethical transactions and decisions. Sometimes others will disagree, even want to override your point. If it's important, don't let it go. You have to live with what your group does after the meeting is over and the anonymity of it is gone.

Designated Leaders

As important as shared leadership is, members may choose to have one specific leader, an organization's bylaws may require one, or a corporation designates a manager as group leader. In such cases, a *designated leader* fills certain functions and faces diverse expectations from members. Let's look at personal qualities and specific tasks expected of designated leaders.

Effective Leader Qualities "She's really good leadership material," says the Girl Scout Leader—or perhaps the boss. What does that mean? It depends on whom you ask, as well as on the task and the group. A study of leaders working in the "global marketplace" lists *flexibility, a sense of humor, patience, resourcefulness, positive regard for others,* and *technical competence* as important.[31] Students in another study wanted *enthusiasm, forcefulness, understanding, supportiveness, intelligence, creativity, friendliness,* and *organization* as qualities of effective leaders.[32] Yet another point of view, Chinese, wished for *interpersonal competence* first, but also emphasized *personal morality, goal efficiency, interpersonal competence,* and *versatility*.[33]

We can condense all these effective leaders' qualities to these:

Credibility. Chapter 2 defines *credibility* as competence, objectivity, trustworthiness, coorientation, and dynamism. These attributes are variously interpreted, however, by different cultures. Take choosing a negotiation leader. North American businesses, for example, look more for technical expertise and less for status or socioeconomic background, compared to Mexican teams, chosen for personal attributes and *palanca* (leverage, connections, "clout"), which may or may not be connected with formal status—in contrast to Japanese, Chinese, French, British, and Saudi Arabian teams, where individual status is a high priority. The Japanese, however, also value knowledge and age, while the French value interpersonal ties and similarities.[34]

Proactivity and preparation. A proactive person reaches beyond the moment and creates opportunities, anticipates, thinks of possibilities and contingencies, plans ahead, and acts. Your proactivity shows when you're prepared, organized, and bring information and ideas. You have already anticipated needs and acted without being asked.

Communication abilities. Leadership relies on communication. Even just being talkative and involved makes others feel that you have the potential to be a leader,[35] but the individual likely to *emerge* as leader also shows self-assurance, directs and summarizes, and orients the group toward the goal.[36] Leaders need to be able to laugh, to think creatively, to play with ideas, to enjoy people, and to get other people to do the same. And these communication abilities all help to build the self-confidence you need to serve as leader.

Effective Leader Responsibilities The contemporary leader is, in a sense, a supermember, working to empower others to reach their goal. One writer defines the best leader as "teamplayer: [one who] unites others toward a shared destiny through sharing information and ideas, empowering others and developing trust."[37] In successful research teams, effective leaders fulfill these responsibilities:[38]

- Speaking and acting as representative of the group
- Maintaining cordial relations and having influence with superiors
- Keeping the group in good standing with higher authorities

Choosing Wise Leaders

Mel Lawrenz, *pastor of Elmbrook Church in Brookfield, Wisconsin, shares the following thoughts on selecting church leaders. Would they apply as well to leadership in other contexts?*

At Elmbrook Church, our council selects new elders when a position is vacated. For years, I have advised the council with one plea. "Please, oh please, find candidates who are wise." Passion and vision are important traits, but wisdom points vision in the right direction and keeps passion pushing in the proper places. . . .

Wisdom gives leaders the authority to lead because it gives followers a reason to trust. . . .

A wise leader . . . will reflect a generosity of spirit, a love for mercy, and the ability to forgive. . . .

Wise people influence by planting seeds in the hearts and minds of others. Wise people are trusted. Their words are deep and sound. . . .

We need leaders who are consistent, stable, and whose personal lives are congruent with their public personas. There needs to be integrity or wholeness to who they are, what they think, and how they act. . . .

From Mel Lawrenz, "Choosing Wise Leaders," Christianitytoday.com. Retrieved August 5, 2004, from http://www.christianitytoday.com/global/printer.html?/le/2002/002/11.89html

- Exhibiting trust by giving team members meaningful levels of responsibility
- Providing team members with the necessary autonomy to achieve results

By any standard, a leader's job is demanding. In addition to the responsibilities just listed, leaders should take responsibility for the following roles:

Developing others' self-leadership. "In many modern situations, the most appropriate leader is one who can lead others to lead themselves."[39] As organizational teams take on more responsibilities, the role of "coach" becomes more critical. At one company, supervisors—now called "team facilitators"—who once spent 10% of their time coaching now *spend 60% coaching and training.*[40]

Even in a class project team, the leader (or members sharing in leadership) can coach by explaining, encouraging, and helping others to assume responsibility for their success. One of our students, using her theater background, coached her class project team in presenting skits that portrayed principles the team had chosen to present for the class. She did a great job, the team did a great job—and they got that A.

Setting standards. People often expect a leader to set standards for both work and ethics of the group. You can lead others to brainstorm and set standards for group and task processes. Express high standards and manage your own behavior to model those standards. Prepare yourself for meetings. Encourage others to bring in information, and set standards for analyzing it effectively. Help to create the image of a team that develops expertise in its area and takes pride in its work. Be willing to take risks that help create a star-quality team.

Ensuring meeting processes. As leader, you also are responsible for making meetings function well. We discuss meeting management shortly.

Leadership Styles

One leader takes it easy, another drives members forward, yet another coaches and coaxes. Leaders use a variety of styles, whether in preaching, teaching, counseling, coaching, managing, or politics. Their style is influenced by culture and/or gender socialization as well as by expectations of the group. Sometimes styles fit into one of these three classic categories:[41]

Laissez-faire leader
Leader who uses a neutral, uninvolved leadership style

Authoritarian leader
Leader who makes all decisions and may use coercion or reward to get results

Democratic leader
Leader who facilitates discussion and shares decision-making power

1 A **laissez-faire leader** uses a neutral, uninvolved style in which the leader simply lets the group do what it wants. This is okay for a team of experts who are comfortable sharing leadership and want to charge ahead. In other circumstances, however, productivity, quality, involvement, and satisfaction decrease.

2 An **authoritarian leader** exerts rigid control, making all decisions, running things by the book, setting schedules, and using coercion or reward to get results. Authoritarian leaders often increase short-term productivity—along with dissatisfaction, aggression, and turnover rates among members.

3 A **democratic leader** maintains an open climate, makes sure everyone's heard, facilitates discussion and decision making, and shares power. Meetings take longer, as members have genuine input, but members are less likely to be absent or leave the group and are more likely to generate good ideas, participate, and be committed to their decisions.

There's no question leaders affect how teams function. One study found that *team citizenship behavior*—that is, team-mindedness, teamwork, altruism, civic virtue, conscientiousness, and courtesy—all relate to the leader's support of the team and emphasis on teamwork and commitment.[42] Likewise, positive feedback strengthens positive feelings about team prestige, competency, and belonging, whereas from negative feedback members perceive more loafing in the group.[43]

Transactional leader
Leader who uses rewards in return for effective performance

Transformational leader Leader who motivates, inspires, and develops members to meet goals

These days, you still see plenty of authoritarian leaders in all venues, but many try for a democratic style, and some strive to be a **transactional leader,** whose style avoids coercion and uses rewards that fulfill members'—or teams'—needs, wants, and values in return for effective performance.[44] Teams pull together better when rewards are for the team as a whole rather than for individuals.

Although these terms probably describe how most leaders actually work, the ideal is to empower groups and individuals to move forward on their own. People who have studied remarkable business leaders talk about the **transformational leader,** the charismatic individual who coaches and advises individuals and teams to provide vision, instill pride, and inspire and stimulate team members to use their own intelligence, rationality, and problem-solving skills.[45] An even higher ideal is the **visionary leader,** who shapes and gains a team's acceptance of a long-term vision—a direction setter, change agent, spokesperson, and coach, a person who leads superteams to success by providing clear and uplifting goals.[46]

But what works with one group won't with another. The answer often is **situational leadership,** using whichever style addresses unique requirements of each group. Fisher notes that leaders "behave differently with different people; they behave differently at different stages of group development; and they behave differently when the task situations differ."[47] A leader may adapt to situations according to the stage the group is in (how self-motivating and directed it is)[48] and the type of task the group must accomplish.[49]

A Group's First Steps

When you start a brand-new group, all of you must figure out how to work together. It's worth taking time to get to know one another and build rapport, as well as to make decisions about leadership and standards.

Getting to Know One Another

A group that meets just once may have only 5 minutes for making connections among members; a team that will meet for weeks (or even months or years) may take an entire meeting or two to lay its foundation. Members need to know something about one another, to identify abilities they can bring to their task, and to discuss their expectations for the experience. Even in a brief meeting, however, you can move the group through a getting-acquainted process this way:

1 *Take the initiative.* Suggest spending a few minutes on introductions. Say something like, "Could we take time to find out something about each other? I think we'll work together better if we do."

2 *Learn—and use—everyone's name.* Attaching a name to a face, after all, is the first step to seeing another person as a distinct individual, and it makes communication more comfortable.

3 *Create dialogue.* Show interest in people, ask questions, disclose a bit about yourself. Start, of course, with basic information, such as where you're from, what you do, and so on.

4 *Identify special strengths* each individual brings to the group, such as access to resources or relevant talents, interests, or experience. Ask something like, "Let's each make a list of what we think we can do for this team."

5 *Share values* and individual feelings that might reflect the importance members attach to the work, their particular needs or wants and expectations

about how the group will interact. Ask questions such as, "What is important about our assignment?" "What will we need to do? What ethical issues will we face?" and, "How will we deal with them?"

6   *State personal agendas.* Members bring their own goals and sometimes bring a **hidden agenda,** individual objectives based on motives the individual would rather not talk about but could affect teamwork. People may not reveal their agendas, but early discussion of individual expectations can create a norm for sharing information that allows members to meet both individual and group needs.

Hidden agenda Team member's personal goals that affect the team's interaction but that the member does not share with the group

Deciding on a Leader

Maybe someone has already appointed a leader for you, maybe not. Do you want to choose one?

Discuss the issue early on and decide whether you want to select a leader immediately or not. If time is crucial and you need someone to take charge, you may want to go ahead and choose a leader. If not, you can take some time to assess individuals' abilities to fulfill leader functions. One who seems like a dynamo right now may turn out to be full of hot air on closer scrutiny. Further, designating one person can make it too easy for a group to dump all responsibility on the leader while they disregard group-building and task leadership needed to develop a real team.

If there is any doubt, we suggest waiting for a few meetings before choosing a leader. Even then, there are alternatives:

Leadership and learning are indispensable to each other.

John F. Kennedy,
American president

- Distribute all leader functions among various members according to their inclinations and talents.
- Distribute some leader responsibilities for specific functions, and share the rest among the entire group.
- Take turns as primary leader according to a specific schedule.
- Wait and allow a leader (or leaders) to emerge as the team works together over time.

Whatever alternative you choose, discuss precisely what the team expects of a leader or of people fulfilling leadership functions. Potentially good teams can fall apart when everyone "just assumes" that others will take care of the agenda, minutes, resources, and so on.

Preparing for Work

Over time, groups develop norms—usual, expected ways of behaving. However, some norms need to be discussed and set at the beginning, such as clear expectations for members' commitment and accountability and regular meeting times and places. You can reassess and modify norms as your group progresses.

How Culture Affects Meeting Planning

People from varying cultures may come to a meeting with very different expectations, as meeting planners have found out. Advice for meeting planners points out that lower-context cultures, which tend to be high-technology, industrialized, and competitive cultures, are likely to follow their agendas rigidly, whereas higher-context members might prepare an agenda—or, preferably, a simple list of items—and change it at the meeting according to their need. Sandra Mumford Fowler, a Washington, D.C., consultant and trainer, says that lower-context folks, such as Germans, would be offended at the idea of changing an agenda. Higher-context people, such as some Asian groups, are more comfortable letting things evolve.

Lower-context cultures also want to begin and end meetings promptly at the scheduled moment, whereas people from higher-context cultures are happy to let the time adapt to the situation. "I was at a meeting in Sweden when an African speaker started telling stories to illustrate his point and went overtime," recalled Margaret Pusch, president of the Intercultural Press in Yarmouth, Maine. "People thought it was so rude."

From R. Reisner, "How Different Cultures Learn," *Meeting News* 27:6 (June 1993), pp. 30–32.

Commitment and Accountability Suppose you've worked hard on your group's task only to have someone say, "Who cares?" or, "I didn't have time." If your group sets standards for commitment and accountability *early*, that will help avoid later problems. As a group, explore the following:

- How much time (per day, per week, per month) can each member reasonably commit to meetings and outside preparation?

- What happens if a member misses a meeting or does not produce work on time?

- How will you deal with unanticipated problems such as illness or a family crisis?

If members have different expectations, conflict is probable. Question one another, understand expectations, and decide on norms. But also, expect the unexpected—set up a system for contacting one another and dealing with crises.

Meetings "I didn't know we had a meeting" or, "I went but nobody was there." You never want to hear these excuses, so your group needs to set up the details at your first meeting.

Meeting times. Share all members' schedules and identify a meeting time. Ask members to put those meeting times on their calendars, but also designate someone to send out reminders.

Meeting places. Consider accessibility, comfort, and available resources—and ambience, too. Someone's home might be most comfortable, for example, but a classroom could provide better access to all members and to the library if it's needed.

Preparing Agendas

Agenda Written plan for a meeting

An **agenda** is simply a written plan to guide the order of discussion for a meeting, but what an important plan it is. Whether formal or informal, a good agenda is vital to an effective meeting. It's designed, ordered, and phrased to identify participants, purposes, issues, and time needs of the meeting. Members need to prepare for meetings, so some groups mandate that they receive an agenda in advance.

Formal and Informal Agendas   Large organizations and committees often use formally structured parliamentary rules such as *Robert's Rules of Order*.[50] Parliamentary rules are designed for democratic groups set up on adversarial, political premises, meaning members try to persuade one another to their side. Without rules and structure, the weakest voices will not be heard, and meetings will be bedlam. Formal, parliamentary agendas usually guide meetings in which there are officers, regular committee reports, and issues or plans to discuss and bring to a vote.

An informal agenda is custom designed for a specific meeting, which could be anything from a short, one-time discussion to a workshop extended over several days. Even a group that meets only once should discuss their agenda. The group needs a road map. Suppose you're meeting with a group of students to plan a class project. You might use an agenda like this:

1   Introduce yourselves.

2   Ask someone to take notes if necessary.

3   Ask someone to lead if necessary.

4   Decide on your goals—what you must accomplish by the end of the meeting.

5   Plan steps to achieve the goal.

6   Get all the information about your task on the table.

7   Analyze the information in terms of the goal.

8   Summarize what you've accomplished.

Although this general agenda must be adapted to your group's task, it provides a checklist to help your group work through its task efficiently.

Formats for Agendas   A team that meets over a period of time needs to design and publish an agenda for each meeting. The wording of a topic can affect the way you think and talk about them. For example:

Topical agendas are brief and to the point. If your sole purpose for meeting is to review and discuss some information, for example, the agenda need only list the order of topics:

1   Review information from the last meeting.

2   Hear Bob's report.

3   Discuss information relating to Dale's proposal.

4   Set up the next meeting.

Discussion question agendas stimulate thinking, guide the order, and kick off discussion, but leave leeway for thinking critically and creatively. Suppose your college task force has created a proposal to solve the parking problem, and this meeting is to evaluate that proposal. You might use a question format:

1   How well does the proposal meet our goals to provide better parking?

2   What are the advantages and disadvantages of the proposal?

3   What are the ethical implications?

4   What are the legal implications?

Managing the Meeting

Members sometimes are shockingly grateful when someone keeps the discussion unpolluted by extraneous issues and helps them move toward the goal. Yet these are probably the easiest skills to learn and to provide for a team.

You can help members avoid compromising the team's objective with political issues and weakening it with extraneous issues by:

Exhibiting personal commitment to the goal

Reminding members to avoid too many priorities

Encouraging fairness and impartiality toward all team members

Encouraging members to confront and resolve inadequate performance by team members

Encouraging openness to new ideas and information from team members[51]

Whether you are designated as leader or a member who shares in leadership, you can guide development of an effective meeting by:

- *Facilitating participation.* Encourage and motivate members to participate. Ask for and give information and ideas.

- *Managing participation.* Make sure everyone gets a chance; keep people from dominating; consider differences and needs of members.

- *Keeping discussion coherent.* Make connections among ideas. Refer, when appropriate, to previous information or to related information from other experiences.

- *Building ideas and analysis.* Synthesize concepts, identify relationships, or find new interpretations or applications of ideas within the discussion topic.

- *Controlling discussion inhibitors.* Try to keep people from sidetracking the discussion, withdrawing, criticizing negatively, or contributing to confusion in the group.[52]

The idea is to draw the best of individual and collaborative effort from the group—to achieve your goals as a "superteam."

Summary

You will need group communication skills in all aspects of your personal life and career. All venues today use group and teamwork. Organizations, including virtual organizations, have learned that groups and teams are often more effective in accomplishing tasks and securing commitment to the goal. Developing group communication as a student helps you to practice and demonstrate leadership abilities that employers want. The ideal is for your work groups to evolve into teams and then into superteams—highly committed, collaborative groups characterized by clear vision, firm goals, excellent communication, and solid teamwork. Members develop a team culture and image as they move through developmental phases and face midpoint crises.

In effective teams, all members share leadership responsibility by fulfilling roles that build the group and accomplish its tasks. Leaders are appointed, elected, or emerge as leaders because of their contributions to the team. Good leaders are credible, adaptable, proactive, prepared, and effective communicators.

Leadership styles vary from classic laissez-faire, authoritarian, or democratic guidance of group processes to more inclusive approaches such as transactional, transformational, or visionary leadership that seek to empower team members. Leaders often must adapt their styles to situational contingencies revolving around circumstances, tasks, purposes, or members.

Getting a good team started requires getting to know one another, deciding whether to choose a leader immediately, and setting standards and procedures for work, including personal commitments, accountability, and meeting times and places. The group should prepare and distribute an agenda prior to a meeting and modify it at the beginning of the meeting as needed.

Exercises

1   To assess your leadership skills, complete Form 10.1 in Cyberpoint 2 (see Cyberpoints following). Then make an additional copy of Form 10.1 and ask a friend to rate your leadership behavior on that copy.

Discuss the completed forms with your friend. What does your friend see that you do not? How can you use that feedback? List your strengths and the skills you'd like to develop.

2   Select one behavior from the leadership survey (see results from Form 10.1 used in Exercise 1 and Cyberpoint 2) that you would like to use more often (for example, *summarizing issues for the group*). For a couple of weeks,

consciously use the new behavior in group meetings or in classes. Keep a journal of how you use the behavior, how you think it affected the group, and how you feel about expanding your repertoire of group behaviors in this way. When you feel comfortable with this new skill, select another one and use the same process to develop it.

3   The student organization has appointed a new committee to consider requests for funds made by student groups. The committee is meeting for the first time. A portion of some of the committee's discussion is shown here. In a small group, discuss this meeting and then respond to the questions following it. Report your findings to the class.

Chris (the chairperson): Let's get this over with, I've got a date in 10 minutes. We've got five requests here. I think the first one's legitimate. How many are in favor of it?

Sue: Whoa, I don't even have a copy of these requests. What are they?

Chris: Oh. Well, this one is from the Spanish Club and they want $100 to help with their banquet.

Shawn: Are there other ethnic clubs who want money, too?

Chris: I don't know. Let's see—here's the Irish Club. They want money for the St. Patrick's Day parade in the city. And here's one from . . . who cares? Let's just go through and decide. . . .

Nicola: Wait, wait . . . how much money do we have to allocate? Are there any policies about how we decide?

Sue: What other requests are there?

Shawn: Is this the whole committee? I don't know any of you . . . and who else should be here?

Chris: I have to go in 5 minutes. Can we just say these are all granted?

- What is happening with the leadership in this group? Who's the leader? Who is trying to provide leadership? What could be done to improve it?

- Will this group become a team? Can it become a superteam? Why or why not? Think of the characteristics of a group versus a team versus a superteam. How does this group fit right now?

- What should have happened at the outset? What could happen now to make this group work more effectively?

4   Think of a group to which you currently belong (social, religious, school—whatever). Create an agenda for the next meeting of your group using what you learned about the issues described in this chapter for good agendas. Then make a short presentation to the class in which you describe your group, its goals, and the agenda you have designed for the meeting. Explain why you chose the type of agenda and the order of items that you did for this group. Explain how your group might benefit if they were to follow the agenda you created.

Cyberpoints

The following Cyberpoints can be easily accessed from the Student Companion website for this text at http://academic.cengage.com/communication/lumsdenccc3. Click on *Student Book Companion Site* and select this chapter from the pull-down menu at the top of the page that says "Select a chapter." Click on *Cyperpoints* under *Chapter Resources* and you will find links for the exercises following.

1   Use the InfoTrac College Edition and the keyword *leader* to locate current articles about leading and leadership. Choose three articles to review. How do these articles relate to the leadership information in this chapter?

2   Go to the *Communicating with Credibility and Confidence* website at http://academic.cengage.com/communication/lumsdenccc3. Measure your leadership skills by clicking on *Form 10.1, Self-Assessment of Leadership*. What do you think you do well? Which skills can you improve to help a group or team experience be more effective and less frustrating? What steps can you take at your next group meeting?

3   How can groups help foster personal development? Access one of these websites to see how some groups provide support for people: http:www .alcoholics-anonymous.org; http://www.overeatersanonymous.org; or http://www.emotionsanonymous.org. After visiting and browsing each site, consider and record concepts of group dynamics and communication from this chapter that are used by these groups to promote personal growth.

4   Are you a transformational leader? Use Infotrac College Edition to search the key terms: *transformational leadership*. Browse the articles to find one that will help you understand more about what transformational leadership is and how you can apply it in a group. Record your answers to the following questions:

- What is transformational leadership?
- What are the benefits of transformational leadership for a small group?
- How can you apply transformational leadership in your next group meeting?

Chapter 11

Problem Analysis and Decision Making: Achieving Group and Team Goals

Objectives for This Chapter

Knowledge

- Understand the functions of goal setting for decision-making groups
- Know steps in a decision-making sequence
- Identify criteria for analyzing possible solutions and instilling confidence in team decisions

Feelings and Approaches

- Value thorough vigilance in decision making
- Want to be vigilant in problem-analysis and decision-making activities
- Appreciate the value of group approaches to decision making
- Feel confident about using group problem-analysis and decision-making processes

Communication Abilities

- Be a credible communicator in group problem-analysis and decision-making situations
- Guide your group through decision-making tasks
- Apply critical and creative thinking in group problem analysis and decision making
- Use analysis tools and techniques when investigating problems and possible solutions
- Recognize and minimize groupthink conditions in decision-making groups

Key Terms

group goals	applicability	risk
charge	practicality	desirability
instrumental objectives	advantages	consensus
brainstorming	disadvantages	groupthink

"**N**ow, what did that meeting accomplish, besides taking an hour of my life?" No doubt you'd rather not leave a meeting feeling like this, but we'll bet it's happened. Perhaps it's happened at meeting after meeting when a group *could* have become a real team but never quite made it. It's possible to *develop* a group into a team, through identifying goals, finding needed information, systematically selecting a solution—and using vigilance to avert problems that can destroy your decision-making effectiveness.

Identifying Your Team's Goals

Group goals Results that a team has been assembled to achieve

A team project is like taking a trip—you need to know where you're going to know if you've arrived. Like planning that trip, a team needs to identify **group goals** early to clarify its destination and develop a *plan* for working toward it. You start with why the team was created and what it's meant to do.

Identifying Purposes

You may belong to many groups—social, religious, service—but when a team is gathered by an organization, it's usually to do one of the following:

■ *Information gathering*. Research and investigate a specific problem or issue and prepare a report, often as a first step toward other purposes.

■ *Problem analysis*. Investigate, report, and perhaps make recommendations about scope, causes, and impact of a problem. A university problem-analysis team might focus on anything from parking to plagiarism.

■ *Decision making*. Gather information and use problem-analysis processes to make decisions.

■ *Implementation* might be up to the same team or it might go on to another team. A corporation's quality teams, for example, might "identify areas that can be improved and implement changes to improve them." Such teams might be responsible for their ideas from creation through implementation and assessment.

Technology meets human interaction: Two groups of people, meeting at different places, can interact via videoconferencing that allows them to talk, to see one another, and to study the information they need to make good decisions—all without leaving their workplace.

Jon Feingarsh/corbistockmarket.com

Defining Goals

Those who created your team presumably gave you a task description or assignment called the **charge,** which may or may not be specific. Your student government committee, for example, might be charged to "look into the problem of low involvement in student activities." At work, you might be assigned to a task force with the vague charge to "improve community relationships."

Charge Task or assignment that defines the purpose of a team

These charges are so general the team must define them more specifically. After an initial discussion, the team needs to ask its founder, "This is what we think we should do; is that what you want?" Then you write a goal statement, in clear, unambiguous terms, of *what* will be done, *who* will do it, *when* it will be accomplished, and what the *criteria* for success are. A goal statement for a written report might be:

- *Major goal.* On October 1 (*when*), the Community Relations Task Force (*who*) will present to Ms. Fernandez, Director of Community Relations, a written report on the investigation and recommendations on Community Relations (*what*).

- *Criteria.* The report will be approximately 20 pages, complete, well written and documented, and professionally prepared.

Instrumental objectives The lesser tasks that lead to achieving a team's goal

To move from a goal statement to final results, the team identifies **instrumental objectives,** all those smaller tasks essential to reaching the ultimate goal. Identifying instrumental objectives and planning how to reach them forms a blueprint for achieving major goals. For example:

1 Major goal: Written report

2 Major goal: Oral report

3 Instrumental objective: Get information on current relationships between the company and community

4   Instrumental objective: Get information on what citizens see as a helpful corporate role

5   Instrumental objective: Design and suggest ideas for what your company can do

6   Instrumental objective: Write and edit report

7   Instrumental objective: Plan and rehearse oral presentation

You now have two major goals with five instrumental objectives: two information-gathering tasks (3 and 4), one problem-analysis, idea-generating task (5), and two report-preparation tasks (6 and 7). Each instrumental objective moves toward your major goals (1 and 2), and each may also require still smaller steps. For example, to find out what current relationships are, other tasks might include designing a survey, surveying local organizations and institutions, and analyzing survey results. Each instrumental objective should be constructed just as carefully as final goal statements, with clear terms and criteria for achievement.

If you set clear goals and instrumental objectives at the outset, you can save a lot of trouble later. You may need to clarify, alter, expand, or reduce some of your goals as you go along, but at least you know what you're trying to do and how to go about it. We've seen, for example, a team carefully research, design, and duplicate a survey—and then discover they should have gotten the institution's permission to distribute it. What a terrible waste of time, energy, and money.

Understanding and Committing to Goals

Often, members think they are in agreement and then find out they don't understand one another at all. You can reduce confusion by confirming what people intend by their goals. These communication techniques can really help:

1   *Paraphrase stated goals and discuss whether the paraphrase is accurate and complete.* If discussion unearths differences you didn't know were there, you can fix the problem early.

2   *Hypothesize interpretations, examples, or applications for the goals.* Someone might say, "When we say 'well documented,' does that mean an annotated bibliography?" Another member might say, "Good grief, no! I thought we'd just list any sources we used!"

This process helps the team negotiate mutual understandings of goals and objectives. Still, the team's effectiveness is diminished if some work hard for those ends and others do not, so the team still may need to negotiate members' commitment to the goals, both by asking members to commit and by building norms for full involvement as you go along. One method is *census taking*, asking each member's position—in this case to what extent she or he can take responsibility for achieving these goals. Individuals vary in ability to commit, and you'll never have a total match among members, but you do want to be sure everyone's in the same boat, rowing at approximately the same pace.

Gathering Information

The first breakthrough in corporate and public cooperation to achieve socially responsible ends occurred when McDonald's Corporation and the Environmental Defense Fund (EDF) joined forces. They assembled a task force of representatives from both organizations to propose ways to reduce waste and increase recycling in McDonald's restaurants. Each organization's members had extensive expertise in their field, which they enlarged by consulting books and materials to gain information about the other organization.

McDonald's brought in experts from various departments to explain corporate issues; EDF staff, as well as experts from other environmental organizations, provided background on issues beyond solid waste. In addition, EDF team members spent numerous hours in various McDonald's restaurants to understand operations. Each EDF member worked a day in a restaurant . . . and the team toured facilities of two McDonald's food suppliers, five packaging suppliers, and one of McDonald's largest distribution centers as well as a polystyrene recycling facility and a composting facility. Most visits included tours, formal presentations, and extensive question and answer sessions with top management and technical experts.

The end result was a collaboratively developed task force report from which McDonald's adopted every proposal to "reuse, reduce, and recycle" waste. This effort introduced a new method for solving problems through cooperative forces and a new standard for achieving both corporate success and socially responsible behavior.

From Environmental Defense Fund/McDonald's Corporation Task Force Report, 1991, p. iv. Used by permission.

Planning Your Team's Inquiry

There is a lot of work between setting goals and achieving them—and often that work falls into four broad phases identified by Herbert Simon: intelligence, design, choice, and review.[1] We'll talk about intelligence (meaning information) here, and then we'll discuss the other parts as they fit into the rest of the chapter.

Information: What, Where, and How to Get It

As Hirokawa and Scheerhorn write, "A group's information base is directly or indirectly tied to all phases of the decision-making process. Therefore, any errors occurring within the base are likely to contribute to faulty decision-making."[2]

Your team's immediate job, then, is to figure out the kind of information you need to reach your instrumental objectives and end goals. Make an open-ended list of things you need to get. Then consider who should get what.

Figure 11.1 *Re-search assignment worksheet format*

Research Planning Form				
What information is needed?	Resource location	Reporting format	Possible resources	Date needed

You can start by finding out what expertise members may have, what they know, what can they do, and how they can contribute to your team's goals. From that, you can plan a strategy for getting other information you will need. The team may need specific research, using public resources such as print and media materials in libraries, public offices, museums, and archives, computerized databases and indexes, or interviews with experts on the topic.

Now what? This is where many teams slip up. Everybody gets an assignment; half of the people do it, half don't. Of the half who do it, half do it halfway. The team winds up lacking information it needs, drastically undermining its effectiveness.

Before anyone leaves the meeting room, do these things:

1 Determine who will do what, set deadlines, and establish guidelines for reporting information to the team. First, divide responsibilities. Consider each person's talents, interests, contacts, and time—but also equity and balance in getting the work done. Then assign appropriate tasks to each member.

2 Create a work plan: a complete list of assignments including *who, what, when,* and, if you're working in subgroups, *with whom.* Calculate time for research, discussion, and planning, and leave a bit of time for the unexpected. Set deadlines for completing each piece and for progress reports. A form such as the one in Figure 11.1 helps create your work plan covering all responsibilities and deadlines. Give everyone a copy.

3 Set guidelines for documentation. They can be simple, just so everyone gets full documentation for sources (author, date, title of article, title of book or journal, edition, publisher, page numbers). Not only does documentation show both you and your source are credible, but it also ensures that if you need to go back for further information, you'll know where to find it.

Each member's report should include brief, concise handouts clearly summarizing critical information, including glossaries for new terms. If members run across information that could be useful for someone else's assignment, copy it for the other person or provide a full bibliographic citation and where to locate the resource.

Information: How to Share and Analyze It

The team may have a mile-high stack of data, but sharing it is important. Everyone needs to understand it. First, if there is a change in membership, the team can pick up the threads and weave the work back together more easily. Second, sharing information helps achieve goals and develops team vision and cohesiveness. And third, the process vitalizes and focuses team synergy. Sharing information effectively is one of the ways you become a superteam. So that may well be the sole agenda for some meetings. *All* members need to understand *all* information to analyze it, draw conclusions, and apply it to the goals. This requires allowing time for feedback and questions.

A report to your team, like any other presentation, should be well organized and presented interestingly and directly, with clear and credible data and good visual aids. (You'll find a lot more on presentations in the next four chapters.)

Remember to keep everyone's attention focused on the ideas. It's a big help to post information—that is, use visual displays so everyone else can see the data while you talk about it. You can present information visually with PowerPoint, handouts, overhead projectors, or flipcharts to show data or relationships among ideas so everyone can focus on information and recall it.

Making Team Decisions Systematically

Watch out when a group just shrugs and jumps at a decision—it isn't likely to be a good one. The degree to which members are *vigilant* about the quality of their decisions is the degree to which they will be successful. Vigilant critical thinking and analysis proceed through a series of smaller decisions in examining the problem, clarifying objectives, developing available choices, and examining potential consequences.[3]

These activities, combined with Simon's four-stage decision-making process mentioned earlier (intelligence, design, choice, review) and reflective thinking stages identified by John Dewey[4] many years ago, provide useful strategies for work plans and meetings.

> *All decisions are made about imaginary worlds.*
>
> Kenneth Boulding, 20th-century philosopher

1 Analyze the problem.

2 Collect and analyze information.

3 Establish criteria for solutions.

4 List possible solutions.

5 Evaluate possible solutions.

6 Decide on the most appropriate solution(s).

7 Implement the decision.

8 Evaluate the effectiveness of the decision.

These tasks may provide the agenda for a single meeting if the goal is relatively simple, or they may guide a team's work over a period of months or even years. Because problem solving is so detailed, however, and because team decision making does not always occur in this order, agendas may be modified considerably as meetings move along. Teams often overlap the tasks, loop back, and jump forward in vigilant analysis and achievement.

A systematic plan doesn't *guarantee* clear thinking. As you move through decision making, you might use **brainstorming** to create multiple perspectives and options. Brainstorming helps produce more ideas to improve your chances of making the highest-quality choices.

The best way to brainstorm is with a group, so you get a lot of ideas from diverse sources, but you can use the same process alone. The goal is to think of as many ideas as you can, noting them as you go. Reach to the outer limits for wild and crazy thoughts. Look at the problem from every angle. Here are some guidelines:

1   Appoint someone to facilitate if you're in a group.

2   Don't stop to evaluate ideas.

3   Keep the flow of ideas moving fast.

4   Write down as many ideas as you can.

5   Do not "own" ideas, good or bad—keep egos out.

6   "Piggyback" or "hitchhike" ideas onto previous thoughts.

7   Sweat out silences and plateaus; sit quietly and let your brain incubate until something emerges.

8   After many ideas are on the list, analyze and winnow them down.

9   Start serious selection from the remaining possibilities.

Try it. You'll discover ideas you didn't dream you could have.

Analyzing Problems

Dewey[5] states that feeling a difficulty is the first step in problem exploration. You perceive something is wrong. What then?

The first task is to move from intuitions about difficulties to identifying the nature and scope of specific problems. The team must ask questions, gather information, and think analytically, critically, and creatively to identify problems and find their causes and effects.

Problem Identification   Identifying problems is not as easy as it sounds. From knowing there's a problem you explore the general area of concern to find trouble spots. Then you start isolating problems by tracking them. You analyze how things presently *are* functioning and compare that with the ways things *should* work.

Assume you have been appointed to a college task force charged with improving registration procedures. First, your team might track the registration process as staff and students actually experience it. To identify issues, you could create a step-by-step flowchart of process and problem spots. A flowchart can

---

Brainstorming Process of generating solutions by thinking of as many ideas as possible without constraint

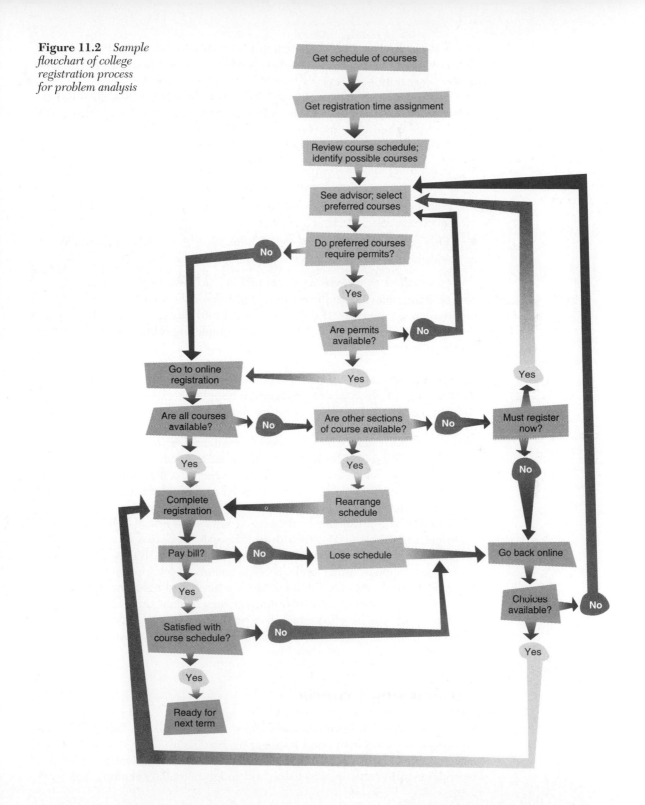

Figure 11.2 *Sample flowchart of college registration process for problem analysis*

be used at any stage of information sharing or problem solving, but it is particularly useful for identifying problems. Figure 11.2 shows a flowchart of one university's registration process.

Next, compare your flowchart to registration procedures described in university policies and procedures. This will aid in identifying possible problem areas in the process and isolating policies that need more careful examination. Your analysis can begin by seeking answers to some of these questions:

- What difficulties are people experiencing? Where are bottlenecks? At what points are many people encountering obstacles?

- What harms are being done? What is the scope of the problem? How many people are affected? How seriously?

- What conditions are relevant to the difficulties? Are policies, procedures, objectives, or criteria missing or inappropriately applied?

As you start to analyze registration problems, you might detect patterns. One difficulty may be insufficient classes at times convenient for students. The negative results are clear: If students can't get into classes or must take them at inconvenient times, they may have trouble completing requirements or getting course prerequisites.

Causes and Effects   As you track problems you'll see possible causes. If you don't identify causes correctly, though, you're not going to solve the problem—and you may create new ones. But it can be difficult to determine if one factor causes a problem or just happens to occur at the same time, another symptom rather than the cause. Chapter 3 develops guidelines for logical cause-effect reasoning, which should be applied in your team's problem analysis.

Some teams find a fishbone diagram, created on a flipchart or large board with all members participating, helps identify, track, analyze, and visualize multiple cause-effect relationships.[6] See Figure 11.3 for an example.

You construct a fishbone by drawing a long line—vertical or horizontal—to represent the problem. You then draw diagonal lines—like fish ribs—off the problem line, labeled with issues relating to the problem. Figure 11.3 shows a registration fishbone listing students, departments, resources, and methods as potential components of registration. Shorter horizontal lines drawn off the diagonal lines are labeled with subordinate issues or categories affecting larger problems. Now you have a diagram showing relationships among issues pertaining to the problem. The fishbone doesn't solve problems or prove causes, but it might clarify relationships among issues.

Establishing Criteria

Problem solvers and decision makers make a huge mistake in failing to decide on criteria for a solution—and it's amazing how many make this mistake. To make quality choices you have to know what you want the solution to be like. *Criteria* are standards by which you will judge potential solutions. You can't

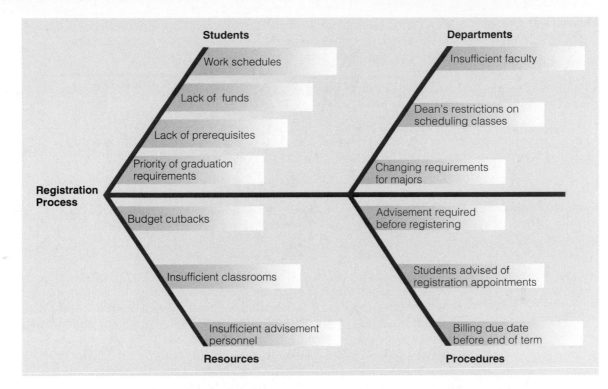

Figure 11.3 *Sample fishbone analysis of registration process to identify problems' causes and effects*

assume you'll "know it when you see it." You might not. Establishing clear criteria is extremely important to your success.

To set criteria, first brainstorm a list of what conditions would be like with the perfect solution. If your task is to create a class project, for example, criteria will include meeting assignment requirements plus acquiring learning and grades as well as conditions that you, as a team, have decided to include in your project. For example, suppose you're on a creative team for a film-making class. Your criteria for an "ideal" project could look like this:

- Be original and unique.
- Involve each member in a specific role.
- Deal with a controversial or timely topic.
- Demonstrate skill in each area listed on the syllabus.
- Write a good script.
- Use graphics effectively.
- Cut and edit smoothly.
- Achieve demonstration quality for each member's portfolio.
- Have fun.
- Earn an A for each member.

Figure 11.4 *Sample T-chart for analysis of one solution to registration problems*

PROPOSAL: Offer additional sections of "high demand" courses	
PROS	**CONS**
Makes more sections available	Requires more faculty
Schedule flexibility allows for more employment opportunities	Requires more classroom space
Will speed up registration process	May reduce enrollment in other courses, leaving faculty without students

I have a few ideas. Together with yours, we may have something.

Max DePree, corporate founder, developer, CEO, and author

As you might surmise, some criteria are dictated by the assignment, but some are produced by the team's thinking about what will make a good film. Probably, this team would add and subtract criteria according to possible projects they might do.

Once you've drafted criteria, try to visualize what things would be like with a solution that meets those criteria. Members need to share a team vision—a mental picture of what that final result will be like, how it will feel, what it will provide. As you visualize and discuss the ideal solution together, you clarify any misunderstandings or assumptions that could cause problems later on. Further, the vision you hold in common motivates members to achieve it.

Finally, and very importantly, *record your criteria* clearly and unambiguously and post them in big print on a flipchart so you can check potential solutions against each criterion.

Generating Possible Solutions

You've analyzed and documented a problem's causes, effects, and seriousness. If that's all your team is to do, fine (though you probably still have to submit a report to someone). But if you are to propose a solution, you need to start by generating possible solutions, and this takes time, energy, and dedication. It takes teamwork and creative thinking from all members to gather every imaginable solution. Use brainstorming to get as many ideas as possible on the table. Don't be afraid to get silly, and don't evaluate ideas yet. You want quantity now; later, you'll evaluate the quality of the ideas.

Then, when your team has a list of criteria and possible solutions, you're ready to make decisions. The best may just jump out at you, but if you diagram each visually, the team can apply criteria and compare ideas. One useful technique is to prepare large charts of solution options and criteria—on flipcharts, whiteboard, or taped-up butcher's paper.

Figure 11.5 *Decision matrix for comparing possible solutions*

Possible Solutions	Criterion #1: Reduce waiting	Criterion #2: Use classroom space efficiently	Criterion #3: Have students get classes when needed
Register by phone	Shorten wait Etc.	No effect Etc.	Immediate confirmation Etc.
Register online	No waiting Etc.	Yes—rooms assigned after all requests in Etc.	Little control over 2nd and 3rd choices Etc.
Register without advisors	Less wait, but reduces personal attention Etc.	No effect Etc.	Negative impact— may take wrong courses Etc.

Analysis Tools   Here are two ways to visualize and analyze possible solutions that can help your team make a good decision.

1   *T-chart.* To keep everyone focused on one solution, try a T-chart (also useful in making personal decisions). On a large sheet of paper or blackboard, draw a T, with a line down the middle and a bar across the top; label one side "Pros" and the other "Cons." As members discuss one solution, record them in the appropriate column. Figure 11.4 shows a sample T-chart for one possible solution for registration problems.

2   *Decision matrix.* For comparing several solutions, a decision matrix lays out information and jogs members' memories. As Figure 11.5 shows, a decision matrix is simply a large grid. Across the top, you label each column with one criterion for the ideal solution. Down the left-hand side, you label each row for one solution. Then, as a team, you fill in each cell with notes as to how each plan meets each criterion. When you've completed the grid, you have a concise, easily comprehended set of comparisons for the proposals.

You've got a clear, visual representation of how solutions compare; now what? Now your team can start examining critical issues by focusing on each solution's applicability, practicality, advantages versus disadvantages and risks, and desirability or ethicality.

Applicability How well a solution meets the criteria for solving a problem

Applicability   Different solutions have varying levels of **applicability,** that is, how well they may meet your criteria. You could consider:

- Will the proposed solution solve the entire problem?
- If a proposal solves only part of the problem, how significant is that part?
- How does the idea compare to others on goal achievement?

Suppose your service club needs $500 to buy holiday gifts for needy kids. You've brainstormed solutions, including a bake sale. Somebody will have to bake a lot of cookies for *that* solution to earn $500. A bake sale is inadequate and doesn't meet criteria, so your team will either eliminate that solution or combine it with other possibilities.

Practicality Sticky issues of **practicality** can prevent a solution from being implemented successfully. Before you decide, consider these practical questions:

Practicality The likelihood that a solution to a problem can be implemented successfully

- How much time and money will it take, and will they be available?
- What kinds of support (perhaps from other teams, agencies, parent organizations, individuals) will be needed to implement the idea?
- What kinds of barriers will have to be overcome?
- Will it be possible to sell the idea to those who will implement it?

If any of these issues are significant barriers, then *that* solution can't be implemented. You might, however, see ways to adapt a proposal to solve practical issues—just be sure that the adapted proposal is superior to other plans.

Advantages Positive effects of a solution to a problem

Disadvantages Negative consequences of a solution to a problem

Advantages, Disadvantages, and Risks Once you've decided a solution will work, the next issue is implementation. In practice, would this plan yield extra advantages—or disadvantages or risks. To identify both **advantages** and **disadvantages,** consider what could occur with implementation. For example:

- How might the implemented solution affect *other* individuals or groups?
- Would advantages flow automatically from implementation or require some other action?
- Would some minor modification eliminate some disadvantages?
- How do advantages and disadvantages weigh against each other?
- How do advantages and disadvantages weigh against those of other proposed solutions?

Risk Potential gains of solving a problem weighted against potential losses

In addition to revealing advantages and disadvantages, these questions might also highlight **risks,** potential gains that you weigh against possible adverse consequences, such as cost, damage, or even failure. Any innovative and potentially successful idea involves some risk, because, by definition, a new idea isn't proven by long experience. It necessarily carries the possibility of failure. Without risk taking, however, there would be no new ideas, no progress, no exciting possibilities. The reality is, people must weigh risks and make the most informed choices they can.

Desirability No matter how perfect a proposed solution may seem—applicable, practical, low risk, and advantageous—it may rise or fall on its desirability. Desirability is a value judgment of a potential solution. That is, you evaluate probable outcomes by weighing them against your team's values and ethics. How valuable and how worthwhile will the plan be?

Once, in a notorious incident, an automobile manufacturer considered, and rejected, recalling a model because the number of people *killed* due to its safety defect was not enough to justify the *expense* of recalling the cars. Management's cost-benefit analysis weighed potential profit against people's lives, and profit won. How many deaths would have been needed to tip the scale?

As your team looks at its proposals, ask:

- How desirable are probable effects of the proposal?

- Will the implemented proposal serve the team's vision?

- Will the proposal harm anyone spiritually, psychologically, physically, economically, and/or socially?

- Is any team member uncomfortable with the ethics of the proposal?

As you discuss ethical issues, you will find some answers are easy. "No, that's against our values," or, "Yes, that's ethically acceptable." But some issues are not simple at all; they may present a dilemma when choices are among competing people and competing values.[7] You have an ethical dilemma, for example, when one team member believes a specific solution is unethical while another's values are violated by the only other practical alternative. How do you handle these competing values? First, team members must recognize that a dilemma exists by listening to and analyzing one another's ideas. Then, they must discuss issues and try to reach a consensus. Sometimes, resolving dilemmas requires a more objective outsider to facilitate the discussion.

Analysis starts with identifying precisely where the issues are. As Jaksa and Pritchard point out, "Seeking exact points of difference can help solve disagreements by eliminating false distinctions and evasions."[8] Don't brush the dilemma off with "Everyone's entitled to an opinion," or, "Value judgments are subjective." That might bring discussion to a quick end, but although these statements seem to express an attitude of tolerance, they also suggest you do not have much to learn from one another.

Gouran[9] suggests five questions for examining ethics of both its decisions and processes:

1   Did we show proper concern for those who will be affected by our decision?

2   Did we explore the discussion question as responsibly as we were capable of doing?

3   Did we misrepresent any position or misuse any source of information?

4   Did we say or do anything that might have unnecessarily diminished any participant's sense of self-worth?

5   Was everyone in the team shown the respect due him or her?

Decision Modes

A team could go on analyzing alternatives indefinitely, but at some point it must decide. Take time to be sure any second thoughts are discussed, then choose a method of decision. All too often, groups make "twofer" decisions: two people speak for a decision—and silence from other members is interpreted as consent. Twofer decisions lead to disgruntlement and lack of commitment. Better modes include decision by consensus, voting, and even decision by authority.

Consensus decisions.   Theoretically, consensus represents full agreement of all members. Actually, **consensus** is a sufficient degree of agreement by all members achieved through intensive discussion and negotiation. Individualistic North Americans are trying hard to learn consensus techniques of the Japanese because they work so well. Japanese teams typically hammer out decisions in exhaustive round-the-clock discussion until everyone agrees—a harrowing process, but once consensus is reached, decisions move swiftly with full support of all concerned. Striving for consensus is worth the effort, even if a final decision requires another method. A team that achieves a high degree of consensus develops stronger commitment to its decisions and is more likely to follow through than a team that does not.

Voting.   When time constraints or strong disagreements prevent consensus, voting is an option. Many people prefer voting as a quick and easy method to decide between alternatives. If discussion has been thorough, and all individuals have had opportunity to express their ideas and feelings, most people will accept a majority decision. Much too frequently, however, a vote is a cop-out, a lazy way of pushing to a conclusion without vigilant and vigorous problem analysis. Voting is quicker, but it leaves more people dissatisfied and results in less cooperation down the road than does a consensus decision.

Decision by authority.   In some cases, a team's job is to conduct inquiry, think critically and creatively and make recommendations. Deciding is up to someone with higher status, perhaps a manager, executive committee, or president of an organization.

Creating Implementation Plans

Teams often have superb ideas, but when plans are put into action, overlooked details keep them from working. Successful implementation of an idea requires a carefully developed plan and a mental picture of the final product. We suggest the following steps for developing your plan:

1   *Brainstorm a checklist.* Include everything that must be done to implement the proposal. Use the formula "who does what, when, where, how, and from what resources."

2   *Divide the checklist into categories.* For example:

- Resources needed: Money, information, technological support, permissions and cooperation from authorities, agencies, and organizations

- Actions that must be taken, such as making contacts, acquiring equipment and materials, applying for permissions or licenses, and perhaps arrangements for space and/or media.

- Instrumental objectives for each action, step by step

- Person(s) responsible for each action

- Time required for each step

3 *Decide precisely who is responsible for completing each step.* Be specific, make sure each member commits to his or her responsibilities, put the list in writing, and make sure everyone has a copy. When you have implementation meetings, go over the checklist to see if things are being done and if revisions are necessary. Humans have a touching faith in their memories; unfortunately, it is often unjustified. No matter how many previous times a flight crew has flown a Boeing 747, we expect them to scrupulously review the flight safety checklist each time we are on board.

4 *Plan how to evaluate the proposal.* You will need objective, systematic feedback to know how well the solution works. Evaluations could include questionnaires and surveys directed to people affected by your plan and assessments by objective, expert observers.

Ensuring Open Group Process

None of this works if people can't communicate openly, cooperatively, and vigilantly. In Chapters 7 and 9, we discussed managing conflicts and game playing—skills teams need frequently. There can be other problems as well.

Even the best of teams can slide into what Janis calls **groupthink:** "a mode of thinking that people engage in when they are deeply involved in a cohesive group, when members' striving for unanimity overrides their motivation to realistically appraise alternative courses of action. . . . Groupthink refers to a deterioration of mental efficiency, reality testing, and moral judgment that results from in-group pressures."[10] Groupthink is a kind of mindlessness, or perhaps single-mindedness, that blinds team members to everything except what they assume and/or want to be true.

When the space shuttle *Challenger* exploded just after takeoff, people were thunderstruck and wondered how this tragedy could have happened. With inquiry, it became painfully obvious that information about a possible defect in an O-ring had been available, but decision makers were shielded from analysis that might have delayed the blast-off to correct that fatal flaw.

These decision makers were far from stupid, but groupthink swept them into a bad decision. The entire crew died as a result. Groupthink undermines credibility and causes bad decisions. Teams need to know how groupthink happens, how decisions are affected, and how to prevent it.

How Groupthink Happens

Groupthink can grow from previous team experiences or "antecedent conditions" such as structure and situation in which the team functions.[11] For example:

Cohesiveness. Cohesiveness is characteristic of superteams, yet cohesiveness can block good decisions if members protect it with an unwritten "group harmony rule" that silences dissenting members so problems are not discussed.[12]

Structure. Structural conditions, such as homogeneity, inadequate group processes, and insulation from the outside world, can instill groupthink in decision making. Without diversity, homogeneous members tend to think in narrow channels. Without vigilant decision-making processes, teams shortcut critical thinking steps and impartial, principled leadership that could encourage members' openness to ideas and dissent. Insulation from outside information leaves members unaware of data and perspectives that might affect their decisions.

Situation. Situational stress can pressure a team into groupthink. Members are more likely to remain closed to new or different ideas when facing a crisis, threat, or high-stakes competition. This is particularly true if a powerful leader advocates a solution and members see no viable alternative, or if morale is low because of recent failures—or the task seems impossible—or a moral dilemma seems to have no solution that meets members' ethical standards. A team in this depressed situation may accept alternatives that, as individuals or under other circumstances, they might reject.

What Groupthink Does

"Antecedent conditions" don't *always* push teams into the groupthink trap. But when they do, teams' decision making is warped. You can see the effect of groupthink in the following warning signs:

- *Illusion of invulnerability.* Members feel their group is stronger than any counteracting forces. This leads them "to become over-optimistic and willing to take extraordinary risks and causes them not to respond to clear warnings of danger."[13]

- *Belief in the team's inherent morality.* The team assumes it has "right" on its side, so anyone who is in opposition must necessarily be "wrong." This belief builds a "we against them" mentality by stereotyping others as incompetent, inferior, or immoral.

- *Closed-mindedness and collective rationalizations.* Members resist new ideas and information and build rationalizations for their preconceived positions. They exclude or fail to seek information that could increase their understanding, paying attention only to those facts that support a position they favor.

- *Self-censorship.* Team members rationalize their positions and don't allow themselves to say, or even to think, something that counters the team's thought or might "rock the boat."

- *Pressure on dissenters.* Members exert pressure to conform on anyone who expresses a dissenting thought, and leaders may encourage this pressure by ignoring, downplaying, or even ridiculing a dissenting view.

- *Mindguards.* Just as bodyguards protect people from harm, mindguards protect leaders from hearing anything that might disturb or upset their viewpoint. Members deflect bearers of bad news and filter, distort, or hide information that might disturb groupthink illusions.

- *Illusion of unanimity.* Members have an illusion that they all agree, which comes around full circle to reinforce all of the behaviors that led to the illusion in the first place.[14]

These patterns, which certainly protect a group's feeling of superiority, cohesiveness, and strength, also strangle members' abilities to think rationally and critically. Scary, isn't it, when you consider that the failed U.S. invasion of Cuba in the Bay of Pigs fiasco, the Watergate scandal that led to the resignation of President Nixon, the Iran-Contra affair, the *Challenger* tragedy, and many more disastrous decisions were precipitated by groupthink?[15] A report from the Senate Intelligence Committee concluded groupthink led U.S. and British leaders to believe erroneously that Iraq held weapons of mass destruction. That belief was the justification for a preemptive strike and a war that killed and injured thousands.[16]

In smaller tragedies, groupthink even besets student teams. We remember a group who got together to study for an exam. Under stress but overconfident, they failed to research their topic and relied on one student's recollections without confirming them. As they talked, the students created a rubric of misconceptions all members used to write their exams. Their professors were boggled at the extent of inaccuracies—and the students were shocked they had done so poorly. Groupthink had convinced them they had the right information.

How to Reduce Groupthink

Here are some groupthink-busting approaches to help avoid this blight on teamwork:

1   *Set norms.* Value openness, right of dissent, and principled leadership.

2   *Test assumptions.* Examine assumptions about facts, values, or people. Look for evidence of illusions of invulnerability, moral superiority, or unanimity. Check for stereotyping of other groups and assumptions about their behaviors or values.

3   *Scout for information.* Aggressively seek outside resources, experts, and relevant information to challenge members' views. Make it a team expectation that each member will discuss ideas with outside groups and communicate responses to the team.

4   *Challenge ideas.* Have all members act as "critical evaluator," regularly challenging ideas, information, and suggestions. Appoint someone to be devil's advocate, arguing as persuasively as possible for the "other side."[17]

5   *Shift the structure.* Set up outside groups or subgroups to work separately on the same issues, and compare deliberations. Then regather the full team and hash out the results.

6   *Hold focus meetings.* Hold special meetings to focus on single issues when policy decisions may involve serious risks.[18]

7   *Review.* Hold "second chance" meetings for people to review decisions and to raise new ideas or concerns about them.[19]

Bill Dewitt reports on his experience with a Burlington Northern team that transformed the company's intermodal (combining forms of transportation—trains, trucks, ships) business from the bottom of the industry to setting the standards. Note the emphasis on protecting the team from groupthink.

If you would take an idea to this team you would get a wealth of testing on any relevant issue.

Everyone knew about the marketplace and knew about operations and knew about equipment and so on. You didn't blow smoke by anybody in this group. That was part of why we trusted each other so much. You knew that if there was something missing in your logic or application, the others would say, "Wait a minute. Come again."

From J. R. Katzenbach and D. K. Smith, *The Wisdom of Teams: Creating the High-Performance Organization* (Boston: Harvard Business School Press, 1993), p. 34.

At every stage, review and assess team processes to be sure everyone is heard and pressures to conform are within bounds. If all members are vigilant in avoiding groupthink traps, you can develop a cohesive, productive team that investigates and analyzes issues openly, clearly, and critically.

Summary

Good group decisions depend on every member's credible, principled leadership to help identify purposes, define goals specifically and clearly, plan and execute research, share information, and follow systematic, analytical steps to identify potential solutions.

An orderly process includes analyzing problems and identifying possible causes and effects; establishing clear, specific criteria by which the group can later judge its potential solutions; and generating a range of ideas. The group then applies analytical techniques to determine each proposal's applicability, practicality, advantages, disadvantages, and risks as well as desirability or value. The best proposal may be chosen by consensus, majority vote, or an authority. Finally, the group may make plans for implementing the decision and for following up with an evaluation.

Throughout this process, members must vigilantly avoid groupthink. Especially under stress, members may be highly cohesive and strive too hard for harmony, and this can lead to groupthink, a mistaken unanimity blocking out information and hindering analysis. Members may believe they are invulnerable and morally superior to other groups, rationalizing their attitudes, becoming closed-minded, censoring themselves and others to block contrary ideas, and/or "mindguarding" their leaders from contradictory information. They may agree on a disastrous decision under the illusion that they are unanimous. Members can avoid groupthink by setting norms for vigilant analysis, testing assumptions, seeking full information, and challenging ideas, information, and suggestions. It helps to have someone play devil's advocate and/or use outside groups, subgroups, or focus meetings to shift group structure and expose different analyses. Finally, it is important to have special follow-up meetings to review, and possibly to revise, a decision after it has been made.

Exercises

1 Recall a time that you've been in a group (school, work, family, community) that had a problem to analyze and a decision to make. Using what you've learned in this chapter, compare your experience to the prescriptions offered in this chapter for:

- Analyzing problems
- Generating and analyzing solutions
- Making decisions, and
- Implementing and assessing decisions

Focus on at least two of these areas. Record the similarities and the differences you notice as you compare your experience with the text.

2 Consider how a working group creates their own decision-making process by doing the following:

- Select a working group that has recently made a decision that is procedural (regarding how things are done) or legislative (regarding instituting or repealing a law, rule, or policy). For example, student government; college administration; local, state, or federal government.

- Learn the group's decision-making process. Investigate the process by which the decision was reached using interviews, articles, minutes, news articles, and so on.

- Evaluate the group's decision-making process. Compare its choices to the information in this chapter to determine how effectively the group used the steps of problem solving and decision making.

- Look for groupthink. Were there any sign of groupthink? What were the possible causes? What were the effects?

- Prepare a report of your investigation to make to the class.

3 Form a small classroom group. Assume you are a task force in a large corporation. Your attention has been called to issues related to these facts:

- The plant is in a rural industrial park.
- The closest town is 10 miles away.

- People with families sometimes are distracted from work by family concerns.
- The town has one small day care center.
- Two churches have preschools that operate until five o'clock.
- The company has no maternity/paternity leave benefits.
- Many employees live 20 or more miles away.
- Parents of small children are frequently late or absent.
- Parents of school-age children miss work on many school holidays.
- Some personnel have left the company when they started families.
- Recent productivity declines are primarily among people ages 25–45, normally a productive age group.
- Morale in the company is low.
  a Using this information, analyze the problem(s) these facts suggest and create a fishbone diagram (see Figure 11.3) to illustrate the causes and effects of the problems.
  b Using the cause-effect (fishbone) diagram you created, set goals your task force would like to achieve and establish criteria for a satisfactory solution. Then generate possible solutions to the problems and create an implementation and assessment plan.
  c Report your analysis and plans to the class.

 4 Observe a group or team as the members try to solve a problem. This could be a college or community committee, a work team, and so on. Choose Chapter 11 from the pull-down menu on the *Communicating with Credibility and Confidence* website (see Cyberpoint instructions following). You will find Form 11.1, which you can use as a guide to analyze the team's processes. What worked well? What didn't? Where did members seem to conform to what you've learned in this chapter? Where did they not?

Make a brief oral report to the class on your findings. Identify the most important thing this group did well and the processes it used to achieve it. Also identify one place where the decision-making sequence broke down and what members might have done to work through the difficulty.

Cyberpoints

The following Cyberpoints can be easily accessed from the Student Companion website for this text at http://academic.cengage.com/communication/lumsdenccc3. Click on *Student Book Companion Site* and select this chapter from the pull-down menu at the top of the page that says "Select a chapter." Click on *Cyberpoints* under *Chapter Resources* and you will find links for the exercises following.

1   Need some help with researching your topic? Go to the Web Center for Social Research Methods at http://www.socialresearchmethods.net/. Make a short list of the ideas that you found here that will help you do planning and analysis.

2   Looking for additional library resources? According to Morreale (Morreale's Mailbag, *Spectra 11,* April 2001, 4), the following are the top ten libraries on the Web: (1) Internet Public Library: www.ipl.org; (2); http://sunsite3. berkeley.edu/Libweb/; (3) Library Spot: www.libraryspot.com; (4) Stanford University: www-sul.Stanford.edu; (5) University of California: http://infolib. berkeley.edu/; (6) Harvard College Library: www.hcl.harvard.edu; (7) Yale University: www.library.yale.edu; (8) UCLA Library: http://www2.library. ucla.edu/; (9) Carnegie Mellon: www.library.cmu.edu; and (10) Penn State: www.libraries.psu.edu. Visit at least three of these sites and browse around. What are three features or resources you discovered that will be useful for you in problem analysis and decision making?

3   Do you think that cultural differences can affect decision making and communication in groups? Use InfoTrac College Edition to locate the article, "Decision Making by Chinese and U.S. Students," by Karen L. Harris and Roger Nibler. Use the PowerTrac function to search by the author's last name. Read the article and pay special attention to how the cultural differences influence decision making. Are the differences important? How do you suppose culture might account for these differences? How should we think and communicate based on this information?

Chapter 12

Research and Development: Creating Public Speeches

Objectives for This Chapter

Knowledge

- Understand how speech preparation affects credibility and confidence
- Know steps for preparing and organizing a public speech
- Understand approaches for selecting and refining a speech topic
- Know how to research and use supporting material for speeches

Feelings and Approaches

- Recognize the importance of research and development for a speech
- Feel confident in your abilities to research and develop a speech
- Appreciate a speech as a creative product resulting from extensive work
- Value the confident feeling generated by thorough preparation

Communication Abilities

- Select and refine a topic for a speech with a specific purpose
- Identify audience characteristics relevant to a particular speech occasion
- Research and organize material to reach the goals of a speech
- Develop speeches that increase self-confidence and credibility

Key Terms

speech to inform

speech to persuade

thesis statement

demographics

psychographics

speech body

organizational pattern

supporting material

speech introduction

speech conclusion

transition

visual message

A good speech is like a good business—both rely heavily on research and development. Known as "R & D" in the business world, research and development are key to creating new ideas or products to stay competitive.

Equally, R & D is critical to your success as a public speaker. You will be more confident when you are thoroughly prepared and know what you're talking about. And you'll certainly be more credible with a speech you've structured clearly with well-supported ideas.

Effective presentations are products of intensive preparation. President Woodrow Wilson, who took pride in his public speaking, was once asked by a reporter, "How long does it take you to prepare a 10-minute speech?" Wilson thought for a moment and replied, "About 2 weeks." "How long, then, does it take you to prepare an hour's speech?" the reporter probed. Wilson answered, "About a week." The reporter pursued it further. "What about a 2-hour speech?" "I could make that right now," Wilson quickly responded.

The *public* in public speaking provides an important perspective. You "go public" through your speeches, providing a window through which others see you and assess your competence and credibility. Of course, that's one reason public speaking creates such high anxiety. But speeches are also opportunities to demonstrate your command of information and situations. That's why your R & D requires serious attention.

Speech R & D follows a simple process—simple, but not easy. Preparation uses your analysis and creativity through nine essential steps; a shortcut at any point will make success less likely.

1   Determine your purpose and topic.

2   Gather research information.

3   Analyze your audiences.

4   Organize your ideas.

5   Develop your ideas to achieve your goal.

6   Create your introduction, conclusion, and transitions.

7   Plan visuals to supplement your text.

8   Prepare speaking notes.

9   Rehearse your presentation.

This chapter guides you through the first seven of these steps. Chapter 13 covers the last two R & D stages.

Determining Your Purpose and Topic

People often describe a speaking task in terms of what they have to *do*, such as "I have a report to give" or, "I have to prepare a 5-minute speech." It's better to focus on the *results* you want from the speech, asking yourself: *Why* do I have a speech to prepare, and *what* do I want listeners to know or to do? For example, "I want the oversight committee to approve our proposal for prisoner training." To set and achieve that goal, you first must clarify your purpose, select your topic, and develop a clear thesis statement.

Clarifying Your Purpose

No matter what the specific purpose, all speeches have the goal of getting listeners to change in some way. That change may be to increase listeners' knowledge (when you speak to inform) and/or to influence them to shift their attitudes, values, beliefs, and/or behaviors (when you speak to persuade).

You can use Speech Builder Express, a web-based speech outlining and development tool, to help you create your speech goal. To access Speech Builder Express, use the pass code included in your new copy of *Communicating with Credibility and Confidence*. When you log on, you'll be prompted to set up an account, and then you can start on a speech outline by choosing a speech type. To work on your exact purpose, select "Goal/Purpose" from the left-hand menu and follow the instructions. For short reminders from this chapter about speech goals, click on the *Tutor* button.

These two goals—informing and persuading—often overlap. All persuasion must provide information so that listeners can understand arguments, and all informative speaking must persuade people to listen and value your message. Nonetheless, we talk about informative and persuasive speaking separately to help you learn how to approach each task.

Speeches to Inform   A **speech to inform** provides listeners with new information or shows them new relationships among known materials. These speeches may teach a process, a skill, or ideas; they may provide background and facts that let people mentally experience new places or increase their understanding of a subject.

You seek to inform when you coach a team, report on your research, talk about a trip you took, or discuss a book you read. Managers explain health benefit plans to employees; religious workers teach their doctrine to potential or actual followers; judges instruct juries; people give directions for getting to specific locations; and parents share family history with children. (Chapter 14 covers how to prepare a speech to inform.)

Speeches to Persuade   A **speech to persuade** gives listeners ways to fulfill needs and reasons to alter attitudes, values, beliefs, and/or behaviors, motivating

---

Speech to inform Provides listeners with new information or shows them new relationships among known materials

Speech to persuade Gives listeners ways to fulfill needs and reasons to alter attitudes, values, beliefs, and/or behaviors, motivating them with logical and emotional appeals to change established ways of thinking or acting

When you get people to listen to what you believe, you get on fire yourself—big fires, little fires—that never do go out. I met Everett Dirkson in the airport in St. Louis, one of the greatest speakers of the day. He said, "You are a great speaker. I know. I've heard you."

"Where was it?" I asked.

"I forget the circumstances," he answered, "but you said the following. . . ." and he repeated what I had said verbatim. That is the greatest compliment you can have as a speaker. It lights a real fire in you.

I remember a young fellow who wanted me to advise him on how to be a good speaker! I told him, "Be interesting, be enthusiastic, and don't talk too much!"

From Norman Vincent Peale, in L. Walters, *Secrets of Successful Speakers*, p. xiii. Copyright © 1993 The McGraw Hill Companies, Inc.

them with logical and emotional appeals to change established ways of thinking or acting.

Persuasive communication is essential to democratic decision making, not to mention capitalistic enterprise. Politicians influence voters to elect them, lobbyists work to influence legislators, and legislators seek to influence one another. Salespeople influence buying decisions; teachers influence students to complete assignments, to aspire to higher goals, and to develop self-esteem. (Chapter 15 develops strategic approaches for persuasive speeches.)

Speeches for Special Occasions   On a special occasion, you might find yourself up there making any one of the following speeches:

Introducing a speaker. Usually the audience knows who is to speak, but your job as introducer is to enhance that speaker's credibility. It's best to summarize (briefly) the speaker's expertise as it relates to the occasion, mention special awards or recognition the speaker has received, and refer to the speaker's background, experiences, perhaps special projects, that may provide common ground with the audience.

Presenting an award. Critical information when presenting an award includes criteria for selection and how the recipient fulfilled them. If the audience doesn't already know who won the award, you may build suspense by withholding the name until the end of your presentation.

Accepting an award. Receiving an award is an honor, but focuses the spotlight on you in ways that can make you especially nervous. You've probably watched Oscar winners go on and on with disorganized thank you's. Short and sweet should be the rule here. If you're surprised to have won, say so, but also express your pride—don't cover it under a cloak of humility.

Thank those who confer the award and *very few* others who are important to this recognition, and indicate any ways in which the award might challenge you in your future efforts.

Entertaining. Most speeches should have some entertainment value to keep audiences listening, but some presentations are purely to entertain. They can range from stand-up comedy to a dramatic reading. Each requires you to have a sense of your role and the audience's expectations.

Speaking after dinner. Combining a meal with a presentation is challenging for the speaker. People tend to relax after eating—perhaps even to want a nap—and that makes them a tough audience to engage. You need dynamism and appropriate humor to grab and hold attention. Frequently, an after-dinner speech serves as entertainment, and the audience expects lighter, more humorous fare. When you can, get your audience involved in your speech in some way: give them a task to perform, solicit questions, or interact with them to keep them energized.

Making a business presentation. At work or in class, you will present research findings and proposals—often as part of a team, so you need both teamwork skills (covered in the previous two chapters) and presentational skills. You and your team will cooperate to develop the content, assign specific responsibilities for each part of the speech, and rehearse together. An advantage is that you can take turns speaking, and this variety can help keep your audience's interest.

The more you sweat in advance, the less you'll have to sweat once you appear on stage.

George Plimpton, 20th-century American writer

Selecting a Topic

Students spend a lot of time trying to find the "perfect" topic for a classroom speech, something to seize the audience's interest and hold them spellbound. "Perfect" topics are not discovered, however; speakers create them. You no doubt have heard dull speeches about potentially fascinating issues and mesmerizing speeches about seemingly boring subjects.

In the "real world," a speaking commitment usually includes some expectation about your topic. Students have a wider choice for their classroom speeches, but they may wrestle so long with selecting a topic that they have too little time to develop their speech adequately. Here are some ideas to help you in your quest for a topic:

Your own interests. Consider your hobbies, reading interests, work experiences, organizational memberships, or places you've visited. One of our students, a dedicated mountain biker, spoke on the sport and the controversies that impinge upon it.

Family background and heritage. Everyone's roots provide unique ethnic, cultural, and historical issues that you could research further. A student of Irish heritage, for example, might speak on historical, religious, or geographic topics relating to Ireland.

Ideas from other courses. You might use this chance to delve into something a professor said that sparked your interest. A geography instructor mentioned there is still more gold in California mountains than was mined during all the Gold Rush years, inspiring a student to speak about the current status of gold mining in the state.

Social or political issues. Look for a topic that interests you in media coverage of social causes and pending legislation. A student who heard discussions about roles in the military for people who are gay or lesbian developed her speech about the need for laws protecting equal rights for people with different sexual orientations.

Topics you select should meet six important criteria:

1   *Time limits*. Usually, you have a time limit, and you need to plan a talk you can communicate within that limitation. For instance, in 5 minutes you might be able to explain finding a good travel buy on the Internet, but you couldn't describe a 2-week tour of Europe.

2   *Timeliness and resource availability*. For a current topic, research materials should be readily available from libraries, offices, interviews, or the net. Some sources may be available through interlibrary loans, but usually not in time.

3   *Spirited interest*. You need enough enthusiasm about your topic to communicate interest, concern, or involvement to your audience—if you're bored, your audience will be, too. Find something exciting or intriguing to you.

4   *Occasion*. Frequently, the topic is dictated by the event. A holiday celebration, your fraternity's or sorority's anniversary dinner, or a wedding toast dictate your topic but allow creativity in your approach.

5   *Purpose*. If you want to inform your audience, you start with what they know and expand it from there; if you want your listeners to *change,* you need to give them reason and motivation to shift their attitude or behaviors from their present status.

6   *Adaptability to audience*. A topic may be new to your listeners, but you need to draw on their backgrounds and motivations to interest them, perhaps taking them to another level of understanding without stretching them impossibly far beyond their present knowledge or attitudes.

Even a very good subject may be too broad for the time limit on your speech, so you'll need to narrow it. (Skipping this step is one reason President Wilson required less preparation time for a longer speech.) You narrow a topic by getting more and more specific until you reach a manageable scope. Think of the process as an inverted pyramid, moving from broader, abstract to very concrete issues. Figure 12.1 provides three examples of narrowed topics.

Let's develop the broad subject of "crime" into a workable speech topic. The topic of crime can take us in several directions, so we'll start with rehabilitation of prisoners. You might begin with the general level of *crime* and narrow it to the more specific topic, *repeat offenders*. You might limit it with more specificity to *lack of rehabilitation for offenders* and even further to *how prisons prepare inmates for independent living and self-management*, and, more specific yet, *training prisoners to take greater financial responsibility* is a doable topic.

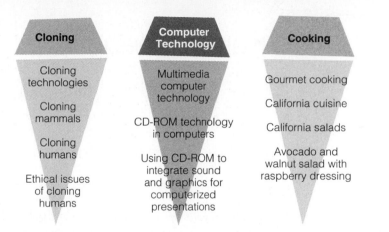

Figure 12.1 *Three broad topics narrowed for speech time limits*

Stating Your Thesis

Thesis statement Clear, concise declarative sentence stating the central idea of your speech

The refinement of your topic and clarification of your purpose leads you to a **thesis statement,** a clear, concise declarative sentence stating the central idea of your speech, the idea you want your audience to understand or to act on. The statement must be specific enough to identify precise ideas, yet general enough to summarize the speech's content. The speech on the refined topic of crime, for example, might have this thesis: "Prisoners need to develop greater financial responsibility while incarcerated."

You can use Speech Builder Express to help you create your thesis. Select "Thesis Statement" from the left-hand menu and follow the instructions. For short reminders from this chapter about thesis statements, click on the *Tutor* button.

A clear thesis statement helps you identify specific issues you will need to develop in your speech. An examination of our sample thesis statement suggests the following issues you may need to consider:

Is developing prisoners' financial responsibility desirable?

Does greater financial responsibility enhance self-esteem?

Does greater financial responsibility reduce recidivism (chances of returning to prison)?

Can prisoners pay any part of their living expenses?

Can prisoners reimburse victims?

Can prisoners plan for their finances after release?

Does paying for one's living expenses help develop financial responsibility?

Does reimbursing one's victims help develop financial responsibility?

Does financial planning for one's release help develop financial responsibility?

Identifying issues guides your research to answer questions you have identified. As you seek answers, you may identify more issues and questions, which may even lead to rephrasing your specific topic and thesis statement.

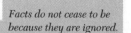

Facts do not cease to be because they are ignored.

Aldous Huxley, 20th-century American writer

Researching Your Speech

The computer term *GIGO* (garbage in, garbage out) applies to building a speech as well—you only turn out a good speech when good information goes into it. You build a speech on finding, evaluating, and recording good information.

Finding Research Information

Before you even start your research, please, please plan your approach to documenting what you find. Remember that you will need to *quote and attribute your sources accurately,* and may have to go back and check something. With that in mind, keep a clear, well-organized record of your notes and their sources—these could be on note cards, a voice recorder, a photocopy, or a print from a scanner/computer. Every note needs to include the name of the source, qualifications, author of the material (if it's a secondary source), article title, publication title, date, page numbers, publisher, and specific information from the material. If you use media sources, you need the title, artist, director, possibly concept creator; copyright date; and specific information from the material.

Information on websites is not necessarily reviewed by anyone—it could be accurate, but it could be fabricated. One authority says articles on the Internet can be considered reliable if they are "written and/or issued by an authoritative source such as the federal government or a reliable organization . . . authenticated as part of an editorial or peer review process by a publisher . . . [and/or] . . . evaluated by experts, reviewers, or subject specialists/librarians as part of collection development."[1] Check the header, body, and footer on a web page to find out author, source, and whether the source is a moderated or unmoderated list, or even an anonymous site. You also can check online directory sources to find out about the source's affiliations and biographical information.[2] Internet sources may not give all the data, but be sure to record the URL and date you retrieved it.

With that plan ready, you can start your research, which is simply finding answers to questions through information from various sources. Good research asks penetrating questions and finds credible information to answer them through a variety of sources—electronic, print, and human.

Electronic Sources   Most libraries have collections of films, videos, and audiotapes, including CD-ROM discs incorporating many other resources listed here, as well as multimedia resources accessible by computer.

The Internet has vast sources of information on just about anything, and probably, like many students, it's your habit to go there first when you need information. Useful sites to look for include:

> *Organizational and government websites* for information on products, issues, research, or enterprises.
>
> *News groups'* bulletin boards for various topics, transmitted through an electronic bulletin board system, *Usenet.* There are more than 20,000 news

groups,[3] "organized in categories called *hierarchies,* in which each level is separated by a period. These levels become more specific after each period. For example, 'soc.culture.african.american' is a social news group with an interest in African American cultural issues."[4]

University files and programs provide anything from library indices to departmental or university information. Many universities now have developed special discs to guide students through research methods in given fields or across the university, and some of these, such as those at Cornell University or Purdue University, are available to you on the web.

Advertised addresses that organizations relevant to your interests have published in newspapers, magazines, journals. You may or may not find what you want, but there's a better chance that the site address will be current if you find it advertised in a current publication.

Print Sources   Some things are not available electronically, and some are easier to read and ponder in print. Most libraries list research sources in computerized databases; these include:

Books. Still "best friends" for some of us—great for discovering just the right quotation, insight, or reference for a speech.

Reference works. Encyclopedias, atlases, almanacs, and related resources, many or most of which also are available electronically.

Documents. If it exists, some governmental agency has studied it. Some libraries are designated as depositories and receive all documents published by the federal government. Again, most of these are available online or on library discs as well.

Periodicals. Indexes, many on disk (such as Socio File and Psych Lit), use key words to identify professional journal, magazine, and newspaper articles.

Human Sources   People can help you enormously in finding and understanding information. For example:

Reference librarians. These people are experts on tracking down resources, and most of them get great satisfaction from applying their expertise to help a student.

Yourself. You may have taken a course, traveled to a relevant location, or developed knowledge through a hobby that relates to your topic. This gives you a lively, interesting view that you can supplement with other resources to give you a broader picture.

Surveys. You can expand your knowledge by surveying classmates, fellow employees, or a randomized group. Focus your survey directly on questions you seek to answer for your speech. Although you can only generalize your findings to the group you survey (that is, if you survey only women, you can't generalize to men), when your audience is part of that group, responses are directly relevant.

Interviews. Professors and experts in the community usually are willing to share their knowledge with students. Interviews, face to face or by phone, can give you firsthand information. Sometimes, you can get permission to tape-record your interview and use a short excerpt in your speech.

Evaluating Research Information

The challenge is to sort through your information for quality and relevance. We talked about some of this in Chapter 3, but we want to remind you to examine a source's qualifications, reputation, and ethical behavior; if any of these is questionable, so is what the source says.

When possible, use a *primary source,* the first publication or person to provide information. A *secondary source* (one that repeats or summarizes the original material) is an abstraction or compilation of information and, because it's one step or more removed, it may contain inaccuracies or biases. For example, *Readers' Digest* articles often are abstracted from other publications. Newspaper articles and television reports are the writer's synthesis and interpretation of events. Examine your information to see if it is consistent with other findings or if it stands out as an exception. Differing points of view should be noted and evaluated, but, generally, the thinking that has greater consistency with other findings tends to provide more dependable answers to your research questions.

Finally, check the timeliness of the information. Sometimes, old information is fine—for example, contemporaneous reports of historical events and quotations from original sources. More recent information, however, is often more reliable than older data. Research findings grow, and later studies may build upon or contradict earlier studies. Information about television in the 1980s, for instance, may not apply to today's programming.

Analyzing Your Audience

The more you know about your listeners, the better you can tailor your messages to win their understanding and acceptance of your ideas. Corporations spend large sums to research customer preferences for marketing a new product. Political campaigns take daily polls to track subtle shifts in voters' attitudes. You might not be able to use *these* audience analysis techniques for your speeches, but you will need to get as much information as you can about your audience's characteristics and expectations.

Audience Characteristics

Demographics Categorize people according to external attributes: age, sex, ethnicity, income, educational level

Psychographics Categorize people based on internal factors: attitudes, values, needs

Audience analysis examines the demographic and psychographic characteristics of your listeners. **Demographics** categorize people according to external attributes: age, sex, ethnicity, income, educational level. **Psychographics** categorize people based on internal factors: attitudes, values, needs. These analyses tell you what to include and what angle to take in your speech. Be careful not to make assumptions about people based on stereotypes about their identity groups, but try to learn about their:

Knowledge. How much does the audience know about the topic? What they already know tells you how much background to give for a clear frame of reference. Obviously, well-informed individuals with a prior interest in the topic require less introductory material than those who know little about it.

Attitude. What is the audience's present attitude about the subject? If listeners already tend to support your position, then you need to focus more on reinforcing and strengthening their attitudes. If you intend to "sell" a proposal to people who might oppose it, however, then your presentation must change their attitudes with more documentation and strategic appeals.

Values. What audience values are relevant to the issues? People try to act in ways consistent with their values, so sometimes you must show them your ideas are grounded in their values. For example, if you propose to the college president and board of trustees that the college invest in its music program, you might choose to spotlight the economic value of potential alumni contributions, or public relations benefits that might accrue—depending on how important to your president you believe each benefit might be.

Expectations. What does your audience expect of this presentation? Brief or long? Formality or informality? If you speak for 30 minutes to a group that expected a 15-minute presentation, for instance, or if you are breezily informal in a more formal situation, your audience may be annoyed and your credibility may suffer. Before you prepare a speech, ask what is expected. Start with your speaking assignments for this class. Suppose you present a brilliant 10-minute, memorized persuasive speech—but your instructor has assigned a 5-minute informative speech, using notes as well as three different sources and visuals. You might be disappointed in your grade.

Sensitivity. What issues are sensitive? Your approach and language should always be sensitive to issues of gender and culture. We've seen well-meaning people undermine their presentations with tasteless jokes, thoughtless cartoons, and inappropriate examples. Sexist or racist language and material offensive to members of other cultures or identity groups both reduce your credibility and adversely affect the listeners' response to the content.

Audience Analysis Sources

You can find reliable information about your audience with good research techniques. Here are some ideas:

Asking. Talk with people who know about your audience. Start with the person who arranged for you to speak. For example, one of our colleagues was asked to talk to the student council about using parliamentary procedure. He prepared by asking several council members and the group's

Audiences differ widely. In which of these photos would you suspect the audience members to have the most in common? Why? How many different audience characteristics can you identify in these groups? What characteristics can you not identify in a photo? What does the presence of cameras and microphones suggest to you about audiences?

Spencer Grant/Photo Researchers, Inc.

Bob Daemmrich/The Image Works

advisor about procedures they used, problems they encountered, their familiarity with the topic, and their level of concern over the issue.

Reading. Obtain literature—newsletters, mission statements—from the group to gain insight into their values and priorities, as well as other activities to which you can relate your material.

Observing. Think about your classroom speeches. You spend time with this audience each week. What have you learned about their interests and backgrounds? What do they know or value that you can use as a foundation for enhancing your speech?

Organizing Your Ideas

All the good stuff you've collected must be sifted and framed so your audience can understand and accept it. Your intuition may be to prepare the introduction, body, and conclusion in that order, but ignore your intuition. The best way is to start with the **speech body,** the substance of it, structured with main points and subpoints.

Only after you have clearly delineated and organized your main points do you create an introduction to prepare the audience for what follows and a conclusion to provide a strong closing. Then you develop transitions to communicate clearly the relationships among these major sections as well as among the main points, subpoints, and supporting material.

Organizational Patterns

As you'll recall, well-organized messages are easier for listeners to process and understand. Miller explains that people process information in "chunks," or groups of related items.[5] This concept should guide your approach to organizing the body of your speeches.

An **organizational pattern** logically orders ideas in relationship to one another. Main ideas that build your thesis may be organized in a linear order, they may follow a more conceptual approach that relates various parts of the topic to a larger whole, or they may use a psychological strategy designed to move the audience from where they are to where you want them to be. Patterns include:

Chronological organization links ideas or events sequentially, such as past to present to future or through a step-by-step process. A speech that teaches or demonstrates how to do something normally has this structure.

Spatial or geographic organization relates ideas in terms of space. A report on the U.S. economy could be organized by major regions (Northeast, South, Midwest, and West), or you might organize a speech about your college in terms of the activities in various buildings: Travis Hall, Williams Lounge, and Melendez Center.

Parts-to-whole or topical organization develops related ideas under the same main topic. If a speech answers the who, what, when, where, why, and how of an issue or event, it uses this structure because each answer is a "part" of the whole story. Or dividing an issue into political, economic, and environmental aspects uses a parts-to-whole pattern.

Speech body The substance of a speech, structured with main points and subpoints

Organizational pattern Logically orders ideas in relationship to one another

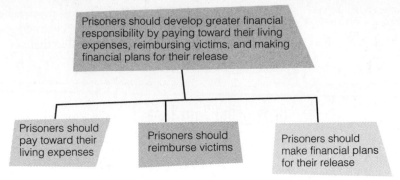

Figure 12.2 *Sample division of a thesis statement into its main points*

Prisoners should develop greater financial responsibility by paying toward their living expenses, reimbursing victims, and making financial plans for their release

Prisoners should pay toward their living expenses

Prisoners should reimburse victims

Prisoners should make financial plans for their release

Ascending or descending organization orders ideas in numerical order, size, or status. David Letterman's "Top 10" lists are always presented in ascending order—from the least important to the most important—the "top" of the hierarchy. Or a descending-order speech about taxes could flow from federal to state to county to local governments.

Problem-solution organization divides the speech in two main ideas: a perceived problem and ways to solve it. Sometimes, you can add a third main point, the advantages or benefits of the proposed solution.

Logical format organization subdivides the ideas into in a sequence that reflects a pattern of reasoning. For example, the points could be divided between cause and effects (or effects and causes).

Organizational Process

Developing the organization of your speech is detailed work. The first step is to sort your research notes into groups, one for each general idea. The theme of each group suggests main points for the body of the speech, as shown in Figure 12.2.

The next step is to structure the material within each main point. Take the notes for each main division and separate them into subcategories. This provides subpoints for the main points. Figure 12.3 gives an example of the results of this step.

You can use Speech Builder Express to help you create your outline. Select "Outline" from the left-hand menu and follow the instructions. For short reminders from this chapter about outlining, click on the *Tutor* button.

The process of creating subdivisions continues until all material you want to use is in place. As you divide the information into categories, keep these principles in mind:

- *Use no more than five major chunks for any division*. That's about all people can process when they hear it; after all, there is no instant replay. So the speech should present a maximum of five main points (three is better), and each main point should contain no more than five subpoints.

Figure 12.3 *Sample subdivision of a main point into subpoints*

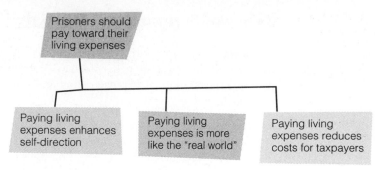

- *Show clear relationships among parts within any subdivision.* All "chunks" within a group should link clearly to one another in keeping with the organizational pattern. You would not organize main ideas into "past, present, future, and implications," for example, because the first three chunks are chronological and "implications" is inconsistent with the time sequence pattern. Mixing the categories upsets the relationships and makes it harder for an audience to follow and comprehend.

Under each main point, however, you could use a different pattern of subpoints. That is, a first main point, "the past," might fall into subpoints of who, what, and where in a parts-to-whole pattern. Under the second main point, "the present," you might use another pattern, such as spatial; just follow the basic principle that each grouping or subdivision should include only subpoints that are clearly related to one another.

Developing Supporting Material

Supporting material Additional information that holds up the body of a speech and gives it shape, substance, and energy

The organization of your speech is a skeletal structure; **supporting material** is additional information that holds the body up and gives it shape, substance, and energy. From your research base, select supporting material to accomplish three objectives:

1 *Clarify.* A statement may give your audience a fact or a position; you add supporting material to help them understand it.

2 *Prove.* Any statement may or may not be true. Supporting material provides data to convince your audience that what you say is probably true. Proof helps establish your credibility as a speaker.

3 *Vivify.* No matter how factual or reasonable a point may be, an audience needs to "see it" to understand its relevance and feel its impact. Supporting material can help to make an idea stand out over other ideas, and to gain an audience's attention and understanding.

Types of Supporting Material

Some say the presentation software explosion is part of a general decline in public speaking—as Stanford professor of communications Cliff Nass puts it, "Try to imagine the 'I have a dream' speech in PowerPoint."

Geoffrey Nunberg, *Fortune*, December 20, 1999

In conversations, in reports, in papers—you find ways to clarify, prove, or vivify what you mean. In a speech, you have the advantage of thinking ahead and planning specific support for each point and subpoint. Some types of supporting material include:

- *Examples* make a point real and vivid, so it's a good rule to: Let no generalization stand without an example. Several types of examples are shown here as they might be used in a speech on the subject of marriage:

    A *hypothetical example* is made up. You've just said, "Holidays can create major conflicts in a marriage," and support it with, "For example, suppose Jan's family and Terry's both insist on the couple coming for the big holiday meal?"

    A *real example* is an actual occurrence: "When my parents were married, my father's mother refused to speak to the newlyweds for 3 weeks because they went to Mom's mother's house for the holidays first."

    Instances are brief examples, usually presented in a series. "There's the matter of whose house the couple goes to; the question of when gifts are opened; the value clash over religious beliefs; the issue of how much money each family spends. . . ."

    An *illustrative narrative* is a story told from beginning to end to illustrate the point: "Family conflict almost broke up my friends, Donnell and Shoshanna, when Donnell's father proudly announced he was *taking* the couple on a honeymoon cruise. . . ."

- *Comparisons and contrasts* show similarities to and differences from something else, using either direct comparison or analogy. A direct comparison might be, "Marriage is like a legal contract—it binds the two partners in economic and civil matters." An analogy clarifies by comparing an idea to another thing: "Marriage is like setting out in a little boat on a big sea—it takes both people working together to keep it steady."

- *Facts* are statements that can be proven, as opposed to *opinions,* which cannot. A fact would be, "There are more interracial marriages in the United States now than ever before," whereas an opinion might be, "It's a sign of progress that more people are marrying people of other races."

- *Statistics* are useful to prove a factual point or to emphasize and clarify a value, but they need to be understood easily by the audience. You might support the preceding fact with, "According to Dr. Frazier in the book *Psychotrends,* 'Every year, about 600,000 interracial marriages are made in the U.S., about a third of which are between whites and African Americans.'"[6]

- *Testimony* is quoted from an expert in a specific field or from a nonexpert who has observed or experienced something. Expert testimony helps establish the probability of a fact or the desirability of an action. "Lay" or nonexpert testimony can add clarity or vividness to a point. Both add to the power of a speech. You see both expert and lay testimony on television newscasts, where the reporter asks an expert to explain or prove a phenomenon but also interviews people on the street for their observations or reactions.

■ *Explanations* may use any of the preceding methods in the process of describing, elaborating, or detailing what a point means. An explanation can include:

Restatement uses different words to elaborate on a previous statement. A first statement might be, "Marriage as a civil contract is one thing and as a religious commitment is another." The restatement: "That is, a civil contract should be available to all citizens but spiritual commitments should be made according to a couple's religious institution."

Definition may take many forms. Dictionary definitions report common usage, but you can also define ideas with other types of support such as example, testimony, and comparison: "My mother divorced my father because, in the end, she felt he held all the power in their relationship [an example]. As gender expert Julia Wood says, 'The social view of women as less powerful than men carries over into intimacy'[7] [expert testimony]. And, for many women of my mother's generation, marriage was like childhood—controlled first by Dad, then by husband [comparison]."

Choice and Use of Supporting Material

Think of yourself as an artist painting a picture for a special client—your audience. You need to decide where to put strong lines, where to add color, where to create shapes so your audience will see the picture you want them to see. To do that, you have to decide what supporting material to use and how to use it most effectively.

At this stage in developing your speech, look over your structure to find any gaps in information or logic. Often, you will find that you need more information on some issue, and this is the time to get it. Remember you have been intensely involved in the topic, so you may know much more about it than the audience. That can lead to underestimating the amount of explanation and supporting material your listeners need to understand connections that are obvious to you. You don't want to insult the intelligence of your audience, but neither do you want to overestimate their level of prior knowledge. Answers to these questions will help you analyze your speech:

What support will help reach your purpose and your goals?

Where do you need proof? Clarification? Vivification for attention and interest?

Which specific material will appeal to your audience's needs, goals, and values?

Which material will best show your objectivity, competence, and coorientation with your audience?

What material will vivify the speech with contrast and color?

Then there is your time limit to consider. Don't just try to talk faster or slower or hope it doesn't matter. It does. If you need to cut, look for entire sections to eliminate rather than bits and pieces of supporting material. That just strips the flesh from the bones. Cutting an entire main point is usually better than trying to cover too many points in too little time.

Creating Introductions, Conclusions, and Transitions

Once the speech is mapped out, you can plan how to prepare your audience to listen, understand, and stay with you all the way.

Speech Introductions

Plan the introduction after you have worked out the body. If on the first class day of a new term your professor asks you to introduce someone to the class, don't you need to meet the person first and find out about him or her? That's why introductions should be prepared *after* you know what you are introducing.

Furthermore, a plan for the speech gives you a better idea of how to get it started. As a general guideline, your introduction should take about 10% of your total speaking time. In a 5-minute speech, you have only about 30 seconds to achieve several important objectives.

Speech introduction
Opening of a speech that gets the audience's attention and prepares them to listen to your speech

Objectives An effective **speech introduction** gets the audience's attention and sets them firmly on the path into your thinking. For most speeches, four goals are paramount:

1 *Gain attention.* You need to engage listeners' minds and involve them immediately in your speech topic.

2 *Motivate listeners to stay tuned.* Many years ago, Borden warned that listeners are always thinking, "So what?" or, "Who cares?"[8] So you need to tell the audience "what's in it for them" and make them see how they can benefit from listening to you.

3 *Establish your credibility.* Your coorientation and involvement with listeners show—perhaps with a story or an example—that you share similar interests. Equally important, your competence, trustworthiness, and objectivity come through when you show interest and preparation, perhaps by relating, subtly, what motivated you to research the topic.

4 *Focus your topic.* The introduction should preview the main points of the speech. For example, you might say, "I'll first discuss the scope of the trade deficit with China, and then look at ways it might be reduced." You might also tell your audience what you will *not* cover, for instance, "I won't cover all aspects of U.S. international trade deficits—I will look only at those with China." This is the first step in proverbial advice to speakers: "Tell them what you are going to tell them, then tell them, then tell them what you've told them."

Types of Material   If you don't hook your audience in the first few moments, you might never get them. Recall that human beings can pay attention to only one thing at a time.[9] You have a brief moment when listeners pay attention simply because you've gotten up and faced them—and that's the moment you must bring their attention directly to your speech.

You can select your introduction from a wide variety of options:

Reference to the occasion. Tie your speech to circumstances surrounding the speaking event. A college recruiter speaking to a high school senior class, for example, might say, "They tell me this is 'college week' at Hampton High. This is the week you go crazy, trying to decide about the next four or five years of your life. Maybe I can help."

Reference to the audience. Comments about your audience can help establish coorientation and goodwill, perhaps by recalling mutual experiences offer sincere compliments to listeners. At a meeting of professionals, a speaker commented, "I am so impressed with the supportive feeling in this room. It's great to be with people who care about one another the way you do."

Startling or challenging statement. You can phrase ideas in surprising or novel ways to highlight the scope or impact of an issue: "Look around you. There are 50 people in this room. A local poll found that 25 of you drove drunk even before you graduated from high school."

Narrative. A narrative is a brief story that sets the scene or the tone for the speech. A student in her forties used this introduction to her speech: "About 20 years ago, Elizabeth faced a tough decision. She found out she was pregnant. Her husband had just left her and she already had a young child. She knew she could not depend on her ex-husband for any help, and she had no job nor source of support. After careful consideration and consultation, she decided to have an abortion. It was a difficult decision, but at least she was able to do it legally, privately, and with minimal additional anguish." The student then developed her presentation about protesters' harassment and violence at abortion clinics.

Quotation. A quotation can serve several purposes: to intrigue your audience, to recount a startling statement, to relate material that appeals to audience values and needs, and certainly to establish your credibility. Perhaps you're introducing a speech on the need for bipartisan solutions to social problems. You might open with, "In Africa, the Kikuyu have a saying: 'When the elephants fight, it is the grass that suffers.' In the United States, the elephants are trampling on the needs of American citizens."

Rhetorical questions. Rhetorical questions focus the audience's thinking; you do not expect answers. They require careful timing; following the question, you need to pause long enough for people to think, but not so long that they respond verbally. You can cue the audience with your vocal inflection—a pace and pitch that lets the listeners know they are only to think about their responses. Rhetorical questions are most effective when you use two or three in a series (even if they are only slight rewordings) rather than just one. You might ask, for example, "How would you feel if you found out that your best friend told a secret that you had shared in confidence? [pause] Would you feel betrayed? [slight pause] Angry?"

Appropriate humor. Humor can create a bridge into the speech with a brief ironic or witty reference appropriate to the audience, yourself, and the occasion. Once, Phyllis Diller got up to speak with her arm in a cast. She began, "I'd like to begin with a public service announcement: If there is anyone here who has just bought the new book *The Joy of Sex*, there is a misprint on page 206."[10] Whatever you do, *don't* start a speech with an irrelevant or old "joke," followed by, "But seriously, folks . . ." You'll lose your audience as soon as you say "seriously."

Reference to a previous speaker. A speech before yours may have touched on your topic. Don't just cringe: the worst thing you can do is ignore what the audience will surely see. Instead, look for ways to adapt your introduction and, if necessary, the speech body. Suppose your speech is on the abolitionist movement of the 1800s and a previous speaker talked about the women's rights movement of the 1900s. You might say, "The fight for human rights—both women's rights, as Randi has just described, and the rights of African Americans—goes back a long way. That fight took shape in the 1800s. . . ."

Speech Conclusions

Speech conclusion
Ending of a speech that drives home your ideas or makes the sale

Your **speech conclusion** is your opportunity to drive home your ideas or "to make the sale," but, as important as this is, conclusions are often neglected in preparation. Too often, speakers end with a limp, "Uh . . . well, I guess that's it. Thank you." They lose the chance to give their speeches impact and aesthetic balance and to ensure their listeners remember and act on what they have said.

A good conclusion isn't long—also about 10% of your total speaking time—but it needs to accomplish specific objectives.

Objectives   You have three objectives to achieve in your conclusions. To some extent, they are mirror images of the introduction's purposes.

1   *Summarize the speech.* Here's the place to "tell the audience what you told them." A summary, which repeats the main points, may include an illustration that encompasses the key ideas of the speech.

2   *Tell the audience what to do.* You want your speech to have an impact, so give your audience specific responses they can make to your material. How can they apply the information? How can they get more details? Do you want them to approve your proposal or seek more information? Should they lobby or contact legislators? What behaviors should they change? Don't assume these steps will be obvious—give your listeners some direction.

3   *Provide a strong finish.* First and last impressions are the most powerful, and you want the audience to remember your message. Most speakers realize

they must start the speech with strong material to get the audience's attention. You need to close it with equal impact.

Types of Material Most types of material for introductions are also appropriate for conclusions: you can refer back to the occasion or the audience; you can sum up with a quotation; you can startle or amuse or challenge the audience. You can combine all of these to provide closure and impact. Here are three more approaches specifically for conclusions:

1 *Synopsis*. Pulling your main points together into a concise restatement helps hammer home your thesis. For example, you could say, "In the past few minutes, I have explained how costly it is, both economically and spiritually, to neglect the problem of homelessness. I also have described the way one group is working to solve that problem, an approach that any group can take on as a service project. . . ."

2 *Call for action*. Suppose you've just explained why you believe the Federal Communications Commission (FCC) should set stricter guidelines for children's television programming. You might conclude with a summary of your arguments, followed by this statement: "What can you do? You can write directly to the FCC and you can write to your congressional representative and senators. I have copies of the addresses here. Four letters may take you 30 minutes to write and less than $2 to mail—and they may help improve the quality of life for countless American children. It's a small investment to make."

3 *Reference to the introduction*. Conclusions that go back to the introduction can balance the speech, bringing ideas full circle. The student who opened her speech with the narrative about Elizabeth's abortion closed this way: "At least Elizabeth was spared the difficulty of battling through harassing throngs to get to her doctor. Her decision to have the abortion was excruciating enough, and the additional agony would be more than she should suffer. I know, because I am Elizabeth."

Speech Transitions

Transition Statement that connects ideas and tells the audience when a speaker is changing topics

Transitions are statements that link points, serving both as bridges between ideas and as "road signs" telling the audience when you are making turns or going in a different direction. You want to keep the audience's mind in the same place as your own, so you need to signal clearly every change. Here are examples for each connection point:

> *From introduction to the body*. Suppose you've just used an ironic, startling statement as an introduction: "It's nice to know we're educating the young. It seems 10-year-olds today can name more brands of beer than they can name U.S. presidents!" Your transition might be, "Some experts—like Dr. George Gerbner of Pennsylvania's Annenberg School of Communication—believe marketing is creating our culture and narrowing the perspective of our people. Let me tell you why communication experts have reached this conclusion— and what they're trying to do about it."

From a main point to a subpoint. If the main point is long, it's a good idea to preview all subpoints just as you preview the speech's main points in the introduction. If it's a briefer speech, less detail is needed—for example, "Three reasons support this idea. Let's look at the first."

From a subpoint to supporting material. This transition uses short phrases to bridge one to the other and provide documentation as an ethical, credible communicator. If you're citing facts or statistics or quoting another source, use phrases such as "According to . . . ," "In the words of . . . ," "Sen. Roberts has said . . . ," "Confucius expressed it this way . . . ," or, "Here's an example of . . ."

From one main point to the next. This transition can remind listeners of the previous point and bridge to the next one with a brief summary and preview, for instance, "We've seen that, morally, this proposal is the right thing to do. But pragmatically, is it something we can afford to do?"

From the last main point to the conclusion. This transition often leads into a summary. An example might be, "So what do we know? We have seen (summary of your main points)" or, "Based on the evidence I've given you, we can only conclude that . . ."

Using Visuals to Enhance Supporting Material

Visual message
Graphic image that helps listeners understand a speech's content

Spoken words usually have greater impact when accompanied by **visual messages.** A study at the Wharton School of the University of Pennsylvania found that when spoken messages were supplemented by visuals, receivers understood more of the content, and, when asked to process the information to make decisions, they arrived at better decisions more quickly.[11]

Graphic images help people "to see relationships, processes, and problems in a way that textual descriptions do not,"[12] both because ideas take shape in graphic form and because people take in more messages through their eyes than through their ears. When the eyes are not focusing on the speaker and supporting visuals, they wander—and the mind follows. Visuals are a big help.

Remember, however, visual aids are not the speech, nor should they only repeat what you say. In fact, visuals can be a detriment when the speaker uses them to escape responsibility for engaging the audience and listeners' eyes glaze over under the onslaught of slides. The point is to *enhance your oral messages* with visual cues.

Visual Formats

"The ability to prepare a slide presentation has become an indispensable corporate survival skill," says *Fortune* magazine.[13] Fortunately, this skill is easy for speakers to learn, and slides are easier to use, because software packages allow you to control the entire presentation alone.[14]

To cool off the presentation escalation, General Hugh Shelton, Chairman of the Joint Chiefs of Staff, recently took the unusual step of ordering military personnel around the world to limit their slide shows to the basic information.

Shelton isn't the only one who's fed up. Navy Secretary Richard Danzig complains, "The idea behind most of these briefings is for us to sit through 100 slides with our eyes glazed over, and then do what all military organizations hope for . . . surrender to an overwhelming mass."

From "'Friendly Fire' of the Electronic Variety," *Dollars & Sense,* July 2000, p. 4.

PowerPoint and similar software packages are easily used even by what one writer calls the "graphically challenged"[15] to create visuals for presentation by providing templates to construct an image (charts, illustrations, drawings, business graphics, and such) that can be shown on slides operated by the speaker. There also is software for adding audio to your presentation[16] and for digital editing.[17] The sky's pretty much the limit.

You can use Speech Builder Express to help you create visual aids for your speech. Select "Visual Aids" from the left-hand menu and follow the instructions.

Even without all this high tech, however, you can produce visuals the old-fashioned way, with overhead projectors, flipcharts, slides, whiteboard, posters, handouts, and/or audio- or videotape segments. Whichever you use, visual aids should support, prove, clarify, or vivify your information—but not overwhelm your presentation or your audience.

To plan your visuals, you need to consider audience size, formality of the situation, and available resources. Chapter 13 develops ways to use your visual materials effectively. Whatever format you choose, remember your credibility is enhanced by high-quality visuals.

Guidelines for Creating Visuals

To be effective, each visual needs to meet three criteria:

1 *Big.* Be sure the visual can be seen easily from any point in the room. Check this with the equipment and in the room where you will be speaking.

2 *Bold.* Give your visuals life and interest. Use vivid colors, engaging graphics, appropriate humor, and audience-involving formats.

3 *Brief.* If your visual uses text, use only key words or phrases of four or fewer words. In both text and graphics, limit each visual to five or fewer key ideas; use

Figure 12.4 *Story-board for planning visuals to supplement a speech*

Outline	Description of Visuals
I. Main point	_____
A. Subpoint 1	_____
1. Supporting detail 1	_____
2. Supporting detail 2	_____
B. Subpoint 2	
1. Supporting detail 3	_____
2. Supporting detail 4	_____
II. Etc.	

multiple slides for complex ideas, laying one over the other if necessary to bring multiple "chunks" together. Round off numbers where possible and set up figures so there's plenty of room for relationships to be seen vividly.

Plan for your visuals as you develop your speech, although final decisions must wait until you're close to completion. A visual should supplement your oral text, not substitute for it, so coordinate the two carefully. In most cases, your visuals allow you to increase the impact of your supporting material—your clarification, proof, and vividness—by involving your listeners' eyes as well as their ears. A *storyboard* is a good way to plan for visuals by providing space—a box or a column—for identifying visuals in your speech notes. Figure 12.4 shows an example.

A good speech is a work of art that uses your thinking, language, and graphic representations to create a message that will inform or persuade your audience to reach the goals you have set.

Summary

Research and development for a speech begin with identifying specific purposes and preparation of a clear, concise thesis statement. Your goals will be achieved through the thinking and/or actions of the audience, so you need to analyze their demographics and psychographics to know how the listeners' knowledge, attitudes, and values might influence their responses.

Speakers demonstrate credibility by delivering a speech that has a clear structure, contains sound evidence and careful reasoning, and uses a style and format that command attention. You develop speech content from your research, selecting the best information and organizing ideas strategically. An organizational structure moves listeners from point to point with appropriate transitions—from a purposeful introduction, through a cohesive body, to an effective conclusion.

Supporting materials clarify, prove, and vivify points for an audience. Examples, comparisons and contrasts, facts, statistics, testimony, explanations, and repetition increase your effectiveness when speaking to inform or persuade listeners to change their attitudes, values, beliefs, and/or behaviors. Effective visuals, whether prepared through specialized software or by hand, should provide variety and clarity to enhance, but not supplant, your oral presentation.

Exercises

1 Choose four of the following and refine the general subject to a specific speech topic. See Figure 12.1 for examples.

Politics	Television	College life	Careers
Technology	Friendship	Civil War	Waterways
Religion	Agriculture	Health	Bioethics

Next, select any two of your refined statements and write a thesis statement that could be used for a speech on the topic.

2 With a partner, select one of the thesis statements that either of you prepared in the previous exercise.

a Create an organizational structure for a speech developing that thesis statement by creating main ideas, subpoints, and possible supporting material.

b Use either an organizational chart (see Figure 12.2) or the traditional outline format to develop the structure.

c Use a specific organizational pattern (chronological, spatial, parts-to-whole, and so on) for each subdivision you create.

3 In a small group, brainstorm as many possible resources for information as you can for the following speech thesis statement:

Visiting Hong Kong provides great opportunities for sightseeing, shopping, and dining.

4 Prepare a brief presentation for the class in which you do the following:

a State an idea in a single declarative sentence.

b Provide one item of supporting material to clarify the idea, identifying the source of the material as you use it.

c Have your audience identify the type of supporting material you have used (for instance, example or testimony).

d Discuss with the audience the quality of the material and its effectiveness in terms of achieving your goal. Would you need different material or sources depending on whether you're using the support to prove as opposed to clarifying or vivifying a point?

5 Review the section in this chapter on analyzing your audience. In a small group, create a two-part audience profile: a general profile, including the audience demographics, and a topic-specific profile, including audience psychographics. Develop your general profile as a group. Then, focus on each group member's topic, one at a time to develop a topic-specific profile for each speaker. The multiple insights of group members will be helpful here. Present your profiles to the class.

Cyberpoints

The following Cyberpoints can be easily accessed from the Student Companion website for this text at http://academic.cengage.com/communication/lumsdenccc3. Click on *Student Book Companion Site* and select this chapter from the pull-down menu at the top of the page that says "Select a chapter." Click on *Cyperpoints* under *Chapter Resources* and you will find links for the exercises following.

1 The Internet can be a tremendous resource for topic ideas and for research. Here are some websites to get you started.

Current News groups lists (http://groups.google.com/)

Public newsletters that you can "search by keyword or category and in thirteen different languages" (http://www.meta-list.net/)

The Invisible Web, "the search engine of search engines," indexes "over 10,000 data bases, archives, and search engines offering links to targeted search sources instead of hundreds or thousands of web pages." (http://www.profusion.com/)

"The Drum Beat, a publication of the Communication Initiative, electronic magazine that features selected articles from developing world newspapers relating to communication, development and change trends, programs and policies" (http://www.comminit.com)

"The National Data Book of the Census Bureau offers a collection of statistics on social and economic conditions in the U.S." (http://www.census.gov/prod/www/statistical-abstract-us.html)

"1stHeadlines links to thousands of headline news stories each day from over 300 newspapers, broadcast, and online sources . . ."(http://www.1st headlines.com)

2 To see some sample speech outlines and storyboards, go to the *Communicating with Credibility and Confidence* Web site at http://academic.cengage.com/communication/lumsdenccc3. Pay special attention to the types of supporting material and how it is used to clarify, prove, and/or vivify. How is support placed in the outline or storyboard? Write a brief summary of what you noticed and how you can use it as you construct your next speech.

3   For up-to-the-minute sources on software for creating visuals, use InfoTrac College Edition and enter the keywords *PowerPoint, visuals,* and *public speaking.* Review 2–5 articles of interest to you. Based on your reading, create a set of 3–7 guidelines you should remember so that your use of PowerPoint is successful.

4   Are you qualified to evaluate your Internet research sources? Read the criteria for evaluating Internet sources in the article by Robert Harris, Professor of English at Vanguard University (http://www.virtualsalt.com/evalu8it .htm). Harris has also authored a book on the topic: *WebQuester: A Guidebook to the Web.* Take notes or download his article for immediate use.

- Summarize what you will apply into a short checklist.
- Use your checklist by finding and recording three Internet sources you can use in your next speech.
- Evaluate each source against the criteria on your checklist.

Chapter 13

Rehearsal and Delivery: Speaking to Audiences

Objectives for This Chapter

Knowledge

- Identify characteristics of different modes of speech presentations
- Know techniques for rehearsing and refining a speech
- Understand how to get set for the moment of presentation
- Know what makes a speech presentation credible to an audience

Feelings and Approaches

- Enjoy preparing, rehearsing, and presenting a speech
- Feel confident in presenting a speech
- Feel that the listeners are partners in a conversation

Communication Abilities

- Select the best presentation mode for an occasion
- Rehearse and polish a speech through visualization and practice
- Manage notes, media, and visuals effectively
- Speak confidently and credibly
- Manage feedback and questions effectively

Key Terms

impromptu speaking   manuscript speaking   memorized speaking

extemporaneous speaking

At the end of every term, we teachers are impressed and gratified when a student who started the class scared, trembling, and inarticulate delivers a confident, credible, well-prepared speech. That successful speaker has prepared material *and* chosen the best mode for presenting the speech, *and* visualized and rehearsed—out loud, with the visuals—until she or he is confident of success. That's what it takes to make a successful speech.

With the right approach to developing and rehearsing your speech, you can go to the podium with confidence and deliver your speech so that your audience engages with you and with your ideas. This chapter discusses how to select your mode of presentation and rehearse so that it will be second nature for you to use notes, manage visuals, and respond to your audience confidently and credibly.

Selecting Your Mode of Presentation

Think about some of the best speakers or lecturers you've heard. Consider them as models for what you want to do. Study their content and their behavior. What made you sit up and listen? What made you feel these speakers were talking directly with *you*? Chances are, their vitality and energy and involvement captured you, whichever type of presentation they chose. Still, successfully reaching your audience depends partly on the type of presentation you choose.

There are four basic modes of speech presentation:

Impromptu speaking
Presenting your ideas in an organized and thoughtful fashion without formal preparation or rehearsal

1   **Impromptu speaking** presents your ideas in an organized and thoughtful fashion *without* formal preparation or rehearsal. You might give a short impromptu speech to support a position or provide information when you're at a meeting. The quality of your impromptu speech depends on how much you already know and have thought about the topic, as well as on your skill in organizing and presenting ideas quickly and articulately. Impromptu speaking is appropriate only for a quick, to-the-point response to a situation; the lack of preparation quickly undermines your effectiveness in longer impromptu presentations.

Extemporaneous speaking Presenting a speech, with key word notes, that has been outlined and rehearsed

2   **Extemporaneous speaking** is a well-prepared, well-organized, and well-rehearsed—but not written-out—presentation for which you have first prepared a complete outline but speak from a few, key-word notes. The wording is developed through repeated oral practice—"talking it out"—rather than writing it out, so precise words may change every time the speech is presented. Extemporaneous speaking is the most flexible, adaptable, and dynamic method for engaging your audience. Usually, an extemporaneous speech gives you the best opportunity

to be a credible communicator by showing both your careful preparation and direct involvement with the audience.

Manuscript speaking
Reading aloud a speech that has been written

3 **Manuscript speaking** is reading aloud a speech you have carefully written with specific wording and notations to indicate emphasis and gestures. Newscasters—and political speakers—read from a paper manuscript or from a TelePrompTer, a monitor that scrolls up the script for the speaker to read. You may need a manuscript when the event is formal, or contains crucial information for a large audience, or when the slightest mistake might have serious repercussions. In other situations speakers may think they will be safer with a manuscript, but they are wrong—a manuscript is difficult to use well, and it creates a wall between speaker and audience.

Memorized speaking
Speaking a written text from memory and rehearsal

4 **Memorized speaking** takes manuscript speaking to a more difficult preparation level through memorization and rehearsal of the written text. Memorizing a speech is difficult, and you lose the spontaneity and flexibility of an extemporaneous presentation. If you forget a word, you're likely to forget the entire flow of the speech.

You may not believe it, but extemporaneous speaking is usually far better than other methods. Why? Because your extemporaneous speech will be more polished and professional than an impromptu speech, and you will be able to communicate more directly and comfortably with the audience than if you are using a manuscript.

Generally, the way you speak normally—your *oral language*—is more dynamic and interesting to listen to than a written message, no matter how well you might recite it. Oral language is more direct, informal, concrete, spontaneous, and often, more believable. Written language is usually more formal, uses a more complex vocabulary level, and often seems more remote. As soon as listeners feel they could more easily read your speech for themselves than listen to you speak it, you've lost them, and their apparent boredom will undermine your confidence.

Another advantage in extemporaneous preparation is that a speech is a dynamic event—so it is not entirely predictable, no matter how well you have planned. You can adapt to the unexpected more easily than if you are reading from a manuscript. With few notes, you are free to observe listeners' responses and to monitor your own. You know your organization, goals, and information, but you are not locked into a word-by-word development. When necessary, you can explain further, omit a point, or add an illustration to help your audience understand and connect with your ideas. You can change your wording on the spot, shifting from abstract words to concrete words—or vice versa—to build coorientation with your audience. If you forget a word or an idea, you can fill in or shift direction without anyone knowing you missed something. Further, you have freedom to move around, gesture, and maintain direct eye contact, because you don't have to battle with a manuscript.

With a manuscript, you're boxed in. If you lose your place, you have to scramble around to find your place. A manuscript burdens you in other ways as well. Reading or memorizing takes much more preparation and performance skill than working from notes and usually results in a less effective presentation. Further, if a problem arises with a manuscript—such as misplaced pages—you may have to shift to extemporaneous speaking anyway. When former President Clinton

Figure 13.1 *Extemporaneous versus manuscript speaking*

Extemporaneous	Manuscript
Oral language, natural delivery	Written language; formal delivery
Flexibility of content	Less flexibility
Adaptability to audience	Little opportunity to adapt
Speaker confidence in communicating directly	Less confidence, less directness
Freedom of movement and gestures	Less freedom of movement and gestures
Greater freedom with technological aids	Less freedom with technological aids
Less certainty that every word will be the same as planned	More certainty that every word will be as planned

presented a health care speech to Congress and the nation, the wrong speech started scrolling on the TelePrompTer. He looked at the screen, realized that the speech was wrong, and proceeded extemporaneously until the problem was corrected. Fortunately, Mr. Clinton is an adept extemporaneous speaker, and he knew his material well.

Figure 13.1 compares manuscript to extemporaneous speaking.

We strongly believe extemporaneous speaking is the place for you to start, so we do not develop manuscript speaking in this text. If, however, you absolutely must use a manuscript for a specific occasion, you might want to consult the *Communicating with Credibility and Confidence* Web site at http://academic.cengage.com/communication/lumsdenccc3 and select Chapter 13 from the pull-down menu.

Visualizing Your Success

We've emphasized throughout this book the impact visualization can make on your effectiveness and self-confidence. Once again, and with feeling, we say: *Envisioning yourself as an effective speaker is important from the moment you start preparing.* Too often, people do just the opposite: They see themselves as nervous and ineffective. Research reveals a circular relationship: Speakers who are very anxious are likely to "see" their upcoming speech negatively,[1] and negative images of a speaking situation make a speaker more anxious.[2] Your anxiety can undermine you from the moment you start preparing, let alone at the moment you get up to speak. Visualizing yourself as confident, credible, and communicative, however, stresses positive images and helps you direct your energy to speak effectively.[3] You manage your anxiety *and* improve your speaking ability.

Although we have discussed positive visualizations and writing affirmations before, we want to stress these things:

1   Take time out to sit down, relax, close your eyes, and focus on positive images of your presentation, both before you practice and before you actually present your speech. Choose a quiet place where you won't be disturbed.

2   Mentally create a visualization for the entire day of your speech[4] (review Chapter 2 for how to do this). See yourself getting up in the morning, dressing appropriately—so you feel and look good—and preparing for an excellent experience. Develop an image of the entire speaking experience. Envision the room; sense what it's like; see yourself entering the room, feeling comfortable and confident. Visualize yourself in front of the audience communicating dynamically and engagingly. See what you are doing and how listeners are responding. Create clear, moving pictures—mental video previews—of yourself succeeding in the presentation and gaining the audience response you desire. Take your visualization all the way through your successful conclusion. Replay the scene in your mind in full living color; concentrate on your positive emotional responses as the successful presentation proceeds.

3   Write out an affirmation—a complete, positive, present-tense description—of your image, feelings, and the audience response you are receiving (see Chapter 2). Make it terrific.

4   Read your affirmation over to yourself before each practice session, and replay the scene, focusing on how positive the experience is.

Preparing and Using Notes

Your notes really do make a difference. Notes have a place in actually developing your speech, in rehearsing it, and certainly in presenting it to an audience. Brief, to-the-point notes unobtrusively remind you of what you want to say without distracting you or the audience and allow you to be communicative and spontaneous in your delivery.

Good notes will remind you of where you are and what you're talking about but *will not tell you precisely the words to use*. Your original outline will use complete sentences and annotations, but your notes will be brief and adapted to changes you make during your rehearsal. Here's our advice to make your notes work for you:

1   Avoid using sheets of paper or large cards—they are awkward, noisy, and distracting to your audience.

2   Put your notes on cards: If you might not have a lectern, use 4" by 6" cards, vertically, that fit easily in your hand. If you know you will speak at a lectern, you can use 5" by 8" cards that you can put down in front of you.

Figure 13.2 *Three sample note cards for an extemporaneous speech*

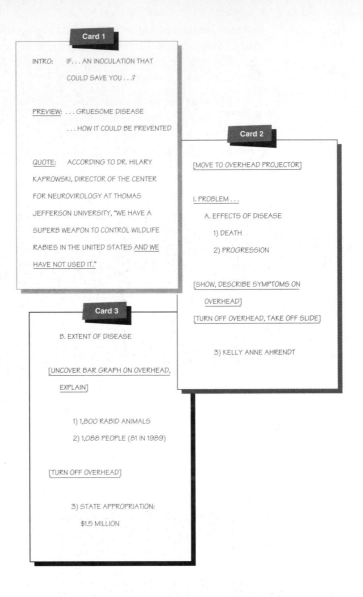

Card 1

INTRO: IF. . . AN INOCULATION THAT

COULD SAVE YOU . . .?

PREVIEW: . . . GRUESOME DISEASE

. . . HOW IT COULD BE PREVENTED

QUOTE: ACCORDING TO DR. HILARY

KAPROWSKI, DIRECTOR OF THE CENTER

FOR NEUROVIROLOGY AT THOMAS

JEFFERSON UNIVERSITY, "WE HAVE A

SUPERB WEAPON TO CONTROL WILDLIFE

RABIES IN THE UNITED STATES AND WE

HAVE NOT USED IT."

Card 2

[MOVE TO OVERHEAD PROJECTOR]

I. PROBLEM . . .

A. EFFECTS OF DISEASE

1) DEATH

2) PROGRESSION

[SHOW, DESCRIBE SYMPTOMS ON

OVERHEAD]

[TURN OFF OVERHEAD, TAKE OFF SLIDE]

3) KELLY ANNE AHRENDT

Card 3

B. EXTENT OF DISEASE

[UNCOVER BAR GRAPH ON OVERHEAD,

EXPLAIN]

1) 1,800 RABID ANIMALS

2) 1,088 PEOPLE (81 IN 1989)

[TURN OFF OVERHEAD]

3) STATE APPROPRIATION:

$1.5 MILLION

3   Use large print so the notes are easy to see quickly.

4   Use only key words in the notes, not full phrases or sentences.

5   Start every new main point on a new note card; it helps to maintain a better sense of your organization during the presentation.

6   Indicate clearly on your notes where you will use visuals or other aids.

7   Number the cards so you won't have to shuffle them to find your place.

Figure 13.2 shows three sample note cards for an extemporaneous presentation. You can see how these note cards would remind you of your main points, ensure that you quote a source correctly, and still give you freedom to adapt and change as you speak.

Rehearsing and Adapting Your Speech

You are ready now for the next three stages of preparing a speech: Practice, practice, and practice. Mark Twain once said that the only way to prepare a speech is to *talk* it. That is, to speak it out loud, feel how it flows, hear how it sounds, and improve it as you go. Good rehearsal is another stage of developing your speech, because *your speech continues to change as you develop your notes, practice, revise, practice, and polish it with a clear image of an effective presentation.* Constructive feedback helps, too.

When you rehearse, practice using your notes as reminders while you talk out loud about the ideas. As you "talk" the speech, you may well modify it by adding supporting material, eliminating a joke, or embellishing an idea, until the speech sounds natural, confident, credible, and communicative. If, after repeated practice, you find that the key words on your note cards don't serve your memory well, add a word or rephrase.

Here are some guidelines to help you get the most from your practice time:

Practice out loud. If you simply look over your notes, you're practicing only part of the actual presentation. Silent rehearsal is like practicing with only two balls for a three-ball juggling act. Moving from idea encoding to transmitting is a significant leap in the communication process.

Rehearse in sections. Instead of starting every practice session with the introduction and going straight through the conclusion, some rehearsals may be more productive if you work repetitively on short sections with which you're having difficulty. In 10 minutes, you might run through an entire speech once, but you could work through a 20- to 30-second segment 20 times.

Use visual and/or audio support as you practice. You want to be sure that any aid you use flows smoothly with the presentation, so it supplements your talk rather than distracts the audience.

Remember you can use Speech Builder Express to help you create visual aids for your speech. Just follow the instructions in Chapter 12 (page 275).

Time yourself. As you develop your presentation, you may add or subtract material. You also will develop a good conversational pace as you "talk it out." Time yourself frequently, and be sure that you are within the allotted time limits.

Rehearse with eye contact. Even if there's no one in the room but you, a tape recorder, and a mirror, talk to imaginary people. Move your eyes to focus on different places in the room, as if there were people there. (We'll discuss more about this shortly.)

There are two kinds of speakers: those that are nervous and those that are liars.

Mark Twain, 19th–20th-century North American writer

Practice in the most realistic location.   Ideally, you would rehearse your speech in the room where you are to present it. If this isn't possible, try to familiarize yourself with the site so you can see the place in your visualization. *And* look for as similar a place as possible to rehearse. Consider:

- *Size and sound.* Get a feel for how much you need to project your voice to reach everyone in the room and how much space you have to move around in without landing in someone's lap.

- *Lighting.* Find out how much light there is, where it falls, and how to control it. If the lighting in the room is dim, you need to be more dynamic and active than if it's bright, because people's attention drifts in low light.

- *Equipment.* Figure out precisely how you will present your audio or visual aids. Know where the electrical outlets are and ensure that the equipment you need is there and working.

Rehearse with feedback.   When you get and use feedback, you perform better.[5] You can get helpful feedback with:

- *Videotape.* If videotape is not available, use audiotape. In either case, focus on what you do well and how you can do it better. Listen for places where you could increase vocal inflection, or pick up or slow down the pace, or pause for greater effect. Find specific things you can do to improve. For instance, don't just look at a tape and say, "My hands are awkward," and then glue them to your sides. Awkward might be better than rigid. Instead, try putting one hand into a pocket briefly, or gesturing to emphasize a point as you would in a conversation with a friend.

- *A friendly audience.* Video replay is more useful if you combine your own assessment with that of a skilled observer to coach you. Ask people who are on your side to listen to you—people who will give you feedback that honestly helps you improve your performance.

> *Effective public speaking is 95 percent mental preparedness and 5 percent technique.*
>
> Dilip Abayasekara, founder of Speaker Services Unlimited

"Getting Set" for Your Speaking Opportunity

"On your marks—get set—go!" Public speaking is much like running a race. You've been "toeing the mark" as you developed and practiced your speech. When the day comes, you have to get set before you go. This means, first, managing your anxiety, and then getting yourself involved in the entire event and analyzing ways in which you need to adapt—and finally, taking command of the room.

Managing Your Nerves

With all that practice and preparation, will you be completely calm? No. You're a reasonable person. You know your presentation can affect your credibility and possibly your grades or career. Of course, it's natural to be apprehensive when you are about to make a speech, but the flow of adrenaline can be a positive force for you. In fact, an overly calm person is usually a boring speaker. Who wants to listen to someone who doesn't seem to care? Your challenge is simply to manage your nervousness and use its energy to enliven your performance—that is, to get all those butterflies to fly in formation.

Here is our advice:

1   *Dress so you look both attractive and professional*. Even for a classroom speech, think of yourself as a career person. How you look affects your credibility and confidence.

2   *Eat a nourishing—but light—meal*. You want the energy food gives you, but you don't want to feel bloated or sleepy.

3   *Do some loosening-up exercises*. Do what actors do. Before you enter the room, go to a private spot—possibly, the restroom—and stretch all of your muscles, one at a time. Consciously work to relax the muscles in your throat, shoulders, and neck. Breathe slowly and deeply. Wiggle your face around, blow air through your lips, make open-throat sounds—"ah, hah, ho"—and think about relaxing your throat and breathing from your diaphragm. Your body is your instrument for speaking, so it must be both relaxed and alert.

4   *Rerun your affirmation statements and visualizations in your mind*. Be sure your mental picture of yourself giving your speech is complete and fresh.

5   *Focus your thoughts on your purpose*. You have a message to share with the audience; so concentrate on that.

Finally, keep the focus on *communicating*. Your listeners aren't there to criticize you—they are there to hear what you have to say. If you're a little less than perfect, that's okay. The audience knows you're human; so are they.

Adapting to Circumstances

When you arrive at your speaking site, become involved with the people and the event. Talk with others prior to the meeting, and participate if other activities are scheduled. When other speakers are making their speeches, concentrate fully on their delivery and their message. This does four things:

1   It keeps your mind off your nerves and on the moment.

2   It keeps your energy up so you can carry it into your presentation.

3   It maintains your connection with the people who will be your audience, keeping the focus on them as your listeners, rather than on yourself.

4   It gives you information you could use in your speech. For example, you may decide you want to shift your visual aid from the left side of the room to the right side because the light is better, or you may hear something from another speaker you'd like to refer to when you talk.

With even the best preparation, you may arrive at a speaking occasion and find unexpected conditions. There could be a power failure, making it impossible to use your overhead projector. There could be a change in the agenda, resulting in your speech being last when you thought it would be first—or vice versa. A previous speaker could cover some material you had planned to discuss. Or another speaker could go overtime, leaving you with fewer minutes than you expected. These possibilities require:

- *Preparing for the unexpected.* Consider in advance where you can elaborate on information, how you can present it differently, and how you can adapt to changes of agenda or equipment. If, for example, technology should fail, it's a lot easier to adapt if you have handouts or are ready to draw on a blackboard, describe verbally, or simply cut out the parts that absolutely require visuals. Knowing you can adapt gives you confidence, and listeners either are not aware of your adaptations or are impressed by your ability to make them.

- *Using the unexpected to your advantage.* You can mention a change, but don't complain about it. Your audience will find you both credible and confident if you deal with the unexpected calmly and smoothly. Suppose, for example, two students speak on the electoral college. The second speaker, Kira, might start with, "Shue has told you how the electoral college works—now I am going to tell you about how it worked in the last presidential election and about current proposals to change it." In this way, Kira provides a credible bridge from the previous speech into her own.

- *Maintaining flexibility.* If someone stops you to ask a question that covers one of your points, you can answer the question, skip over the point, and save the time for other items or for more questions. The goal is to have the audience understand and respond to your speech. If you adapt your presentation—even if you omit something you had intended to cover—that's okay as long as you achieve your overall purpose.

Talking with Your Audience

When you deliver a speech, you are simply talking with people—there are just more of them than in a normal conversation. As in a conversation, you want each person to feel connected with you, to feel you are talking directly with her or him. Because of the larger number of people, however, your communication needs to be bigger—farther ranging and more dynamic—than it would be with one or two people. From the moment you get up to speak, you need to take command in these ways:

Remember you're ready.   At this moment, you are the expert on your topic. You've researched and prepared. That doesn't mean you know everything—but it does mean you have something to which people will want to listen.

Own the room.   In your visualization and in your actions, you want to walk up there and make the audience feel you are in command of yourself and your material. When it's time for you to speak, take a deep breath, look around, and move confidently to the speaking area. Arrange your notes or visuals so they are properly set for you to use. If you are to use a microphone and a lectern, check the microphone height and test it to be sure it's working properly. Unless you are compelled to stay at the lectern and/or microphone, however, you get a much stronger start if you step away from the lectern so you own the entire space, with no barricade between you and your audience. You can put your notes on the lectern and use it as a stage prop, but not as a crutch. If you must use a microphone that's attached to the lectern, stand behind it. The best guideline is, don't touch the lectern—touching leads to leaning on it, wrestling with it, and scrunching behind or over it.

Take a moment to settle in before beginning your speech. Your listeners *want* you to succeed—they are there to hear you—so start by focusing on them. Engage individuals in the audience, eye to eye. Smile. Act friendly. Take a deep breath, and focus on what you want your audience to know or to do. The short period from when you are called up to speak through the first minute of your presentation is critical to managing your overall anxiety during the speech.[6] Don't rush into it!

Introduce the speech firmly.   Give your introduction the way you have practiced it. Don't preamble with, "My speech is about . . ." You deliberately have planned and rehearsed an introduction to get your audience's attention and prepare them to understand and accept your words. Use that introduction. Adapt it to a previous speaker or the situation, if need be, but keep your original strategy in mind, and don't weaken it with a preamble.

Enhance your credibility.   Your listeners measure your credibility, as you know, in the way they see your competence, objectivity, trustworthiness, coorientation, and dynamism. They see it in the honesty and care with which you've done your research and prepared your presentation and in the credible support you provide. You show your credibility, too, in the competence of your preparation and in the dynamism of your delivery.

Communicate with—not at—your listeners.   We talked, in Chapter 1, about a *dialogical ethic;*[7] this feeling of "dialogue" is as important in public speaking as it is in interpersonal conversation. Even though you are one person speaking to many, communicating as in a dialogue means you respect your audience and are providing them information and freedom to choose among options. Even though they are not speaking aloud, you are listening to them—that is, you are considering their perspectives, watching their feedback, considering them your partners in communication. When you do so, you invite listeners into a discussion on the topic, creating genuine listener involvement.

Keep your goals clearly in mind.   Even if you forget something entirely, you can adapt and work toward your purpose—and your listeners probably won't even know you missed a point. If the point you missed is important, try to bring it in later, for instance: "But before I explain just why this is a problem, let me go back for a moment and define what I mean by . . ." Sometimes, humor can help, too.

Don't jump to conclusions about nonverbal reactions. Somebody's frown may indicate thoughtfulness, not displeasure. A person rolling her eyes may only be trying to remember something relating to what you've said. You can't be sure that such cues are negative. If nonverbal cues from one person are distracting you, look at someone else.

Using Nonverbal Delivery

A consultant and trainer for political candidates says, "Think of all the memorable speakers you've ever heard. One trait they all share is their uniqueness."[8] The point is not to be like everyone else, but to learn ways to enhance your nonverbal communication so it engages the audience and fits the situation.

Although some speaking situations are more formal than others, you will feel more confident and your audience will be more interested if you start with the attitude that you're having a conversation with them. Think of it this way: If you're talking with one person, what is your nonverbal communication like? Take a look at Figure 13.3.

As you converse with one person, you feel free to express yourself and to respond to the other person naturally and easily. You easily adjust your gestures and voice to fit within a small area around the two of you, making frequent eye contact as you speak. If two other people join you, what do you do? You speak a little louder, you move your eye contact from person to person, your gestures become just a bit broader, and you shift position to include the other listeners.

If a larger group of people gathers around you, then what? You simply raise the volume of your voice, expand the range of your eye contact, and use broader gestures so you can communicate with everyone in the group. Simple, isn't it? This easy expansion of space is the foundation for talking with an audience of 25 or 250. Whatever the size of the audience, it's just a collection of individual people, each of whom wants to be able to hear you, see you, and understand you.

In that context, your delivery of a speech starts with what you already know and do regularly—the art of conversation. Then it extends to skillful use of your eyes and face, your body and gestures, and your voice and articulation to make it all clear and interesting.

Eyes and Face

Your face and eyes give your audience the first impression of your credibility and goodwill. "But I'm not an actor," students say. "How do I make my face expressive? And if I make eye contact I'll forget what I want to say."

You don't have to be an actor. Expressiveness starts from within and works its way out. Beginning with your visualization, and continuing as you introduce

Figure 13.3 *Expanding audience size, "conversation," and amplitude of movement and voice*

Conversation with one

Conversation with three

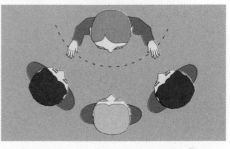

Speech/conversation with many

and develop your speech, see yourself as lively, expressive, and focused on your interest in the topic and the audience. As you develop that approach, your face will reflect what you feel inside. When you ignore your self-consciousness and concentrate on your topic and your listeners, you will show your involvement and confidence. People will react with trust and interest.

The worst thing is to immerse yourself in your notes; you'll drown in them. But if you make eye contact, will you forget what you want to say? Actually, it's

Your eyes, face, hands, and body are all part of your nonverbal delivery.

Al Campanie/Syracuse Newspapers

just the opposite. Your eyes will help you to connect personally with audience members—and that will increase both your confidence in yourself and their belief in your credibility. Here are important guidelines for using eye contact:

Sustain your contact.   When you make eye contact with someone, hold it for several seconds, long enough to actually feel you are speaking to *that* person—one speaker calls that moment a "mind lift"[9]—then move on to someone else. Avoid using the flicker or sweep system of eye contact. That is, don't touch on one person like a firefly and then flit off to someone else or just sweep your eyes back and forth across the room. If you've ever been in the audience when a speaker did these things, you know they're unnatural, unnerving, and uncommunicative.

Look at everybody.   Be sure you make eye contact throughout the entire room. Be careful not to focus mostly on one side or the center of the room; this makes other listeners feel they might as well not be there. What if the audience is too large? That's okay; in a very large audience, your eye contact with one listener makes those behind that person feel as if you are looking at them as well. Just divide your audience into imaginary squares, like a tic-tac-toe pattern. Then focus on a front-center person in each section until you have made full contact, and move on to another section.[10]

Adapt to listeners' responses.   Once in awhile, you have to adjust or break the eye contact rule. If, for example, your eye contact seems to make someone squirm, move on to someone else. Sometimes, culture influences a listener's responses; often, for example, people from Asian cultures are not comfortable with sustained eye contact. If you have a listener who seems hostile, you might try sustained eye contact and a smile or two to try to win the person over. If that doesn't work, just concentrate on the rest of the audience. Finally, some listeners are so friendly and supportive it's a temptation to talk only to them. Appreciate the support, but resist the temptation to carry on a private conversation for too long.

Body and Gestures

You want your audience to be vitalized by your speech—and to accomplish that, you must be vital, too. You develop energy through visualization, relaxation, exercise, and practice. You continue to build enthusiasm for and involvement in your speech just by the way you walk up and own the room. And you carry that energy through your straight, tall, relaxed, and energetic posture.

Does that mean a person in a wheelchair, for example, can't be a powerful speaker? Not at all, but it does mean that the speaker must convey energy and involvement with other cues—eyes, face, gestures, voice. Franklin D. Roosevelt used a wheelchair, but he was a powerful speaker and was elected president four times.

Here are some additional guidelines, to supplement those in Chapter 5, for using body movement and gestures effectively in a speech:

Use your space.   People need change and contrast to keep their attention; your movement helps them stay involved and increases your contact with all parts of the audience. Even in a large room, you can use a clip-on mic or a hand mike, and move around on the stage to emphasize points and convey energy.

Move naturally—but strategically.   If you were having a simple conversation, you would move naturally to emphasize your points, indicate your thoughtfulness, or regulate the conversation. Often, however, public speakers stay glued to one spot, or else they pace like caged tigers. To find natural movements that will emphasize your ideas, think about these guidelines: When you transition from one point to another, walk to the other side of the room. To strengthen the importance of an idea, take a few steps forward. You might move briefly behind the lectern to read a quotation or move to your visual. Move to the side of the podium to feel like you are sharing a conversation with the audience about an important topic.

Let your thoughts dictate your gestures.   Some people use more gestures when talking on the phone than when speaking before an audience. But, don't say to yourself, "I'll slam my fist into my hand here." That kind of planning produces gestures that miss a beat, look unnatural, and make you feel uncomfortable. Remember, audiences believe in you and your message when your words and gestures match.[11] So, let your gestures develop in the context of what you want your audience to know or do. Use your gestures as illustrators to show and as regulators to guide your listeners through your ideas.

Adapt the size of your gestures to the size of your audience.   As you develop gestures, make sure they are appropriately large and broad for your audience—but not so grand that they draw attention away from your point. Look back at Figure 13.3. If you're talking to one person, your gestures are relatively narrow. As your audience expands, your gestures expand as well to encompass the most distant members, using a range about as wide as the distance from the person

An Accent Is No Problem!

Dr. Dilip R. Abayasekara, born and raised in Sri Lanka, spoke mostly Singalese as a child. But he became fascinated with public speaking and, when he came to the U.S.A. to earn his B.S. and Ph.D. in organic chemistry, he pursued his speaking interest through classes and contests. When he entered his first oratorical contest, Dr. Abayasekara says, "It didn't even cross my mind that my accent might be an obstacle. . . . Looking back, I think the professor who organized the contest was surprised that a foreign student entered. I placed second."

Today, Dr. Abayasekara shares his expertise in public speaking through the consulting firm he founded, Speaker Services Unlimited, coaching clients from such diverse areas as professional organizations, colleges, and the Pentagon.

Summarized from Azriela Jaffe, "So Long, Stage Fright," in *Success*, June 2000, p. 70.

---

farthest to your left to the person farthest to your right. Unless you're demonstrating something, keep your gestures above your waist or the lectern so that they are visible to your audience.

Voice and Articulation

A communication trainer notes that "in a clearing in the woods of the Green Mountains of Vermont there is a stone marker with an engraving commemorating that 'on July 7 and 8 in the year 1840, Daniel Webster spoke at this place to 15,000 people.' Without a mike!" The trainer goes on to say that speakers who can't be heard tend "to put the blame on the listener when, in fact, speaking-to-be-heard is becoming a lost art."[12]

She is so correct. When you're speaking to an audience, remember two things. First, each listener does not have constant eye contact with you and may not be close enough—or see well enough—to read your lips or pick up your more subtle facial expressions. Your vocal inflection and pace may be the best cues to what you want to convey. Second, audience members usually won't stop you to ask, "What did you say?" Nor, as when reading a book, can they flip back to review a previous page. So clear pronunciation of your words is crucial to your success.

No one voice is best, nor is any one dialect superior. There is, however, a best way to use your voice, and there are ways to articulate clearly so that people understand you no matter what dialect you speak. Our advice is this:

1 *Develop the most effective use of your voice.* You have the best vocal quality and appear most confident and relaxed when your throat is open, although you adjust the degree of openness for the meaning you want to convey.[13] Try the

exercises at the end of this chapter to develop an open throat, and practice speaking like that in conversation as well as in speeches.

2 *Focus on the meaning you want to convey.* Practice with a tape recorder and stretch your ability to communicate your ideas. Develop variety in your pitch, rate, and volume to help your listeners understand your meaning and reinforce your credibility.[14] Try various combinations of inflections, pace, volume, and pitch for conveying the emphasis, feelings, and impact you want to communicate.

3 *Pronounce your words correctly and articulate them clearly.* When you're with a group of old friends who know you well, they know how you speak and are quick to grasp your meaning. Public speaking, however, demands that you make your ideas clear for an audience who doesn't have that advantage. If people can't understand you, you lose credibility and, probably, listeners. Wolvin, Berko, and Wolvin point out that "if you say 'air' for 'error' or 'din't' for 'didn't,' you are being lazy in your use of articulators."[15] People stereotype others on the basis of their speech, and you don't want a prejudgment to reduce your credibility. Check correct pronunciation of words, listen to yourself on tape to pick up sloppy or unclear speech, and have others listen to you and give you feedback.

4 *Use pauses, rate, and emphasis to clarify meaning.* Your speech is clearer and more interesting if you pause between thoughts, vary your rate of speech to suit your audience as well as your meaning, and emphasize ideas with changes in volume and pitch. Some of our students whose first language was not English have been brilliant speakers—not because they lost their accents, but because they used pauses, variation in rate, and emphasis to make their meaning clear.

5 *Reduce detractors to a minimum.* Everyone occasionally uses vocalized pauses like "um" or verbalized pauses such as "y'know." Silences are preferable to such sounds, but don't worry about a random filler in your speech. If you use these detractors habitually, perhaps while you gather your thoughts or as a punctuation sound between many phrases, then they become distracting and annoying. To eliminate them from your speech, you need to become aware of them (video, audio, or personal feedback helps), and then consciously edit them from your oral speech. Surprisingly, it isn't very hard to do. You have to stop yourself a few times, sometimes in mid-"um," but that's okay. Just stop and then go on with your statement.

Using Visuals

Visuals—whether old-fashioned and simple or technological and sophisticated—are only as good as you make them and as effective as you are in using them. At the year 2000 Republican National Convention, Laura Bush looked at her TelePrompTers for her speech only to find that enthusiastic delegates had besieged them with confetti—and made them inoperable. Fortunately for Bush, she was able to see a TV screen that also displayed her text.[16] She was lucky.

It's not about "acting" a speech, it's about getting to the "truth" of what it is you're trying to say, and what you want from your audience.

Bill Crounse, president of a firm specializing in media and speech coaching for political candidates

Sometimes you just have to know what you're going to say and do if your visuals—or TelePrompTer—fail you.

This incident is a reminder of the need to *rehearse* with your visual, audio, or demonstration aids as well as to prepare alternatives if they fail you. Learn how much time it takes to switch from talking to presenting the visual and back again. Among other things, get a feeling for how the visual aids can help relax you as a speaker; both your focus and the audience's attention are diverted temporarily from you. Not only can this reduce anxiety, but your physical movement as you turn from the audience to the visual and back to your notes actually helps your body relax.

Here are a few other things to remember when using visuals of any kind:

- *Use visuals to supplement speaking, not supplant it.* The point is to keep attention and reinforce information. It's so easy to create overhead visuals by computer that some people project their entire speech on the screen. Boring! Snooze time! Don't do it.

- *Talk to the audience, not to the visual.* A rule to guide you is "TTT—touch-turn-talk." Touch—identify the visual area you want the audience to focus on. Turn—redirect your attention to the audience by engaging them with direct individual eye contact. Talk—continue with your oral message.

- *Cover everything but what you want the audience to focus on.* If you're using an overhead projector to show a list of items, for example, only reveal one at a time as you talk. Keep the others covered. When you are finished using a visual, turn it off, cover it, or remove it so the audience doesn't continue to concentrate on the aid and miss what follows.

- *Beware of passing around handouts, pictures, or objects.* If you must give the audience material to hold or pass, do it only as you go over it with them. Otherwise, they get absorbed in reading or looking at your handouts and stop paying attention to you.

Answering Questions

Inexperienced speakers tend to fear questions, but questions can be your best friends. Questions allow you to be sure your message has been understood correctly and to respond to concerns or objections audience members may have.

Before you start, be aware of how the situation, people's expectations, and cultural differences may affect questioning, so you can plan ahead. Some situations allow little time for questioning, so you have to manage the session tightly. Or there is too much time and people aren't asking questions. It's wise to think ahead so you can fill that time with added information.

Some groups, too, do not expect to ask questions or, the reverse, to engage in a full dialogue. For example, many Asian people do not expect to respond with questions—whereas the French ask a lot of them.[17] You need to inquire beforehand what listeners expect.

Digital Presentations: Make Your Delivery Effective

Most presentation software includes graphics and images that can be used as part of a presentation. A word of warning, though: Don't get carried away! While graphics can be pleasing and humorous, try to keep them to a minimum so they don't detract from the content.

But Web pages and other documents on computer monitors are another story altogether. They are designed to be viewed by one person at a distance of less than 20 inches. Ironically, some presenters fail to take this into account because even during the presentation they are staring at a 15-inch monitor or small laptop screen.

Unfortunately, the audience gets seasick while the mouse glides swiftly across the screen or while a page goes scrolling by in a blur. Most trainers learn, through experience, to slow down, to tell the audience what they are about to do, and to repeat movements as needed. Project your work onto a large screen and see what it looks like.

From D. Scott Brandt, technology training librarian at Purdue University Libraries in West Lafayette, Indiana, "Digital Presentations: Make Your Delivery Effective," *Computers in Libraries* 18:4 (May 1998): 35, 38, 39.

Even with the best preparation, question sessions can be intimidating. Martel gives this very good advice for question-and-answer sessions: "Don't participate in the session until you have a positive attitude regarding how it can help you accomplish both your substance and image goals."[18] Of course your speech answered some questions, but time limits may prohibit covering everything. So rehearse for your friends (or coaching team, if you're running for president!) and have them ask practice questions (perhaps about data, sources, consequences) as well as identify points listeners might challenge. Anticipate both honest and hostile or trick questions so you can get a feel for potential answers—how might you respond to demonstrate your competence, objectivity, and trustworthiness and still make your point?

Your credibility can be enormously enhanced by masterful responses to questions; the skills are fairly simple, but impressive in action. Start by assuming questions are well intentioned. Even if they aren't, treating them as if they were puts the ball in your court and reflects favorably on you. Then listen intently, and answer questions as concisely and directly as possible, maintaining a friendly and cooperative approach.

When questions are confusing or tricky, try these techniques:

1 If the question is hard to hear or is long and complicated, take a moment to analyze it and restate it more briefly for the audience.

2 If the question really involves two or more questions, separate them and state your intention to answer them individually.

3   If the questioner makes a speech instead of asking a question, don't disagree or argue. Listen courteously, and then phrase a question from it or ask the speaker to phrase the question.

4   If the question is loaded ("Why would you spend money on a dead-end project?"), do three things: Point out how the question is loaded, reject it as stated, then shift to a better question ("I disagree that this is a dead-end project, and I can't logically answer that question as it is phrased. Now, if you mean what will this project do to justify the expense, I can give you three benefits it will bring to this community").[19]

5   If the answer to a question is complicated, organize your response into concise chunks and begin with a preview: "Four concerns are involved here. The first is . . ."

6   If you already answered the question, don't mention that fact. Just answer it again, perhaps expanding your response slightly.

7   If you don't have an answer, say so; don't fake it. If appropriate, promise to find out the answer and get back to the questioner.

8   If the information is on one of your visuals, go back and show it as you discuss the answer.

You may someday face a questioner who is overtly hostile. Remember that hostility from one person doesn't cancel out the majority who are supportive and favorable to your message. The key is to stay cool and friendly; don't get sarcastic or defensive, because that's giving control to the questioner. Sometimes, you can "bridge" the question—that is, start with what the questioner said and move the topic to your ground. For example, after your speech about oral vaccine for rabies, a listener asks, "How can you talk about spending money on this vaccine when there isn't even enough money to build new schools?" You might answer, "Whether oral vaccine is the best priority for funds is a legitimate question. As you recall, one state spent $1.5 million to treat people who were exposed to rabies. So the issue is not whether to spend the money, but whether to spend it on prevention or on treatment."

Summary

Preparing for a speech starts with deciding whether to present it as an impromptu, extemporaneous, orally read manuscript, or memorized speech. Extemporaneous delivery uses more oral language and enables you to adapt more readily to the situation and audience, although sometimes a manuscript is essential for specificity or control of public messages.

You need to prepare careful notes for extemporaneous speaking. Use numbered cards, large print, and key words as cues. Notes allow you to "talk" the development of the speech using key words to trigger memory while using conversational language.

The process of rehearsing and adapting the speech starts with visualizing and affirming yourself successfully presenting it. You also need extensive practice (preferably at the site, but certainly in a quiet place) with videotape and personal feedback from friends to help you polish the presentation. Practice also involves handling the visuals until using them is second nature and identifying possible questions and preparing answers for them.

Before delivering the speech, get set mentally and physically by visualizing, relaxing, exercising both body and articulators, and becoming fully involved in the audience and the situation. Sometimes, you need to adapt your approach to accommodate changes in agenda, other speakers, or technological difficulties. Being prepared to adapt increases your confidence and your credibility. When you approach the lectern, take command and engage your audience in such a way that you demonstrate your credibility and interest in them. Maintaining your confidence as you speak is easier if you keep the focus on the audience and your message rather than on yourself.

Delivering your speech effectively involves using the same nonverbal abilities as in a one-to-one conversation, but simply expanding the range of your voice, gestures, eye contact, and body movements to accommodate your conversation to a larger group. Upright posture, good eye contact, expressive gestures, vocal variety, and clear articulation are essential to communicating well in a public speaking situation.

Finally, handling questions in a cool, well-organized, friendly manner enables you to clarify ideas and enlist the cooperation of the audience.

Exercises

1   Attend a public presentation—a lecture, a sermon, a business presentation, or the like. Evaluate the speaker's presentation. Consider:

   a The mode of presentation, the management of notes or manuscript, and the use of visuals or other aids

   b The language (Does it seem oral or written?), the adaptation to the audience, and the speaker's credibility

   c The degree to which the speaker appeared to be confident and the way she or he handled questions

   d The speaker's presentation abilities—uses of body, face, eyes, gestures, voice, and speech

   What was effective and what would you suggest the speaker do to improve his or her presentation? Report your observations to the class.

2   Select a short essay on a controversial topic from a book or magazine. Then do the following:

   a Read it over once. Then, for a small group of fellow students, make a 3-minute impromptu speech with an introduction, body, and conclusion, on the essay's topic. (Don't look back at the essay.)

b   After making your impromptu speech to your group, refer back to the essay. Now take 30 minutes to select specific points to develop a thesis and supporting information. Organize, practice, and present—*in your own words, not the author's*—a 3-minute extemporaneous speech with an introduction, body, and conclusion for your group.

3   Voice and breathing. With a partner, tape-record a session in which you take turns doing the following exercises. Listen carefully and coach each other. Then, for one week, do the exercises privately three times a day, trying to build up stronger breath support, a more open throat, and crisper articulation of sounds. At the end of the week, have another session with your partner and tape-record yourselves again. Play back the first recording and the last. Do you hear any differences in either of your performances? Do you feel any differences in the amount of breath support or in your articulation of words?

a   To develop strong breath support and open throat, draw your breath in evenly as you slowly count (mentally) to six, pursing your lips so you can hear the air pushing into your lungs. Next, hold the air for another six counts, keeping your throat open. Then exhale slowly and evenly as you count (mentally) to six, again keeping your lips pursed so you can hear the exhalation. Be careful not to exhale too fast at first. Repeat once.

b   To learn to control your breathing, say each of these words but try to control your breath so it doesn't all rush out at once:

   hit—home—half—hot—head—heavy

   Feel how the air tends to rush out because the h sound is made with a panting movement of air. Try to hold back some of that air so it is more evenly available for the full word.

c   Try to say this in one breath:

   Have you ever seen such a wonderful, splendiferous sight as a spider spinning, swirling, sending its silky, slender string amongst the stickily, prickly boughs of a tree trembling in the nebulous night?

   Now, do it again, trying to parcel out enough bits of breath for each portion of the sentence.

4   Articulation. Reread the instructions for Exercise 3 and follow them with your partner as you practice the exercises following:

a   Recite this phrase:

   lots of hot coffee in a proper coffee pot

   Listen for the clarity of *t* and *p* sounds; these should be crisp. Also listen for an *ah* tone in the *o* sounds. If you make an *aw* sound, try to make the sound farther back in the mouth with a more open throat.

b Try this one:

> *Theophilus Thistle, the successful thistle sifter, in sifting a sieve full of unsifted thistles, thrust 3,000 thistles through the thick of his thumb. Since thousands of successful thistle sifters have sifted unsifted thistles without thrusting thistles into their thumbs, Theophilus Thistle is an unsuccessful thistle sifter indeed. We wish success to Theophilus Thistle, the faithful, if clumsy, thistle sifter.*

Listen for clear *th* sounds, made by pushing air through the tip of the tongue against the top teeth, and for clear *s* sounds, made by pushing air through the tip of the tongue just barely touching—briefly—the ridge behind the top front teeth. On the *s* sounds, if you make a *th* sound, the tongue is a bit too far forward and flat; if the *s* whistles, the tongue tip is placed too hard against the ridge.

c Now try this one:

> *If Axelrod only would ask Askew to drop the axe nicely, Askew would act in accordance and Axelrod's accelerating anxiety about an axe-induced ache would no longer accrue.*

Listen for clear *x* sounds, made starting in the back of the mouth and moving the tongue forward quickly from a *k* to an *s* position. And listen for a clear *s*; sometimes, people reverse the order of the *s* and *k* sounds in words, which substitutes *x* for *sk*, resulting in *axe* instead of *ask*, for example.

Cyberpoints

The following Cyberpoints can be easily accessed from the Student Companion website for this text at http://academic.cengage.com/communication/lumsdenccc3. Click on *Student Book Companion Site* and select this chapter from the pull-down menu at the top of the page that says "Select a chapter . . ." Click on *Cyperpoints* under *Chapter Resources* and you will find links for the exercises following.

1 Do you need to make a manuscript speech? Go to the *Communicating with Credibility and Confidence* website at http://academic.cengage.com/communication/lumsdenccc3 and select Chapter 13 from the pull-down menu for some hints on how to prepare a manuscript. What do you feel were the most helpful hints presented? Why?

2 Would you like to improve your voice or your speech? Go to Chapter 13 on the *Communicating with Credibility and Confidence* website for exercises that will specifically help you to develop your delivery skills. Or check out the Virtual Presentation Assistant at http://www.ku.edu/~coms/virtual_assistant/vpa/vpa.htm for further help on preparation and presentation. What are three ideas for improvement you discovered?

3 For additional help on using visuals effectively, see the advice of the Oceanography Society for the Office of Naval Research at http://www.onr .navy.mil/about/speaking%5Ftips/handouts.asp. Scroll down to the "Visual Aids" title and the section called "The Ten Commandments of Visual Aids." What are three ideas you could use to improve your use of visuals?

4 At http://www.lib.msu.edu/vincent, you can listen to excerpts from the speeches of a number of U.S. presidents. You'll find a wide variety of styles and ways of using the voice among these speakers. Whom did you listen to? Of those you heard, whom would you choose as a role model? Why? Whom would you definitely *not* choose as a role model? Why not?

Chapter 14

Public Presentations: Speaking to Inform

Chip Henderson/Getty Images

Objectives for This Chapter

Knowledge

- Identify purposes and contexts of informative speaking
- Know ways to help audiences understand and remember information
- Understand methods to help listeners learn

Feelings and Approaches

- Feel confident in communicating information
- Approach speaking to inform with the audience's benefit as a central focus
- Enjoy interacting with audiences to help them understand

Communication Abilities

- Present information credibly
- Design a presentation that motivates others to learn
- Set measurable objectives for enhancing listeners' understanding
- Present information effectively in various contexts

Key Terms

audience motives   parallel structure   mnemonic device

learning style   associate ideas   reinforcement

Did you ever try to explain something, only to see the listener's eyes glaze over, and you try again—and again—to make the information clear? Talk about frustrating! This happens to teachers every day, and to the rest of the world almost as often.

This is an information age, they say, and ours is an information society. From classes to study groups to researching projects, you are gathering information. From giving reports to coaching Little League to explaining an idea to a friend, you are providing information.

Sharing information is so important that some communication theorists list it as the second key role of communication, after gaining cooperation.[1] The problem is, people are presented with too much to know and remember; it's estimated that the "sum of all knowledge is now doubling every seven years."[2] As a speaker, therefore, you compete for your listeners' comprehension against a multitude of unrelated facts and ideas. That's why you must be both credible as a source of information and confident of your ability to inform people effectively.

This chapter will help you develop the ability to impart information and enhance others' understanding in a variety of contexts.

Speaking to Inform

Almost any speech includes some explanation and data that informs the audience, but many presentations focus specifically on sharing ideas or information. You hear lectures—that is, speeches to inform you about a topic—every class day. It's true, of course, the same data presented solely to inform you may also serve in another speech to support a persuasive appeal to vote for your candidate or donate to a cause. Either way, the speech design depends, in part, on the occasion and specific content of the speech.

Occasions for Informative Speaking

The most relevant occasion, at the moment, probably is a class speaking assignment meant to prepare you for future speaking opportunities, including:

- *Reports.* As a student, you give research or project reports to your classmates, but soon, you may give reports to colleagues or managers in your job. Health care professionals report on treatment and patient progress to their teams; managers report on sales and marketing campaigns to executive boards; members of organizational teams report research to teammates and superiors; your professors report research results or academic projects at conferences and, sometimes, to administrative committees or boards.

- *Briefings.* Many jobs include briefing people on information about some action they must take. A briefing specifically focuses information and analysis on what receivers need to know. A major part of a researcher's or analyst's job is preparing someone else to answer questions and convey information intelligently. Executives, politicians, and top newscasters often rely on briefings for research and analysis they will subsequently use in presentations, meetings, press conferences, or broadcasts.

- *Lectures.* If you're good at what you do, you may find yourself lecturing about it, perhaps using slides or other visual aids to present your information. You probably will carry on a dialogue with your audience through question-and-answer sessions, and you might combine lecture with discussion and other teaching methods.

- *Training.* You may train someone else to play a sport, do a job, make a presentation, understand the way an organization works—almost anything. A primary objective of corporations these days is to train people to work together and manage themselves.[3] One communication career option, therefore, is in training business, social, religious, academic, and community organizations. Such training develops not just people's skills but their understanding of theories and data so they can assume more responsibility for a wider range of individual and team activities.

Types of Content

Whatever the topic or purpose, when you speak to inform the audience you normally talk about objects, events, processes, and/or concepts.[4] Here's an example: Your art history professor's lecture about Michelangelo might touch on:

Objects.   The speaker describes or explains something tangible and concrete; your professor shows you a slide of paintings on the ceiling of the Sistine Chapel and describes the details of their composition and color, enhancing your understanding of the object.

Events.   The speaker gives a description and, perhaps, a chronology of events to clarify how a given occurrence fits into a larger context; perhaps she explains events that led Michelangelo to lie on his back for years, painting a ceiling he never wanted to paint in the first place.

Processes.   The speaker shows relationships among various components in developing some outcome; the professor might explain Michelangelo's process of cartooning, projecting, preparing, and painting a mammoth depiction of the biblical story of creation on a ceiling. Sometimes, a speech about processes includes demonstration and/or hands-on experience to help the learner internalize the information.

Training is everything. The peach was once a bitter almond; cauliflower is nothing but cabbage with a college education.

Mark Twain, 19th–20th-century American author

Concepts. The speaker defines complex ideas about theories, beliefs, values, philosophies, and/or viewpoints, often using a variety of perspectives to help listeners grasp the concept. Your lecturer might explain Michelangelo's concept of how a form emerges, through the artist's sculpture, from its prison in a piece of marble—and why the artist found sculpture so much more satisfying than painting.

Audience Motivations and Learning Styles

You set the objectives—but only your listener can reach them. Your job is to be credible and confident in shaping and presenting information so your audience can use it. Part of that job is knowing how to draw on your audience's motivations and ways of comprehending and learning.

You can apply principles of motivation (see Chapter 3) to planning your speech. The object is to use **audience motives**—their needs, wants, and values—as a foundation for motivating the audience to listen.

Remember, too, that individuals process information differently. Each person has an individual **learning style** that uses one or both sides of the brain[5] and reflects such influences as our abilities, personalities, culture, and perhaps gender. These differences can affect your speech in a number of ways. For example:

- *Your audience's cultures affect how they respond to information.* Research finds, for instance, that Anglo and Asian learners are likely to use analytic learning, breaking ideas down into component parts. Native Americans, Hispanics, and African Americans, however, tend to use a relational style, relating ideas to one another holistically.[6]

- *Your listeners' styles may be different from yours.* Speakers may unconsciously reflect a cultural bias in the ways they present information,[7] imitating their own teachers without recognizing that the method may not help a diverse audience to learn.[8] In North American classrooms, for example, most students *need* more visual information that uses their right brains intuitively and creatively, but what they often *get* is more lectures or abstract symbols on a whiteboard. This is due to a Western bias toward linear or analytic left-brain thinking.[9]

- *Some listeners expect to interact and question; some don't.* Powell and Andersen note that in Asian cultures, students "receive information and then reflect upon it," neither disagreeing nor asking questions because "such behavior would threaten the 'face' of the teacher who is a revered and respected individual."[10] Native American students also tend to learn silently, through observation and imitation, whereas North American Anglos often question, respond, and discuss ideas.[11] Figure 14.1 summarizes the relationship between culture and learning.

If your listeners all are just like you, maybe they learn the same way you do. Your best bet, however, is to vary your presentation so individuals can process your information in the diverse ways best suited to them.

Audience motives
Listeners' reasons for wanting to know what a speaker presents to them

Learning style The way an individual processes information, influenced by the side of the brain used and individual ability, personality, culture, and, perhaps, gender

Figure 14.1 *The relationship between culture and learning*

Low-Context Cultures:

- Provide information in words
- Are less aware of nonverbal cues, environment, and situation
- Lack well-developed networks
- Need detailed background information
- Tend to segment and compartmentalize information
- Control information on a "need to know" basis
- Prefer explicit and careful directions from someone who "knows"
- View knowledge as a commodity

High-Context Cultures:

- Draw much information from the surroundings
- View nonverbal cues as important
- Exchange information freely
- Rely on physical context for information
- Take environment, situation, gestures, and mood into account
- Maintain extensive information networks
- Are accustomed to interruptions
- Do not always adhere to schedules

Monochronic People:

- Do one thing at a time
- Concentrate on the job
- Take time commitments (deadlines, schedules) seriously
- Are low context and need information
- Adhere religiously to plans
- Are concerned about not disturbing conversations
- Emphasize promptness

Polychronic People:

- Do many things at once
- Are highly distractible and subject to interruptions
- Consider time commitments an objective to be achieved if possible
- Are committed to people and human relationships
- Change plans often and easily

Methods to Aid Understanding and Memory

How can you help your audience to understand and remember? American students retain about 10% of what they read, 26% of what they hear, 30% of what they see, 50% of what they see and hear, 70% of what they say, and 90% of what they say *as* they practice what they are learning.[12] This is good news for your own learning; giving your presentation will teach *you* a lot. If you can design a speech that helps your audience to hear what you say, perhaps also to see it, and even to practice it, then they, too, will remember what you've taught them. To help your audience understand your information, you can start by wording your points to help them remember the connections among them and by supporting your ideas with material that strengthens and clarifies the points in your listeners' minds.

Organizational Patterns

You already know some effective patterns for organizing the body of a speech from Chapter 12. Now let's look at some additional patterns that specifically help to enhance your listeners' understanding and memory.

Extended Analogy or Example *Analogies* and *examples* are a great way to clarify concepts—the analogy draws on previous knowledge and the example illustrates the idea. Extending an analogy or an example throughout your speech can serve as an organizational pattern.

Suppose your speech is to inform the local Chamber of Commerce of how management structures in the city's corporations are changing from vertical to horizontal organizations. The body of your speech might be an analogy comparing an urban skyscraper to a traditional Spanish home, in which case you would structure your subpoints to show spatial relationships:

    I. Traditional organizations and skyscrapers are tall.
        A. Communication from the bottom to the top is limited.
        B. Creative flow from the bottom to the top is limited.
        C. Participation from the bottom to the top is limited.
   II. Contemporary organizations and Spanish homes are horizontal.
        A. Communication among all parts of the organization flows freely.
        B. Creative flow among all parts of the organization is free and open.
        C. Participation among all parts of the organization is encouraged.

Using drawings of each type of building, you could show how the skyscraper has levels piled on one another, with the power offices at the top and specialized areas underneath them. Only elevators and staircases provide communication from level to level. You would compare this to the Spanish home, with all the rooms on one level, arranged around a central patio accessible to all areas of the house so people can interact openly and freely.

Acronym Arrangement An *acronym* is a word you create out of the first letters of several related ideas. As an organizational pattern, you create an acronym from the first letters of each of the main points of a speech. This helps your audience (and you) remember the specific ideas. Recalling the acronym triggers

Dr. Samuel Betances

Dr. Samuel Betances, internationally known "edutainer," consults with businesses and educational institutions—teaches and entertains—writes and lectures—on how to communicate and get along in this widely diverse society. A professor of sociology at Northeastern Illinois University, Dr. Betances earned his masters and doctorate at Harvard University. He is a funny, wise, and incredibly communicative teacher, as well as an agent of change in a changing world. Dr. Betances has said, among other things:

I remember coming from Puerto Rico and going to school being intelligent and yet unskilled. My teachers looked at my generation and said, "Speak English," and we said, "Si." And they said, "Forget Spanish," and we said, "OK." But before we learned English we forgot Spanish, and soon we were illiterate in two languages. How dumb to tell us to forget what we know. . . . You need to learn middle-class English, [but] do not forget what you knew, because in order to be good Americans, you don't have to know less, you have to know more.

I came to school, I did not understand the language of English. . . . The teachers gave a demonstration of what they wanted us to know in English, . . . and I missed out on the explanation, not because I lacked intelligence, but because I lacked the symbolism. And sometimes the teacher did not know how to express something in the way that I could understand it. . . . I was failing for not knowing what I had not been taught. She . . . gave us 14 problems in arithmetic for homework. Victor told me that in Spanish. So I went home and I began to work on my 14 problems in arithmetic, and I had missed out on the explanation, and I did not know what to do. . . . By the time I got to the fourth one I was almost crying. [My mama] said, "Don't worry, I will help you," and she did the next one, and I kissed her and she did the next one, and I kissed her, and soon we were on a roll, she was doing, I was kissing, and then I copied all of them in my own handwriting, handed them to the teacher ('cuz I'm Puerto Rican, but I'm not a fool), the teacher came back, the first four that

memory of all the message. If your speech is on maintaining optimal health through weight control and physical conditioning, your acronym organization might be VEER:

    I. **V** is for "Visualize yourself as thin."

    II. **E** is for "Eat sensibly."

    III. **E** is for "Exercise faithfully."

    IV. **R** is for "Reward yourself appropriately."

Your organization also gives you ideas for introducing and concluding your speech. You might start with, "How would you like to VEER from the fat lane,

I did had four red "x" marks, and then the ten that my mama did had ten red "x" marks. So I said, "Victor, come here. She marked them all wrong!" Victor said, "Teacher, Sammy's got a confession to make. He did the first four, but what you don't know is that his mama did the next ten! And you marked all wrong!" And Miss Carmel said, "Tell him his mama doesn't know what she's doing." She said something about my mama! So I said something about her father! And stupid Victor translated it. Next thing I know, I'm at the principal's office writing 500 times, something that to this day, I don't know what I wrote. But I suspect it has something to do with somebody's mama.

Listen to me. I was intelligent. Harvard-bound. Sometimes corporations today send their helicopter to pick me up. And when colleges think of freshman orientations, and think about the future, they send for me. Intelligent, yes, but unskilled. My mother loved me, but she was unskilled. The teachers worked hard, but they did not know how to communicate with us. And I'm telling you something, you who are now entering this freshman class: Learn to collaborate with other young people and those of you that know how to do it, learn how to do it better by helping those of us who are intelligent but unskilled. To give them the opportunity, to tutor, to collaborate, and to make coalitions of interest instead of coalitions of color so that we can march to the front door, all of us helping each other. The one that tutors learns it better by teaching it to those that don't know, and the ones that don't know get it from other students, because sometimes some of us teachers don't know how to do it, and some of the parents love us but do not know how to give us what we need. . . . Are you ready to collaborate and to make those coalitions of interest and to help each other out so that you can all be successful?

Amen! Well all right, let's do it.

From Dr. Samuel Betances's presentation at Kean University, Union, New Jersey, August 30, 1993. Used by permission.

to drive down the thin lane, and enjoy the view in your mirror? I'm going to show you how to do that in four easy steps."

Journalist's Formula In a journalism class, you learn to write stories that answer the *who, what, when, where, why,* and *how* questions. These questions provide an excellent pattern for a briefing, report, or explanation of an event, arranging some or all of the categories to suit your topic. You might organize a report to your employer this way:

I. What do we want to accomplish?

II. How can we do it?

III. Who should be responsible?

IV. When can we implement the program?

Another way to apply this formula is in subpoints under any other pattern, such as problem-solution:

I. We had a problem with our product's quality.

    A. The problem was a defective spring. (What?)

    B. The problem was caused by the manufacturer's error. (Why?)

II. We solved the problem with our product's quality.

    A. We changed the contract with the manufacturer to require quality testing before they ship the springs to us. (How?)

    B. We implemented our plan at the plant during last quarter. (When?)

Demonstration   Often, a speech to inform demonstrates how a procedure works through a chronological, step-by-step procedure that shows as well as tells your listeners what they need to know. Methods to help your audience grasp the process include:

Grouping steps.   Group ("chunk") the steps into no more than five logical main points. Don't commit the common error of going straight down a list of 10 or so steps. They are too hard to remember. For example, one of our students spoke on how to prepare a résumé. She started preparing with a long list of ideas: Brainstorm, request references, check transcripts, organize ideas, state objectives, list education, note academic and extracurricular experiences, draft, edit, type, print—it was far too much to remember. So she organized the body of the speech like this:

I. Analyze your qualifications.

    A. Identify important academic experiences.

    B. Identify important extracurricular experiences.

    C. Identify important skills and abilities.

II. Assemble the pieces.

    A. Request letters of recommendation.

    B. Order transcripts.

III. Create the résumé.

    A. List important elements.

    B. Emphasize important points.

    C. Set up for visual impact.

    D. Write for clarity.

    E. Edit for accuracy.

Seest thou not how God hath coined a parable? A good word is like a good tree whose root is firmly fixed and whose top is in the sky. . . . And a corrupt word is like a corrupt tree which has been torn off the ground, and has no fixity. . . .

Koran 14:24–27

IV. Publish the résumé.
    A. Have the résumé professionally typed.
    B. Have the résumé professionally printed.

Using visuals. Plan your demonstration with visuals that develop each step on the outline. Then rehearse carefully to be sure you can develop each step sufficiently in the length of time you have. Demonstrations are worse than useless when the speaker rushes through without proper equipment. The résumé speaker communicated effectively within her time limits by projecting slides to show her audience, step by step, how she had prepared a professional-looking résumé.

Preparing in advance. Plan ways to prepare portions of your demonstration ahead of time. The perfect example of this is when television's many cooking show hosts grate a bit of chocolate and put it on the stove to melt—but then use chocolate that was previously grated and melted. They mix the chocolate mousse and slip it into the oven as the viewers salivate—but when a lucky guest savors a taste of the mousse at the end of the show, it's a mousse that was baked earlier.

Outline Wording

The way you *phrase* the main and subpoints of your speech makes the logical connections between your ideas. It just isn't enough to have a list of topics. "Let's see," you may say to yourself, "I'll talk about how aerobics helps the heart and respiratory system and how to do aerobics." To weave these points into a logical and memorable development you need to:

- *Connect phrased points logically.* In this case, you may think you have three main points, but close examination shows that you really have two: how aerobics can help one's health (the subpoints would deal with benefits to the heart and respiratory system specifically), and how one can do aerobics.

- *Word points to help you with the extemporaneous development of the speech.* You do not want a prewritten manuscript, but your talk should carry through the logical development of your outline. If you clearly state each point on the outline, you will more easily remember and develop the ideas.

- *Word points to help listeners follow and understand you.* We can't emphasize this enough. Plain old word lists, such as "Economy—Living—Success," just won't do. You need full statements of each main point and subpoint that make your idea clear and have logical relationships to the other points.

Parallel structure
Organization or material that uses same phrasing for each of a series of ideas

    An excellent way to phrase main points, as well as subpoints for each, is to use parallel structure. **Parallel structure** is repeatedly using the same phrasing to introduce or complete each of a series of new and equal ideas so the wording reinforces and intensifies the impact of the ideas. You'll notice that our sample speech outlines use parallel structure. Parallel structure doesn't just make the outline seem smooth and seamless—though it does that, too. Hearing the same phrases to introduce each idea helps your audience to see and remember the logic of your speech. Further, the very process of thinking through and phrasing points serves you in these critical ways:

> Using parallel structure helps you create logical categories that are equal to one another.
>
> Using parallel structure helps you remember what you want to say with few notes.
>
> Using parallel structure allows you to adapt as you speak.

Look, for example, at the brief outline at the end of this chapter for a student's speech about preparing for a career in physical therapy.

As you can see, the body of the speech uses a parts-to-whole organizational pattern with main points focusing on equal topics of motivation, discipline, and involvement. With the parallel wording "*A physical therapy student* must . . . ," the speaker and listener can see each point as immediately related to one another and to the whole process of preparing to become a physical therapist. Similarly, under each main point, the parallel use of "*Your . . .*" underscores personal responsibility for developing qualifications for this major.

After preparing the body of the speech with clear parallel points, the introduction is easier to craft. This speech opens with a personal anecdote that leads directly into the preview and the body. The parallelism also makes the transitions easy to design so they bridge the points with a few words that summarize the previous point and preview the next one. Finally, the clear parallel structure simplifies creating a quick summary and a conclusion that brings all of these points together. In this case, that goal is accomplished by using a conclusion with a rhetorical question and a reference back to the introduction.

Support for Ideas

You already know a lot about supporting your ideas from Chapter 12. We will expand those concepts specifically for speeches to inform. The criteria for support in an informative speech, of course, is that it be clear and specific; the first criterion for clarity is using the simplest, most concrete language possible. Sometimes, however, you will be introducing complicated concepts and new vocabulary to your listeners. Supporting such new material often involves defining terms, associating ideas, and using language that enlivens and clarifies the information in some way.

Defining Ideas   Dictionaries are fine, but sometimes other methods of definition are more accurate or clearer—or more interesting. Suppose, for example, you were speaking of love. You could define it by using:

Quotations from authorities.   Look for experts' quotations in reference books or specialized dictionaries or articles or books on the subject. You might go to psychology textbooks or scholarly books on the nature and types of love.

Negation.   Showing what something is *not* is "definition by negation," as when Apostle Paul writes to the Corinthians that love "does not envy, it does not boast, it is not proud. It is not rude, it is not self-seeking, it is not easily angered, it keeps no record of wrongs. Love does not delight in evil but rejoices in the truth."[13]

Comparison and contrast.   Weigh the concept against other, more familiar, ideas. For instance, you could use an analogy or an example to compare attributes, such as, "Love is like a flowing stream, moving and nourishing those it touches." Or you could quote a poet's or philosopher's analogy, such as Kahlil Gibran's "Stand together and yet not too near together for the pillars of the temple, in order to hold the temple up, stand apart. The oak tree and the cypress do not grow in each other's shadow."[14]

Components.   Break the concept down to component parts and define each separately—then put them back together. Perhaps you would define love by citing psychologist Branden's concept that love involves spiritual, emotional, and sexual attachment,[15] and then proceed to use those terms as the foundation for the three main points of your speech.

Historical roots.   You can use history as a foundation for defining a concept. One way is to trace the etymology of the term in a given language and culture. Love often is defined in terms of the classic Greek concepts of filial love, spiritual love, and erotic love. You might talk about all three, or you might focus your speech on romantic love and trace that concept through the centuries. Alternatively, you might compare and contrast the views of love held by different cultures through history.

Associating Ideas   Your listeners already have ideas and information you can use to help them learn. When you link that information to new material, or **associate ideas,** the new material seems more familiar, less threatening, and easier to learn than if it were presented as totally unfamiliar. Maybe you're trying to explain the concept of ethics to people who have never heard the term, so you start from their religious frame of reference. The study of ethics goes far beyond one religion, but understanding can start with the familiar concept.

Another aid to your listeners' memories (and your own!) is a **mnemonic device,** a memory aid that connects ideas to other ideas. It's something like remembering where a place is by remembering what you had for lunch there. Useful mnemonic devices include:

Acronyms.   We talked about using acronyms as organizational patterns for speeches, but you can also use them for subpoints or to summarize a single point. Suppose you were speaking on stress management; you might say, "Remember to 'ALF'—Always Laugh First."

Similar symbols.   You can relate a visual symbol to a word so the association triggers a memory. People often use this trick to remember a new acquaintance's name. If the name is "Fawcett," for example, you rehearse it mentally, picturing a faucet with the person's face. A speaker can give listeners a similar hint to help them remember a concept. You might help your listeners remember

Associate ideas New material that is directly linked by a speaker to existing ideas and information

Mnemonic device Memory aid used to connect ideas

Michael Siluk/The Image Works

that it was Theodore Roosevelt who said, "Walk softly and carry a big stick," by telling them to think of a teddy bear carrying a baseball bat.

Metaphors and analogies. These devices express the similarities between two ideas, show logical relationships, and help an audience to associate a new concept with a strong or familiar bit of support. For example, a statistics professor helped one of your authors—Gay—by saying, "Statistical analysis is like language—it just uses mathematical symbols instead of words to show relationships among ideas." With just one analogy, that teacher melted away a mental block and opened the road to understanding statistical concepts.

Reinforcing Ideas   Reinforcement is repeatedly underscoring an idea and intensifying its importance so it stands out in the mind of the listener against competing demands for attention and memory. You can reinforce your ideas with:

Reinforcement Process of repeating an idea and underscoring its importance so it stands out in listeners' memories

Rewards. You can link your main points to a reward—to something the audience wants or values. People find rewards in the reasons you give them for listening. Your listeners might see a reward in listening to your speech on physical fitness, for instance, if you remind them that fitness can benefit their sex lives.

Repetition. You can repeat ideas in the same words. Repetition is especially important in helping people remember a concept by giving the idea extra importance and strength. In a speech on animal husbandry, for example, you might repeat the phrase, "The welfare of your stock is the welfare of your family," to emphasize the economic importance of learning how to care for your animals properly.

Ways to Use Participation and Feedback

Today's audiences are a restless bunch. As Wolvin, Berko, and Wolvin observe, "Most of us who have been raised on television have come to expect a seven-to-ten-minute viewing format, followed by a commercial break."[16] People fade out or squirm when they get bored and also tend to forget anything that didn't involve them. That means the more you can get your listeners involved in ideas and feedback, the better. The extra dividend is that when you're really engaged in transactions with your audience, you are less nervous—and when you get feedback, you feel even better.

Audience Participation

You can get an audience to participate actively in your presentation in a number of ways. For example:

1   *Ask them questions, get them to think about the topic, and open up discussion.* Keep the questions nonthreatening, and give people a little time to answer. Speakers too often ask the question and immediately proceed to the next point. If you were giving a speech on job interviewing, for example, you might ask, "What would impress a potential employer with your leadership ability?" After having listeners brainstorm ideas and write them on a flipchart or whiteboard, you could select one and then ask, "Now, how could you show this in an interview?"

2   *Give them hands-on opportunities as you speak.* In a speech on selective perception, for example, you might ask audience members to close their eyes and listen intently for 60 seconds—and then have them make a list of everything they just heard.

3   *Use guides, quizzes, or exercises as you speak.* A student reporting on gender differences in communication, for example, gave listeners a list of statements about male versus female language and had them mark "True" or "False." She then referred to the quiz as she spoke, asking her audience for their responses and opinions, and relating her research findings to the statements.

4   *Enlist audience members to role-play a situation with you.* You can demonstrate a point quickly by asking a person in the audience to be someone else for a moment. We once heard a speaker ask someone to role-play her employee. Then she asked, "Now, how would you respond if I said, 'You really do lousy work, don't you?'" Of course, the role-player answered defensively. Then the speaker said, "Right. Now, let's do it another way. Suppose you've handed me a

report and I've looked at it. I say, 'I can see you've put a lot of effort into this. There are just a couple of things I'd like to go over with you.'" Naturally, the role-player's response was much less defensive, and the speaker had effectively used her audience to make her point about using supportive communication. If you have plenty of time for your presentation, you can vary this by having two members of your audience role-play for you.

Feedback Opportunities

Everybody needs feedback to find out what they've done and what they want to do next time. The most effective feedback lets you know how well you met your objectives and indicates what changes you need to make. Approaches for getting and giving mutually helpful feedback include the following:

- *A presentation assessment by your listeners*. You can use a handout sheet on which you ask for general or specific information about how effective they found your presentation. You'll find some sample feedback forms on the *Communicating with Credibility and Confidence* website at http://academic.cengage.com/communication/lumsdenccc3 (select Chapter 14 from the pull-down menu) that you may want to try or adapt for your own purposes.

- *A quiz that tests information or concepts you tried to teach*. If people are to take this quiz immediately, it should be brief, easy to read and check, and questions should focus on one point at a time.

- *A hands-on demonstration of specific skills you wanted people to learn*. You can ask people to show you what you've told or taught them; for example, if you demonstrated how to cross-stitch, you might give each participant a small bit of cross-stitch to do for you.

Feedback only helps if you can use what it tells you, either for yourself or for your audience. If you're testing listeners' learning, for example, try to summarize the results and discuss them in general terms with your audience. This can clarify and reinforce information that the listeners may have misunderstood or missed entirely. If you're asking for feedback to improve your presentations, then view it purely as potential help for you. Summarize them, read comments, and isolate one or two objectives to strive for next time. Most people give you good, honest, supportive responses.

Your Source Credibility and Confidence

When you set out to inform people, you are acting as an intermediary—someone who researches and refines information for others. Before you speak, you will have researched the topic thoroughly. You will know more about the topic than your listeners do, and have analyzed and interpreted your data for them. Most of your listeners' understanding will come from what you choose to tell them and from your responses to their feedback and questions. As the listeners' intermediary, then, you bear an ethical responsibility for what they learn.

A credible and ethical speaker should always have the good of the audience in mind and be open to discussing alternative ideas.[17] In addition, the speaker should present information that is,

Accurate. The information is specific and precise.

Complete. The information includes all important factors.

Relevant. The information relates directly to the point.

Understandable. The information is explained clearly and fully.

Reasonable. The information is developed logically.

Socially useful. The information can serve good purposes.

Meet these criteria and you will be both credible and confident—you will know what you're talking about, and your audience will know you're on their side.

Summary

At school and in your career, you may give many presentations to inform, including reports, briefings, lectures, and training sessions. Your presentations should be based on learning objectives—clearly stated, specific, measurable, and reasonable goals that you want your listeners to accomplish. Your confidence and credibility rely, in part, on your using basic principles of learning to tap into your listeners' motivations. Then you can get them to attend, listen, and remember through techniques of definition, association, and reinforcement.

Proper wording of your outline aids both your own memory and presentation and your audience's understanding and memory. Each main point should be carefully worded in full, declarative sentences and coordinated with each other main point in parallel structure. Each subpoint, too, should be a complete declarative sentence that parallels other subpoints under a main point. The summary of your information should be clear and focused, followed by a conclusion that reinforces the information and listeners' motivation to remember and use it.

In addition to the organizational patterns explained in Chapter 12, extended analogies or examples, acronym arrangements, the journalist's who-what-when-where-why-how formula, and step-by-step demonstrations work well in speeches to inform. Seek to involve your audience as much as possible with questions, hands-on experiences, guides and exercises, and role-playing with or between audience members. You can get and give feedback relating to your objectives by asking listeners to fill out an evaluation of your presentation, to take a quiz or test on the content you presented, and/or to demonstrate what they learned to do with a hands-on exercise.

Exercises

1 Identify a hypothetical audience (for example, a civic or religious group, a political setting, a school group). Select any chapter of this book and plan a 5-minute speech for this audience to inform them about some part of the chapter's content. Remember that a 5-minute time period will allow you to cover only two to four concepts from the chapter you select.

2 Get together with a partner and share the plans you developed for Exercise 1. Then work together to refine the plans. Compare your perceptions of the audiences' needs and expectations. Now create an outline together, using a specific organizational pattern worded with parallel structure (see "Outline Wording" in this chapter). Under each point, suggest the kind of supporting materials (from both the text and other sources) you might use, and create an introduction and conclusion. Then work together to present your plan, and your thinking behind the plan, to the class.

3 With a small group, click on and print a *Speech to Inform Assessment Sheet* from the *Communicating with Credibility and Confidence* website using the following Cyberpoints instructions. Then observe a short videotaped speech (your college resource center, library, or your instructor may have a collection of these) or a live speech on television. Now meet with your group and compare each member's ratings on the assessment form. In what places are your ratings similar? On what items do you differ? What aspects of the speech led to similar assessments? What tended to make your responses differ? As a group, present your findings to the class.

4 Plan and present to your class a 5-minute speech to inform using this chapter and the Sample Speech to Inform Outline & Commentary as resources. Your speech can be a lecture, a report, or a demonstration of a process (see "Occasions for Informative Speaking" earlier in this chapter). Make a complete, parallel structure outline with a bibliography of the resources you used. Write a brief (5–10 questions), objective quiz (true/false or multiple choice questions), duplicate it, and have your classmates complete it to assess how well they learned the principles you set out to convey.

Cyberpoints

The following Cyberpoints can be easily accessed from the Student Companion website for this text at http://academic.cengage.com/communication/lumsdenccc3. Click on *Student Book Companion Site* and select this chapter from the pull-down menu at the top of the page that says "Select a chapter." Click on *Cyperpoints* under *Chapter Resources* and you will find links for the exercises following.

1 To help you plan a PowerPoint presentation, try: www.presentersuniversity .com/visuals.php. Look under the heading, "Designing Effective Visual Aids," for the February 2004 article titled, "The Deadly Sins of Modern PowerPoint Usage." Also look under the heading, "Using Visual Aid Effectively," for "3 Quick PowerPoint Tips to Keep the Punch in Presentations" (October 2003) and "Top Ten Tips for PowerPoint Slide Shows" (June 2000). Summarize what you learned that will improve your next use of PowerPoint.

2 How's your research for your informative speech going? Save time and frustration by using InfoTrac College Edition for your research. Locate articles by using the keyword search field by entering key terms that relate to your topic. Record the search terms that you used and the resources you found that you plan on using to prepare your speech. What were your frustrations? What search strategies got you your best results?

SAMPLE SPEECH TO INFORM

Commentary

Topic: What is involved in preparing to be a physical therapist
Purpose: For the audience to understand the personal effort to become a physical therapist
Thesis: A career in physical therapy takes motivational, academic, and experiential preparation.
Introduction: The speaker uses a personal narrative with strong imagery and descriptive wording to get the audience's attention, to build rapport with the audience, and to develop her credibility on the topic.

Preview

The speaker summarizes smoothly the three main points of the presentation so her audience will know precisely what she will discuss. As she develops the speech through practice, she may add a brief transition, such as, "What do I mean, first, by 'motivational preparation'?"

Body of Speech

Organizational pattern. The points are organized as parts relating to the whole picture—a parts-to-whole pattern.

Main points. Each of the three main points is worded as a declarative sentence parallel to each of the other two, each starting with "A physical therapy student must be. . . ." This helps both speaker and audience to follow the logic of the speech.

Outline

Introduction

Three years ago, an automobile accident changed my life forever. I found myself lying in a hospital bed, twisted in pain, unable to move my legs, and scared to death. I thought I might never walk again. Today, I ride horseback, swim, run—I feel great. I feel great because 2 years of physical therapy restored my body and my confidence. That's why I've decided to become a physical therapist—so I can help others get their bodies and their confidence back, too. But I have discovered that becoming a physical therapist is nearly as hard as my recovery was.

Preview

I'm going to share with you what I've learned about becoming a physical therapist—what it takes in motivational, academic, and experiential preparation.

Body of Speech

I. A physical therapy student must be highly motivated to overcome discouragement along the way.
   A. Your ability to meet the heavy requirements is essential.
   B. Your ability to compete against many other well-qualified, motivated students is essential.

   Transition: Not only do you have to be motivated to meet requirements and compete against other equally motivated students, but you also have to be extremely well disciplined to succeed academically.

(continued)

SAMPLE SPEECH (continued)

Commentary

Subpoints. Under each main point, all subpoints are of equal type and weight, with each subpoint worded parallel to the other two. As the speaker plans the speech, she will add supporting materials to develop the subpoints. These should include examples, statistics, quotations from physical therapists or researchers, and explanations.

Transitions. Between the first and second and the second and third main points, the speaker has planned a transition that bridges the two points. The first transition ties together motivation and discipline. The second transition ties together discipline and experience. This way the "parts-to-the-whole" are woven together into the total picture for the audience.

Conclusion
The speaker weaves together four methods of conclusion: A rhetorical question (answered by her personal testimony), a brief summary, a reference back to the introduction, and a strong concluding statement. In so doing she reminds the audience of all she has said and reaffirms her convictions and her credibility.

Outline

II. A physical therapy student must be highly disciplined to succeed academically.
   A. Your social life is a dream of the past.
   B. Your professional life is a dream of the future.
   C. Your college life is a nightmare of studying in the present.
   Transition: All this academic discipline and sacrifice isn't enough, however. You also must be highly involved in the field itself.
III. A physical therapy student must be highly involved in the field to be admitted to a program.
   A. Your application must demonstrate extensive volunteer experience in the field.
   B. Your interview must demonstrate extensive knowledge of the field.

Summary
I've told you a little bit about how motivated a person must be to overcome discouragement in such a demanding and competitive field—how much discipline it takes to succeed in academic and hands-on requirements—and how thoroughly involved in volunteer activities and the field a student must be to get admitted into a physical therapy program.

Conclusion
Do you think it's worth it? I do. I think becoming a physical therapist is worth every bit of motivation and discipline and involvement it takes—because, without physical therapy, I would not be standing here today to talk about it. Now I can help someone else to have that same new chance at life. Yes, I definitely think becoming a physical therapist is worth it.

Chapter 15

Public Presentations: Speaking to Persuade

Bob Adelman/Magnum

Objectives for This Chapter

Knowledge

- Identify components of the persuasive process
- Know principles of influencing change
- Understand strategies for organizing persuasive messages
- Identify appeals that motivate audiences to change
- Know how language affects audience responses

Feelings and Approaches

- See persuasion as an artistic transaction between speaker and audience
- Feel confident in designing a persuasive speech
- Feel credible in influencing an audience to change
- Honor ethical standards in using persuasive strategies

Communication Abilities

- Analyze audiences and goals as a foundation for persuasive speeches
- Organize speeches psychologically and logically to move audiences
- Select emotional, logical, and psychological appeals to motivate audiences
- Develop an audience's belief in your credibility
- Use persuasive language that moves the audience to understand and accept your position

Key Terms

persuasion

self-persuasion

beliefs

attitudes

values

behaviors

social judgment theory

deductive speech pattern

inductive speech pattern

problem-solution speech pattern

motivated-sequence speech pattern

residues speech pattern

Persuasion is about influencing others to change how they feel, or think, or act. Whether you're selling shoes or running for president, your ability to influence others is important to you in many ways—in your career, maintaining relationships, contributing to your community. Democratic societies depend on members to advocate all sides of important issues persuasively so citizens can make reasoned and ethical decisions that affect the good of all.

As a member of a democratic society, you engage in what Barber calls "political talk."[1] By this he means not just talk about politics, but communication about values, options, and decisions within the political framework of your religious organization, your business, and your community. Political talk could include working with others on social or religious issues—for example, to change a school's curriculum or to get a new stop sign to protect children from injury.

As political talk, then, persuasion often is the basis for your relationships with other citizens. More than just speech, says Barber, the process includes listening, thinking, setting agendas, and engaging in mutual inquiry; this transactional communication "makes and remakes the world."[2]

Although this chapter focuses on designing speeches to get public audiences to change, the principles of persuasion apply any time you try to get even one person to accept your point of view. Here we examine persuasion as a process to influence change, and we discuss ways to use your knowledge about your audience to adapt persuasive messages. Then we give you some strategies for organizing persuasive speeches, we develop methods for achieving credibility, and we examine ways that effective language enhances persuasive messages.

Process of Persuasion

Persuasion *Process of moving an audience to change willingly its beliefs, attitudes, values, and/or behaviors*

Persuasion is the process of moving your audience to change their beliefs, attitudes, values, and/or behaviors—and to change them willingly. Let's consider what each part of this definition implies.

Willingness to Change

If you get what you want by holding a gun to someone's head, that's not persuasion, it's coercion. Coercion uses fear or blackmail to force someone to comply; it may win submission but it doesn't win minds or hearts or ensure future commitments. You might be compelled to hand over your money to a robber, for instance,

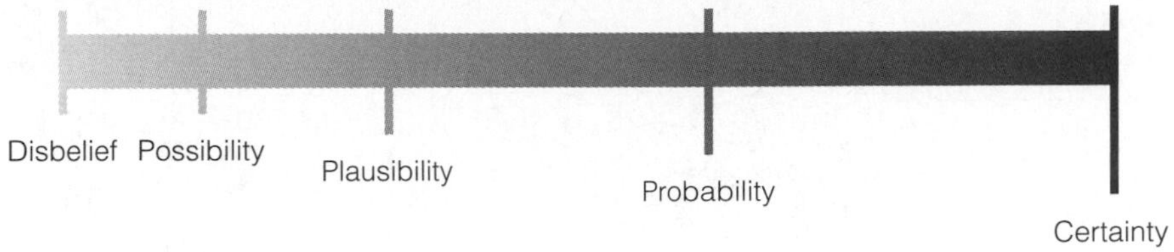

Figure 15.1 *Scale showing range for beliefs*

Disbelief Possibility

Plausibility

Probability

Certainty

but the experience won't persuade you to seek out another robber to whom to give money the next day.

Persuasion starts with people's motives and gives them reasons for change and action. As a persuader, you are ethically concerned with the benefit and free choice of the audience. Far from manipulating your audience to do something they wouldn't do otherwise, you maintain respect for your listeners' rights to agree or disagree and give them reasons to agree with you.

Ultimately, any change your audience makes is through **self-persuasion.** As a speaker, your influence depends on providing material that activates the audience members' motives—their needs, values, beliefs, attitudes, and goals. From these motives, individuals develop their own rationale for changing in some way. In that sense, persuasion is transactional, building change on elements contributed by you and by the audience itself. Centuries ago, Aristotle identified the speaker's challenge as "finding all available means of persuasion."[3] He didn't guarantee that any method would always be successful, because audiences still have individual choices and motives.

Self-persuasion
Process by which an audience develops a rationale for change because of information provided by a speaker

Beliefs

Often a person doesn't know enough about a subject, or "knows"—that is, believes—mistaken information. In persuasion, you give your audience information necessary to change beliefs relating to your goals. If you and your message are credible and audience members accept the information, then you have inspired them either to adopt new beliefs or to change old ones. As beliefs change, related attitudes, values, and behaviors may change as well—and that's persuasion.

Beliefs Degree to which a person accepts something as true

We previously defined **beliefs** as "what people have learned or come to know through experience; they are either true or represent what they think is true."[4] Think of beliefs along a continuum, ranging from 0% (no belief that something is true) to 100% (total certainty that something is true).

Figure 15.1 shows a belief scale. Once you acknowledge the slightest chance something is true, you categorize it as "possible." When you have more reason to believe the statement, you consider it "plausible." When you conclude that something is more likely true than not, you view it as "probable." When you have no doubt in your mind, your belief is "certain." You might believe it is highly probable that money put in Salvation Army kettles during the December holidays will provide help for needy people. But are you equally confident that money given to *all* charitable organizations provides *all* the services the groups claim?

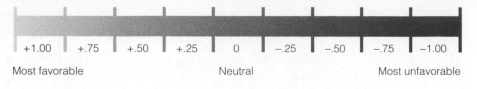

Figure 15.2 *Scale showing range of possible attitude positions*

+1.00   +.75   +.50   +.25   0   −.25   −.50   −.75   −1.00

Most favorable   Neutral   Most unfavorable

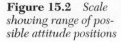

I see the world verbally. You say truth, you say justice, you say democracy, you say development—words don't create them, but if they do not exist in words they will never exist.

Carlos Fuentes, 20th-century Mexican writer and diplomat

Attitudes Internal degree of favor or disfavor an individual holds about people, objects, or ideas

---

Although you may believe something is probable if it has better than a 50% chance of being true, you may want a higher degree of confidence than that to take action. Certainty, however, is even more elusive. You know true/false test items that state "Always" or "Never" are usually false, because few things are that absolute. Fortunately, you don't usually need to persuade your audience that something is certain; simply persuading your listeners to be less sure or more sure—a move in either direction—represents a change. Suppose you're asking people to give money for hungry children, and your audience believes it is only *possible* your program will actually feed the kids. That isn't good enough; you have to persuade them that their donations *probably* will provide food.

Attitudes

Even though persuaders seek to change others' attitudes all the time, the actual attitude is an unobservable, internal degree of favor or disfavor, like or dislike, that an individual feels about people, objects, or ideas. **Attitudes** are, as we defined them in Chapter 3, preset responses, stable and enduring dispositions to evaluate things in particular ways. "Virtually anything that is discriminable can be evaluated and therefore can function as an attitude object."[5]

Attitude Scales   While the continuum for describing a belief ranges from "I don't believe that" to "I totally believe it," an attitude is different. You can measure an attitude along a scale from a positive to a negative side, perhaps from "It's wonderful" down to "It's horrible." As Figure 15.2 shows, an attitude might be shown on a scale anywhere from a positive extreme of +1.00 to a negative extreme of −1.00. The "0" point indicates a neutral attitude—neither favorable nor unfavorable.

Suppose at the beginning of a new term somebody hands you a scale like this one and asks you to identify your attitude toward each class you've enrolled in. If you have no previous knowledge for a class, your attitude may be neutral. Maybe you've heard one is excellent, so your attitude is, perhaps, a +.50—you think you might like it. Another class could be known as boring or excessively difficult, so you might rate it −75. Attitudes can change with new experiences, however; you may find the difficult-class instructor to be brilliant and would rate the course positively by the end of the term. Or vice versa.

Attitude Change   People often think of persuasion as getting your audience to shift all the way from one side of the scale to the other, but really, an attitude change is any movement along the continuum. For example, a shift from +.50 to +.60 is change in a positive direction, and from +.50 to +.40 in a negative direction. Those small attitude shifts may be sufficient for your purposes.

Imagine you're speaking on behalf of Julie Coldwell's candidacy for mayor. One voter, Ishi, has a −.15 attitude toward Coldwell, while her attitude toward Coldwell's opponent, Bob Pawley, is −.10. If she were voting now, Ishi probably would select Pawley as the lesser of two evils. But if her attitude changed as little as .06, she would move to Coldwell. That .06 change could occur in several ways: Coldwell could move ahead of Pawley (from −.15 to −.09), or Pawley could fall behind (from −.10 to −.16). Or they could both move in some combination that adds to .06 (such as Coldwell moving from −.15 to −.12 and Pawley moving from −.10 to −.13).

That's just Ishi's shift, of course. How about the rest of the audience? Another misconception is that you need to get all or most of the audience to change attitudes. You can be very successful by convincing only a small *portion* of the audience. Just enough to put you over the top. In sales, marketers talk about "share" (proportion of the overall market your product sells to), and you can have a very successful business if you sell toothpaste to only a 5% share of the U.S. market. The same is true in other persuasive efforts.

Let's return to the election example. Say Coldwell trails her opponent by 4% (that is, Pawley 52% to Coldwell 48%), so she could win by influencing a small attitude change in just over 2% of the voters from the group favoring Pawley. If she has analyzed her audience to choose the best strategies to persuade that 2+%, Coldwell could win.

Values

You might change specific beliefs or even attitudes. You can rarely change values. You *can*—and in fact do—use your audience's values as a foundation for building their motivation to accept your position. Why? **Values** are, as previously defined, "conceptions of The Good or The Desirable that motivate human behavior and that function as criteria in our making of choices and judgments."[6] Values become most evident when people assign priorities (often, unconsciously) to decide not just what is important but what is more—or most—important to them. Values are central to an individual's concept of self. A challenge to a value is a challenge to all the person believes she or he is, and trying to change it will create resistance in your audience. When you recognize, accept, and appeal to individuals' values, however, you can persuade your audience to change a belief, attitude, or behavior.

You may detect that audience members do not see that their values are in conflict with their attitudes, beliefs, and/or behaviors. That inconsistency becomes a basis for persuasion. Here's an example: A couple has little money and always spend as little as possible, so they plan to buy the cheapest available car seat for their new baby. If you can persuade them a more expensive car seat is significantly safer, their value for baby's safety might outweigh their value for saving money—and they might well buy your product.

Values Concepts of good or desirable that motivate behavior and serve as criteria for choice and judgments

And a Little Child Shall Lead Them

The May 7, 1992, issue of the Clayton (Georgia) Tribune *reported on a Ku Klux Klan march in that city the previous weekend:*

[The KKK] had anticipated as many as 50 members might participate in the march, but only about 13 were on hand. . . .

The Klan members started their slow march across the street from where members of the Persimmon Church of God were conducting a car wash and bake sale to raise money for their church building fund. . . .

When one of the youngsters started singing, "Jesus Loves the Little Children," every one of them joined in to serenade the Klan members—men and women—as they walked by in single file. To the observers, it was a powerful statement, a touching moment befitting the occasion.

"It was spontaneous from the children," [Raburn] Wilson [an adult member of the church group] said. "The adults had wanted them to remain silent."

In the same issue, an editorialist added:

It set the stage for the remainder of a lousy day for the Klan. "Jesus Loves the Little Children" is a very old, very familiar religious song. It has been sung louder by much larger choirs many times before, but we doubt it has ever been more magnificent.

The article concluded:

"We washed 120 cars and sold 100 cakes," Wilson said. "I don't understand it. We usually average only about 20."

Excepts from Dick Gentry, "Only 13 March in Klan Parade; It Was a Non-event, Official Says," *Clayton Tribune*, May 7, 1992, p. D5, and Editorial, "A Child Shall Lead Them," p. A4.

Behaviors

Behaviors External, observable actions that interact with beliefs, attitudes, and values

Behaviors are external, observable actions—things people consciously and unconsciously say and do—that interact with their beliefs, attitudes, and values. You can't always know what's behind a behavior. You might see two people give a homeless person some money and a third one walk right by. Perhaps the first one accepts biblical teaching to give to the poor, and does so because of her religious belief. Perhaps the second one has felt good about giving before, decided that's the kind of person he is, and now always gives because that's his belief about himself. And, perhaps, the third one has heard authorities say that giving to beggars only keeps them from working at an honest job, so she doesn't give because she believes what the authorities say. To get a contribution from the third, the beggar may need to convince her that he is seeking a job. Indeed, you see people holding signs, "Will work for food," an appeal to just that person.

An example of relationships among values, attitudes, beliefs, and behaviors can be seen in one researcher's reports on interviews with both "pro-life" and "pro-choice" advocates. The subjects were only those highly involved in behalf of each cause. Their radically different activist behaviors were intertwined with very different beliefs, attitudes, and values. In the interviews, pro-life activists said people should engage in sexual intercourse only for procreation, and parenthood is not primarily a social role, but a natural and necessary human function. Pro-choice proponents, on the other hand, contended sex is to foster intimacy and give pleasure, and wanting a child, and giving it psychological, social, and financial resources, are essential to parenthood.[7] Obviously, to get members of either group to change their behaviors on this issue would demand substantial internal changes as well.

Another example of conflicts between behaviors and values is reflected in the phenomenon called "NIMBY" (Not In My Back Yard). NIMBY is the attitude of neighborhood residents who may acknowledge the need for certain facilities but oppose putting such services as recycling sites or homes for juvenile offenders in their neighborhoods because that conflicts with their values, attitudes, and beliefs about family comfort, safety, and property values.

To persuade someone to change, then, you must know as much as possible about them, and consider how their attitudes, values, beliefs, and needs might compete to influence behaviors. It may be that a reasonable persuasive goal is to get people to apply a higher priority to some values than others. This shift, then, may influence their behaviors.

Think of your own responses. Perhaps individuals who speak hatefully against a specific group deeply offend your *value* for equality; you may *believe* such speakers feed a dangerous level of anger; and your *attitude* may be very negative toward them. Yet, your *value* of freedom of speech may be stronger and lead you to tolerate their right to speak at your college.

Audience Adaptation

Throughout this book, we emphasize the importance of understanding your listeners—their backgrounds, cultures, genders, needs, attitudes, beliefs, values, expectations, and goals. In preparing and presenting a speech to persuade, this analysis provides a psychological foundation for every choice you make, including goals you set, audience motives you connect with, and preparation you make to refute opposing arguments.

Setting Your Goals

Your goals in persuasion involve the change you seek and the degree of shift you expect from your audience. These objectives need to be specific and realistic.

Specific Goals   Setting specific goals starts with what kind of audience change you want to achieve. That change determines which of these general purposes will advance your goal:

- *Speech to reinforce or stimulate.* A speech to people who already agree with you should intensify attitudes and values and reinforce or strengthen behaviors consistent with those feelings. Sometimes called "preaching to the converted," a speech to reinforce uses material to evoke feelings and responses and more than to prove your ideas. For instance, motivational speakers often use a speech to stimulate a group of salespeople to get out there and sell.

- *Speech to prove.* In this speech, you focus primarily on changing beliefs—on making audience members more or less certain that something is true. A lawyer, for instance, develops evidence and reasoning (which does include emotional premises) to convince a jury.

- *Speech to get action.* In this speech, you want your audience not only to believe, but to *act* on those beliefs. This goal requires you to prove, stimulate, and *motivate* listeners to respond, physically or mentally. A political speech should get the audience to believe your candidate is best *and* to vote for that person; being stimulated by your enthusiasm is insufficient if the listeners don't go to the polls and vote based on their new beliefs.

A good persuasive message plan states clearly and specifically the changes you want the audience to make. For example, suppose you want to persuade your audience to give blood at a drive next week. You might state your specific goals as "My listeners will sign the pledge form" and "My listeners will give blood next week." You may choose not to tell listeners these goals, but stating them for yourself helps you to design and deliver the message.

Realistic Goals   Just how much change can you realistically achieve? Persuaders are often tempted to advocate extreme changes in hopes an audience might move to *some* degree. But that can backfire—you risk having the audience simply reject the whole message.

Social judgment theory, also known as *ego-involvement theory,* provides insight into how much an audience is capable of changing.[8] This theory suggests individuals' attitudes anchor them in their positions. From that anchor point, all statements about the topic can be ordered in terms of how far from the anchoring attitude they fall. The scale in Figure 15.3 shows three categories of audience responses, starting with those closest to the person's present attitude anchor.

1   *Latitude of acceptance* is a range of statements close enough to a person's attitude anchor to make a change to that position seem reasonable.

2   *Latitude of noncommitment* is a range of statements too far from the anchor position for an individual to accept easily, but she or he might change if the persuasive message appeals strongly enough.

3   *Latitude of rejection* is the range of statements too far away from the anchor for a person even to consider; listeners quickly reject proposals that fall in this range.

Social judgment theory Individuals' attitudes influence how much they may change to another attitude position

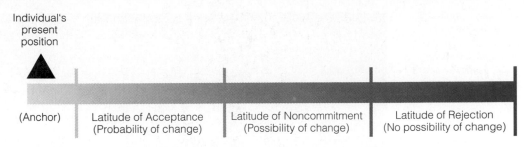

Figure 15.3 *Social judgment theory: Latitudes of acceptance, noncommitment, and rejection with regard to persuasive messages*

How ego-involved a person is determines how wide his or her latitude ranges will be. Ego involvement is the degree of a person's commitment to, and identification with, an issue. Ego involvement can be strong in a person publicly identified as spokesperson for a cause, or whose life experiences have led to personal commitment, or the issue symbolizes important values. When ego involvement is high, latitude of acceptance shrinks, allowing little consideration of alternative attitudes, while latitude of rejection increases, leaving a small area of noncommitment. When you're analyzing your audience and planning your goals, then, consider how listeners' present attitudes and ego involvement may determine how extreme they consider your ideas to be. If your position is far outside their latitudes of acceptance, therefore, you would work on gradual moves to new positions closer to their anchors.

Suppose, for example, you are to speak *against* stricter control of pornography to a women's group that wants stronger laws. The group has taken a public position and, therefore, seems highly ego-involved, so members' latitudes of acceptance will be very narrow. In this case, your goal may be only to get them to reconsider one aspect of the issue—for example, "My message will get listeners to believe that current definitions of pornography make stricter control impossible," or, "My listeners will invite me back to discuss proposals for legal redefinition of pornography."

Considering Diversity

There's no one just like you. So you know you won't have an audience just like you to persuade. If you're speaking to one person or a thousand, it's likely you will speak to people of different genders and sexual orientations, various economic strata and classes, and multiple cultures. You need to take this diversity into account for two very good reasons. First, you want them to find you credible and to hear your message receptively. Second, it's considerate, ethical, and decent to accommodate your message to listeners' expectations.

Some people dismiss attempts to consider others' feelings as "politically correct." It implies you are hypocritical if you use language choices that are sensitive

Can you visualize the audience that this speaker is trying to persuade? In what ways could she adapt to this setting to maximize her effectiveness?

David Young-Wolff/PhotoEdit

to people and situations. If you call the head of a committee a "chairperson," instead of a "chairman," it's not that you're being "politically correct." If you say your friend is an "African American" instead of "Black," or if you adapt your message to customs or language expectations of a culture different from yours, you're not being "politically correct"—you're being a good communicator. Some people say things such as, "I am who I am, and they (their audience) can like it or leave." They don't know that when you consider how people feel, you are being cooriented with them. If you fail to take these factors into account, you are neither credible nor competent in reaching your audience.

Obviously, you can't know everything there is to know about an audience's expectations. But you can learn as much as you can and adapt as well as you can to possible differences by preparing yourself all along for considering audiences, including reading all you can about cultures and genders[9] and:

- *Using feedback and observation* to get a clear understanding of your own communication culture, your attitudes, and your style of communication so you can adapt it to a variety of people.

- *Knowing about others' expectations and adapting to situations,* so you can adapt to your audience's expectations about time, setting, and customs. Learn and use insights from communication styles of various groups, including their expectations of formality or informality; of appropriate humor; and acceptable levels of slang or idiom.

- *Observing, listening, seeking to understand, and developing empathy for others.* It's true you cannot know perfectly what another person feels, but focusing on others, paying attention, trying to understand their feelings, and studying various groups can help a lot. Your objective must be to create messages that consider individuals in your audience, not only to avoid building cultural blocks to communication but to develop appeals that genuinely reach their values and needs.

Connecting with Motives

Understanding your audience will help you find ways to draw on their motives. In its simplest terms, successful persuasion makes listeners see that their own motives will best be served by following your lead or adopting your proposal than by maintaining their present position. As you look for ways to draw on your audience's motivations, keep in mind that they probably have some awareness of what they want to get out of listening and personal objectives that relate to your message. As they listen, they may select and prioritize their plans and adapt them to what you say. As a persuader, show how your ideas can help them achieve their goals. The following insights can help in motivating your audience:

- *People may be aware of a given need only when previous, more fundamental ones have been satisfied* (remember Chapter 3). Appeals to self-esteem needs are not effective, for instance, if your listeners are still motivated by needs for safety and security. Connect your message to audience needs and show how adopting your position will satisfy them more completely.

- *People often respond based on their evaluation of what is likely to be most rewarding and least costly among alternative options*. Your task is to make them see how what you advocate will fill needs and offer rewards *they* value more, with less risk, than other options.

- *People seek consistency among values, attitudes, beliefs, and behaviors*. When a persuasive message alerts listeners to an inconsistency or conflict among their values, attitudes, beliefs, and/or behaviors, they feel dissonance and are motivated to relieve it by making a change.[10] The persuader's job is to show them their inconsistency and how and why the advocated change is the best way to find balance.

This example incorporates all three principles: You're speaking to a community service club; you want members to volunteer in a phonathon to raise money for a new hospital. In your speech, you get them to feel that someone who volunteers for this drive is a good person. You point out that this behavior would be consistent with their value of community service. You show how making telephone contacts for the cause helps them become known to others in the community who will appreciate their efforts and remember them for future business relationships. The listeners may have come for no more than a free lunch, but you appeal to their need for belonging, help them to achieve balance between their values and their behavior, and show them rewards for participating in this drive. As a result, some will decide to volunteer for your phonathon.

Anticipating Opposing Positions

How do you deal with opposing arguments that listeners may hear before or after your speech? You anticipate opposition and help your audience to resist it. Should you acknowledge other points of view and anticipate and refute what advocates on the other side might say? These questions are tough to answer, especially when you consider the time constraints of all speeches.

Research indicates you should include (and refute) opposing viewpoints if your audience members are better educated, are initially opposed, or are familiar with or probably will encounter the other sides.[11] *Inoculation theory* suggests raising opposing views and giving reasons to reject them prepares listeners to reject those positions when they hear them later. It's like a vaccination with a weakened form of a disease creates antibodies to protect against getting the illness.[12]

Organizational Strategies

We talk a lot about organization in this book. That's because the order in which you present ideas influences listeners' perceptions of the relative importance and relationships of all other message elements. A persuasive speech is built to achieve three goals: (1) present the message clearly so the audience understands it; (2) move the audience strategically so listeners don't reject your ideas prematurely; and (3) motivate the audience to accept and act on your proposal.

Persuasive speeches can use any organizational pattern we discussed in Chapter 12 (chronological, spatial, parts-to-whole) to communicate your ideas in clear "chunks," but any format must be developed within a broader strategy that considers audience traits and your persuasive goals. This section gives you several choices with examples to illustrate organizational strategy decisions.

Deductive

Deductive speech pattern Structure that begins with general conclusion and is supported by specific statements

If your proposal is not controversial and falls within the audience's latitude of acceptance or slightly into the latitude of noncommitment, you might present recommendations in the first part of your speech. You could even state the idea of the thesis statement in the introduction, and follow with supporting arguments and evidence. This is a **deductive speech pattern** because, as with deductive reasoning, you start with a conclusion and develop it with specific statements.

Deductive structure follows a parts-to-whole pattern with each main point a reason to support the response you want from the audience. For example, if you were asking an audience that has already contributed to the Red Cross for additional funds, you might organize the body of your speech this way:

Thesis: We all should give whatever we can to the Red Cross to help people struck by Hurricane Yolanda.

    I. The Red Cross needs your help in this terrible disaster.

    II. The Red Cross is the best organization to help people get back on their feet.

    III. The Red Cross can only go so far on what they have.

In this case, both your introduction and your conclusion would zero in on your goal, and your speech subpoints would develop reasons your listeners should make a special donation.

Inductive

Inductive speech pattern Structure that moves from specific points to a general conclusion

When your listeners are strongly opposed, stating your goal in the beginning would cause them to reject it. That's when an **inductive speech pattern** works well. This pattern is subtle and may allow your listeners to change their previously held positions and still "save face." That's an important consideration for most audiences, but especially for those for whom saving face is a significant cultural norm.

Like inductive reasoning, this pattern moves from specific points to the conclusion you want your audience to accept. When you organize inductively, you don't reveal your position early in the speech but develop each subdivision, progressively leading to the inference you want the audience to make. You might, for example, move from the audience's values to ways these values are being violated, to reasons it's important to correct the violation of those values, to your proposal for ending the violation. When you proceed slowly and get listeners' agreement at each point, asking them to accept your ideas one part at a time, they are less likely to resist.

Suppose you are speaking to persuade state legislators who oppose tax increases to vote for a special tax. If you organized your speech deductively, they would turn you off the moment they heard the word *tax*. However, you might move them toward accepting your proposal if you organized the body of the speech inductively:

    I. Our state offers tourists a wealth of entertainment possibilities.

    II. Our state offers our children a poorer education than those provided in the tourists' home states.

    III. Our state could offer our children a quality education if tourists provided more funding for education.

    IV. Our state could fund educational improvements with a 3% tax on tourists' entertainment park admissions.

This inductive development could start with an introduction calling attention to the quality and importance of the state's tourist business. You might use a statement such as, *"American Traveler* magazine lists our state among the top tourist attractions in the United States. Last year, millions visited our entertainment parks alone. . . ." From there, the speech body would lead listeners, step by step, to see a contrast between what the state gives tourists and what tourists give the state that could support children's education. As an inductive pattern, the speech would conclude with a "therefore" statement—in this case, an appeal to support a new tax. The summary and conclusion might go something like this: "We give a world of entertainment opportunity to tourists, but a world of failure to our kids. Our tourists can afford to pay for their fun, but we can't pay for our kids' future. Let's get behind a small tax that will cost so little and yield so much."

Problem-Solution

The **problem-solution speech pattern** is a popular approach to persuasive messages. The first main point develops the need to respond to an alarming situation, and the next main point provides ways to eliminate the difficulty. The problem section develops dissonance to motivate the audience by showing a conflict between the way things are and the way they should be. The solution section shows how the dissonance can be reduced. Let's use college financial aid as an example:

I. Many of our citizens do not have equality of opportunity because they do not have access to higher education. (Problem)

  A. College education is essential to competing in this society.

  B. College education has become too expensive for many of our young people.

  C. College education cannot be supported by current financial programs.

II. Many of our citizens could have equality of opportunity if we provided them access to higher education. (Solution)

  A. Equitable financial aid would guarantee all qualified students enough support to complete a bachelor's degree.

  B. Equitable financial aid would include grant packages and interest-free loans.

  C. Equitable financial aid would consider students' ability to pay and academic qualifications.

With this development, the introduction would underscore the inequity between American cultural values of equality of opportunity and lack of a national economic commitment to education. The summary and conclusion, then, would drive home the point that only by increasing financial aid can this country fulfill its value of equal opportunity for all.

Motivated Sequence

***Motivated-sequence
speech pattern*** Need-
satisfaction pattern that
follows a psychological
sequence to move the
audience to speaker's
desired conclusion

The problem-solution approach becomes more powerful when developed along motivational lines such as those in the **motivated-sequence speech pattern.**[13] This approach uses a problem-solution pattern as an internal structure, but implements a psychological strategy to move the audience through five steps:

1   *Attention.* This is the introduction; as with every speech, you must immediately get the audience's attention and commitment to listening.

2   *Need.* This step lays out issues and makes the audience understand—cognitively and emotionally—why something needs to be done. This requires explanation and proof of what the problem is and why it's serious.

3   *Satisfaction.* After making the audience feel the need, you explain the solution and ways it would meet the need that has already been established.

4   *Visualization.* In this critical step, you create an image of the solution in action. You want the audience to see and feel how things will be when the need is satisfied by the proposal.

5   *Action.* Here, you give the audience a clear call to fulfill the goal of the speech. The more concrete and definitive this step is, the better. Even if your goal is not to get listeners to take specific action, but only to persuade them to think about an issue, the action step should ask them to do that in such a way it both concludes the speech and motivates listeners to act.

Television commercials often follow this sequence. A first shot may show a couple in bed, turning away and covering their mouths rather than kissing each other. Then the voice-over says something about disgusting "morning breath." That gets your *attention* and shows you the *need* for fresh breath if you want a morning kiss. Then, you see the couple brushing their teeth or gargling with the product, the *satisfaction* step. Next, you see them happily smooching, obviously no longer afflicted with the revolting aroma of morning breath—that's *visualization.* Finally comes the *action* step, in which a spokesperson tells you how great the product is and suggests you buy it immediately.

The outline at the end of this chapter is an example of a speech asking listeners to petition for a new water purification system.

Residues

***Residues speech pat-
tern*** Parts-to-whole
structure that considers
alternatives one at a
time, providing reasons
to reject each, until only
desired alternative
remains

When your audience is likely to be thinking of ideas opposing yours, it's a good idea to use the **residues speech pattern.** This parts-to-whole structure considers alternatives one at a time, providing reasons to reject each, until only one choice remains—like boiling away the liquid in a beaker to examine the residue. By presenting multiple alternatives, this pattern applies concepts of inoculation theory and is useful for several objectives:

■   *To compare options.* Reviewing alternatives approaches may help "inoculate" listeners to reject other options when they are considered later.

Databases like Info-Trac College Edition are an excellent source of supporting materials you can use to bolster your persuasive appeals.

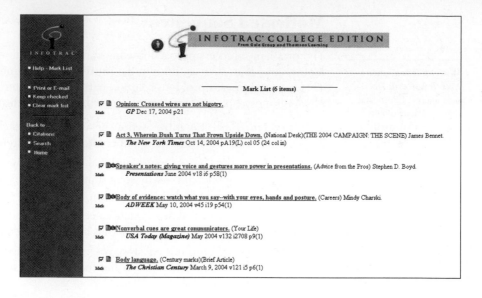

- *To persuade resistant audiences.* The residues approach may be appropriate when audiences are somewhat opposed to your proposal, as the pattern explores the shortcomings of alternative approaches.

- *To combine with other patterns.* The residues pattern can be used with other structures. For example, the solution section of a problem-solution approach or satisfaction step in a motivated sequence could follow a residues pattern.

One of our students used a residues pattern to show the class why they should invest in a specific computer system. Presenting excellent PowerPoint slides, he first established the audience's high value for owning a user-friendly, convenient system. Next he previewed criteria that would make a computer system desirable, to all of which his listeners could agree. He then went through three competing systems, one by one, showing how they met some criteria but not others. This brought him to the system he was proposing, for which he used good evidence to demonstrate that it, in fact, met all of the criteria for the best system to buy. It was an effective way to sell a computer system.

Persuasive Appeals

Years ago, Karl Wallace summarized the substance of effective persuasive messages in two words: *good reasons*.[14] "Reasons" implies your ideas are well thought out and developed logically; "good" means the reasons are consistent with your audience's values.

Wallace's advice echoes that provided centuries before. Aristotle identified three approaches to getting audiences to accept persuasive messages: *logos,* appeals based on logic; *pathos,* appeals based on emotions; and *ethos,* appeals based on the speaker's credibility. Let's examine each.

Appeals Based on Logic

Chapter 3 develops the role of critical thinking in communication and provides guidelines for ensuring logical messages. Here, we expand that discussion to look at specific ways you can use logical principles in your persuasive speeches with evidence and proof.

Requirements for Proof   As noted previously, people can be 100% certain about few things, so you do not need to prove every idea in your speech is absolute fact. But you are obligated to prove probability.

Establishing probable truth so listeners will accept your point requires you to develop evidence and logical reasoning. You need to show that the preponderance of evidence—the largest proportion of convincing supporting material—favors your position.

Supporting Material for Proof   A list of assertions is neither persuasive nor interesting to people, but supporting evidence tends to strengthen your message's impact.[15] Supporting material clarifies, proves, and vivifies ideas; it catches people's imaginations and convinces them of what you say. Here, we'll focus on proof, because the other purposes of support are emphasized in Chapters 12 and 14. You can use the following materials to prove a point:

Examples.   Real examples can help to prove inductively when you draw a general conclusion from them. (Hypothetical examples may clarify and enliven your speech but do not prove because they are not true cases.) One true example, however, still is not enough. Remember inductive reasoning requires sufficient instances to draw general conclusions. A speech about financial aid might use one real example of a brilliant person who had to drop out of school because of financial difficulty. That would clarify and vivify your point. For proof, however, you would also need statistics showing that a significant number of students had the same problem.

Statistics.   Often, multiple examples are collected and reported as statistics. One example of an automobile death attributed to driving under the influence (DUI) doesn't establish a convincing link. Statistics connecting DUI with more than half of all automobile deaths credibly supports an argument that drinking and driving is a serious problem. Statistics must be carefully evaluated to ensure they actually support your particular point and come from reliable sources and research methods.

Testimony.   As personal testimony, a layperson's report can establish facts (what he or she saw, heard, smelled, tasted, or felt), but only an expert's testimony can help you prove interpretations or conclusions about facts. For example, you may describe an event you think violated someone's right to speak and you quote the

First Amendment of the Constitution, but you'll need expert interpretation, such as a Supreme Court Justice's opinion, to prove your claim.

Appeals Based on Emotion

Emotional appeals and logical appeals have been treated separately in speech textbooks since Aristotle's time, but that is largely a matter of convenience and cultural bias. The convenience simply makes discussion easier; the bias is something else. Western societies tend to prize rationality highly, whereas some societies value emotions tied to cultural myths, taboos, and aesthetics.[16]

The emphasis on rationality in Western societies tends to lead individuals in those cultures to be leery of emotion, to feel emotional responses are somehow illegitimate. Pretending people are not emotional, however, is akin to asserting that birds are not aerodynamic. Emotions propel ideas and give them wings. To appeal effectively and ethically to your listener's emotions, your arguments need to flow logically from them.

Premises for Arguments   Though an argument may be rational, emotional appeals often provide premises and/or warrants connecting evidence and reasoning with individual motivations, feelings, and values to build an argument and make a judgment.

Here's an example of how emotion and logic fit together in the appeal for money to feed starving children. Your analysis of the audience suggests they value life, humanity, and generosity. You might show pictures as part of your appeal. Clearly, pictures of emaciated, sick children can have a powerful emotional impact. Look at the underlying argument as a logical appeal:

If children are starving, you should help by donating money.

Children are starving. (Supported by pictures, statistics, and expert testimony)

Therefore, you should help by donating money.

The first line is the major premise in a deductive logical pattern. The second is a minor premise, supported by evidence. The last is the conclusion that, drawing from the first two premises, meets all the rules for logical reasoning. Yet, it has emotional impact because it uses premises that tap into audience values and photos that move their passions.

Now, consider another setting for which you have the same objective of getting donations. Your audience analysis tells you that this group values money higher than the welfare of children. Your appeals to these values and emotions might look like this:

If giving to help starving children provides an income tax deduction, you should donate money.

Giving to help starving children will provide an income tax deduction. (Supported by quotations from the tax code)

Therefore, you should donate money.

This structure, too, meets all the rules for a logical argument, but the conclusion is drawn from premises from that reflect different values and passions. In each case, you can achieve your objective: getting the donations.

Impact on Listeners People respond emotionally when issues touch their values and sense of self. The effectiveness of emotional appeals relates to how listeners may feel about the topic or about life in general at the moment.

Fear appeals. Speeches on tragic problems (AIDS, crime, addiction, cancer, for example) often try to make people afraid. Needless to say, fear appeals must be valid and substantiated to be ethical or relevant to the topic—but with little validity, political commercials often exploit voters' fears by promising the candidate will somehow make problems go away. Research has questioned what level of fear appeal works effectively; for example, a recent study found advocating breast self-examination is more persuasive to women than fear-inducing messages.[17] Fear can cause a defensive reaction that denies the claim. But Eagly and Chaiken conclude that, overall, "the vast majority of experiments have found that higher levels of threat lead to greater persuasion than lower levels, [although] the persuasive impact of fear tends to be stronger on attitudes (toward behavior) and intentions than on behavior itself."[18]

Moods. Listeners who are in a good mood are more easily persuaded, and they make quicker decisions, based more on source expertise and intuitive appeals, than on merits of logical arguments. People in neutral moods are more critical and less persuasible.[19] A persuader who pays attention to mood-inducing effects of the environment and context of the speech, therefore, may be able to build a more positive emotional state in the audience, which will promote openness to emotional or intuitive appeals.

Appeals Based on Source Credibility

It does make sense that audiences will agree with messages more when the sources are more credible, a conclusion supported by most research.[20] In fact, your credibility as a speaker can literally multiply your message's impact.[21]

Both your previous reputation—the audience's view of you *prior to* a specific speech—and your actual words and actions during the speech affect the audience's perception of your competence, trustworthiness, objectivity, dynamism, and coorientation.

Your credibility based on your reputation *is* within your control—you influence these perceptions with everything you do. You make impressions on your listeners in their day-to-day experiences with you, responses to previous speeches you have given, and what they hear about you. You may recall that one of the communication principles covered in Chapter 1 is "Communication is irreversible." That fact builds positive future credibility positively when your actions earn it—but reduces your future impact as a persuader when negative behaviors tarnish your credibility.

What can you do to enhance your credibility during your speech presentation? Specific behaviors include finding common ground, demonstrating competence and objectivity, and speaking with appropriate dynamism.

Finding Common Ground   Much of this book focuses on coorientation and finding ways to identify with audience members and enable them to identify with you. You can show coorientation with listeners with these three components:

1   *Work for coorientational accuracy.* To be cooriented with your listeners you need to perceive correctly their needs, wants, beliefs—their emotional and intellectual states. The key is to focus on your audience—think about *them.* Study, watch, listen, and process feedback to help you relate to your audience's feelings, values, and beliefs.

2   *Use self-monitoring.* As you relate to your audience, also observe your own behavior.[22] Monitor your verbal and nonverbal communication in relation to your audience's responses to you.

3   *Adapt your communication.* As you observe your listeners' responses, make appropriate changes in your approach to help them receive your ideas more positively.[23]

Demonstrating Competence and Objectivity   To trust what you say, your audience needs to know you are qualified and you handle information responsibly. These approaches will show listeners it's worth their time to listen to you:

1   *Explain your research and experiences.* Be descriptive and honest; don't be falsely modest about your qualifications, but also don't be pompous or inflate what you know. If you have had personal experience with the topic, conducted several interviews, consulted scholarly sources, or have a degree in the subject, let your audience know these qualifications.

2   *Use credible sources.* Sources known for objectivity and competence reflect well on your own credibility. Sources such as popular magazines are fine for quotations or examples to vivify your message, but they are not enough to give you credible expert testimony or statistics that prove a claim.

3   *Use a variety of types of support.* Lee and Lee point out that as an advocate speaking to a heterogeneous audience, you need "to look for a variety of supporting materials that will appeal to the different predispositions various segments of the audience bring."[24]

4   *Document your material.* Giving listeners the sources of your information adds to the credibility of both your information and yourself. In fact, without documentation, you may be guilty of plagiarism. In a paper, you document by citing your sources in notes and bibliography. In a speech, you must give the audience this information orally. Artistically build the information into your language so it becomes part of your message. For example, say, "As communication philosopher Richard Johannesen points out in his book, *Ethics of Communication,* 'Plagiarism stems from the Latin word for kidnapper. It involves a communicator who steals

A t a public meeting of white academics and black community activists in Chicago, communication was problematic precisely because style of arguing differed. The whites thought that they couldn't discuss the differences that the meeting was called to resolve because the blacks were "too emotional": they suggested waiting to discuss the differences later, when the others had "calmed down." The black activists, in contrast, considered it quite appropriate to argue with emotion and vehemence: to them, such behavior reflected commitment and honesty. When the whites at the meeting argued dispassionately, according to their own norms of "effective" speaking, they were considered hypocritical by the blacks who judged them, as everyone does, by their own communicative norms.

In my own study of communicative norms in the Mexican-origin community in Chicago,

Mexican immigrants display a very different rhetoric in public speaking than do members of other groups, including Mexican Americans. People enculturated in Mexico weave an elaborate, and poetic, "tapestry" with their words, and when they use this style to argue in public meetings, they are sometimes, depending on the context (and, crucially, their audience), interrupted impatiently by those who prefer concise statements of particular "points," values associated with a U.S. "mainstream" style of communication.

From Marcia Farr, "Response to Daly and Witte Papers," in A. Greenwood (ed.), *The National Assessment of College Student Learning: Identification of the Skills to Be Taught, Learned, and Assessed* (NCES 94-286, pp. 220–226) (Washington, DC: National Center for Education Statistics, 1994), 222–223.

another person's words and ideas without properly acknowledging their source and who presents these words or ideas as his or her own.'"[25]

5 *Acknowledge other positions.* As discussed previously, talking about other views and providing reasons to reject them may inoculate your listeners against opposing positions they hear later. In addition, acknowledging opposing positions shows the audience that you have done your homework and are aware of more than one limited perspective. Audiences tend to attribute less bias, more objectivity, and more credibility to speakers who acknowledge there are other sides to an issue.[26] For example, celebrities appear more credible and likable when their messages acknowledge some negative feature about products they endorse.[27]

Communicating with Appropriate Dynamism   Your nonverbal communication—your voice, speech patterns and articulation, body movement, facial expressions, gestures—carries your verbal message. Although people in different cultures and contexts respond variously to different styles, the intensity and commitment you convey will affect perceptions of your credibility. The dynamism with which you present your ideas should be appropriate to you, to the audience, and to the occasion. Our best advice is to practice your speech so it has *energy*, *vitality, variety,* and *sincerity.* Credible dynamism starts with your passion for the topic and concern for your audience. As you speak, watch feedback and self-monitor, adapting your speaking vigor to audience responses. If they seem bowled over, moderate your approach. If they seem uninvigorated, step up your intensity. Your delivery should engage your listeners with you and your message and keep them with you until the last word of your conclusion.

Being Ethical   Your ethical choices certainly are part of your credibility, but they are much more. They are who you are. Samovar and Porter put it this way: "Because of the potential power of messages, you must always be aware of the *effects of your message on other people.* This focus on your actions and the results of those actions is called, in the Buddhist tradition, *being mindful.*"[28] This means being mindful of your audience, mindful of how what you say will affect them, and mindful of the truth.

One writer says, "'The truth shall make you free' is a phrase I have heard all my life but only recently have I understood how fundamental it is. I find that at every level—body, individual, couple, group, organization, nation—the more truth, the more success. . . . Not telling the truth is the source of most problems."[29] Scores of articles and books have been written about the American crisis in confidence, about how people simply don't believe anyone. It's amazing how much people want a little truth—and how refreshing it can be.

Being mindful of your ethics implies careful minding of your emotional appeals to an audience. To help you keep an ethical perspective, pay attention to:

Choice.   To be ethical, emotional appeals should expose, not obscure, individuals' decision choices. Their emotions should be respected as an important element in their rational decision making.

Relevance.   Emotional appeals should relate directly to the argument and audience values. Unethical uses exploit or manipulate an audience's emotional responses by, for instance, causing listeners to transfer emotions from one object to another, to generalize illegitimately, or to conclude from limited examples—or the appeal is inconsistent with known evidence and/or has no evidence to support the point. In other words, the appeal to emotion is unethical if it "clearly flies in the face of what the receivers, given time, would find in their own investigations."[30]

Language Choices

Your choice of words, and the way you use them, can win or lose your audience. You remember that *connotative meanings,* the personal reactions individuals have to specific words, include attitudes about a concept.[31] A menu might get many orders if it says "charbroiled aged prime filet of beef" but far fewer with "burned piece of decomposing dead steer."

Excerpts from Dr. Martin Luther King Jr.'s speech, "I Have a Dream," provide wonderful examples for some language techniques that can have psychological and emotional effects on your listeners. Look at these:

Metaphor.　A metaphor, you'll remember, is a figure of speech that replaces one word or phrase with another to imply a comparison. King uses metaphor to respond to critics' complaints that the civil rights movement should slow down and wait for gradual change: "This is no time to engage in the luxury of cooling off or to take the tranquilizing drug of gradualism."

Imagery.　King's words evoke strong sensory images. He gets listeners to see and feel vividly, often by combining imagery with his metaphors. Note how he evokes the senses when he says, "seared in the flames of withering injustice," and, "from the quicksand of segregation to the solid rock of brotherhood."

Sounds.　Sounds can have aesthetic appeal to the ear, and language that incorporates pleasing sounds helps give life and artistry to a speech. One method is by *alliteration,* using words with the same initial sound: "not by the color of their skins but by the content of their character." Another method is *assonance,* using words with similar vowel sounds. King achieves both alliteration and assonance when he states, "America has defaulted on that promissory note insofar as her citizens of color are concerned."

Repetition.　King develops power in his words by repeating key phrases for emphasis. His repetition of the phrase, "I have a dream," gives strength to the phrase that became the title of the speech. Another powerful phrase used repeatedly comes near the end: "Let freedom ring."

Allusion.　Allusion makes indirect references or suggestions without identifying directly an object or idea. For example, King (standing in front of the Lincoln Memorial) begins his speech, "Five score years ago, a great American in whose symbolic shadow we stand, signed the Emancipation Proclamation." Listeners understood he referred to Abraham Lincoln, of course; he didn't have to say it. (And he also worked in another alliteration.) Similarly, King's allusions often evoke the religious heritage of many listeners. Some examples: "solid rock," "dark and desolate valley," and the emotional words of an old spiritual, "Free at last. Free at last. Thank God Almighty, I'm free at last."

　　Few speakers ever achieve a comparable level of effectiveness in terms of their strategic language choices, and King's model can help you develop your own powerful persuasive style.

Summary

Persuasion, as the process of moving your audience to change willingly their beliefs, attitudes, values, and/or behaviors, involves analyzing members' motivations and understanding their existing positions on issues. Often, successful persuasion causes audience members to shift a few degrees on either side of neutral on an attitude scale or to move from a position of disbelief to some degree of belief that an assertion is true. Values are difficult to change because they are central to a person's self-concept, so the persuader often must get listeners to reorder important values or reinterpret the way a given attitude or behavior relates to particular values.

Persuasion requires analyzing your listeners and defining reasonable goals for the audience and context. To design a speech, start with a clear goal, then select an organizational pattern that considers the extent to which you will ask listeners to change and strength of audience values pertaining to the issue. The strategy may be deductive when the change is relatively slight or inductive when audience members must be led slowly to a change. A common organizational pattern is to present a problem and then provide the solution. Often, this problem-solution pattern is embedded in a motivated sequence in which listeners are led through psychological steps of attention, need, satisfaction, visualization, and action. The solution step may take listeners through a "residues" development by rebutting alternative options until the speaker reaches the advocated solution.

Effective, ethical persuasive speeches respect the audience and develop logical and emotional appeals as well as enhance the speaker's credibility. Persuasive language is important in influencing change, because audience members bring their own connotative meanings to interpreting a persuader's symbols. Colorful, rhythmic, and expressive language such as imagery, metaphor, assonance, alliteration, and repetition all contribute to successful persuasion.

Exercises

1   For each of the following, estimate where your belief, attitude, or value might fall on the scales provided.

a   *Beliefs*. On a scale of 0 to 100%, estimate your degree of certainty for the following:

I can develop my speaking skills.	_____%
Higher taxes cause recessions.	_____%
I will get a satisfying job after college.	_____%
Everyone should have a college education.	_____%
Cattle farming is very profitable.	_____%

b   *Attitudes*. On a scale of −1.00 to +1.00, estimate your attitude about each of the following: (See Figure 15.2 for example of this scale being used.)

Federal funding for abortions	_____
Voting in congressional elections	_____
The United Nations	_____
Parking on your campus	_____
Making public speeches	_____
Protecting the environment	_____

c *Values.* On a scale from L (low importance) to M (moderate) to H (high), estimate the degree to which you value each of the following:

Financial security   _____

Ethnic heritage   _____

Your credibility as a speaker   _____

Your competence as a speaker   _____

Education   _____

Equality among people   _____

Go back and think about your ratings. On which item in each category (beliefs, attitudes, values) would you be most susceptible to change because of a persuasive message? Which would you be less likely to change? What generalizations can you draw from your responses about how people's belief, attitude, and value positions relate to their persuadability on issues?

2 Working with a partner, select a topic that clearly has more than one side to it. Together, identify a position you could propose in a persuasive speech and write a purpose statement for getting an audience to accept that position. Separately, each of you do one of the following:

a Assume you would be presenting this speech to an audience that would not be too strongly opposed to your position. Identify possible main points and subpoints for a persuasive speech that reflect a *deductive* approach.

b Assume you would be presenting this speech to an audience that would be strongly opposed to your position. Identify possible main points and subpoints for a persuasive speech that reflect an *inductive* approach.

Compare the outlines each of you has prepared. Do they both seek to achieve the same objective? In what ways do the approaches differ? Would it be realistic, assuming that each speech would have the same time limitations, to expect both speeches to achieve the same goal?

3 In a group, select one of the attitude statements from Exercise 1. Then brainstorm a list of motive appeals (see "Connecting Motives") that *might* apply to an audience for which a speech on that topic could be prepared. Make the list as long as you can.

Then, identify a specific audience for the speech and create a plan for finding out which motive appeals would have the greatest likelihood of succeeding with that specific group.

4 Using the motivated sequence(see Sample Persuasive Speech at the end of this chapter), prepare and present a 5-minute speech on a topic of your

choice to persuade your classmates. Be sure you accomplish each of the following steps:

a Get the audience's attention.

b Develop a need with careful use of logical and emotional appeals. Seek to create dissonance in your audience's minds as you develop this section.

c Develop a proposal for satisfying the need. Include ways in which the solution reduces the dissonance developed.

d Get your audience to sense and feel what things will be like as they visualize their lives after adopting your proposal.

e Call your audience to specific action. Consider what they should do as well as how and when they should do it.

Cyberpoints

The following Cyberpoints can be easily accessed from the Student Companion website for this text at http://academic.cengage.com/communication/lumsdenccc3. Click on *Student Book Companion Site* and select this chapter from the pull-down menu at the top of the page that says "Select a chapter." Click on *Cyperpoints* under *Chapter Resources* and you will find links for the exercises following.

1 Do you know how to apply the Toulmin model of argument developed in Chapter 3 to prepare your persuasive speech? Go to *The Toulmin Project Home Page* at http://www.unl.edu/speech/comm109/Toulmin/index.htm. Use your time on this teaching site to learn about Toulmin's model, understand how to use it, and ponder how you can maximize its use as a speaker and consumer of argument and persuasion. Answer the following questions, ending with the creation of your own argument:

What is the Toulmin model?

Why did he create it?

How will you use the Toulmin model to improve the *logos* (appeals based on logic) of your persuasive speech?

Show what you have learned by creating an argument related to your persuasive speech containing, at least, data claim and warrant.

2 Interested in communication careers? Take a look at workinpr.com, a website for the Public Relations and Communications industry. Another possibility is http://lamar.colostate.edu/~pr/prcareers.htm. Browse these sites and look for ways the skills of persuasive speaking could serve you in a public relations career. Record two skills that would be useful.

3 A source for researching your speech is the *National Data Book of the Census Bureau* at http://www.census.gov/prod/www/statistical-abstract-us.html. What are three ways the information at this site could be helpful to the persuasive speaker?

4 Have you wondered, "How can I start my research? Where can I get topic ideas? What's been in the news lately?" Another source for researching your persuasive speech uses headline stories from newspapers, broadcast, and online sources at http://1stHeadlines.com. Find five headlines that suggest topics you think would make good persuasive speeches.

SAMPLE PERSUASIVE SPEECH USING MOTIVATED SEQUENCE STRATEGY

Commentary

Topic: The problem of community water pollution and a desirable solution to the problem

Purpose: To motivate the audience to support a new system of water purification for the community

Thesis: Potential poisoning of our water supply through pollutants and chemicals can be prevented by adopting one of three new technologies already shown to be effective.

Organizational Pattern: This speech uses a motivational sequence to involve and move the audience through recognizing a threat and considering a response to it. Within the motivational steps, points are ordered in logical arguments to show a problem and solution.

Attention Step

The speaker uses a series of rhetorical questions, a shocking statement and statistic, and further quotations, concluding with a strong quotation to which the audience can relate as a community. These methods serve to make the topic important to the audience, develop the speaker's credibility, and motivate the audience to hear more.

Need Step

It is essential that the audience personally feel the need for a new water supply. The speech provides two main reasons, with subpoints, for the belief that this community's water could be poisoned. Each main point is worded parallel to the other one, with

Outline

Attention

Pour a clear glass of water from a pitcher. Hold it out, and ask, Would you drink this water? Would you bathe in it? Wash your dishes in it? How safe do you think it is? Maybe you'd better rethink your confidence in our community's great water. People in a lot of other communities have. The *New York Times* reports that last year in Milwaukee, 43 people died from drinking the water, and many, many more became ill, one of them from drinking just enough water to take an aspirin. Seagulls polluted their water with a disease called cryptosporidiosis. Jim Elder, the head of the Environmental Protection Agency's Office of Ground Water and Drinking Water, says that "professional leaders in the water supply industry have admitted to me privately that they were scared to death by what happened in Milwaukee. They didn't think their source-water situation was that much different."

Need

I. Our community could be poisoned by our water supply at any time because of increased pollutants.

    A. Sources of pollutants from people and animals are increasing rapidly.

    B. Current water purification methods can't keep up with the increased sources of pollutants.

II. Our community could be poisoned by our water supply at any time because of dangerous chemical purification methods.

    A. Current water purification methods rely on chlorine.

    B. Chlorine is now suspected to be carcinogenic.

Commentary

wording that emphasizes the connection of the community to the potential disaster. Each subpoint would be developed with strong, credible evidence to prove the probability of water poisoning and to develop the audience's concern that their community water supply could be threatened.

Satisfaction Step
To meet this need the audience now feels, the speaker lays out two main points, showing that technologies to fix the problem exist and that these technologies are already working in other communities. The subpoints for each main point give specific examples with evidence to show that both are valid points.

Visualization Step
Here is when the audience must begin to see the solution working. The speaker creates for the audience an image of what it would be like to know they have healthy water. It is vivid and satisfying as a visualization.

Action Step
In referring to the water board, the speaker provides a way to achieve the image the audience has just examined. Mentioning a petition introduces a way to take action; restating the need in strong images reinforces the dreadful possibilities if action is not taken; and, finally, calling for action by signing a petition is coupled with a reaffirmation of the visualized success of new technologies for water purification.

Outline

Satisfaction
I. New technologies are available for purifying water.
   A. Ozone treatment methods kill more microorganisms than chlorine does.
   B. Granular-activated carbon systems clean out pollutants and other contaminates.
II. New technologies are working in other communities.
   A. Milwaukee has turned its situation around in a year's time at reasonable costs.
   B. Cincinnati has succeeded with granular-activated carbon systems that clean out other contaminants and eliminate chlorine at reasonable costs.
   C. One hundred communities already are using ozone treatment at reasonable costs.

Visualization
Imagine a child drinking a tall, cool glass of crystal-clear, pure water, playing in a pool, eating off of dishes without danger of becoming ill or poisoned from chlorine. Imagine a community in which we can truly say, "We've got good water."

Action
Our public water board can select and implement a new system if we have the will to motivate them. Let's all sign this petition and get our water board moving on this problem. We can't wait until our children are sick and old people are dying from a drink of water—or until we suddenly find our cancer rate has risen in town and we don't know why. We have to do it now. Please sign the petition, and take the first steps toward a community with truly clean water for its citizens.

Glossary

Active listening Process in which listener focuses on and silently questions speaker's ideas to shape and understand the speaker's meaning

Advantages Positive effects of a solution to a problem

Affinity seeking Communication behavior in which participants look for ways to feel similar and close

Affirmation Positive, present-tense description of a desired achievement

Agenda Written plan for a meeting

Aggressive communication Communicating one's needs and wants, disregarding what others might feel or want

Applicability How well a solution meets the criteria for solving a problem

Artifacts Things living people use to symbolize themselves

Assertive communication Communicating one's needs and wants, with awareness of self and concern for others

Associate ideas New material that is directly linked by a speaker to existing ideas and information

Attitudes Internal degree of favor or disfavor an individual holds about people, objects, or ideas

Audience motives Listeners' reasons for wanting to know what a speaker presents to them

Authoritarian leader Leader who makes all decisions and may use coercion or reward to get results

Behavioral question Asks respondent about ways they have acted in previous situations

Behaviors External, observable actions that interact with beliefs, attitudes, and values

Beliefs Degree to which a person accepts something as true

Brainstorming Process of generating solutions by thinking of as many ideas as possible without constraint

Cause-and-effect reasoning Drawing the conclusion that one event is responsible for the occurrence of another

Channel Means by which cues are carried from sender to receiver

Charge Task or assignment that defines the purpose of a team

Closed question Question that limits the answer of respondent: yes/no, either/or, multiple choice

Codependency Patterns of behavior that "enable" participants to behave in dysfunctional ways

Cohesiveness Degree to which group members are attracted toward each other and the group

Collaborative listening and questioning Dialogue in which speaker and listener work as a team to develop shared understanding

Communication Using verbal and nonverbal cues to transact meanings

Communication accommodation Methods used by people to adapt to others' communication behaviors

Communication apprehension Level of fear or anxiety associated with communication

Communication climate A set of conditions that affect the quality of communication and relationships

Communication dilemma Conflict between need to communicate and desire to avoid risk

Competence Perception of a person's expertise, authoritativeness, and skill

Confirming In dialogue, one person listens and asks questions that value the speaker and the message

Confirming response Message that acknowledges worth of the receiver

Conflict Tension people feel in a relationship when they perceive that they have differing goals or feelings

Connotative meanings Meanings of words that are based on an individual's personal experiences

Consensus Agreement of all group members achieved by intensive discussion and negotiation

Consistency needs Striving to maintain balance among attitudes, beliefs, values, and behaviors that motivates people to choose among conflicting information

Coorientation Perception of a person's similarities to and concern for listeners

Credibility How your message and character are perceived

Critical thinking Deliberate analysis of data, reasoning, and conclusions

Culture Systems of beliefs, values, customs, behaviors, and artifacts shared within a society

Decode Translate symbols and cues into meaning

Deductive reasoning Drawing a conclusion about a specific case from a generalization

Deductive speech pattern Structure that begins with general conclusion and is supported by specific statements

Defensive climate A communication environment in which listeners disregard a speaker's feelings and importance

DELs Derogatory Ethnic Labels; names that attribute negative characteristics to a person or group

Democratic leader Leader who facilitates discussion and shares decision-making power

Demographics Categorize people according to external attributes: age, sex, ethnicity, income, educational level

Denotative meanings Meanings of words that are shared by speakers of the language

Depenetration The process through which partners end a relationship

Detractors Sounds and words interjected between words and sentences

Dialogical ethic Process based on the value of sharing ideas and feelings with another

Disadvantages Negative consequences of a solution to a problem

Disconfirming response Message that renders the receiver invisible or undesirable

Dyadic communication Interactions between two people

Dynamism Energy with which a person compels the interest of others

Dysfunctional relationship Interactions in which participants play games and manipulate one another, which breaks down the optimal relationship

Effective communication Communication that achieves its objectives, enriches people involved, and

provides foundation for future communication

Emergent leader Person who becomes a leader by helping groups develop effective processes

Empathic listening Listening that focuses on the speaker's feelings

Empathy Understanding ideas and feelings of another person

Encode Represent an idea with a symbol

Ethics Codes or beliefs used for making moral judgments and determining acceptable behavior

Ethos A speaker's believability: "good character, good sense, and goodwill"

Euphemisms Words or phrases that gloss over offensive aspects of a message

Extemporaneous speaking Presenting a speech, with key word notes, that has been outlined and rehearsed

Family An interdependent couple or group that creates its own structure within a larger culture

Feedback Responses from message receiver that give the sender information about how symbols were received and interpreted

Forum Open meeting in which audience makes comments and asks questions

Game playing A competitive manipulation of communication so that one player can achieve a personal goal

Gender How one sees oneself in relation to society, sex, and roles

Goal conflicts When your personal and career goals differ from each other or from your management's objectives

Group Two or more persons interacting to influence and be influenced by each other

Group-building roles Functions that help manage members' feelings and create harmony in the group

Group and team communication Socializing or working with a small number of other people

Group goals Results that a team has been assembled to achieve

Groupthink Mode of thinking within a group that emerges when the desire for agreement overrides critical analysis of issues

Haptics Communication by touching

Hidden agenda Team member's personal goals that affect the team's interaction but that the member does not share with the group

Hierarchy of needs Ascending levels of need, each of which must be fulfilled before next level can be achieved

High-context society A society with close family and community groupings, in which people share the same knowledge about each other and their environment

Humanify View a person as one with feelings, rights, values

Images Vivid "pictures" drawn with words

Impromptu speaking Presenting your ideas in an organized and thoughtful fashion without formal preparation or rehearsal

Individual interest/blocking roles Functions that draw attention away from group tasks or goals to serve individual member's needs

Inductive reasoning Drawing a general conclusion from specific cases

Inductive speech pattern Structure that moves from specific points to a general conclusion

Information overload State in which listener has received more data than can be processed and remembered

Instrumental objectives The lesser tasks that lead to achieving a team's goal

Interactive listening and questioning Dialogue in which listener analyzes speaker's ideas and asks and answers questions

Interpersonal bonding The process of forming individual relationships

Interpersonal communication Dynamic process among two or more people

Interview A goal-oriented conversation in which participants follow a question-and-answer structure

Intimate relationships Mutually supportive, trusting, enduring associations between partners

Intrapersonal communication Communication to yourself in response to your environment, other people, or yourself

Job-qualification question Question intended to assess one's ability to meet the criteria of a job

Kinesic Movements of the eyes, face, and body people perceive as meaningful

Laissez-faire leader Leader who uses a neutral, uninvolved leadership style

Leader Person holding a designated title or position in a group

Leadership Verbal and nonverbal communication behavior that influences team processes to achieve goals

Leading question Misleading, manipulative, or unethical question whose wording forces a respondent's answers

Learning style The way an individual processes information, influenced by the side of the brain used and individual ability, personality, culture, and, perhaps, gender

Low-context society A society with scattered family, community, and socioeconomic groupings, in which people do not share the same knowledge about each other and their environment

Manuscript speaking Reading aloud a speech that has been written

Mediated communication Communication channeled through written or electronic medium

Memorized speaking Speaking a written text from memory and rehearsal

Metaphor The comparison of two things by calling one the other

Midpoint crisis Moment when team members realize that time is half-gone but work is less than half-finished

Mnemonic device Memory aid used to connect ideas

Monochronic cultures Cultures in which people attend to one thing at a time, with focus on deadlines and schedules

Motivated-sequence speech pattern Need-satisfaction pattern that follows a psychological sequence to move the audience to speaker's desired conclusion

Noise Stimuli that compete with a message in a channel

Nonstandard language A dialect or style that differs from the standard language within a community

Nonverbal communication Communication that accompanies, replaces, or carries verbal messages

Nonverbal cues Body postures, facial expressions, and other personal behaviors or objects that communicate

Objectify Treat as a thing rather than as a person

Objectivity Perception of a person's ability to look at different points of view and suspend personal biases

Open-ended question Question that allows the respondent to answer in a variety of ways: How? What? Why?

Organizational culture The way things are done within a specific organization

Organizational pattern Logically orders ideas in relationship to one another

Panel Group that presents information to an audience through members who share ideas and ask and answer questions informally

Parallel structure Organization of material that uses same phrasing for each of a series of ideas

Passive communication Using silence or false agreement to appease others while building up resentment or frustration

Passive-aggressive communication Acting like one agrees and accepts, but seeking to undermine the process with later behavior

Perception Process of becoming aware of and interpreting stimuli

Person-centered messages Conversational behavior that recognizes each participant's worth

Personal space Space surrounding an individual actively maintained to protect against threats

Persuasion Process of moving an audience to change willingly its beliefs, attitudes, values, and/or behaviors

Polychronic cultures Cultures in which people do many things at once, with focus on relationships and immediacy

Practicality The likelihood that a solution to a problem can be implemented successfully

Presentational communication Speaking before an audience

Primary question Question that interviewer has planned in advance

Principled leadership Leadership that works to promote ethical values in communication and decision making

Problem-solution speech pattern Structure that begins with need to respond to a problem and offers possible solutions

Process An ongoing, constantly developing and changing operation

Professionalism Communication that shows involvement, competence, pride, and ethical standards in one's work

Proxemics The perception, use, and restructuring of space as communication

Psychographics Categorize people based on internal factors: attitudes, values, needs

Receiver Person who picks up cues using the senses

Redefinition The use of language to change perceptions by changing the words used

Reinforcement Process of repeating an idea and underscoring its importance so it stands out in listeners' memories

Rejection response Message that discards the worth of the receiver or the receiver's ideas

Relational "rules" Expectations of how couples should relate to each other

Relational themes Aspects of their relationship that emerge from couples' conversations

Relaxation techniques Methods used consciously to help you reduce anxiety

Residues speech pattern Parts-to-whole structure that considers alternatives one at a time, providing

reasons to reject each, until only desired alternative remains

Risk Potential gains of solving a problem weighted against potential losses

Secondary question More focused question that follows from respondent's answers to primary question

Selective attention Process of focusing on one detail and not noticing others

Self-disclosure The act of sharing information about yourself with another person

Self-persuasion Process by which an audience develops a rationale for change because of information provided by a speaker

Self-talk Messages to yourself to improve your approach or performance

Semantics The study of how people use words as signs or symbols for ideas and perceptions

Sender Person who transmits a message

Sensory fatigue State in which senses become tired while processing stimuli

Shaping Perceiving a stimulus through personal filters or screens

Shared leadership Group situation in which all members take leadership responsibility

Simulation Demonstration in which interviewee role-plays a job-related situation

Situational leadership Leadership style that adapts to needs and maturity of individual groups

Situational question Asks how respondent would behave in a hypothetical situation

Social exchange theory Choosing an action based on the weighing of rewards and costs

Social judgment theory Individuals' attitudes influence how much they may change to another attitude position

Social penetration The process of gradual widening and deepening of a relationship as two people develop mutual trust and empathy

Speech body The substance of a speech, structured with main points and subpoints

Speech conclusion The ending that drives home your ideas or makes the sale

Speech introduction Opening of a speech that gets the audience's attention and prepares them to listen to your speech

Speech to inform Provides listeners with new information or shows them new relationships among known materials

Speech to persuade Gives listeners ways to fulfill needs and reasons to alter attitudes, values, beliefs, and/or behaviors, motivating them with logical and emotional appeals to change established ways of thinking or acting

Standard language Language associated with power and status within a community

Stereotypes Screens of expectations and judgments through which people filter their perceptions

Strategic ambiguity The deliberate use of words that may have more than one possible interpretation

Style In communication, the way a person uses language

Superteam High-performance team that achieves exceptional results

Supporting material Additional information that holds the body of a speech up and gives it shape, substance, and energy by clarifying, proving, and vivifying

Supportive climate A communication environment in which listeners respect a speaker's ideas and feelings, allowing for open communication

Symposium Formal group session in which each participant gives a speech to an audience, without interaction among group members

Synchronous messages Hand, body, and head movements coordinating with spoken words

Synergy Combination of team members' energy, drives, needs, motives that affect how successful the team is

Syntactics The way languages arrange and order words to convey meaning

Syntality Personality of the group

Task roles Functions that help a group establish structure, develop flexibility, and set goals and objectives

Team Group of people who share an identity and have a mutually defined goal

Territory A specific place you feel is yours

Thesis statement Clear, concise declarative sentence stating the central idea of your speech

Thought speed Time between the rate of human speech and rate of listener's ability to process information

Transactional leader Leader who uses rewards in return for effective performance

Transactional process Interaction in which each person gives and takes to achieve understanding

Transformational leader Leader who motivates, inspires, and develops members to meet goals

Transition Statement that connects ideas and tells the audience when a speaker is changing topics

Transmit Speak or act so that symbols are available to the other person

Trustworthiness Perception of a person's consistent and honest behavior

Turning point Moment when a relationship undergoes an incremental change

Values Concepts of good or desirable that motivate behavior and serve as criteria for choice and judgments

Verbal communication Using language to communicate ideas

Verbal cues Words used to convey and interpret ideas

Visionary leader Leader who shapes and gains a team's acceptance of a long-term goal

Visualization Creation of mental image of a successful performance

Visual message Graphic image that helps listeners understand a speech's content

Vocalics The sound of your voice and the way you speak, which affect how you are perceived

Notes

Chapter 1 Communication Dynamics: Exploring Concepts and Principles

1. G. R. Miller and M. Steinberg, *Between People: A New Analysis of Interpersonal Communication* (Palo Alto, CA: Science Research Associates, 1975).

2. Miller and Steinberg.

3. J. Stewart, "Introduction to the Editor and to This Book," in *Bridges Not Walls: A Book about Interpersonal Communication,* 7th ed., J. Steward, ed. (Boston: McGraw-Hill, 1999), 6.

4. J. J. Lynch, "The Language of the Heart," in *Bridges Not Walls: A Book about Interpersonal Communication,* 5th ed., J. Stewart, ed. (New York: McGraw-Hill, 1990), 32–37.

5. N.Y. Department of Labor, *The Workplace of the Future,* 1996, retrieved October 7, 2000, from http://www.nyatop.org/nyskills.html

6. G. Lumsden and D. Lumsden, *Communicating in Groups and Teams: Sharing Leadership,* 4th ed. (Belmont, CA: Wadsworth, 2004), 9–12.

7. U.S. Department of Labor, *Futurework: Trends and Challenges for Work in the 21st Century* (Washington, DC: Government Printing Office, 1999).

8. F. E. X. Dance, "Toward a Theory of Human Communication," in *Human Communication Theory: Original Essays,* F. E. X. Dance, ed. (New York: Holt, 1967), 288–309.

9. W. V. Haney, *Communication and Organizational Behavior: Text and Cases,* 3rd ed. (Homewood, IL: Richard D. Irwin, 1973).

10. D. J. Cegala et al., "An Elaboration of the Meaning of Interaction Involvement: Toward the Development of a Theoretical Concept," *Communication Monographs* 49 (1982): 233.

11. See D. B. Wackman, "Interpersonal Communication and Coorientation," *American Behavioral Scientist* 16 (1973): 537–550.

12. L. R. Anderson, "Toward a Two-Track Model of Leadership Training," *Small Group Research* 21 (1990):147–167.

13. R. L. Duran, "Communicative Adaptability: A Review of Conceptualization and Measurement," *Communication Quarterly* 4 (1992): 253–268.

14. J. A. Jaksa and M. S. Pritchard, *Communication Ethics: Methods of Analysis,* 2nd ed. (Belmont, CA: Wadsworth, 1994), 3.

15. R. L. Johannesen, *Ethics in Human Communication,* 4th ed. (Prospect Heights, IL: Waveland, 1996), 66–68.

16. J. Stewart and R. Zediker, "Dialogue as Tensional, Ethical Practice," *Southern Communication Journal* 65 (2000): 224–242.

17. Jaksa and Pritchard, 17.

18. "From Corporate America to the White House, Solid Communication Begins with Listening," *PR Week,* February 16, 2004, p. 8.

19. Johannesen, 153.

Chapter 2 Your Communication: Developing Credibility and Confidence

1. C. Pornpitakpani, "The Persuasiveness of Source Credibility: A Critical Review of Five Decades' Evidence," *Journal of Applied Social Psychology* 34 (2004): 266.

2. Aristotle, *Rhetoric,* trans. W. R. Roberts (New York: Modern Library, 1954), 91.

3. See J. Whitehead Jr., "Factors of Source Credibility," *Quarterly Journal of Speech* 54 (1969): 59–63; C. Tuppen, "Dimensions of Communicator Credibility: An Oblique Solution," *Speech Monographs* 41 (1974): 253–266.

4. G. Lumsden, "An Experimental Study of the Effect of Verbal Agreement on Leadership Maintenance in Problem-Solving Discussions" (PhD diss., Indiana University, 1972), 8.

5. C. H. Dodd, *Dynamics of Intercultural Communication,* 3rd ed. (Dubuque, IA: Wm. C. Brown, 1991), 221.

6. K. H. Basso, *Western Apache Language and Culture: Essays in Linguistic Anthropology* (Tucson: University of Arizona Press, 1990), 59.

7. C. W. Carmichael, "Intercultural Perspectives of Aging," in *Intercultural Communication: A Reader,* 6th ed., L. A. Samovar and R. E. Porter, eds. (Belmont, CA: Wadsworth, 1991), 130.

8. V. P. Richmond and J. C. McCroskey, *Communication: Apprehension, Avoidance, and Effectiveness,* 4th ed. (Scottsdale, AZ: Gorsuch Scarisbrick, 1995), 48.

9. R. D. Ireland, M. A. Hitt, and J. C. Williams, "Self-Confidence and Decisiveness: Prerequisites for Effective Management in the 1990s," *Business Horizons* (January/February 1992): 36–37.

10. B. Asker, "Student Reticence and Oral Testing: A Hong Kong Study of Willingness to Communicate," *Communication Research Reports* 15 (1998): 168.

11. Richmond and McCroskey, 34.

12. E. A. Folb, "Who's Got the Room at the Top? Issues of Dominance and Nondominance in Intercultural Communication," in Samovar and Porter, 122.

13. R. R. Behnke and C. R. Sawyer, "Anticipatory Anxiety Patterns for Male and Female Public

Speakers," *Communication Education* 49 (2000): 187–195.

14. K. K. Dwyer, *Conquer Your Speech Anxiety*, 2nd ed. (Belmont, CA: Wadsworth, 2005), 24.

15. D. E. Mastro, "A Social Identity Approach to Understanding the Impact of Television Messages," *Communication Monographs* 70 (2003): 98–113; G. Smitherman-Donaldson and T. A. van Dijk, eds., *Discourse and Discrimination* (Detroit: Wayne State University, 1988).

16. L. Tice, *Investment in Excellence* (Seattle: Pacific Institute, 1983), 1B, 1–8.

17. L. K. Smith and S. A. Fowler, "Positive Peer Pressure: The Effects of Peer Monitoring on Children's Disruptive Behavior," *Journal of Applied Behavior Analysis* 17 (1984): 213–227.

18. G. E. Coover and S. T. Murphy, "The Communicated Self: Exploring the Interaction between Self and Social Context," *Human Communication Research* 26 (2000): 125–147.

19. W. W. Wilmot, *Dyadic Communication*, 3rd ed. (New York: McGraw-Hill, 1987).

20. M. L. King Jr., *Why We Can't Wait* (New York: Signet., 1964), 81.

21. J. H. Harvey, T. L. Orbuch, and A. L. Weber, eds., *Attributions, Accounts, and Close Relationships* (New York: Springer-Verlag, 1992).

22. V. P. Richmond and K. D. Roach, "Willingness to Communicate and Employee Success in U.S. Organizations," *Journal of Applied Communication Research* 20 (1992): 101.

23. J. A. Keaten and L. Kelly, "Reticence: An Affirmation and Revision," *Communication Education* 49 (2000): 166–167.

24. Richmond and McCroskey, 41.

25. W. R. Zakahi and R. L. Duran, "Loneliness, Communication Competence, and Communication Apprehension: Extension

and Replication," *Communication Quarterly* 33 (1985): 50–60.

26. P. M. Ericson and J. W. Gardner, "Two Longitudinal Studies of Communication Apprehension and Its Effects on College Students' Success," *Communication Quarterly* 40 (1992): 127–137.

27. Richmond and McCroskey, 42–48.

28. L. J. Carrell and S. C. Willmington, "The Relationship between Self-Report Measures of Communication Apprehension and Trained Observers' Ratings of Communication Competence," *Communication Reports* 11 (1998): 87–95.

29. Richmond and McCroskey, 46.

30. G. M. Phillips, *Communication Incompetencies* (Carbondale: Southern Illinois University Press, 1991).

31. Y. Lin and A. S. Rancer, "Ethnocentrism, Intercultural Communication Apprehension, Intercultural Willingness-to-Communicate, and Intentions to Participate in an Intercultural Dialogue Program: Testing a Proposed Model," *Communication Research Reports* 20 (2003): 62–72.

32. S. Clement, "The Self-Efficacy Expectation and Occupational Preferences of Females and Males," *Journal of Occupational Psychology* (1987): 257–265.

33. L. A. Lefton and L. Valvatne, *Mastering Psychology*, 3rd ed. (Boston: Allyn & Bacon, 1988), 123.

34. T. Hopf and J. Ayres, "Coping with Public Speaking Anxiety: An Examination of Various Combinations of Systematic Desensitization, Skills Training, and Visualization," *Journal of Applied Communication Research* 20 (1992): 183–198.

35. J. Ayres, B. Heuett, and D. A. Sonandre, "Testing a Refinement in an Intervention for Communication Apprehension," *Communication Reports* 11 (1998): 73–85.

36. K. K. Dwyer, "The Multidimensional Model: Teaching Students to Self-Manage High Communication Apprehension by Self-Selecting Treatments," *Communication Education* 49 (2000): 72–81.

37. S. Ungerleider, "Visions of Victory," *Psychology Today* (July/August 1992), p. 48.

38. A. Anderson, "Learning Strategies in Physical Education: Self-Talk, Imagery, and Goal Setting," *JOPERD—The Journal of Physical Education, Recreation & Dance* 68 (January 1997): 30–36.

39. C. P. Neck and A. W. H. Barnard, "Managing Your Mind: What Are You Telling Yourself?" *Educational Leadership* 53:6 (March 1996): 24.

40. J. Ayres and T. A. Ayres, "Using Images to Enhance the Impact of Visualization," *Communication Reports* 16 (2003): 47–55.

41. Tice, 12–3, 12–4.

42. J. Ayres, T. Schleisman, and D. A. Sonandre, "Practice Makes Perfect But Does It Help Reduce Communication Apprehension?" *Communication Research Reports* 15 (1998): 171–179; and R. D. Roach, "Teaching Assistant Communication Apprehension, Willingness to Communicate, and State Communication Anxiety in the Classroom," *Communication Research Reports* 15 (1998): 138.

Chapter 3 Perception and Thought: Making Sense

1. R. Plotnik, *Introduction to Psychology*, 5th ed. (Belmont, CA: Wadsworth., 1999), 565.

2. M. Fitch-Hauser, D. A. Barker, and A. Hughes, "Receiver Apprehension and Listening Comprehension: A Linear or Curvilinear Relationship?" *Southern Communication Journal* 56 (1990): 62–71.

3. R. W. Preiss and L. R. Wheeless, "Affective Responses in Listening: A Meta-analysis of Receiver Apprehension Outcomes,"

Journal of the International Listening Association 3 (1989): 71–102.

4. A. Baum, J. D. Fisher, and J. E. Singer, *Social Psychology* (New York: Random House, 1985), 54.

5. A. H. Eagly and S. Chaiken, *The Psychology of Attitudes* (Fort Worth, TX: Harcourt Brace Jovanovich, 1993), 1.

6. R. L. Johannesen, *Ethics in Human Communication,* 4th ed. (Prospect Heights, IL: Waveland, 1996), 1.

7. L. A. Samovar, R. E. Porter, and L. A. Stefani, *Communication between Cultures,* 3rd ed. (Belmont, CA: Wadsworth, 1998), 36.

8. J. Wood, *Gendered Lives,* 6th ed. (Belmont, CA: Wadsworth, 2005), 22.

9. D. Tannen, *You Just Don't Understand: Women and Men in Conversation* (New York: Morrow, 1990), 47.

10. E. T. Hall, *Beyond Culture* (Garden City, NY: Doubleday, 1976), 74.

11. D. L. Whorf, *Language, Thought, and Reality* (Cambridge, MA: MIT Press, 1964).

12. C. H. Dodd, *Dynamics of Intercultural Communication,* 3rd ed. (Dubuque, IA: Wm. C. Brown, 1991), 125.

13. Whorf.

14. A. Maslow, *Motivation and Personality,* 2nd ed. (New York: Harper & Row, 1970).

15. H. H. Kelley and J. W. Thibaut, *Interpersonal Relationships* (New York: John Wiley, 1978).

16. L. Festinger, *A Theory of Cognitive Dissonance* (Evanston, IL: Row, Peterson, 1957).

17. M. Clayton, "Rethinking Thinking," *Christian Science Monitor,* October 14, 2003, p. 18.

18. B. Piper, "Critical Thinking Skills," *Professional Builder* 69:1 (January 2004): 54.

19. National Education Goals Panel, *The National Education Goals Report* (Washington, DC: U.S. Government Printing Office, 1991), 237.

20. D. F. Halpern, "A National Assessment of Critical Thinking Skills in Adults: Taking Steps toward the Goal," in *The National Assessment of College Learning: Identification of the Skills to Be Taught, Learned, and Assessed,* A. Greenwood, ed. (Washington, DC: National Center for Educational Statistics, 1994), 29.

21. D. Perkins, E. Jay, and S. Tishman, "Assessing Thinking: A Framework for Measuring Critical Thinking and Problem Solving Skills at the College Level," in Greenwood, 68.

22. Perkins, Jay, and Tishman, 73.

23. J. H. Lipps, "Judging Authority," *Skeptical Inquirer* 28:1 (January–February 2004): 35.

24. S. Toulmin, *The Uses of Argument* (Cambridge, UK: Cambridge University Press, 1958).

25. *New York Times,* January 22, 1993, p A10L.

26. K. Egan, *Teaching as Storytelling: An Alternative Approach to Teaching and Curriculum in the Elementary School* (Chicago: University of Chicago Press, 1986), 41.

27. G. A. Miller, "The Magic Number Seven, Plus or Minus Two: Some Limits on Our Capacity for Processing Information," *Psychological Review* 63 (1956): 81–97.

28. Miller, 81–97.

29. S. Booth-Butterfield and M. Booth-Butterfield, "Individual Differences in the Communication of Humorous Messages," *Southern Communication Journal* 56 (1991): 206.

Chapter 4 Listening and Questioning: Negotiating Meanings

1. R. G. Nichols and L. A. Stevens, *Are You Listening?* (New York: McGraw-Hill, 1957).

2. J. J. Floyd, *Listening: A Practical Approach* (Glenview, IL: Scott, Foresman, 1985), 2–15.

3. J. Flowerdew, "Research of Relevance to Second Language

Lecture Comprehension: An Overview," in *Academic Listening: Research Perspectives,* J. Flowerdew, ed. (Cambridge, UK: Cambridge University Press, 1995), 7–29.

4. W. B. Legge, "Listening, Intelligence, and School Achievement," in *Listening: Readings,* S. Duker, ed. (Metuchen, NJ: Scarecrow, 1971), 121–133.

5. T. Russell, "Make the Connection: Only by Listening Carefully to What Clients Have to Say Will Advisers Truly Understand Their Needs," *Money Marketing,* June 10, 2004, p. 47.

6. M. Brody, 'Learn to Listen: Closing the Mouth and Opening the Ears Facilitates Effective Communication" (Strategies: Managing and Marketing through Motivation). *Incentiv,* 1788:5 (May 2004): 57–58.

7. N. K. Austin and T. J. Peters, *A Passion for Excellence: The Leadership Difference* (New York: Random House, 1985), 5.

8. L. Brown, *Communicating Facts and Ideas in Business* (Englewood Cliffs, NJ: Prentice-Hall, 1982).

9. J. J. Salopek, "Is Anyone Listening?" *Training and Development* (September 1999): 58–59.

10. A. D. Wolvin and C. G. Coakley, "A Survey of the Status of Listening Training in Some Fortune 500 Corporations," *Communication Education* 40 (1991): 152–164.

11. A. Lucia, "Leaders Know How to Listen," *HR Focus* 74:4 (April 1997): 25.

12. Brody, 57–58.

13. S. H. Elgin, *Success with the Gentle Art of Verbal Self-Defense* (Englewood Cliffs, NJ: Prentice-Hall, 1989), 90.

14. R. Bolton, "Listening Is More Than Merely Hearing," in *Bridges Not Walls: A Book about Interpersonal Communication,* 5th ed., J. Stewart, ed. (New York: McGraw-Hill, 1990), 176.

15. M. J. Beatty, "Receiver Apprehension as a Function of Cognitive Backlog," *Western Journal of*

Speech Communication 45 (1981): 277–281.

16. Brody, 58.

17. W. L. Benoit and P. J. Benoit, "Memory for Conversational Behavior," *Southern Communication Journal* 56 (1991): 24–34.

18. Lucia, 1.

19. Bolton, 185.

20. J. Stewart and M. Thomas, "Dialogic Listening: Sculpting Mutual Meanings," in Stewart, 192–210.

21. Stewart and Thomas.

22. Stewart and Thomas.

Chapter 5 Nonverbal Communication: More Than Words Can Say

1. P. A. Andersen, *Nonverbal Communication: Forms and Functions* (Mountain View, CA: Mayfield, 1999), 247.

2. T. P. Mottet et al., "The Effects of Student Verbal and Nonverbal Responsiveness on Teacher Self-Efficacy and Job Satisfaction, *Communication Education* 53 (2004): 150–163.

3. Andersen, 25.

4. J. K. Burgoon, D. B. Buller, and W. G. Woodall, *Nonverbal Communication: The Unspoken Dialogue* (New York: Harper & Row, 1989), 155.

5. R. L. Woolfolk and A. E. Woolfolk, "Effects of Teacher Verbal and Nonverbal Behaviors on Student Perceptions and Attitudes," *American Educational Research Journal* 11 (1974): 297–303.

6. J. K. Burgoon, L. A. Stern, and L. Dillman, *Interpersonal Adaptation: Dyadic Interaction Patterns* (Cambridge, UK: Cambridge University Press, 1995), 3.

7. P. Ekman and W. V. Friesen, "The Repertoire of Nonverbal Behavior: Categories, Origins, Usage and Coding," *Semiotica* 1 (1969): 49–98; M. L. Knapp, *Nonverbal Communication in Human Interaction,* 2nd ed. (New York: Holt, Rinehart & Winston, 1978).

8. D. Goleman, "Non-verbal Cues Are Easy to Misinterpret," *New York Times,* September 17, 1991, pp. C1, C9.

9. T. H. Feeley and M. J. Young, "Humans as Lie Detectors: Some More Second Thoughts," *Communication Quarterly* 46 (1998): 109.

10. J. Swenson and F. L. Casmir, "The Impact of Culture-Sameness, Gender, Foreign Travel, and Academic Background on the Ability to Interpret Facial Expression of Emotion in Others," *Communication Monographs* 66 (1998): 214–230.

11. D. G. Leathers, *Successful Nonverbal Communication: Principles and Applications,* 2nd ed. (New York: Macmillan, 1992), 49.

12. P. A. Andersen, "In Different Dimensions: Nonverbal Communication and Culture," in *Intercultural Communication: A Reader,* 10th ed., L. A. Samovar and R. E. Porter, eds. (Belmont, CA: Wadsworth, 2003), 239.

13. G. B. Ray, "Vocally Cued Personality Prototypes: An Implicit Personality Theory," *Communication Monographs* 53 (1986): 266–276.

14. Ray.

15. R. L. Street Jr., R. M. Brady, and W. B. Putnam, "The Influence of Speech Rate Stereotypes and Rate Similarity on Listeners' Evaluations of Speakers," *Journal of Language and Social Psychology* 2 (1983): 37–56.

16. D. B. Buller and R. R. Aune, "The Effects of Vocalics and Nonverbal Sensitivity on Compliance: A Speech Accommodation Theory Explanation," *Human Communication Research* 14 (1988): 301–332; H. Giles and R. L. Street Jr., "Communicator Characteristics and Behavior," in *Handbook of Interpersonal Communication,* M. L. Knapp and G. R. Miller, eds. (Beverly Hills, CA: Sage, 1985), 205–261.

17. W. G. Woodall and J. K. Burgoon, "Talking Fast and Changing Attitudes: A Critique and Clarification," *Journal of Nonverbal Behavior* 8 (1983): 126–142.

18. H. Giles and N. Coupland, *Language: Contexts and Consequences* (Pacific Grove, CA: Brooks/Cole, 1991), 32.

19. Giles and Coupland, 63.

20. "Where to Drop a Lisp or Pick Up an Accent: Speech Therapist Tells How It's Done," *New York Times,* August 11, 1993, p. B4 L.

21. S. A. Beebe, "Effects of Eye Contact, Posture and Vocal Inflection upon Credibility and Comprehension," *Australian SCAN: Journal of Human Communication* 7–8 (1980): 57–70; J. K. Burgoon, D. A. Coker, and R. A. Coker, "Communication of Gaze Behavior: A Test of Two Contrasting Explanations," *Human Communication Research* 12 (1986): 495–524; C. L. Kleinke, "Gaze and Eye Contact: A Research Review," *Psychological Bulletin* 100 (1986): 78–100; J. Hornik, "The Effect of Touch and Gaze upon Compliance and Interest of Interviewees," *Journal of Social Psychology* 12 (1987): 681–683.

22. J. K. Burgoon et al., "Effects of Gaze on Hiring, Credibility, Attraction, and Relational Message Interpretation," *Journal of Nonverbal Behavior* 9 (1985): 133–146.

23. J. L. Kellerman, J. Lewis, and J. D. Laird, "Looking and Loving: The Effects of Mutual Gaze on Feelings of Romantic Love," *Journal of Research in Personality* 23 (1989): 145–161.

24. J. F. Dovidio and S. L. Ellyson, "Decoding Visual Dominance: Attributions of Power Based on Relative Percentages of Looking While Speaking and Looking While Listening," *Psychology Quarterly* 45 (1982): 106–115.

25. J. Wood, *Gendered Lives: Communication, Gender, and Culture,* 6th ed. (Belmont, CA: Wadsworth, 2005), 138.

26. E. R. McDaniel, "Japanese Nonverbal Communication: A Reflection of Cultural Themes," in. Samovar and Porter, 27.

27. P. Ekman and W. V. Friesen, "Head and Body Cues in the Judgment of Emotion: A Reformulation," *Perceptual and Motor Skills* 24 (1967): 71–72.

28. M. D. Alicke, R. H. Smith, and M. L. Klotz, "Judgments of Physical Attractiveness: The Role of Faces and Bodies," *Personality and Social Psychology Bulletin* 12 (1987): 381–389.

29. D. S. Berry, "What Can a Moving Face Tell Us?" *Journal of Personality and Social Psychology* 58 (1990): 1004–1014.

30. D. S. Berry and L. Z. MacArthur, "Some Components and Consequences of a Babyface," *Journal of Personality and Social Psychology* 48 (1985): 312–323.

31. P. Ekman, R. J. Davidson, and W. V. Friesen, "The Cuchenne Smile: Emotional Expression and Brain Physiology II," *Journal of Personality and Social Psychology* 58 (1990): 342–353.

32. D. B. Bugental, "Unmasking the 'Polite Smile': Situational and Personal Determinants of Managed Affect in Adult-Child Interaction," *Personality and Social Psychology Bulletin* 12 (1986): 7–16.

33. B. A. Le Poire and S. M. Yoshimura, "The Effects of Expectancies and Actual Communication on Nonverbal Adaptation and Communication Outcomes: A Test of Interaction Adaptation Theory," *Communication Monographs* 66 (1999): 1–30.

34. N. Guéguen and M-A. De Gail, "The Effect of Smiling on Helping Behavior: Smiling and Good Samaritan Behavior," *Communication Reports* 16 (2003): 133–140.

35. P. Ekman, W. V. Friesen, and P. C. Ellsworth, *Emotion in the Human Face: Guidelines for Research and an Integration of Findings* (New York: Pergamon, 1972); G. A. Forsyth, R. I. Kushner, and P. D. Forsyth, "Human Facial Expression Judgment in a Conversational Context," *Journal of*

Nonverbal Behavior 6 (1981): 115–130; Leathers.

36. P. Ekman et al., "Universals and Cultural Differences in the Judgments of Facial Expressions of Emotion," *Journal of Personality and Social Psychology* 53 (1987): 712–717.

37. J. K. Burgoon and T. J. Saine, *The Unspoken Dialogue: An Introduction to Nonverbal Communication* (Boston: Houghton Mifflin, 1978).

38. Andersen, "In Different Dimensions," 247.

39. Burgoon, Buller, and Woodall, 315.

40. V. P. Richmond and J. C. McCroskey, "The Impact of Supervisor and Subordinate Immediacy on Relational and Organizational Outcomes," *Communication Monographs* 67 (2000): 85.

41. M. LaFrance and W. Ickes, "Postural Mirroring and Interactional Involvement: Sex and Sex-Typing Effects," *Journal of Nonverbal Behavior* 5 (1981): 139–154.

42. L. A. Samovar and R. E. Porter, *Communication between Cultures,* 5th ed. (Belmont, CA: Wadsworth, 2004), 177.

43. J. C. Pearson, L. H. Turner, and W. Todd-Mancillas, *Gender and Communication,* 2nd ed. (Dubuque, IA: Wm. C. Brown, 1991), 140.

44. Ekman and Friesen, "Repertoire of Nonverbal Behavior."

45. V. Manusov, "An Application of Attribution Principles to Nonverbal Behavior in Romantic Dyads," *Communication Monographs* 57 (1990): 104–118.

46. W. G. Woodall and J. K. Burgoon, "The Effects of Nonverbal Synchrony on Message Comprehension and Persuasiveness," *Journal of Nonverbal Behavior* 5 (1981): 207–223.

47. Burgoon, Buller, and Woodall, 74.

48. C. M. J. Beaulieu, "Intercultural Study of Personal Space: A Case Study," *Journal of Applied*

Social Psychology 34 (2004): 794–805.

49. Y. M. Epstein, R. L. Woolfolk, and P. M. Lehrer, "Physiological, Cognitive, and Nonverbal Responses to Repeated Exposure to Crowding," *Journal of Applied Social Psychology* 11 (1981): 1–13.

50. E. T. Hall, *The Hidden Dimension* (Garden City, NY: Doubleday, 1969).

51. Beaulieu, 797.

52. C. Z. Dolphin, "Variables in the Use of Personal Space in Intercultural Transactions," *Howard Journal of Communications* 1 (1988): 23–28.

53. N. M. Sussman and H. M. Rosenfeld, "Influence of Culture, Language, and Sex on Conversational Distance," *Journal of Personality and Social Psychology* 42 (1982): 66–74.

54. L. P. Stewart et al., *Communication between the Sexes: Sex Differences and Sex-Role Stereotypes,* 2nd ed. (Scottsdale, AZ: Gorsuch Scarisbrick, 1990), 90.

55. M. S. Marx, P. Werner, and J. Cohen-Mansfield, "Agitation and Touch in the Nursing Home," *Psychological Reports* 64 (1989): 1019–1026.

56. Leathers, 133.

57. B. Major, "Gender Patterns in Touching Behavior," in *Gender and Nonverbal Behavior,* C. Mayo and N. M. Henley, eds. (New York: Springer-Verlag, 1980), 15–37; G. F. Scroggs, "Sex, Status, and Solidarity: Attributions for Nonmutual Touch." Paper presented at the meeting of the Eastern Psychological Association, Hartford, CT, April 1980.

58. L. Copeland, "Learning to Manage a Multicultural Work Force," *Training: The Magazine of Human Resources Development* (May 1988): 48–56.

59. G. Collier, *Emotional Experience* (Hillsdale, NJ: Lawrence Erlbaum, 1985).

60. M. S. Remland, T. S. Jones, and H. Brinkman, "Interpersonal

Distance, Body Orientation, and Touch in the Dyadic Interactions of Northern and Southern Europeans." Paper presented at the meeting of the Speech Communication Association, Chicago, IL, October 1992.

61. D. E. Smith, F. N. Willis, and J. A. Gier, "Success and Interpersonal Touch in a Competitive Setting," *Journal of Nonverbal Behavior* 5 (1980): 26–34.

62. Pearson, Turner, and Todd-Mancillas, 142.

63. B. Major, A. M. Schmidlin, and L. Williams, "Gesture Patterns in Social Touch: The Impact of Setting and Age," *Journal of Personality and Social Psychology* 58 (1990): 634–635.

64. R. Dibiase and J. Gunnoe, "Gender and Culture Differences in Touching Behavior," *Journal of Social Psychology* 144 (2004): 49–62.

65. V. P. Richmond and J. C. McCroskey, *Communication: Apprehension, Avoidance, and Effectiveness,* 4th ed. (Scottsdale, AZ: Gorsuch Scarisbrick, 1995).

66. Leathers.

67. J. S. Seiter and A. Sandry, "Pierced for Success?: The Effects of Ear and Nose Piercing on Perceptions of Job Candidates Credibility, Attractiveness, and Hirability," *Communication Research Reports* 20 (2003): 287–289.

68. R. E. Porter and L. A. Samovar, "An Introduction to Intercultural Communication," in *Intercultural Communication: A Reader,* 8th ed., L. A. Samovar and R. E. Porter, eds. (Belmont, CA: Wadsworth, 1997), 19.

69. L. Skow and L. A. Samovar, "Cultural Patterns of the Maasai," in *Intercultural Communication: A Reader,* 9th ed., L. A. Samovar and R. E. Porter, eds. (Belmont, CA: Wadsworth, 2000), 97.

70. E. T. Hall, "Monochronic and Polychronic Time," in Samovar and Porter, 9th ed.

71. Porter and Samovar, 8th ed., 18.

Chapter 6 Verbal Communication: Connecting with Language

1. H. Giles and N. Coupland, *Language: Contexts and Consequences* (Pacific Grove, CA: Brooks/Cole, 1991), 20.

2. P. Benoit et al., "From 'Jet Screaming Hootie Queen' to 'Talking to Ralph': An Undergraduate Slang Dictionary." Paper presented at the meeting of the Speech Communication Association, Chicago, IL, November 1992, 16.

3. C. M. Feldman and B. J. Walkosz, "Communicating Unclearly: The Adaptive Role of Strategic Ambiguity in Interpersonal Relationships." Paper presented at the meeting of the Speech Communication Association, Chicago, IL, November 1992, 2.

4. J. S. Seiter, J. Larsen, and J. Skinner, "'Handicapped' or 'Handicapable'?: The Effects of Language about Persons with Disabilities on Perceptions of Source Credibility and Persuasiveness," *Communication Reports* 11 (1998): 2.

5. A. Pratkanis and E. Aronson, *Age of Propaganda: The Everyday Use and Abuse of Persuasion* (New York: W. H. Freeman, 1992), 9.

6. R. E. Lee and K. K. Lee, *Arguing Persuasively* (New York: Longman, 1989), 134–135.

7. I. L. Allen, *The Language of Ethnic Conflict* (New York: Columbia University Press, 1983).

8. M. L. King Jr., *Why We Can't Wait* (New York: Signet, 1964), 81.

9. J. Greenberg, S. L. Kirkland, and T. Pyszcynski, "Some Notions and Preliminary Research concerning Derogatory Ethnic Labels," in *Discourse and Discrimination,* G. Smitherman-Donaldson and T. A. van Dijk, eds. (Detroit: Wayne State University Press, 1988), 81.

10. A. Korzybski, *Science and Sanity* (Lakeville, CT: The Non-Aristotelian Library, 1933).

11. G. Philipsen, "Speech and the Communal Function in Four Cultures," in *Readings on*

Communicating with Strangers: An Approach to Intercultural Communication, W. B. Gudykunst and Y. Y. Kim, eds. (New York: McGraw-Hill, 1992), 236; abridged from *Language, Communication, and Culture,* S. Ting-Toomey and F. Korzenny, eds. (Newbury Park, CA: Sage, 1989), 79–92.

12. S. Fox, "The Controversy over Ebonics," *Phi Delta Kappan* 78:3 (November 1997): 237–241.

13. Fox, 237.

14. N. Morris, "Communicating Identity: The Politics of Language in Twentieth-Century Puerto Rico." Paper presented at meeting of the Speech Communication Association, Chicago, IL, November 1992, 3.

15. Morris, 16.

16. "European Union (EU) Concerned that Internet and Other Means of Advanced Communications Could Hurt Region's Culture," *Communications Daily* 16, October 22, 1996, p. 10.

17. Giles and Coupland, 38.

18. Giles and Coupland, 38.

19. Giles and Coupland, 40–45.

20. C. Kramarae, *Women and Men Speaking* (Rowley, MA: Newbury House, 1981).

21. M. Houston, "Multiple Perspectives: African American Women Conceive their Talk," *Women and Language* 23 (2000): 11.

22. J. T. Wood, *Gendered Lives: Communication, Gender, and Culture,* 6th ed. (Belmont, CA: Wadsworth, 2005), 116.

23. N. J. Smith-Heffner, "Women and Politeness: The Javanese Example," *Language in Society* 17 (1988): 536.

24. D. Tannen, *You Just Don't Understand: Women and Men in Conversation* (New York: Morrow, 1990), 78–79.

25. Tannen, 78–79.

26. A. House, J. M. Dallinger, and D. Kilgallen, *Communication Reports* 11 (1998): 11.

27. E. T. Hall, *Beyond Culture* (Garden City, NY: Doubleday, 1976).

28. W. B. Gudykunst and S. Ting-Toomey, "Verbal Communication Styles," in Gudykunst and Kim, 224; abridged from Gudykunst and Ting–Toomey, 99–115.

29. R. C. Anderson and W. E. Nagy, "The Vocabulary Conundrum," *American Educator* (Winter 1992): 18.

30. R. McCrum, W. Cran, and R. MacNeil, *The Story of English* (New York: Elisabeth Sifton Books/ Viking, 1986), 19.

31. Anderson and Nagy.

32. M. C. Aaron, "The Right Frame: Managing Meaning and Making Proposals," *Harvard Management Communication Letter* 2 (September 1999): 2.

Chapter 7 Relationship Climates: Creating Communication Environments

1. L. R. Anderson, "Toward a Two-Track Model of Leadership Training: Suggestions from Self-Monitoring Theory," *Small Group Research* 21 (1990): 147–167.

2. M. Buber, *I and Thou*, 2nd ed. (New York: Scribners, 1958).

3. J. R. Gibb, "Defensive Communication," *Journal of Communication* 11 (1961): 141–148.

4. G. H. Stamp, A. L. Vangelisti, and J. A. Daly, "The Creation of Defensiveness in Social Interactions," *Communication Quarterly* 40 (1992): 177–190.

5. J. Stewart, "Interpersonal Communication: Contact between Persons," in *Bridges Not Walls: A Book about Interpersonal Communication*, 5th ed., J. Stewart, ed. (New York: McGraw-Hill, 1990), 13–31.

6. J. H. Berg and R. L. Archer, "The Disclosure-Liking Relationship," *Human Communication Research* 10 (1983): 269–281; V. J. Derlega et al., "Self-Disclosure and Relationship Development: An Attributional Analysis," in *Interpersonal Processes: New Directions in Communication Research,*

M. E. Roloff and G. R. Miller, eds. (Newbury Park, CA: Sage, 1987), 172–187.

7. J. H. Harvey, T. L. Orbuch, and A. L. Weber, eds., *Attributions, Accounts, and Close Relationships* (New York: Springer-Verlag, 1992), 2.

8. V. Waldron and J. L. Applegate, "Similarity in the Use of Person-Centered Tactics: Effects on Social Attraction and Persuasiveness in Dyadic Verbal Disagreements," *Communication Reports* 11 (1998): 155–165.

9. S. Trenholm and A. Jensen, *Interpersonal Communication* (Belmont, CA: Wadsworth, 1998), 279–280.

10. J. Luft, *Of Human Interaction* (Palo Alto, CA: Mayfield, 1969).

11. A. Demarais and V. White, *First Impressions: What You Don't Know about How Others See You* (New York: Bantam, 2004), 116.

12. S. Ting-Toomey, "A Comparative Analysis of the Communicative Dimensions of Love, Self-Disclosure Maintenance, Ambivalence, and Conflict in Three Cultures: France, Japan, and the United States." Paper presented at the meeting of the International Communication Association, Montreal, Canada, May 1987.

13. W. K. Rawlins, "Communication in Cross-Sex Friendships," in *Women and Men Communicating: Challenges and Changes,* L. P. Arliss and D. J. Borisoff, eds. (Ft. Worth, TX: Harcourt Brace, 1993), 53.

14. R. A. Buhrke and D. R. Fuqua, "Sex Differences in Same- and Cross-Sex Supportive Relationships," *Sex Roles* 17 (1987): 339–532.

15. E. E. McDowell and C. E. McDowell, "An Exploratory Study of Gender, Gender Orientation, Self-Disclosure and Loneliness for Senior High School Students." Paper presented at the meeting of the Speech Communication Association, Atlanta, GA, November 1991.

16. S. Duck et al., "Some Evident Truths about Conversations in Everyday Relationships: All Communications Are Not Created Equal," *Human Communication Research* 18 (1991): 228–267.

17. L. E. Lazowski and S. M. Andersen, "Self-Disclosure and Social Perception: The Impact of Private, Negative, and Extreme Communications," in *Communication, Cognition, and Anxiety,* M. Booth-Butterfield, ed. (Newbury Park, CA: Sage, 1990), 131–154.

18. D. A. Infante et al., "Verbal Aggressiveness: Messages and Reasons," *Communication Quarterly* 40 (1992): 116; D. A. Infante and C. J. Wigley, III, "Verbal Aggressiveness: An Interpersonal Model and Measure," *Communication Monographs* 53 (1986): 61–69.

19. K. J. Tusing and J. P. Dillard, "The Sounds of Dominance: Vocal Precursors of Perceived Dominance During Interpersonal Influence," *Human Communication Research* 26 (2000): 148–171.

20. S. A. Myers and A. D. Johnson, "Verbal Aggression and Liking in Interpersonal Relationships," *Communication Research Reports* 20 (2003): 90–96.

21. B. J. Broome, "Building Shared Meaning: Implications of a Relational Approach to Empathy for Teaching Intercultural Communication," *Communication Education* 40 (1991): 239.

22. Broome.

23. P. Watzlawick, J. H. Beavin, and D. D. Jackson, *Pragmatics of Human Communication: A Study of Interaction Patterns, Pathologies, and Paradoxes* (New York: Norton, 1967).

24. E. Berne, *The Structure and Dynamics of Organizations and Groups* (New York: Grove Press, 1966).

25. Stamp, Vangelisti, and Daly, 186.

26. M. E. Roloff, *Interpersonal Communication: The Social*

Exchange Approach (Beverly Hills, CA: Sage, 1981).

27. P. H. Zietlow and A. L. Sillars, "Life Stage Differences in Communication during Marital Conflicts," *Journal of Social and Personal Relationships* 5 (1988): 223–245.

28. J. T. Wood, *Gendered Lives: Communication, Gender, and Culture,* 6th ed. (Belmont, CA: Wadsworth, 2005), 185.

29. S. Ting-Toomey, "Intercultural Conflict Style: A Face-Negotiation Theory," in *Theories in Intercultural Communication,* Y. Y. Kim and W. B. Gudykunst, eds. (Newbury Park, CA: Sage, 1988), 213–235.

30. J. G. Oetzel, "The Effects of Self-Construals and Ethnicity on Self-Reported Conflict Styles," *Communication Reports* 11 (1998): 133–144.

31. K. H. Basso, *Western Apache Language and Culture: Essays in Linguistic Anthropology* . (Tucson: University of Arizona Press, 1990), 67.

32. Ting-Toomey.

33. W. W. Wilmot, *Dyadic Communication,* 2nd ed. (Reading, MA: Addison-Wesley, 1979).

34. M. Rafenstein, "How to Compromise," *Current Health,* December 2, 1999, p. 30.

35. V. Satir, "Paying Attention to Words," in Stewart, 63–68.

36. Infante et al., 116.

37. D. A. Infante et al., "Verbal Aggression in Violent and Nonviolent Marital Disputes," *Communication Quarterly* 38 (1990): 361–371.

38. D. A. Infante et al., "Initiating and Reciprocating Verbal Aggression: Effects on Credibility and Credited Valid Arguments." Paper presented at the meeting of the Speech Communication Association, Chicago, IL, October 1992.

39. D. J. Goldsmith, "Giving Advice: The Role of Sequential Placement in Mitigating Face Threat," *Communication Monographs* 67 (2000): 1–19.

Chapter 8   Personal Relationships: Growing with Another

1. G. R. Miller and M. Steinberg, *Between People: A New Analysis of Interpersonal Communication* (Palo Alto, CA: Science Research Associates, 1975).

2. G. A. Hauser, *Introduction to Rhetorical Theory* (New York: Harper & Row, 1988).

3. A. Demarais and V. White, *First Impressions: What You Don't Know about How Others See You* (New York: Bantam, 2004), 17.

4. J. K. Burgoon, D. B. Buller, and W. G. Woodall, *Nonverbal Communication: The Unspoken Dialogue* (New York: Harper & Row, 1989), 325–329.

5. S. W. Duck, *Meaningful Relationships* (Thousand Oaks, CA: Sage, 1994).

6. R. A. Bell and J. A. Daly, "The Affinity-Seeking Function of Communication," *Communication Monographs* 50 (1984): 96–97.

7. J. N. Capella and M. T. Palmer, "Attitude Similarity, Relational History, and Attraction: The Mediating Effects of Kinesic and Vocal Behaviors," *Communication Monographs* 57 (1990): 161–183; M. Sunnafrank, "On Debunking the Attitude Similarity Myth," *Communication Monographs* 59 (1992): 164–179.

8. R. Reisner, "How Different Cultures Learn," *Meeting News* 17 (May/June 1993): 30–31.

9. K. H. Basso, *Western Apache Language and Culture: Essays in Linguistic Anthropology* (Tucson: University of Arizona Press, 1990), 84–85, 97.

10. S. Duck et al., "Some Evident Truths about Conversations in Everyday Relationships: All Communications Are Not Created Equal," *Human Communication Research* 18 (1991): 228–267.

11. J. T. Wood, *Gendered Lives: Communication, Gender, and Culture,* 4th ed. (Belmont, CA: Wadsworth, 2001), 125.

12. Duck et al.

13. H. T. Reis et al., "On Specificity in the Impact of Social Participation on Physical and Psychological Health," *Journal of Personality and Social Psychology* 48 (1985): 456–471.

14. A. Garner, *Conversationally Speaking: Tested New Ways to Increase Your Personal and Social Effectiveness* (New York: McGraw-Hill, 1981).

15. J. K. Burgoon, L. A. Stern, and L. Dullman, *Interpersonal Adaptation: Dyadic Interaction Patterns* (Cambridge, UK: Cambridge University Press, 1995), 3.

16. L. R. Wheeless, A. B. Frymier, and C. A. Thompson, "A Comparison of Verbal Output and Receptivity in Relation to Attraction and Communication Satisfaction in Interpersonal Relationships," *Communication Quarterly* 40 (1992): 102–115.

17. T. E. Zorn, "Construct System Development, Transformational Leadership and Leadership Messages," *Southern Communication Journal* 56 (1991): 178–193.

18. S. Booth-Butterfield and M. Booth-Butterfield, "Individual Differences in the Communication of Humorous Messages," *Southern Communication Journal* 56 (1991): 205–218.

19. W. K. Rawlins, "Communication in Cross-Sex Friendships," in *Women and Men Communicating: Challenges and Changes,* L. P. Arliss and D. J. Borisoff, eds. (Ft. Worth, TX: Harcourt Brace, 1993), 52.

20. B. Meeks, S. Hendrick, and C. Hendrick, "Communication, Love, and Satisfaction," *Journal of Social and Personal Relationships* 15 (1998): 755–773.

21. I. Altman and D. A. Taylor, *Social Penetration: The Development of Interpersonal Relationships* (New York: Holt, Rinehart & Winston, 1973).

22. A. P. Bochner, "The Functions of Human Communicating in Interpersonal Bonding," in *Handbook of Rhetorical and Communication Theory*, C. C. Arnold and J. W. Bowers, eds. (Boston: Allyn & Bacon, 1984), 544.

23. J. M. Honeycutt et al., "How Do I Love Thee? Let Me Consider My Options: Cognition, Verbal Strategies, and the Escalation of Intimacy," *Human Communication Research* 25 (1998): 39–63.

24. M. L. Knapp, *Interpersonal Communication and Human Relationships* (Boston: Allyn & Bacon, 1984).

25. I. Altman, A. Vinsel, and B. Brown, "Dialectic Conceptions in Social Psychology: An Application to Social Penetration and Privacy Regulation," *Advances in Experimental Social Psychology* 14 (1981): 107–160.

26. A. Johnson et al., "Relational Progression as a Dialectic: Examining Turning Points in Communication Among Friends," *Communication Monographs* 70 (2003): 230–240.

27. L. A. Baxter and B. M. Montgomery, "Rethinking Communication in Personal Relationships from a Dialectical Perspective," in *Handbook of Personal Relationships*, 2nd ed., S. Duck, ed. (New York: Wiley, 1997), 325–349.

28. C. Bullis, C. Clark, and R. Sline, "From Passion to Commitment: Turning Points in Romantic Relationships," in *Interpersonal Communication: Evolving Interpersonal Relationships*, P. J. Kalbfleisch, ed. (Hillsdale, NJ: Lawrence Erlbaum, 1993), 213–223.

29. A. J. Johnson et al., 230.

30. L. Baxter and C. Bullis, "Turning Points in Developing Romantic Relationships," *Human Communication Research* 12 (1986): 469–493.

31. Altman and Taylor.

32. Knapp.

33. A. J. Johnson et al., "The Process of Relationship Development and Deterioration: Turning Points in Friendships That Have Terminated," *Communication Quarterly* 52 (2004): 54–67.

34. Bochner.

35. J. K. Burgoon and J. L. Hale, "The Fundamental *Topoi* of Relational Communication," *Communication Monographs* 52 (1984): 193–214.

36. J. P. Coughlin and A. L. Vangelisti, "Desire for Change in One's Partner as a Predictor of the Demand/Withdraw Pattern of Marital Communication," *Communication Monographs* 66 (1999): 66–89.

37. D. Borisoff, "The Effect of Gender on Establishing and Maintaining Intimate Relationships," in Arliss and Borisoff.

38. C. Gilligan, *In a Different Voice: Psychological Theory and Women's Development* (Cambridge, MA: Harvard University Press, 1982).

39. F. Pittman, III, "Beyond Betrayal: Life after Infidelity," *Psychology Today*, May/June 1993, pp. 32–38, 78–82.

40. S. A. McCornack et al., "When the Alteration of Information Is Viewed as Deception: An Empirical Test of Information Manipulation Theory," *Communication Monographs* 59 (1992): 17.

41. McCornack et al.

42. J. K. Burgoon, "Applying an Interpersonal Communication Perspective to Deception: Effects of Suspicion, Deceit, and Relational Familiarity on Perceived Communication." Paper presented at the meeting of the Speech Communication Association, Chicago, IL, November 1992.

43. S. A. McCornack and T. R. Levine, "When Lies Are Uncovered: Emotional and Relational Outcomes of Discovered Deception," *Communication Monographs* 57 (1990): 119–138.

44. D. A. Infante et al., "Verbal Aggression in Violent and Nonviolent Marital Disputes," *Communication Quarterly* 38 (1990): 361–371.

45. J. Scheff and S. M. Retzinger, *Emotions and Violence: Shame and Rage in Destructive Conflicts* (Lexington, MA: Lexington Books, 1991); Infante et al., "Verbal Aggression."

46. C. W. Metcalf and R. Felible, *Lighten Up: Survival Skills for People under Pressure* (Reading, MA: Addison-Wesley, 1992).

47. Wood, 312.

48. J. T. Wood, *Gendered Lives: Communication, Gender, and Culture*, 6th ed. (Belmont, CA: Wadsworth, 2005), 280.

49. A. Abbey, "Misperception as an Antecedent of Acquaintance Rape: A Consequence of Ambiguity in Communication between Men and Women," in *Acquaintance Rape: The Hidden Crime*, A. Parrot and L. Bechhofer, eds. (New York: Wiley, 1991), 96–111.

50. P. A. Mongeau and M. Yeazell, "Relational Communication in Male- and Female-Initiated First Dates." Paper presented at the meeting of the Speech Communication Association, Chicago, IL, November 1992.

51. L. A. Samovar and R. E. Porter, eds., *Intercultural Communication: A Reader*, 9th ed. (Belmont, CA: Wadsworth., 2000), 12.

52. J. Trost, "What Do We Mean the Same by the Concept of Family?" *Communication Research* 17 (1990): 431–443.

53. S. Planalp, "Communication, Cognition, and Emotion," *Communication Monographs* 60 (1993): 6.

54. A. L. Vangelisti, "Communication in the Family: The Influence of Time, Relational Prototypes, and Irrationality," *Communication Monographs* 60 (1993): 42–54.

55. N. B. Epstein, D. S. Bishop, and L. M. Baldwin, "The McMaster Model of Family Functioning," *Journal of Marriage and*

Family Counseling 4:4 (1982): 19–31.

56. "How Much Time Do Kids Spend with Dad?" *USA Today Magazine,* August 2000, p. 4.

57. J. Yerby, N. Buerkel-Rothfuss, and A. P. Bochner, *Understanding Family Communication* (Scottsdale, AZ: Gorsuch Scarisbrick, 1990), 312–313.

58. Yerby, Buerkel-Rothfuss, and Bochner.

59. Yerby, Buerkel-Rothfuss, and Bochner.

60. D. B. Bugental, "Communication in Abusive Relationships," *American Behavioral Scientist* 36 (1993): 288.

61. S. P. Policoff, "Children of Chaos," *Campus Voice* (Winter 1987): 12–14.

62. P. Hobe, *Lovebound: Recovering from an Alcoholic Family* (New York: Penguin Books, 1990), 18.

Chapter 9 Professional Relationships: Transacting for Success

1. J. S. Ott, *The Organizational Culture Perspective* (Pacific Grove, CA: Brooks/Cole, 1989), vii.

2. K. Weick, *The Social Psychology of Organizing,* 2nd ed. (Reading, MA: Addison-Wesley, 1979).

3. J. Benjamin and R. E. McKerrow, *Business and Professional Communication: Concepts and Practices* (New York: HarperCollins, 1994), 36.

4. A. Trethewey and K. L. Ashcraft, "Practicing Disorganization: The Development of Applied Perspectives on Living with Tension," *Journal of Applied Communication Research* 32 (2004): 81–88.

5. L. B. Rosenfeld, J. M. Richman, and S. E. May, "Information Adequacy, Job Satisfaction, and Organizational Culture in a Dispersed-Network Organization," *Journal of Applied Communication Research* 32 (2004): 28–54.

6. A. Hylmo and P. M. Buzzanell, "Telecommuting as

Viewed through Cultural Lenses: An Empirical Investigation of the Discourses of Utopia, Identity, and Mystery," *Communication Monographs* 69 (2002): 329–356.

7. T. H. Feeley, "Testing a Communication Network Model of Employee Turnover Based on Centrality," *Journal of Applied Communication Research* 28 (2000): 262–277.

8. T. R. Levine and L. R. Wheeless, "Cross-Situational Consistency and Use/Nonuse Tendencies in Compliance-Gaining Tactic Selection," *Southern Communication Journal* 56 (1990): 1–11; P. King, "Automatic Responses, Target Resistance, and the Adaptation of Compliance-Seeking Requests," *Communication Monographs* 68 (2001): 386–399.

9. J. J. Sullivan, T. L. Albrecht, and S. Taylor, "Process, Organizational, Relational, and Personal Determinants of Managerial Compliance-Gaining Strategies," *Journal of Business Communication* 27 (1990): 332–355.

10. S. Metts, "Face and Facework: Implications for the Study of Personal Relationships," in *Handbook of Personal Relationships,* 2nd ed., S. Duck, ed. (Chichester, NY: Wiley, 1997), 375.

11. J. Oetzel et al., "Interpersonal Conflict in Organizations: Explaining Conflict Styles via Face-Negotiation Theory," *Communication Research Reports* 20 (2003): 106–115.

12. C. L. Carson and W. R. Cupoch, "Facing Corrections in the Workplace: The Influence of Perceived Face Threat on the Consequences of Managerial Reproaches," *Journal of Applied Communication Research* 28 (2000): 215–234; J. C. McCroskey and V. P. Richmond, "Applying Reciprocity and Accommodation Theories to Supervisor/Subordinate Communication," *Journal of Applied Communication Research* 28 (2000): 278–289.

13. D. L. Hamilton, S. J. Sherman, and C. M. Ruvolo, "Stereotype-Based Expectancies: Effects on Information Processing and Social Behavior," in *Readings on Communicating with Strangers: An Approach to Intercultural Communication,* W. B. Gudykunst & Y. Y. Kim, eds. (New York: McGraw-Hill, 1992), 137.

14. J. B. Sweeney, unpublished and untitled student paper, 1994.

15. C. H. Deutsch, "Listening to Women and Blacks," *New York Times,* December 1, 1991, p. F25.

16. D. Goleman, *Emotional Intelligence: Why It Can Matter More Than I.Q.* (New York: Bantam, 1995), 155–156.

17. A. Stephen, "Fondle a Woman: Pay $250,000," *New Statesman* 128, June 14, 1999, p. 20.

18. G. M. Bellman, *Getting Things Done When You Are Not in Charge* (San Francisco: Berrett-Koehler, 1992).

19. W. G. Stephan and C. W. Stephan, "Intergroup Anxiety," in Gudykunst and Kim, 17.

20. Stephan and Stephan, 18–19.

21. P. Amason, M. W. Allen, and S. A. Holmes, "Social Support and Acculturative Stress in the Multicultural Workplace," *Journal of Applied Communication Research* 27 (1999): 310–334.

22. W. B. Gudykunst and Y. Y. Kim, "Communicating Effectively with Strangers," in Gudykunst and Kim, 369.

23. R. Fisher and S. Brown, "A Strategy for Building Better Relationships As We Negotiate," in Gudykunst and Kim, 398.

24. C. J. Stewart and W. B. Cash Jr., *Interviewing Principles and Practices,* 6th ed. (Dubuque, IA: Wm. C. Brown, 1991), 5.

25. R. W. Pace and D. F. Faules, *Organizational Communication,* 3rd ed. (Englewood Cliffs, NJ: Prentice-Hall, 1994).

26. "Getting Past the Gatekeeper," *Black Enterprise* 31 (August 2000): 49.

27. J. Hollwitz and C. E. Wilson, "Structured Interviewing in Volunteer Selection," *Journal of Applied Communication Research* 21 (1993): 45–49.

28. J. M. Cortina et al., "The Incremental Validity of Interview Scores Over and Above Cognitive Ability and Conscientiousness Scores," *Personnel Psychology* 53 (2000): 325.

29. J. A. Weekley and J. A. Gier, "Reliability and Validity of the Situational Interview for a Sales Position," *Journal of Applied Psychology* 72 (1987): 484–487.

30. W. C. Donaghy, *The Interview: Skills and Applications* (Salem, WI: Sheffield, 1990), 6.

31. T. Janz, "Initial Comparisons of Patterned Behavior Description Interview versus Unstructured Interviews," *Journal of Applied Psychology* 67 (1982): 577–580; T. Janz, *Behavior Description Interviewing: New, Accurate, Cost-Effective* (Boston: Allyn & Bacon, 1986).

32. Donaghy, 165.

33. P. D. Ballard, "Dress for Success," *The Black Collegian,* 19 (February 1999): 68.

34. G. M. Goldhaber, *Organizational Communication*, 5th ed. (Dubuque, IA: Wm. C. Brown, 1990), 334.

35. C. Kleiman, "A Good Boss Is Vital for Success on the Job," *The Tribune* (San Luis Obispo County, CA), September 8, 2004, p. D1.

Chapter 10   Groups and Teams: Communication and Leadership

1. L. K. Michaelson, W. E. Watson, and R. H. Black, "A Realistic Test of Individual versus Group Consensus Decision Making," *Journal of Applied Psychology* 74 (1989): 834–839.

2. D. S. Gouran, *An Investigation to Identify the Critical Variables Related to Consensus in Group Discussions of Policy*, Project No. 8–F-004 (Washington, DC: U.S. Department of Health, Education and Welfare, Office of Education, 1969).

3. D. C. Kinlaw, *Developing Superior Work Teams: Building Quality and the Competitive Edge* (Lexington, MA: Lexington Books, 1991), xix.

4. C. Serant, "Enhancing Your Visibility," *Black Enterprise* (February 1992): 39.

5. J. R. Katzenbach and D. K. Smith, *The Wisdom of Teams: Creating the High-Performance Organization* (Boston: Harvard Business School Press, 1993), 81.

6. M. Csikszentmihalyi, *Flow: The Psychology of Optimal Experience* (New York: Harper & Row, 1990).

7. S. G. Cohen and D. Mankin, "Collaboration in the Virtual Organization," in *Trends in Organizational Behavior 6*, C. L. Cooper and D. M. Rousseau, eds. (New York: Wiley, 1999), 105.

8. G. Lumsden and D. Lumsden, *Communicating in Groups and Teams: Sharing Leadership*, 4th ed. (Belmont, CA: Wadsworth, 2004), 14.

9. Katzenbach and Smith.

10. Kinlaw, 12.

11. C. Hastings, P. Bixby, and R. Chaudhry-Lawton, *The Superteam Solution: Successful Teamworking in Organisations* (Aldershot, UK: Gower, 1986).

12. R. B. Cattell, "Concepts and Methods in the Measurement of Group Syntality," *Psychological Review* 55 (1948): 48–63.

13. C. E. Larson and F. M. J. LaFasto, *TeamWork: What Must Go Right/What Can Go Wrong* (Newbury Park, CA: Sage, 1989).

14. Katzenbach and Smith, 62–63.

15. J. G. Bowles, "The Human Side of Quality," *Fortune,* September 24, 1990.

16. C. J. Nemeth and J. L. Kwan, "Minority Influence, Divergent Thinking and Detection of Correct Solutions," *Journal of Applied Social Psychology* 17 (1987): 788–799.

17. B. Tuckman and M. Jensen, "Stages of Small-Group Development," *Group and Organizational Studies* (1977): 419–427.

18. "Teams: Solving the Sophomore Slump," *Harvard Management Update* (July 1999): 6.

19. C. J. G. Gersick, "Time and Transition in Work Teams: Toward a New Model of Group Development," *Academy of Management Journal* 31 (1988): 9–41.

20. Lumsden and Lumsden, 29.

21. S. A. Hellweg, L. A. Samovar, and L. Skow, "Cultural Variations in Negotiation Styles," in *Intercultural Communication: A Reader,* 7th ed., L. A. Samovar and R. E. Porter, eds. (Belmont, CA: Wadsworth, 1994): 286–292.

22. J. L. Nye and D. R. Forsyth, "The Effects of Prototype-Based Biases on Leadership Appraisals, A Test of Leadership Categorization Theory," *Small Group Research* 22 (1991): 360–379.

23. Katzenbach and Smith, 148

24. D. S. Gouran, *Making Decisions in Groups: Choices and Consequences* (Glenview, IL: Scott, Foresman, 1982), 148.

25. K. D. Benne and P. Sheats, "Functional Roles of Group Members," *Journal of Social Issues* 4 (1948): 41–49; C. Pavitt and P. Sackaroff, "Implicit Theories of Leadership and Judgments of Leadership among Group Members," *Small Group Research* 21 (1990): 374–392.

26. Benne and Sheats; Pavitt and Sackaroff.

27. Benne and Sheats.

28. Larson and LaFasto, 125.

29. J. M. Dukerich et al., "Moral Reasoning in Groups: Leaders Make a Difference," *Human Relations* 43 (1990): 473–493.

30. J. W. Gauss, "Integrity Is Integral to Career Success," *Healthcare Financial Management* 54:8 (2000): 89.

31. J. S. Thornton, "Leadership Traits That Work Worldwide," *Association Management* (August 1990): 22–23.

32. Pavitt and Sackaroff, 380.

33. W. Ling, R. C. Chia, and L. Fang, "Chinese Implicit Leadership Theory," *Journal of Social Psychology* 140 (2000): 729.

34. Hellweg, Samovar, and Skow, 286–292.

35. H. Riecken, "The Effects of Talkativeness on Ability to Influence Group Solutions of Problems," in *Interaction in Small Groups,* P. V. Crosbie, ed. (New York: Macmillan, 1975), 238–249.

36. B. Schultz, "Communication Correlates of Perceived Leaders in the Small Group," *Small Group Behavior* 17 (1986): 51–65.

37. Kinlaw, xvi.

38. J. A Kolb, "Leader Behaviors Related to Team Performance in Research and Non-Research Teams." Unpublished paper presented at the meeting of the Speech Communication Association, Atlanta, GA, November 1991.

39. C. C. Manz and H. P. Sims, "Superleadership: Beyond the Myth of Heroic Leadership," *Organizational Dynamics* (Spring 1991): 18–35.

40. R. S. Wellins, W. C. Byham, and J. M. Wilson, *Empowered Teams: Creating Self-Directed Work Groups That Improve Quality, Productivity, and Participation* (San Francisco: Jossey-Bass, 1991), 130.

41. R. K. White and R. O. Lippett, *Autocracy and Democracy* (New York: Harper & Row, 1960).

42. C. L. Pearce and P. A. Herbik, "Citizenship Behavior at the Team Level of Analysis: The Effects of Team Leadership, Team Commitment, Perceived Team Support, and Team Size," *Journal of Social Psychology* 144 (2004): 293–310.

43. M. S. Limon and F. J. Boster, "The Effects of Performance Feedback on Group Members' Perceptions of Prestige, Task Competencies, Group Belonging, and Loafing," *Communication Research Reports* 20 (2003):13.

44. J. R. Hackman and R. W. Walton, "Leading Groups in Organizations," in *Designing Effective Work Groups,* P. S. Goodman et al., eds. (San Francisco: Jossey-Bass, 1986), 84.

45. B. M. Bass, "From Transactional to Transformational Leadership: Learning to Share the Vision," *Organizational Dynamics* (Winter 1990): 22.

46. B. Nanus, *Visionary Leadership: Creating a Compelling Sense of Direction for Your Organization* (San Francisco: Jossey-Bass, 1992).

47. A. B. Fisher, "Leadership: When Does the Difference Make a Difference?" in *Communication and Group Decision-making,* R. Y. Hirokawa and M. S. Poole, eds. (Beverly Hills, CA: Sage, 1986), 205.

48. P. Hersey, K. J. Blanchard, and W. E. Natemeyer, "Situational Leadership, Perception, and the Impact of Power," *Group and Organization Studies* 4 (1979): 418–428.

49. E. P. Hollander, *Leadership Dynamics: A Practical Guide to Effective Relationships* (New York: Free Press, 1978).

50. H. M. Robert, III et al., eds., *Robert's Rules of Order,* 10th ed. (Cambridge, MA: Perseus, 2000).

51. Larson and LaFasto, 123.

52. J. K. Barge, "Task Skills and Competence in Group Leadership." Paper presented at the meeting of the Speech Communication Association, Atlanta, GA, November 1991.

Chapter 11 Problem Analysis and Decision Making: Achieving Group and Team Goals

1. H. A. Simon, *The New Science of Management Decision,* rev. ed. (Englewood Cliffs, NJ: Prentice-Hall, 1977).

2. R. S. Hirokawa and D. R. Scheerhorn, "The Role of Communication in Faulty Group Decision-Making," in *Communication and Group Decision Making,* R. Y. Hirokawa and M. S. Poole, eds. (Beverly Hills, CA: Sage, 1986), 74.

3. D. S. Gouran and R. Y. Hirokawa, "The Role of Communication in Decision-Making Groups: A Functional Perspective," in *Communication in Transition,* M. S. Mander, ed. (New York: Praeger, 1983), 168–185; Hirokawa and Scheerhorn.

4. J. Dewey, *How We Think* (Boston: D. C. Heath, 1910).

5. Dewey.

6. K. Ishikawa, *Guide to Quality Control,* 2nd ed., rev. (Tokyo: Asian Productivity Organization, 1982).

7. B. L. Toffler, *Tough Choices: Managers Talk Ethics* (New York: Wiley, 1986), 21–22.

8. J. A. Jaksa and M. S. Pritchard, *Communication Ethics: Methods of Analysis,* 2nd ed. (Belmont, CA: Wadsworth, 1994), 17.

9. D. S. Gouran, *Making Decisions in Groups: Choices and Consequences* (Glenview, IL: Scott, Foresman, 1982).

10. I. L. Janis, *Groupthink,* 2nd ed., rev. (Boston: Houghton Mifflin, 1983), 9.

11. I. L. Janis, *Crucial Decisions: Leadership in Policymaking and Crisis Management* (New York: Free Press, 1989).

12. Janis, *Crucial Decisions,* 56–58.

13. I. L. Janis, *Groupthink* (Boston: Houghton Mifflin, 1971), 225.

14. Janis, *Groupthink,* 2nd ed.; Janis, *Crucial Decisions.*

15. Jaksa and Pritchard.

16. "The Senate Report," *New York Times,* July 10, 2004; retrieved September 15, 2004, from www.nytimes.com/2004/07/10/op.../ 10SAT1.html?ex=1247198400&en= 65ee53c793e6d98c&ei=5090& partner=rssuserlan; K. Kwiatkowski,

"Flawed Decision Making: Cliques, Groupthink, Deceit Created Iraq Campaign," VAIW Veterans Against the Iraq War Home Page, August 1, 2003; retrieved September 15, 2004, from News&file=articl&sid=116&mode=thread&order=0&thold=0&POSTNUKESID=6D4bB543; J. K. Alter, "Is Groupthink Driving Us to War?" *Boston Globe,* September 16, 2002; retrieved September 15, 2004, from www.boston.com/news/packages/iraq/globe_stories/091602_alter.htm

17. Janis, *Crucial Decisions.*

18. Janis, *Crucial Decisions.*

19. Janis, *Groupthink,* 2nd ed.

Chapter 12 Research and Development: Creating Public Speeches

1. D. S. Brandt, "Evaluating Information on the Internet," *Computers in Libraries* 16:5 (1996): 44.

2. Brandt, 46.

3. D. L. Carlson, "Electronic Communications and Communities," *Antiquity* 71 (1997): 1049.

4. T. K. Muhammad, "The Scoop on Newsgroup: The Internet Is More Than the World Wide Web," *Black Enterprise* 27:8 (March 1997): 37.

5. G. A. Miller, "The Magic Number Seven, Plus or Minus Two: Some Limits on Our Capacity for Processing Information," *Psychological Review* 63 (1956): 81–97.

6. S. H. Frazier, *Psychotrends: What Kind of People Are We Becoming?* (New York: Simon & Schuster, 1994).

7. J. T. Wood, *Gendered Lives: Communication, Gender, and Culture,* 4th ed. (Belmont, CA: Wadsworth, 2001), 212.

8. R. C. Borden, *Public Speaking as Listeners Like It* (New York: Harper & Row, 1935).

9. M. B. Howes, *The Psychology of Human Cognition: Mainstream and Genevan Traditions* (New York: Pergamon, 1990), 71.

10. L. Walters, *Secrets of Successful Speakers: How You Can Motivate, Captivate and Persuade* (New York: McGraw-Hill, 1993), 127.

11. Wharton Applied Research Center, "A Study of the Effects of the Use of Overhead Transparencies on Business Meetings: Final Report," Wharton School of the University of Pennsylvania, September 14, 1981.

12. D. H. Carlson, "Computer-Based Graphics Tools for the Graphically Challenged," *Information Technology and Libraries* 18 (1999): 182.

13. G. Nunberg, "The Trouble with PowerPoint," *Fortune,* December 20, 1999, p. 330.

14. L. Toupin, "Putting the 'Power' Back into a PowerPoint Presentation," *Design News* 54 (December 20, 1999): 39.

15. Carlson.

16. R. K. Ellis, "I Can HotFoot, Can You HotFoot, Too?" *Training and Development* 54:7 (2000): 64.

17. "Make It Snappy," *PC/Computing* 12:6 (1999): 178.

Chapter 13 Rehearsal and Delivery: Speaking to Audiences

1. J. Ayres and B. L. Heuett, "The Relationship between Visual Imagery and Public Speaking Apprehension," *Communication Reports* 10 (1997): 87–94.

2. P. Fanning, *Visualization for Change* (Oakland, CA: New Harbinger, 1988).

3. J. Ayres and T. S. Hopf, "Visualization, Systematic Desensitization, and Rational-Emotive Therapy: A Comparative Evaluation," *Communication Education* 36 (1987): 236–240; J. Ayres and T. S. Hopf, "The Long-Term Effect of Visualization in the Classroom: A Brief Research Report," *Communication Education* 39 (1991): 75–78; J. Ayres and T. S. Hopf, *Coping with Speech Anxiety* (Norwood, NJ: Ablex, 1993).

4. Ayres and Hopf, *Coping with Speech Anxiety,* 31–47.

5. G. E. Mills and R. W. Pace, "What Effects Do Practice and Video Feedback Have on the Development of Interpersonal Communication Skills?" *Journal of Business Communication* 26 (1989): 159–177.

6. R. R. Behnke and C. R. Sawyer, "Public Speaking Anxiety as a Function of Sensitization and Habituation Processes," *Communication Education* 53 (2004): 164–173.

7. R. L. Johannesen, *Ethics in Human Communication,* 4th ed. (Prospect Heights, IL: Waveland, 1996), 63–85.

8. B. Crounse, "Talking the Talk: Helpful Tips on Giving Political Speeches," *Campaigns and Elections* 21:6 (2000): 64.

9. L. Walters, *Secrets of Successful Speakers: How You Can Motivate, Captivate and Persuade* (New York: McGraw-Hill, 1993), 137.

10 Walters, 138.

11. W. G. Woodall and J. K. Burgoon, "The Effects of Nonverbal Synchrony on Message Comprehension and Persuasiveness," *Journal of Nonverbal Behavior* 5 (1981): 207–223.

12. D. Drucker, "How Not to Mumble," *Training and Development* 54:2 (2000): 71.

13. K. C. Crannell, *Voice and Articulation,* 4th ed. (Belmont, CA: Wadsworth, 2000).

14. G. B. Ray, "Vocally Cued Personality Prototypes: An Implicit Personality Theory," 53 (1986): 266–276.

15. A. D. Wolvin, R. M. Berko, and D. R. Wolvin, *The Public Speaker/The Public Listener* (Boston: Houghton Mifflin, 1993), 192.

16. P. Bedard et al., "Blinded," *U.S. News and World Report* August 14, 2000, p. 64.

17. K. L. Allen, "Getting It Across," *Across the Board* 37:1 (2000): 78.

18. M. Martel, *Mastering the Art of Q & A: A Survival Guide for Tough, Trick, and Hostile Questions* (Homewood, IL: Dow Jones-Irwin, 1989), 156.

19. "How Do I Deal with Hostile Questions?" *Public Management* 80:4 (1998): 27.

Chapter 14   Public Presentations: Speaking to Inform

1. D. A. Infante, A. S. Rancer, and D. F. Womack, *Building Communication Theory*, 2nd ed. (Prospect Heights, IL: Waveland, 1993), 25–26.

2. J. Ebersole, "Viewpoint: The Future of Graduate Education," *University Business* (August 2004): 15.

3. J. Byrne, "The Horizontal Corporation," *Business Week*, December 20, 1993, pp. 76–81.

4. J. H. Byrns, *Speak for Yourself: An Introduction to Public Speaking* (New York: Random House, 1981).

5. B. McCarthy, "Using the 4MAT System to Bring Learning Styles to Schools," *Educational Leadership* (1990): 31–37.

6. R. B. Powell and K. Andersen, "Culture and Classroom Communication," in *Intercultural Communication: A Reader,* 7th ed., L. A. Samovar and R. E. Porter, eds. (Belmont, CA: Wadsworth, 1994), 322–330.

7. D. A. Lieberman, "Ethnocognitivism, Problem-Solving, and Hemisphericity," in Samovar and Porter, 178–193.

8. T. F. Blakeslee, *The Right Brain: A New Understanding of the Unconscious Mind and Its Creative Powers* (New York: Anchor Press, 1980).

9. R. Felder and L. Silverman, "Learning and Teaching Styles in Engineering Education," *Engineering Education* (1988): 674–681.

10. Powell and Andersen, 324.

11. Powell and Andersen, 324.

12. Silverman, cited in Lieberman, 185.

13. I Corinthians 13: 4–6, New International Version.

14. K. Gibran, *The Prophet* (New York; Knopf, 1923).

15. N. Branden, *The Psychology of Romantic Love* (Los Angeles: J. P. Tarcher, 1980).

16. A. D. Wolvin, R. M. Berko, and D. R. Wolvin, *The Public Speaker/The Public Listener* (Boston: Houghton Mifflin, 1993), 25.

17. J. V. Jensen, *Argumentation: Reasoning in Communication* (New York: Van Nostrand, 1981).

Chapter 15   Public Presentations: Speaking to Persuade

1. B. R. Barber, *Strong Democracy: Participatory Politics for a New Age* (Berkeley: University of California Press, 1984).

2. Barber, 173 and 179.

3. Aristotle, *Rhetoric,* trans. W. R. Roberts, in *Rhetoric and Poetics of Aristotle,* ed. F. Solmsen (New York: Random House, 1954), 24.

4. A. Baum, J. D. Fisher, and J. E. Singer, *Social Psychology* (New York: Random House, 1985), 54.

5. A. H. Eagly and S. Chaiken, *The Psychology of Attitudes* (Fort Worth, TX: Harcourt Brace Jovanovich, 1993), 5.

6. R. L. Johannesen, *Ethics in Human Communication,* 4th ed. (Prospect Heights, IL: Waveland, 1996), 1.

7. K. Luker, *Abortion and the Politics of Motherhood* (Berkeley: University of California Press, 1984).

8. C. W. Sherif, M. Sherif, and R. W. Nebergall, *Attitude and Attitude Change: The Social Judgment-Involvement Approach* (Philadelphia: Saunders, 1965).

9. L. A. Samovar and R. E. Porter, *Communication between Cultures,* 5th ed.(Belmont, CA: Wadsworth, 2004), 311–318.

10. L. Festinger, *A Theory of Cognitive Dissonance* (Evanston, IL: Row, Peterson, 1957); D. J. Bem, *Beliefs, Attitudes, and Human Affairs* (Belmont, CA: Brooks/Cole, 1970).

11. C. I. Hovland, A. A. Lumsdaine, and F. D. Sheffield, *Experiments in Mass Communication: Studies in Social Psychology in World War II,* Vol. 3 (Princeton, NJ: Princeton University Press, 1949), 201–227; A. Lumsdaine and I. Janis, "Resistance to 'Counterpropaganda' Produced by One-Sided and Two-Sided Propaganda Presentations," *Public Opinion Quarterly* 17 (1953): 311–318.

12. W. J. McGuire, "Inducing Resistance to Persuasion: Some Contemporary Approaches," in *Advances in Experimental Social Psychology,* Vol. 1, L. Berkowitz, ed. (San Diego, CA: Academic Press, 1964), 191–229.

13. B. E. Gronbeck et al., *Principles and Types of Speech Communication,* 12th ed. (New York: HarperCollins, 1994).

14. K. R. Wallace, "The Substance of Rhetoric: Good Reasons," *Quarterly Journal of Speech* 49 (1963): 239–249.

15. C. Pornpitakpani, "The Persuasiveness of Source Credibility: A Critical Review of Five Decades' Evidence," *Journal of Applied Social Psychology* 34:2 (2004): 243–281.

16. Johannesen, 39–40.

17. D. R. Roskos-Ewoldsen, J. Y. Jessy, and N. Rhodes, "Fear Appeal Messages Affect Accessibility of Attitudes toward the Threat and Adaptive Behaviors," *Communication Monographs* 71 (2004): 50.

18. Eagly and Chaiken, 443.

19. A. M. Isen, "Positive Affect, Cognitive Processes, and Social Behavior," in *Advances in Experimental Social Psychology,* Vol. 20, L. Berkowitz, ed. (San Diego, CA: Academic Press, 1987), 203–253); L. T. Worth and D. M. Mackie, "Cognitive Mediation of Positive

Affect in Persuasion," *Social Cognition* 5 (1987): 76–94.

20. Eagly and Chaiken, 429–430.

21. D. L. Lumsden, "An Experimental Study of Source-Message Interaction in a Personality Impression Task," *Communication Monographs* 44 (1977): 121–129; M. H. Birnbaum, R. Wong, and L. K. Wong, "Combining Information from Sources That Vary in Credibility," *Memory and Cognition* 4 (1976): 330–336.

22. L. R. Anderson, "Toward a Two-Track Model of Leadership Training: Suggestions from Self-Monitoring Theory," *Small Group Research* 21 (1990): 147–167.

23. L. R. Duran, "Communicative Adaptability: A Review of Conceptualization and Measurement," *Communication Quarterly* 4 (1992): 253–268.

24. R. E. Lee and K. K. Lee, *Arguing Persuasively* (New York: Longman, 1989), 122.

25. Johannesen, 308.

26. Eagly and Chaiken, 355–363.

27. M. A. Kamins et al., "Two-Sided Versus One-Sided Celebrity Endorsements: The Impact on Advertising Effectiveness and Credibility," *Journal of Advertising* 18 (1989): 4–10.

28. Samovar and Porter, 330.

29. W. Schutz, *The Truth Option: A Practical Technology for Human Affairs* (Berkeley, CA: Ten Speed Press, 1984), 9.

30. R. S. Ross, *Understanding Persuasion,* 3rd ed. (Englewood Cliffs, NJ: Prentice-Hall, 1990), 28.

31. C. E. Osgood, G. J. Suci, and P. H. Tannenbaum, *The Measurement of Meaning* (Urbana: University of Illinois Press, 1957).

Index

Photo Credits

This page is an extension of the copyright page. We have made every effort to trace the ownership of all copyrighted material and to secure permission from copyright holders. In the event of any question arising as to the use of any material, we will be pleased to make the necessary corrections in future printings. Thanks are due to the following authors, publishers, and agents for permission to use the material indicated.